Breakthrough Discoveries in Information Technology Research:
Advancing Trends

Mehdi Khosrow-Pour
Information Resources Management Association, USA

INFORMATION SCIENCE REFERENCE

Hershey · New York

Director of Editorial Content:	Kristin Klinger
Senior Managing Editor:	Jamie Snavely
Assistant Managing Editor:	Michael Brehm
Publishing Assistant:	Sean Woznicki
Typesetter:	Sean Woznicki, Mike Killian, Kurt Smith
Cover Design:	Lisa Tosheff
Printed at:	Yurchak Printing Inc.

Published in the United States of America by
Information Science Reference (an imprint of IGI Global)
701 E. Chocolate Avenue
Hershey PA 17033
Tel: 717-533-8845
Fax: 717-533-8661
E-mail: cust@igi-global.com
Web site: http://www.igi-global.com/reference

Library of Congress Cataloging-in-Publication Data

Breakthrough discoveries in information technology research : advancing trends
/ Mehdi Khosrow-Pour, editor.
      p. cm.
  Includes bibliographical references and index.
  Summary: "This book informs researchers and practitioners of novel and emerging research in information science and technology, allowing for the discussion and dissemination of critical concepts that will promote further study and innovation"--Provided by publisher.
  ISBN 978-1-60566-966-3 (hardcover) -- ISBN 978-1-60566-967-0 (ebook) 1. Information technology--Technological innovations. 2. Information technology--Research. 3. Offshore outsourcing. I. Khosrowpour, Mehdi, 1951-
  HC79.I55B697 2010
  303.48'33--dc22
                                    2009042994

British Cataloguing in Publication Data
A Cataloguing in Publication record for this book is available from the British Library.

All work contributed to this book is new, previously-unpublished material. The views expressed in this book are those of the authors, but not necessarily of the publisher.

Table of Contents

    Mahesh S. Raisinghani, Texas Woman's University, USA
    Brandi Starr, Texas Woman's University, USA
    Blake Hickerson, Texas Woman's University, USA
    Marshelle Morrison, Texas Woman's University, USA
    Michael Howard, Texas Woman's University, USA

    Tapasya Patki, University of Arizona, Tucson, USA
    A.B. Patki, Department of Information Technology, Government of India
    Mahesh Kulkarni, Center for Development of Advanced Computing, India

    Nathan Denny, University of Arizona, USA
    Igor Crk, University of Arizona, USA
    Ravi Sheshu Nadella, University of Arizona, USA

    Igor Crk, University of Arizona, USA
    Dane Sorensen, Raytheon Missile Systems, USA
    Amit Mitra, TCS Global Consulting Practice, USA

    Preeti Goyal, University of Delhi, India
    Bhimaraya A. Metri, Management Development Institute, India

Detailed Table of Contents

Mahesh S. Raisinghani, Texas Woman's University, USA
Brandi Starr, Texas Woman's University, USA
Blake Hickerson, Texas Woman's University, USA
Marshelle Morrison, Texas Woman's University, USA
Michael Howard, Texas Woman's University, USA

The operation of information technology and information systems (IT/IS) offshore outsourcing is being increasingly practiced among firms that are focusing on core competencies and cost effectiveness. With the increase in offshore IT/IS operations, a growing number of companies are encountering negative experiences and unpredicted results. The analysis performed in this chapter reveals the possible risks and perceived success factors of companies outsourcing IT/IS operations offshore. The major points of interest are operational and strategic risks; legal contracts; cultural, security, and financial issues; and noted success factors by companies that participate in offshore outsourcing. The research indicates the importance of risk identification and the formulation of strategic plans that include preventive, detective, and corrective control methods of implementation and evaluation. Effective methods and metrics for measuring the success or failure of IT/IS offshore outsourcing operations is expected to be a continuing development with the increasing growth of this phenomenon.

Tapasya Patki, University of Arizona, Tucson, USA
A.B. Patki, Department of Information Technology, Government of India
Mahesh Kulkarni, Center for Development of Advanced Computing, India

Outsourcing has been conventionally viewed as a solution to generate quick profits and provide business continuity. The previous decades have seen the emergence of the Information Age, where the key focus was on knowledge acquisition and application. We are now progressing towards the era that revolves around "concept" development from an era that was information-dependent. This age, referred to as the

Conceptual Age, will be dominated by six new senses: Design, Story, Symphony, Empathy, Play and Meaning; and shall focus on the human resource development aspects. This creates a need to diverge from the current reliance on linear and sequential algorithmic practices in outsourcing and to adopt cognition based engineering and management approaches. This chapter lays the foundation for Offshore Engineering and Management (OEM) and discusses estimation issues in OEM that have their roots in software engineering. Also, this chapter identifies the limitations of the current methodologies from an outsourcing point of view, and delineates how they can be deployed effectively for an outsourced environment.

Chapter 3
Nathan Denny, University of Arizona, USA
Igor Crk, University of Arizona, USA
Ravi Sheshu Nadella, University of Arizona, USA

The growing adoption of outsourcing and offshoring concepts is presenting new opportunities for distributed software development. Inspired by the paradigm of round-the-clock manufacturing, the concept of the 24-hour knowledge factory (24HrKF) attempts to make similar transformations in the arena of IS: specifically to transform the production of software and allied intangibles to benefit from the notion of continuous development by establishing multiple collaborating sites at strategically selected locations around the globe. As the sun sets on one site, it rises on another site with the day's work being handed off from the closing site to the opening site. In order to enable such hand offs to occur in an effective manner, new agile and distributed software processes are needed, as delineated in this chapter.

Chapter 4
Igor Crk, University of Arizona, USA
Dane Sorensen, Raytheon Missile Systems, USA
Amit Mitra, TCS Global Consulting Practice, USA

Collaborative work groups that span multiple locations and time zones, or "follow the sun," create a growing demand for creating new technologies and methodologies that enable traditional spatial and temporal separations to be surmounted in an effective and productive manner. The hurdles faced by members of such virtual teams are in three key areas: differences in concepts and terminologies used by the different teams; differences in understanding the problem domain under consideration; and differences in training, knowledge, and skills that exist across the teams. These reasons provide some of the basis for the delineation of new architectural approaches that can normalize knowledge and provide reusable artifacts in a knowledge repository.

Chapter 5
Preeti Goyal, University of Delhi, India
Bhimaraya A. Metri, Management Development Institute, India

Alliances, collaborations and networks are synonymous with strategy today. Business Process Outsourcing (BPO) is one such type of alliance. With increasing reliance on outsourcing, the organizational boundaries are blurring. The implications for the client organization can be tremendous, as it now relies on an outside organization to fulfill its operational objectives. Currently, there is no single framework, which can effectively measure performance for BPO arrangements. In its present form, the Balanced Scorecard (BSC) only addresses, the performance measurement needs of a single enterprise and any perspective on any external relationships is completely missing. The traditional BSC does not suffice as a performance measurement framework for BPO. While both the client and the vendor can use a BSC for their respective organizations, the strategic objectives of the organizations may not be met. In this chapter, the authors propose a new perspective as an extension to the BSC, namely the goals alignment perspective. Goals alignment of the two organizations will enable creation of performance measures that will help participating organizations to achieve their respective goals.

Chapter 6

    B. Dawn Medlin, John A. Walker College of Business, Appalachian State University, USA
    Adriana Romaniello, Universidad Rey Juan Carlos, Spain

Business processes refer to the activities that are performed within an organization that are used in order to produce value for the organization and its customers. Through the use of onshore outsourcing, banks as do other industries expect several benefits such as cost savings and reduction in overhead. Using knowledge management concepts, banks can better understand their firm's performance as well as their own needs. This knowledge may also lead to the increase of employees' skill sets. This study surveyed members of the North Carolina Bankers Association in order to determine what if any of their business processes they selected to outsource.

Chapter 7

    Jason McCoy, Global Seawater, Inc., USA
    Johannes Sarx, ALCIMED, France

Offshoring has been adopted as a tool for reducing costs and for gaining strategic advantages by financial services, software development, and other competitive industries. For a variety of reasons, the pharmaceutical industry has been slow to take advantage of the benefits that offshoring can provide. The purpose of this chapter is to explore the internal and exogenous factors motivating global pharmaceutical firms to increase and expand their sourcing activities. And, instead of discussing global sourcing in general, India has been analyzed as a unique and explanatory case study for this new, emerging trend. The reasons behind this decision include India's position as a renowned global IT hub, the country's "home grown" biotechnology and biopharmaceutical industries, the numerous strategic partnerships and offshoring relationships between global and Indian firms, as well as its significant advances in IT and information management.

Chapter 8

Statistical analysis is the universally accepted method by which sense is created from raw data. Successful requirements determination is often dependent upon the gathering customer data over the Internet, and it may be largely limited to collecting the responses such as Yes/No and Likert scale categories. These data are then analyzed to identify customer trends or other items of interest to management. The data can be useful, but key to their usage is the application of suitable mathematical tools. Traditionally little more than standard statistics has been used in the analysis of ordinal, or category, data. This chapter introduces measures of agreement and dissent to the field of e-business analysis and shows how ordinal data can be analyzed in meaningful ways.

Chapter 9

This chapter reviews the development of institutional theory in direct relations to historical changes within the UK's National Health Service (NHS) with an eye to contributing to the theoretical specification of healthcare information processes. This is done partly by extending certain paradigms (see Meyer & Rowan, 1991; Powell & DiMaggio, 1991; Tolbert & Zucker, 1994) through a proposed model of causes and consequences of variations in levels of institutionalisation in the healthcare industry. It reports finding from a 5-year study on the NHS implementation of the largest civil ISs worldwide at an estimated cost of $10 billion over a 10-year period. The theoretical basis for analysis is developed, using concepts drawn from neo-institutionalism, realisation of business value, and organisational logic, as well as mixed empirical results about the lack of IT investments value in the NHS. The findings suggest that large scale, IT change imposed upon a highly institutionalised healthcare industry is fraught with difficulty mainly because culturally embedded norms, values, and behavioural patterns serve to impede centrally imposed initiatives to automate clinical working practices. It concludes with a discussion about the nature of evaluation procedures in relation to the process of institutionalising IS in healthcare.

Chapter 10

This chapter develops the concept of crisis compliance (CC)—defined as making appropriate use of IT, and non-IT methodologies to predict, prevent, and prevail over disasters. CC emerges from Lally's Target Shield and Weapon Model, which is grounded in the theories of crisis management, normal accident theory, and high reliability organizations. CC is then applied to a case study involving Hurricane Katrina, with examples drawn from other recent disasters. Emerging IT-based crisis management initiatives will be examined with an emphasis on how the impacts of Hurricane Katrina could have been mitigated. Recommendations for predicting, preventing, and prevailing over future disasters will emerge from the analysis.

Chapter 11

Kirsten Ellis, Monash University, Australia
Marian Quigley, Monash University, Australia
Mark Power, Monash University, Australia

This chapter examines the issues in conducting ethical usability testing with children including the special complications presented by the unique characteristics of children. It outlines the process of gaining approval of overseeing bodies to conduct research with children and discusses the difficulties in gaining informed consent from teachers, parents and the children themselves; protection of the research subject from harm and the difficulty of empowering children to instigate their right to refuse to participate in the research project. The chapter also discusses practical issues regarding the research design such as age appropriate practice, the duration of testing and recruitment of participants.

Chapter 12

Panayotis Fouliras, University of Macedonia, Greece
Nikolaos Samaras, University of Macedonia, Greece

In recent years many technologies have converged to integrated solutions and one of the hottest topics has been the deployment of wireless personal area networks (WPANs). This chapter presents a generic architecture scheme that allows voice and other real-time traffic to be carried over longer distances. The proposed scheme is a novel framework that combines a wired backbone network including Bluetooth access points (APs) with the mobile Bluetooth-enabled devices of the end users. This scheme is called Bluetooth Promoted Multimedia on Demand (BlueProMoD). BlueProMoD is a hybrid network and provides free-of-charge communication among customers, multimedia advertisements, as well as location-based and other value-added services.

Chapter 13

Yun-Ke Chang, Nanyang Technological University, Singapore
Miguel A. Morales-Arroyo, Nanyang Technological University, Singapore
Mark Chavez, Nanyang Technological University, Singapore
Jaime Jimenez-Guzman, National University of Mexico, Mexico

Conversational agents that display many human qualities have become a valuable method business uses to communicate with online users to supply services or products, to help in online order process or to search the Web. The gaming industry and education may benefit from this type of interface. In this type of chats, users could have different alternatives: text display, photo of a real person, or a cartoon drawing and others. This is an exploratory study that reviews five randomly chosen conversations that an animated chatbot has with Web users. The character simulates human gestures, but they are stylized to reproduce animation standards. The goal of this exploratory study is to provide feedback that will help designers to improve the functionality of the conversational agent, identify user's needs, define future research, and learn from previous errors. The methodology used was qualitative content analysis.

This chapter describes a new voice-based tool for global collaboration. This tool, called EchoEdit, attempts to provide multimedia capabilities to program source code editing for the purpose of eliciting in situ vocal commentary from active developers.

Biometric Systems verify the identity of a claimant based on the person's physical attributes, such as voice, face or fingerprints. Its application areas include security applications, forensic work, law enforcement applications etc. This work presents a novel concept of applying Soft Computing Tools, namely Artificial Neural Networks and Neuro-Fuzzy System, for person identification using speech and facial features. The work is divided in four cases, which are Person Identification using speech biometrics, facial biometrics, fusion of speech and facial biometrics and finally fusion of optimized speech and facial biometrics.

Chapter 16

This chapter investigates the design and development of a hierarchical fuzzy logic system. A new method using an evolutionary algorithm for design of hierarchical fuzzy logic system for prediction and modelling of interest rates in Australia is developed. The hierarchical system is developed to model and predict three months (quarterly) interest rate fluctuations. This research study is unique in the way proposed method is applied to design and development of fuzzy logic systems. The new method proposed determines the number of layer for hierarchical fuzzy logic system. The advantages and disadvantages of using fuzzy logic systems for financial modeling is also considered. Conclusions on the accuracy of prediction using hierarchical fuzzy logic systems compared to a back-propagation neural network system and a hierarchical neural network are reported.

This chapter explores the use of fuzzy logic in the medical field. While giving a comparison of classic and fuzzy logic the authors present the various uses of the applications made possible by fuzzy logic, focusing on diagnosis and treatment. The ever evolving technology making the line between medicine and technology thinner every year, is helping to make the treatment of disease and the mending of injury easier for medical professionals. The authors also propose several questions that arise from, and may by answered by, fuzzy logic and its applications.

The chapter introduces bias-variance decomposition in probabilistic logic learning. The author uses Stochastic Logic Programs for probabilistic logic representation. In order to learn probabilistic logic models the author uses Failure Adjusted Maximization (FAM) that is an instance of the Expectation Maximization (EM) algorithm for first order logic. Experiments are carried out by concentrating on one kind of application: quantitative modelling of metabolic pathways that is a complex and challenging task in computational systems biology. The author applies bias-variance definitions to analyze quantitative modelling of amino acid pathways of Saccharomyces cerevisiae (yeast). The results show the phenomenon of bias-variance trade-off in probabilistic logic learning.

Preface

Information technology is a discipline under constant evolution. The following collection, entitled *Breakthrough Discoveries in Information Technology Research: Advancing Trends*, aims to inform researchers and practitioners of novel and emerging research in information science and technology, allowing for the discussion and dissemination of critical concepts that will promote further study and innovation. Selections explore all facets of the discipline, with specific contributions focusing on outsourcing, ethical concerns in research, biometrics, and information technology's role in disaster prediction and prevention.

Chapter 1, *"Information Technology/Systems Offshore Outsourcing: Key Risks and Success Factors"* by Mahesh S. Raisinghani, Brandi Starr, Blake Hickerson, Marshelle Morrison, and Michael Howard, reveals the possible risks and perceived success factors of companies outsourcing IT/IS operations offshore. The major points of interest are operational and strategic risks; legal contracts; cultural, security, and financial issues; and noted success factors by companies that participate in offshore outsourcing. The research indicates the importance of risk identification and the formulation of strategic plans that include preventive, detective, and corrective control methods of implementation and evaluation. Effective methods and metrics for measuring the success or failure of IT/IS offshore outsourcing operations is expected to be a continuing development with the increasing growth of this phenomenon.

Chapter 2, *"Emerging Trends in Outsourcing"* by Tapasya Patki, A.B. Patki, and Mahesh Kulkarni, lays the foundation for Offshore Engineering and Management (OEM) and discusses estimation issues in OEM that have their roots in software engineering. Also, this chapter identifies the limitations of the current methodologies from an outsourcing point of view, and delineates how they can be deployed effectively for an outsourced environment.

Chapter 3, *"Agile Software Processes for the 24-Hour Knowledge Factory Environment"* by Nathan Denny, Igor Crk, and Ravi Sheshu, contends that the growing adoption of outsourcing and offshoring concepts is presenting new opportunities for distributed software development. Inspired by the paradigm of round-the-clock manufacturing, the concept of the 24-hour knowledge factory (24HrKF) attempts to make similar transformations in the arena of IS: specifically to transform the production of software and allied intangibles to benefit from the notion of continuous development by establishing multiple collaborating sites at strategically selected locations around the globe. As the sun sets on one site, it rises on another site with the day's work being handed off from the closing site to the opening site. In order to enable such hand offs to occur in an effective manner, new agile and distributed software processes are needed, as delineated in this chapter.

Chapter 4, *"Leveraging Knowledge Reuse and Systems Agility in the Outsourcing Era"* by Igor Crk, Dane Sorensen, and Amit Mitra, discusses collaborative work groups and the growing demand for new technologies and methodologies that enable traditional spatial and temporal separations to be surmounted that they create. The hurdles faced by members of such virtual teams are in three key areas:

differences in concepts and terminologies used by the different teams; differences in understanding the problem domain under consideration; and differences in training, knowledge, and skills that exist across the teams. These reasons provide some of the basis for the delineation of new architectural approaches that can normalize knowledge and provide reusable artifacts in a knowledge repository.

Chapter 5, "*Extending the Balanced Scorecard for Outsourcing: The Goals Alignment Perspective*" by Preeti Goyal and Bhimaraya A. Metri, asserts that alliances, collaborations and networks are synonymous with strategy today. Business Process Outsourcing (BPO) is one such type of alliance. With increasing reliance on outsourcing, the organizational boundaries are blurring. The implications for the client organization can be tremendous, as it now relies on an outside organization to fulfill its operational objectives. Currently, there is no single framework, which can effectively measure performance for BPO arrangements. In its present form, the Balanced Scorecard (BSC) only addresses, the performance measurement needs of a single enterprise and any perspective on any external relationships is completely missing. The traditional BSC does not suffice as a performance measurement framework for BPO. While both the client and the vendor can use a BSC for their respective organizations, the strategic objectives of the organizations may not be met. In this chapter, the authors propose a new perspective as an extension to the BSC, namely the goals alignment perspective. Goals alignment of the two organizations will enable creation of performance measures that will help participating organizations to achieve their respective goals.

Chapter 6, "*Business Process Onshore Outsourcing within the Community Banking System: An Investigative Study*" by B. Dawn Medlin and Adriana Romaniello, contains a study surveying members of the North Carolina Bankers Association in order to determine what if any of their business processes they selected to outsource. Through the use of onshore outsourcing, banks as do other industries expect several benefits such as cost savings and reduction in overhead. Using knowledge management concepts, banks can better understand their firm's performance as well as their own needs. This knowledge may also lead to the increase of employees' skill sets.

Chapter 7, "*Offshoring in the Pharmaceutical Industry*" by Jason McCoy and Johannes Sarx, explores the internal and exogenous factors motivating global pharmaceutical firms to increase and expand their sourcing activities. And, instead of discussing global sourcing in general, India has been analyzed as a unique and explanatory case study for this new, emerging trend. The reasons behind this decision include India's position as a renowned global IT hub, the country's "home grown" biotechnology and biopharmaceutical industries, the numerous strategic partnerships and offshoring relationships between global and Indian firms, as well as its significant advances in IT and information management.

Chapter 8, "*Enhancing e-Business Decision Making: An Application of Consensus Theory*" by William J. Tastle and Mark J. Wierman, introduces measures of agreement and dissent to the field of e-business analysis and shows how ordinal data can be analyzed in meaningful ways.

Chapter 9, "*Changing Healthcare Institutions with Large Information Technology Projects*" by Matthew W. Guah reviews the development of institutional theory in direct relations to historical changes within the UK's National Health Service (NHS) with an eye to contributing to the theoretical specification of healthcare information processes. This is done partly by extending certain paradigms (see Meyer & Rowan, 1991; Powell & DiMaggio, 1991; Tolbert & Zucker, 1994) through a proposed model of causes and consequences of variations in levels of institutionalisation in the healthcare industry. It reports finding from a 5-year study on the NHS implementation of the largest civil ISs worldwide at an estimated cost of $10 billion over a 10-year period. The theoretical basis for analysis is developed, using concepts drawn from neo-institutionalism, realisation of business value, and organisational logic, as well as mixed empirical results about the lack of IT investments value , the NHS. The findings suggest that large scale, IT change imposed upon a highly institutionalised healthcare industry is fraught with difficulty mainly because culturally embedded norms, values, and behavioural patterns serve to impede centrally imposed initiatives to automate clinical working practices. It concludes with a discussion about the nature of evaluation procedures in relation to the process of institutionalising IS in healthcare.

Chapter 10, "*Crisis Compliance: Using Information Technology to Predict, Prevent and Prevail Over Disasters*" by Laura Lally develops the concept of crisis compliance (CC)—defined as making appropriate use of IT, and non-IT methodologies to predict, prevent, and prevail over disasters. CC emerges from Lally's Target Shield and Weapon Model, which is grounded in the theories of crisis management, normal accident theory, and high reliability organizations. CC is then applied to a case study involving Hurricane Katrina, with examples drawn from other recent disasters. Emerging IT-based crisis management initiatives will be examined with an emphasis on how the impacts of Hurricane Katrina could have been mitigated. Recommendations for predicting, preventing, and prevailing over future disasters will emerge from the analysis.

Chapter 11, "*Ethical Concerns in Usability Research Involving Children*" by Kirsten Ellis, Marian Quigley, and Mark Power examines the issues in conducting ethical usability testing with children including the special complications presented by the unique characteristics of children. It outlines the process of gaining approval of overseeing bodies to conduct research with children and discusses the difficulties in gaining informed consent from teachers, parents and the children themselves; protection of the research subject from harm and the difficulty of empowering children to instigate their right to refuse to participate in the research project. The chapter also discusses practical issues regarding the research design such as age appropriate practice, the duration of testing and recruitment of participants.

Chapter 12, "*A Generic Framework for Bluetooth Promoted Multimedia on Demand (BlueProMoD)*" by Panayotis Fouliras and Nikolaos Samaras presents a generic architecture scheme that allows voice and other real-time traffic to be carried over longer distances. The proposed scheme is a novel framework that combines a wired backbone network including Bluetooth access points (APs) with the mobile Bluetooth-enabled devices of the end users. This scheme is called Bluetooth Promoted Multimedia on Demand (BlueProMoD). BlueProMoD is a hybrid network and provides free-of-charge communication among customers, multimedia advertisements, as well as location-based and other value-added services.

Chapter 13, "*Social Interaction with a Conversational Agent: An Exploratory Study*" by Yun-Ke Chang, Miguel A. Morales-Arroyo, Mark Chavez, and Jaime Jimenez-Guzman, reviews five randomly chosen conversations that an animated chatbot has with Web users. The character simulates human gestures, but they are stylized to reproduce animation standards. The goal of this exploratory study is to provide feedback that will help designers to improve the functionality of the conversational agent, identify user's needs, define future research, and learn from previous errors. The methodology used was qualitative content analysis.

Chapter 14, "*Voice-Based Approach for Surmounting Spatial and Temporal Separations*" by Kate O'Toole, Srividhya Subramanian, and Nathan Denny, describes a new voice-based tool for global collaboration. This tool, called EchoEdit, attempts to provide multimedia capabilities to program source code editing for the purpose of eliciting in situ vocal commentary from active developers.

Chapter 15, "*Intelligent Biometric System Using Soft Computing Tools*" by Anupam Shukla, Ritu Tiwari, and Chandra Prakash Rathore, presents a novel concept of applying Soft Computing Tools, namely Artificial Neural Networks and Neuro-Fuzzy System, for person identification using speech and facial features. The work is divided in four cases, which are Person Identification using speech biometrics, facial biometrics, fusion of speech and facial biometrics and finally fusion of optimized speech and facial biometrics.

Chapter 16, "*Analysis and Modelling of Hierarchical Fuzzy Logic Systems*" by Masoud Mohammadian, investigates the design and development of a hierarchical fuzzy logic system. A new method using an evolutionary algorithm for design of hierarchical fuzzy logic system for prediction and modelling of interest rates in Australia is developed. The hierarchical system is developed to model and predict three months (quarterly) interest rate fluctuations. This research study is unique in the way proposed method is applied to design and development of fuzzy logic systems. The new method proposed determines the number of layer for hierarchical fuzzy logic system. The advantages and disadvantages of using fuzzy logic systems for financial modeling is also considered. Conclusions on the accuracy of prediction using hierarchical fuzzy logic systems compared to a back-propagation neural network system and a hierarchical neural network are reported.

Chapter 17, "*Fuzzy Logic in Medicine*" by Michelle LaBrunda and Andrew LaBrunda, explores the use of fuzzy logic in the medical field. While giving a comparison of classic and fuzzy logic the authors present the various uses of the applications made possible by fuzzy logic, focusing on diagnosis and treatment. The ever evolving technology making the line between medicine and technology thinner every year, is helping to make the treatment of disease and the mending of injury easier for medical professionals. The authors also propose several questions that arise from, and may by answered by, fuzzy logic and its applications.

Chapter 18, "*On Bias-Variance Analysis for Probabilistic Logic Models*" by Huma Lodhi, introduces bias-variance decomposition in probabilistic logic learning. The author uses Stochastic Logic Programs for probabilistic logic representation. In order to learn probabilistic logic models the author uses Failure Adjusted Maximization (FAM) that is an instance of the Expectation Maximization (EM) algorithm for first order logic. Experiments are carried out by concentrating on one kind of application: quantitative modelling of metabolic pathways that is a complex and challenging task in computational systems biology. The author applies bias-variance definitions to analyze quantitative modelling of amino acid pathways of Saccharomyces cerevisiae (yeast). The results show the phenomenon of bias-variance trade-off in probabilistic logic learning.

Breakthrough Discoveries in Information Technology Research: Advancing Trends examines innovative topics in information science and technology literature. With an eye toward the future of IT research, this collection provides extensive insight into the future of business and society and offers essential research on emerging ideas and trends.

Mehdi Khosrow-Pour
Editor

Chapter 1
Information Technology / Systems Offshore Outsourcing:
Key Risks and Success Factors

Mahesh S. Raisinghani
Texas Woman's University, USA

Brandi Starr
Texas Woman's University, USA

Blake Hickerson
Texas Woman's University, USA

Marshelle Morrison
Texas Woman's University, USA

Michael Howard
Texas Woman's University, USA

ABSTRACT

The offshore outsourcing of information technology and information systems (IT/IS) is being increasingly practiced among firms that are focusing on core competencies and cost-effectiveness. With the increase in offshore IT/IS operations, a growing number of companies are encountering negative experiences and unpredicted results. The analysis performed in this chapter reveals the possible risks and perceived success factors of companies outsourcing IT/IS operations offshore. The major points of interest are operational and strategic risks; legal contracts; cultural, security, and financial issues; and noted success factors by companies that participate in offshore outsourcing. The research indicates the importance of risk identification and the formulation of strategic plans that include preventive, detective, and corrective control methods of implementation and evaluation. Effective methods and metrics for measuring the success or failure of IT/IS offshore outsourcing operations is expected to be a continuing development with the increasing growth of this phenomenon.

It is not the strongest of the species that survives, or the most intelligent, but the one most responsive to change.

—Charles Darwin

INTRODUCTION

Offshore outsourcing with respect to information technology and information systems (IT/IS) or business processes is a key commercial phenomenon. IT/IS offshore outsourcing is the focus of this chapter and is defined as a process undertaken by an organization to subcontract or to sell the organization's IT/IS assets, staff, and/or activities to a foreign supplier, rather than develop IT/IS resources internally. The contractual relationship requires the vendor to assume responsibility for the client firm's IT/IS requirements. IT/IS services include software development and maintenance; network and computer operations; and research and development (see Table 3.1) (Dolan, 2006). An extensive report by the National Academy of Public Administration prepared for the United States Congress and the Bureau of Economic Analysis defines offshoring as follows: "United States' firms shifting service and manufacturing activities abroad to unaffiliated firms or their own affiliates" (Norwood et al., 2006).

In offshore outsourcing work is outsourced to foreign countries that have cost advantages in various tasks such as application development, product manufacturing, and/or call center and back office operations. It involves complexity and risk not found in typical domestic outsourcing due to factors such as cost (i.e., labor, infrastructure, real

Table 3.1. IT/IS common outsourced services

IT/IS Service	Function
Access Controls	Help organization establish and provision authentication needs
IDS Monitoring	Monitor intrusion detection systems on a 24/7 basis
Contingency Planning	Help facilitate crisis plans and responses, that is, disaster recovery sites
Firewall Management	Assist in configuration of software and monitor logs
Antivirus services	Monitor and act upon malicious attacks
Website Blocking	Filter services
Network Scanning	Identify network vulnerability
Remote Management	Monitor network
Encryption Services	Manage PKI
Software Development	Develop software application/s
Business Process Reengineering/ Outsourcing	Reengineer and/or outsource business process to evaluate and eliminate non-value-added activities

estate, and corporate taxes); availability of highly skilled workers; market potential; country risk profile (i.e., disruptive events, security, regulatory risk, macroeconomic risk such as cost inflation, currency fluctuation, and capital freedom), and intellectual property risk; environment (i.e., government support, business and living environment, accessibility of location such as travel time, flight frequency, and time difference); quality of infrastructure (i.e., telecom and IT, real estate, transportation, and reliability of power supply); improved customer service by way of 24X7 call centers and/or fewer environmental regulations (Farrell, 2005, 2006; Kraemer & Dedrick, 2004). Table 3.1 lists the common IT/IS outsourced services.

Industry Analysis

IT/IS offshore outsourcing is one of the fastest growing businesses in the world due to technological advances including the Internet and mobile services. The advances have changed markets by decreasing communication costs and increasing specialization of service production. Given that the Indian software services account for about $9.9 billion, this does not seem like a huge market share until one looks at the exponential growth rate of this sector. This sector managed to grow by 26% in 2005 and Michael Corbett of the International Outsourcing Professionals postulates a 40% compounded annual growth rate over the next decade (Barrett, 2006).

Pressures from dynamic market conditions and market uncertainty have caused business organizations to focus on core competencies and outsource functions in which they that lack expertise in order to show profitability maintain effective cost structures and improve the bottom line. There are increased pressures on management to remain cost effective by accomplishing more with fewer resources at a faster pace. Outsourcing goals and objectives include competitiveness, time to market, round the clock customer service, agility, and access to world class technology. As illustrated in Figure 1, countries and regions with the most outsourced IT professionals are India, Canada, Ireland, China, Philippines, Israel, Eastern Europe, Russia, Mexico, and South Africa (Kripalani, Foust, Holmes, & Enga, 2006).

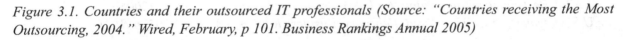

Figure 3.1. Countries and their outsourced IT professionals (Source: "Countries receiving the Most Outsourcing, 2004." Wired, February, p 101. Business Rankings Annual 2005)

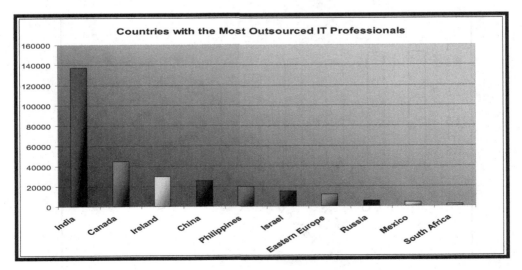

A recent study measured employee cost; quality; English proficiency; infrastructure; and political and economic risk of countries that have outsourced IT/IS professionals. As illustrated in Figure 3.2, according to a recent study, the best countries and regions for the United States to outsource in are India, Philippines, Canada, Ireland, South Africa, Eastern Europe, Russia, Israel, Mexico, and China (Seewald, 2005).

Despite the short-term successes, IT/IS offshore outsourcing has several risks and challenges that increase the possibility of long-term adverse effects on the client company. Studies show that negative effects and consequences of offshore outsourcing such as hidden costs, vendor complacency, lack of vendor flexibility, high employee turnover, and lack of expertise are increasing among major corporations subcontracting IT/IS services (see Figure 3.3) (Dolan, 2006). A recent survey of 25 Fortune 500 corporations indicated that 70% of outsourced operations resulted in numerous negative experiences. Fifty-two percent of the companies surveyed experienced negative experiences and problems three times in two months (Accenture, 2004).

The long-term effects of these negative experiences are difficult to measure because the value of IT/IS is intangible, hidden, and long term (Arbore & Ordanini, 2006; Greaver & Kipers, 2005; Hatch 2005). This obstacle raises the following questions:

What hazards contribute to encountering negative results and how are thriving companies achieving success? What topics and areas are researched the most often in the IS outsourcing field? Risks and success factors seem to be the common threads for the most frequent topics in IS outsourcing. It is also worth mentioning the increase in the number of articles focusing on offshore/global outsourcing. The use of cheaper communications technology, the Internet, economic globalization, and easy access to IT professionals with lower salaries are some of the reasons for this phenomenon. Among the many articles dealing with the economics of outsourcing, involve agency theory, transaction cost theory, game theory, resource-based theory,

Figure 3.2. Best countries and regions for U.S. outsourcing (Source: Seewald, S. (2005). "Best Countries for U.S. Outsourcing, 2005." Wired, February, Business Rankings Annual 2005, p. 101)

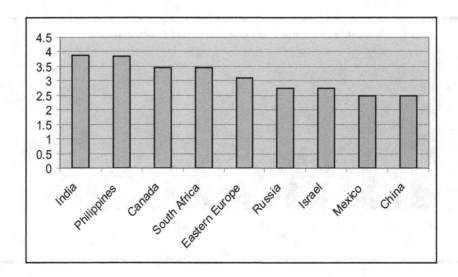

and resource-dependence theory (Dibbern et al., 2004; Gonzalez, Gasco, & Llopis, 2006; Iyengar & Rolf, 2007; Nyrhinen & Dahlberg, 2007). In order to evaluate possible causes for adverse long-term affects, a risk identification and success factor analysis have been developed to gain further understanding.

Risk Identification

Several risks such as cultural, political, financial, technological, commercial, and legal have been linked to the failure of IT/IS offshore collaborations. Adverse risk is heightened because of the geographical distance between the client firm and the vendor firm (Beiling, 2006). Geographical distance, costs, time, and resources prevent the client firm from exercising appropriate control over the vendor. Common risks include operational, strategic, cultural, and financial risks.

Operational Risk

Operational risk is identified as the increased chance of poor quality and output due to limitations of the communications and transmission systems, complexity of operations, and geographic separation between the two firms (Patterson, 2006). Loss of control is a significant threat to the ongoing operations because it decreases the manageability and power of value chains and inhibits client firms to give accurate performance evaluation. Performance evaluation and monitoring is often overlooked due to increased pressures of keeping costs down. An agent's lack of experience for a specific activity also increases the risk of poor quality of services, and the client's inability to measure the performance causes the client firm to become vulnerable to the agent's results and services.

Figure 3.3. Negative effects and consequences of offshore outsourcing (Source: Deloitte Consulting Outsourcing Study, October—December 2004)

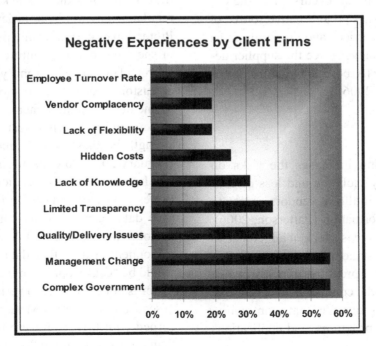

Strategic Risk

Strategic risks result from opportunistic behavior of the vendor client. Shirking is an example of strategic risk. Shirking is defined as deliberate underperformance while claiming full payment (Patterson, 2006). As globalization changes the basis of competition, strategic sourcing is moving from the periphery of corporate functions to the core, and research indicates that service providers are tempted to fail to perform their best work when they know the performance is difficult for their client to measure (Gottfredson, Puryear, & Phillips, 2005; Willcocks & Feeny, 2006). Performance pressures cause a number of offshore companies to cut corners to make certain the product is delivered despite product reliability or product completion (Beiling, 2006). Software development integrity is often violated as a result of the competitive position of providing ISs at the lowest possible cost for the highest achievable quality at the quickest time (Gottschalk, 2006).

Opportunistic recognition is another form of strategic risk. It derives from one party changing the terms of a contract after its inception. Opportunistic recognition occurs when the client discovers that it has no alternative source of support, goods, or services and, as result, must pay the supplier whatever price the supplier demands in the future (Arbore & Ordanini, 2006; Willcocks & Feeny, 2006).

Security Risks

Offshore outsourcing increases the risks on intellectual property violation and loss of confidentiality because it allows vendors access to private business information (Patterson, 2006). In many countries there is a lack of adherence to security and quality standards. Integrity is often violated because of the pressures of performance standards. Many vendor companies have multiple clients and there is no guarantee that a contracting organization's data, programs, and applications will not be duplicated for other clients (Arbore & Ordanini, 2006).

Intellectual property theft is steadily increasing, and protecting rights in foreign countries can be difficult. Countries like China have copyright laws but they tend to favor Chinese companies. Privacy campaigners argue that the processing of sensitive financial and data records in foreign countries do not meet the high privacy standards of the United States (Chan, 2005; Lyons, 2006). Their argument is supported by a particular instance when a woman from Pakistan threatened to post sensitive United States medical records on the Internet (McLean, 2006). As a result, other medical organizations have returned their data processing back to the United States. Other financial companies that offshore ISs are worried they will be open to lawsuits if they can not guarantee acceptable standards of privacy.

In a recent study by Booz Allen Hamilton, information security has become a top concern among companies evaluating offshore outsourcing (Dunlop & Smith, 2005). The respondents also felt there was a significantly higher security risk in working with offshore providers over those in the United States, due to a lack of trust in legal and regulatory environments in developing countries. Protection of corporate and personal data in any offshore outsourcing venture is critical in order to protect the business from cyber crime and theft of customer data. Information security ranked as one of the top three factors when selecting an outsourcing partner. It was rated ahead of financial strength, business stability, and reputation. At the February 20, 2006 Outsourcing World Summit, the International Association of Outsourcing Professionals announced an increasing concern over data security while considering offshore outsourcing (Hunt, 2006). More than 90% of the respondents stated that data security breaches would be "catastrophic "to their business. A key factor is not being able to verify vendor's claims of security capabilities. More companies are concerned with theft or misuse of outsourced data than they are about the threat of terrorism.

Cultural Challenges

Culture is the "totality of socially transmitted behavior patterns, arts, beliefs, institutions, and all other products of human work and thought" (dictionary.com, n.d.). Cultural differences and communication difficulties have numerous effects on business operations including no information sharing, poor communications of decisions, and no interaction between team members. Breakdown in communication often results in inadequate task priority and lack of overall business comprehension. Differences in culture often lead to miscommunication, which can result in considerable chaff. Memories of war and religious animosities make it difficult to build and maintain trust. Another concern is the simulation of a non-foreign facade to the clients who call these centers. Studies show that employees feel alienated from their own culture because of the shrinkage of local traditions to meet client expectations (Beiling, 2006). Workers become exhausted from working in a foreign language and tend to have growing resentments for the American people because of the decreased identity and cultural differences (Willcocks &Feeny, 2006). Although these overseas positions train the employees on the specifics of job expectations, there is little transferable job experience and no preparation for future career growth (Seabrook, 2004).

Financial Risks

As illustrated in Figure 3.4, despite increased cash flow and cost effectiveness, there are many hidden costs associated with IT/IS offshore outsourcing. Tailored contracts, lack of transparency, and bundling of services result in costly unexpected spending. There can be extensive, unpredictable costs due to a lack of due diligence. Vendor firms' unclear pricing and cost structure make it very difficult to understand cost savings. Bundling or grouping of services is a frequent dilemma and causes confusion in unit costs (Dolan, 2006).

Hidden costs are most likely the result of broad and ambiguous contracts that fail to define present and future IT requirements (McLean, 2006). Hidden costs can derive from dismissing or transferring staff, transfer of licenses by software vendors, travel costs, investigation costs, and the cost of developing infrastructure to support off-site operations.

Offshore Outsourcing's Success Factor Analysis

Global giant, Dupont, has developed a framework for its ISs offshore outsourcing operations. The company's IS frame consist of nine core capabilities including: (1) leadership, (2) business systems thinking, (3) relationship building, (4) architec-

Figure 3.4. Financial risks (Sources: Forrester Research, McKinsey & Co, http://pollingreport.com)

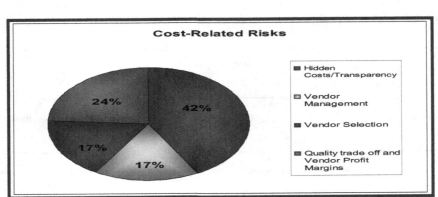

ture planning, (5) making technology work, (6) informed buying, (7) contrast facilitation, (8) contract monitoring, and (9) vendor development (Willcocks & Feeny, 2006; Willcocks, Feeny, & Olson, 2006). IBM has been noted for its exceptional global offshore outsourcing and credits its success to their IBM Relationship Alignment Process (Petershack, 2005). Their model is centered on relationship determinants including: commitment, predisposition, mutual benefits, linkage, unique resources, and shared knowledge. Success factors of IT/IS offshore outsourcing consists of precise risk analysis; detailed cost benefit analysis; relationship management and cultural understanding; understanding legal issues and contracts; and implementing risk controls.

Risk Analysis

Risk analysis enables client firms to determine the financial consequences of risk. As illustrated in Figure 3.5, a risk breakdown structure in risk analysis involves discovering and prioritizing of important risks that need protection and analyzing threats to assets to estimate potential losses.

Successful companies determine the relative importance of each risk and then verify the level of impact it will have on their company in terms of costs, schedule, and quality. Successful firms identify the priority of each risk and determine

the goals of the project accordingly (Bardhan, Whitaker, & Mithas, 2006; Patterson, 2006).

Cost Benefit Analysis

Potential customers need to do a cost-benefit analysis to determine whether database or application server outsourcing is right for them. Cost benefit analysis indicates whether offshore outsourcing is financially sound for companies. As illustrated in Table 3.2, when determining IT/IS offshore outsourcing, a cost benefit analysis should include a review of potential gains, costs, and possible risk(s) of each alternative; appropriate contract period; intangibles and hidden costs; contracting and legal costs; vendor's fee; conversion costs; IS salaries and severance payments; cash; contract cancellations; staff morale; and share price.

Relationship Management and Cultural Understanding

Research indicates that the level of partnership between a client firm and a vendor firm will increase when high levels of cultural similarity exist between them as evidenced by the insurance company USAA (Arbore & Ordanini, 2006; Chakrabarty, Gandhi, & Kaka, 2006). Identification-based trust is associated with successful offshore outsourcing because a mutual understanding allows for both parties to recognize and appreciate

Figure 3.5. Risk breakdown structure

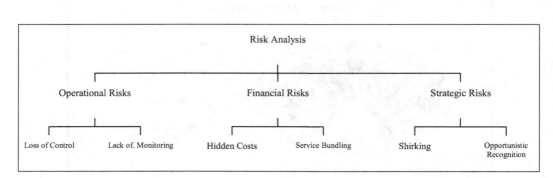

the other's wants. Identification-based trust has been linked to information sharing behavior and the overall quality of communication between the two firms (Bardhan et al., 2006).

The parties involved in an offshore outsourcing relationship belong to distinct cultures and it is vital that these differences are accepted. A recent study by Gartner (Heib, 2006) pointed to culture as a key differentiator to IT success and discussed the need for the IT organization to establish trust, commitment, two-way communication, clarity of purpose, and agility as vital components of the IT organization.

Healthy communication is a crucial element to a working relationship. The effectiveness of the relationship between management personnel of both teams is dependent on the understanding and strong working relationships among the firms. Studies of offshore outsourcing success stories have demonstrated that working chemistry in management and peer friendships among employees have proved to be important determinants in

forming long-term relationships that yield real value (Patterson, 2006).

Industrial relatedness has also been a significant indication of successful offshore outsourcing. IT/IS offshore outsourcing between firms in related industries outperformed firms in unrelated industries (Kripalani et al., 2006). Firms from different industries have more difficulties understanding and collaborating with each other. Firms in related industries communicate their needs more effectively because they share a common language, socialization, institutional history, and organizational practices.

Flexibility, modularity, and process knowledge are important business culture elements to study when determining a vendor firm. The client firm needs to determine the adaptability of the vendor to adjust to the changing demands of business and IT environment. The client firm must also know the vendor's ability or willingness to add, delete, or modify services. Lastly, the vendor firm must know enough about the client firm's industry to successfully deliver needed services.

Table 3.2. Cost analysis

Costs	Factors
Intangibles and Hidden Costs	Administering the outsourcing contract and coordination efforts between internal users and outsourcing company upgrades
Contracting Costs	Legal costs including monetary and opportunity costs involved in contracting, renegotiating, and vendor disputes
Vendor Fees and Prices	Potential increase in costs if initial vendor low-balling of fees/ rough-order-of-magnitude price estimates lead to higher vendor fees and prices after the initial contract
Conversion Costs	Costs associated with transfer of software licenses
IS Salaries and Severance Pay	Staff retained, terminated, and possible legal costs from disgruntled employees
Contract Cancellation Costs	Cost of new negotiation, training of staff, hardware or software replacement
Share Price	Will announcement of outsourcing hurt or help stock prices?

Understanding Legal Issues and Contracts

Legal issues regarding offshore outsourcing of IT/IS functions into emerging economies can be broken down into two parts: (1) the need for laws to govern international business operations, and (2) the ability to enforce international laws. Hall and Liedtka (2007) discussed the implications of the Sarbanes Oxley Act for large-scale IT outsourcing. First, companies and nations realize that international laws and agreements are needed in order to ensure that physical and intellectual properties are protected. Second, countries have different laws and policies regarding ownership and control of physical and intellectual properties, and the ability to enforce the international laws and agreements that have been established is critical.

In 1883, the Paris Convention for the Protection of Industrial Property was established (*WIPO Treaties*, 2006). This became the first international treaty to help people of one country obtain protection in other countries for intellectual properties in the form of industrial property rights (inventions, patents, trademarks, and industrial designs). As the volume and different types of intellectual property grew, there grew new requirements to protect intellectual property. In 1970, the World Intellectual Property Organization (WIPO) came into existence (*WIPO Treaties*, 2006). The WIPO was established to promote the protection of intellectual property throughout the world through cooperation between nations and, where appropriate, in collaboration with any other international organization. In 1974, the WIPO became a specialized agency of the United Nations system of organizations. At present the organization has 181 member nations and the need to expand the scope of laws to protect intellectual property continues to grow as global business grows.

The World Trade Organization (WTO) plays in important part in the establishment of intellectual property rules. The WTO's Agreement on trade-related aspects of intellectual property rights (TRIPS), negotiated in the 1986-1994 Uruguay Round, (*Understanding the WTO*, n.d.) introduced intellectual property rules into the global trading market for the first time. The agreement is supposed to narrow the gaps in how these rights are protected and bring common international rules into play. Although there has been extensive cooperation between many of the nations of the world, there still exist many nations that do not adhere to the international laws that have been established to provide protection to companies. As we look at emerging nations the risk of doing business with these nations increases depending on their acceptance and enforcement of established international laws.

The majority of subjects who participated in the Booz Allen survey felt that the regulatory and legal infrastructure in Asia and South America is not adequate (Dunlop & Smith, 2005). The survey revealed that only 5% of companies surveyed believed that China has a strong and legal infrastructure, South America was 5%, and Southeast Asia was 11%. The 27% of the respondents indicated that India, which is a major country for offshore outsourcing, had a good legal infrastructure. There is a feeling that there is a high potential risk for loss of customer or corporate data in these countries. Companies have to weigh the savings of lower costs that could be realized by offshore outsourcing in these countries to the potential impact to their companies from data loss.

International laws continue to change as outsourcing companies and potential countries to outsource realize the importance of having legally binding contracts. Many countries have worked to improve their legal systems to work with the companies that want to outsource to their country. Russia, for example, has established laws to offer some protection to offshore outsourcing companies (*IT Outsourcing*, 2005). Companies must still do due diligence in advance of any potential outsourcing contract.

What can companies do to protect themselves in emerging countries? First, it is critical to understand the laws and legal infrastructure of the country that the potential vendor is located. Does the company belong to trade groups or industry associations that have established standards for security of company and customer data? A company should have legal counsel that is experienced in the laws of the offshore country and may want to hire local counsel in the country to assist in legal matters. Companies must invest the time to research trade laws of the countries they are looking to outsource in. In addition, a company should research the legal performance history of potential vendors. The company may want to have a third party security audit or an independent security evaluation be completed before any agreements are formalized.

The terms of the contract is an important part of any potential offshore outsourcing agreement. Time should be taken to agree in detail exactly what each party is responsible for. This will lessen the potential of trying to identify which party is to blame when things are not done correctly or on time. The initial development of detailed requirements will make the working relationship operate smoother. If your requirements are not clearly documented in the contract, a company will find it very difficult for any international legal system to rule in their favor.

Another area that needs to be agreed upon is the metrics that will be used to measure progress and success or failure. Service level agreements are necessary and can be an outstanding tool to have if legal issues should arise regarding performance at a future date. The service level agreements should be agreed to and fully understood by both organizations prior to implementing any offshore outsourcing relationship.

Risk Controls

Best practices indicate performing risk controls decrease chances of offshore outsourcing risks (Willcocks & Feeny, 2006). Preventive, detective, and corrective controls are common tools that are implemented for risk reduction. Preventive controls lessen the impact of risk or prevent it before having an impact. Preventive controls include clarifying assumptions, involvement planning, establishment of standards, and hiring translators. Detective controls reveal the existence of a risk and expose future impact under similar conditions. Detective controls include collecting metrics on project performance and conducting frequent audits of offshore vendor sites. Corrective controls involve determining the impact of risk and require establishing measures to prohibit future impacts. Examples of corrective controls are rescheduling of tasks on a critical path, alternate offshore vendor sites, and hiring more translators (Ramanujan & Jane, 2006; Sakthivel, 2007).

DISCUSSION AND FINAL ANALYSIS

Due to the complexity of IT/IS projects and metrics, evaluating the long-term value and effectiveness of offshore outsourcing has been very difficult. Figure 3.6 illustrates that 30% of all these ventures fail to provide the desired outcome and 25% of these partnerships create no cost savings to the firm investing in them.

Due diligence and strategic planning are key elements to achieve excellence in an effort to improve productivity. Dun and Bradstreet's Barometer of Global Outsourcing study indicates that as many as 25% of all outsourcing relationships fail because the client does not clearly communicate its needs, costs exceed expectations, and quality of service is poor (Nair, 2002). As illustrated in Figure 3.7, poor client preparation and joint client-vendor planning accounted for 49% of root failure causes (Telecoms & Technology, 2005).

Despite increased risks and negative statistics, IT/IS offshore outsourcing can still be cost effective and successful if the right combination of due diligence and strategic planning is in place.

Figure 3.6. Cost effectiveness of IS/IT outsourcing

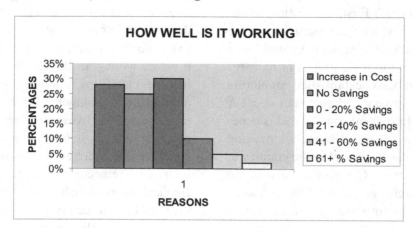

Figure 3.7. Root case analysis of failures in offshore outsourcing projects (Source: Telecoms & Technology Forecast Americas; June 2005, pp. 10-16)

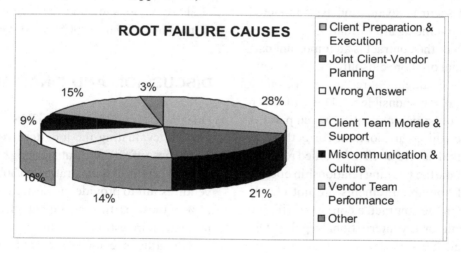

The most cited problem that leads to failure results from ambiguous contracts. Elements of the contract are often overlooked and left out. Many companies have paid a significant amount of money in hidden costs due to vague contract agreements and ambiguous requirements (Kripalani et al., 2006).

In order to decrease risks, companies must first identify those risks and verify the costs of each possibility. A cost analysis is also essential in the planning process. Cost analysis foresees possible cost associated with the production of the desired product. Building and maintaining relationships with the vendor company is an essential success factor that many companies overlook. Statistics show that companies that have healthy working relationships are less likely to have intellectual property laws violated and duplication of applications (Tucci, 2005). IT/IS offshore outsourcing can lead to a long relationship that should be nourished and monitored (Gupta, Seshasai, Mukherji, & Ganguly, 2007).

Next we discuss the eservices capability model (eSCM) and the capability maturity model inte-

Figure 3.8. Overview of eSCM elements, phases and capability levels (Source: Adapted from Hyder, Kumar, Mahendra, Siegel, Heston, Gupta, Mahaboob, & Subramanian, 2002 and Nair, 2002)

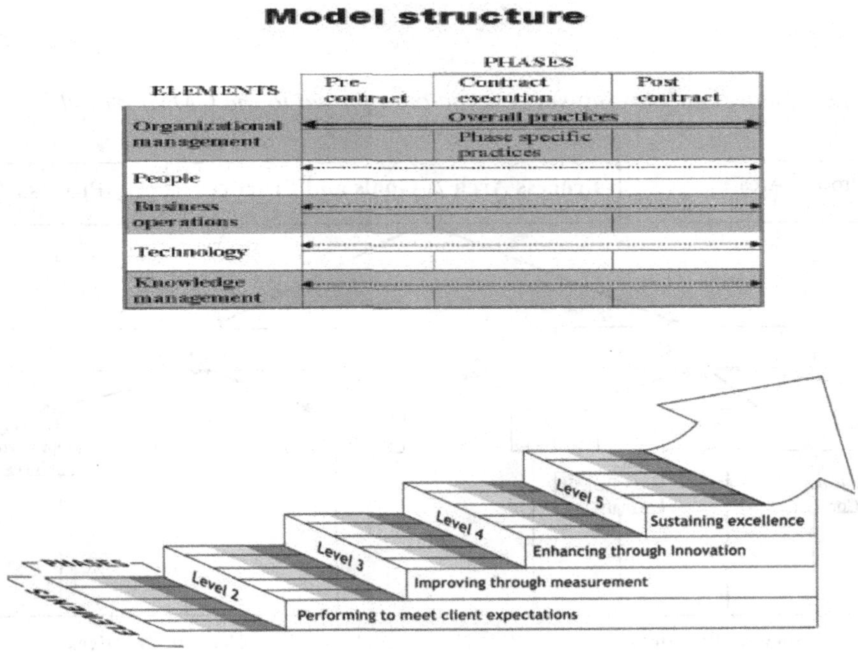

gration (CMMI) framework that help enhance the success factors and minimize negative risk in a offshore outsourcing project. The eSCM best practices framework provides direction on measuring and improving the value of outsourcing relationships by way of enhanced productivity, reduced cycle time, decreased transaction costs and improved time to market. It was developed at Carnegie Mellon University (CMU) to guide organizations doing process outsourcing, especially IT enabled process out sourcing, to form, manage and expand outsourcing relationships. Adopting the eSCM framework (illustrated in Figure 3.8) enables a service provider to implement organization-wide practices required for succeeding in a process-outsourcing situation.

Organizations can consider the eSCM as a holistic reference framework for implementing processes within their organization around critical elements of offshore out sourcing (organizational management, people, business operations, technology and knowledge management) and the different phases in an outsourcing relationship (pre-contract, contract execution, and post contract). The eSCM offers client organizations a means to select capable providers who are committed to delivering consistently high quality services and developing continually improving relationships. Also, we expect this model to provide guidance to service providers so they can more effectively manage IT-enabled outsourcing relationships (CMU, 2001; Nair, 2002;).

The capability maturity model integration (CMMI) developed by the Software Engineering Institute (SEI) at Carnegie Mellon University is used to improve processes for organizations to guide projects, divisions, or entire organizations. Improving processes increases product and service quality when organizations apply them to their business objectives (CMMI, 2005). The success factors have been incorporated into the CMMI model to demonstrate how companies can integrate these factors into their goals and plans (see Figure 3.9). For example, India has far more SEI CMM Level 5 (representing the best software development practices) than any other country

Figure 3.9. IT/IS offshore outsourcing success factors applied to the CMMI model

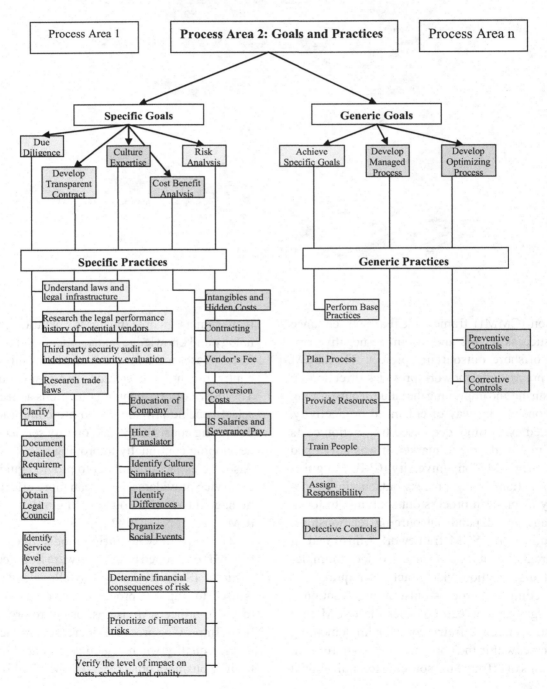

in the world. It had 42 companies at SEI CMM Level 5 assessment and the quality maturity of the Indian software industry can be measured from the fact that already 316 Indian software companies have acquired quality certifications (e.g., ISO 9000) and more companies in India, China, and the Philippines are in the pipeline to do so (www.nasscom.com; Barrett, 2006; Palvia, 2006). Companies can use the CMMI model and become successful in combining their management and engineering processes as well as ensuring that their products or services meet their customers' expectations. Companies can incorporate lessons that they have learned and address additional organizational functions that are essential to their services and products (CMMI, 2005). Companies have also aligned their internal practices with the People CMM framework and by use of Six Sigma methodology for reducing variation and assuring "end-to-end" quality in all company operations (Palvia, 2006).

It is important for the organization to apply the appropriate options such as in-house, outsourced, or hybrid options (e.g., build-operate-transfer or equity investments) to the CMMI model carefully, extend an IT service and measurement culture into business processes; map the offshore location to the organization's global presence; identify appropriate projects for global sourcing; define and measure business process performance and progress from a focus on cost to a focus on value; and focus on measuring business value after IT projects end. Firms expect to benefit from globally recognized quality processes and will outsource offshore to get quality service which would otherwise take the in-house operation several years to achieve.

To conquer the culture dilemma, IT organizations cannot simply try harder or place more pressure on their offshore vendor to deliver. Rather, they must address the issue at the source, within their own organization. Process and project management are the solutions many companies are turning toward. A sign of this trend is found with the 182% increase in companies completing the CMMI assessment from 2005 and 2006 (sei. cmu.edu, 2007).

Table 3.3 illustrates the comparison of the benefits and challenges of CMMI when determining if this model would best fit within the target organization.

Implications for Management

The market is changing as user requirements shift from supporting customized, internally focused

Table 3.3. Benefits and challenges of CMMI level 2 process adoption

Benefits	Challenges
Level 2 processes increase project oversight by establishing project management processes	Requires up to 100% more formal project manager roles than previously existed
Level 2 processes enforce establishing proper project risk monitoring through status and risk reports	Requires organizations understand how to apply resource management and project management simultaneously
Change control is formalized and documented once the project scope is agreed upon	Can be viewed by the internal and external customers as bureaucracy
Establishes processes required to measure work performed for time, quality, and commitments	Requires tools to manage scheduling and project plans
Minimizes the number of different processes used by different groups to accomplish the same thing	May be taken too far, meaning processes become rigid and restricting rather than facilitating
Can create more efficiency by reducing duplicated processes and steps	Similar gains in efficiency, quality, and commitments can be achieved without CMMI; commonly consultant companies are used to recommend process lightening and improvements.

IT environments to shared infrastructure, applications, and processes that are based on open standards. Incremental efficiencies are not enough in the age of outsourcing and offshoring; managers need to shift their emphasis to breakthrough innovation in processes that increase revenue (Koch, 2007). Managing successful IT/IS offshore outsourcing requires the intense strategic planning and full comprehension of the vendor firm culture. Important success factors include tactical entry strategies and planned control strategies. Due diligence and appropriate forecasting of costs and risks are essential for all projects. Appendix A lists the risk assessment factors and their implications for global/offshore outsourcing. In order for offshore projects to reach full potential, there must be a full identification and respect of cultural differences and similarities. Identification of the culture provides a foundation for a stronger relationship and increased job focus. As a result of deficient metrics in the evaluation of IT/IS offshore outsourcing operations, ongoing tests and vendor monitoring can increase the possibility of discovering potential dilemmas as root causes of the problem. Organizations must understand the strategic business value of offshore outsourcing that is instrumental in enhancing growth, cost, speed, and agility. Success will be undermined if the organization focuses solely on cost reduction or tactical problems. To prepare for the future, organizations must assess their sourcing competencies and evaluate their sourcing execution and strategy capabilities.

Implications for Research

Due to the lack of metrics in association with the evaluation of IT/IS offshore outsourcing projects, there is very little research available on the effects of offshore outsourcing on host companies and how these companies are adapting to these changes and challenges. Directions for future research include a survey methodology for cross-sectional or longitudinal data collection using the CMMI framework illustrated in Figure 3.9 and inquiries concerning the client company size and financial stability, countries of vendor firms with increasing negative results, and employee overall satisfaction of offshore outsourcing change. Future researchers may find it interesting to determine if there is a causal relationship between the degree of hierarchy within the organization, formality of relationships, and the success of the offshore outsourcing contracts.

Future research could address what developing countries are doing to increase the availability and caliber of project management professionals; the real cost associated with implementing a CMMI process framework and the process level that has the greatest return on investment; and efficiency improvements in offshore outsourcing projects. IT and corporate executives would benefit from understanding the percentage of onshore versus offshore project success after factoring in the various dimensions of risk.

CONCLUSION

This chapter has explored the risks of offshore outsourcing and integrated the success factors into the CMMI model to demonstrate how companies can integrate these success factors into their goals and plans. It is perceived that offshore outsourcing of IT/IS services allows companies to become more cost effective and focus on core competencies and competitive edge. Despite a growing movement of this offshore development, an alarming number of companies are experiencing negative results while outsourcing. The lack of metrics in this domain has made it very difficult to evaluate appropriate levels of satisfaction. As a result, companies should identify technical and business risks and formulate a strategic plan that includes preventive, detective, and corrective methods of implementation and evaluation. Cultural relationships should also be emphasized in order to develop a dedicated operations focus. To ensure success, firms involved in offshore outsourcing need to make use of more advanced and complex means of communication and coordination in order to overcome issues such as geographical distance and cultural differences; demand economic transparency and a strong business case; adopt flexible contracts; tightly manage service level agreements; keep and build the right skills; and build accountability at all levels. Methods of measuring IT/IS operations is expected to be a key development in years to come with the increased growth of computer technology, and more quantitative measurements and evaluations will provide companies with more precise performance evaluations in the future. Most critically, the significance of achieving win-win relationships by balancing customer savings objectives with vendor margin and overhead goals will help organizations transform competitive advantage into measurable success.

REFERENCES

Accenture. (2004). *Driving high-performance outsourcing: Best practices from the masters.* Executive survey results. Retrieved March 26, 2006, from http://www.accenture.com/xdoc/en/services/outsourcing/ps/global/landing_ps.pdf

Arbore, A., & Ordanini, A. (2006). Broadband divide among SMEs: The role of size, location and outsourcing strategies. *International Small Business Journal, 24*(1), 83-90.

Bardhan, I., Whitaker, J., & Mithas, S. (2006). Information technology, production process outsourcing, and manufacturing plant performance. *Journal of Management Information Systems, 23*(2), 13-25.

Barrett, D. R. (2006). Offshore outsourcing: Key commercial and legal issues. In C. Evans (Ed.), *The Euromoney outsourcing handbook* (pp. 39-48).

Beiling, Y. (2006). Demand for skills in Canada: The role of foreign outsourcing and information-communication technology. *The Canadian Journal of Economics, 39*(1), 53-60.

Capability Maturity Model Integration (CMMI) Overview. (2005). Retrieved May 7, 2006, from http://www.sei.cmu.edu/cmmi/general/general.html accessed 5/8/06

Carnegie Mellon University. (2001, October 4). *Determining capabilities of IT-enabled outsourcing service providers: A capability model and methods.* Retrieved May 25, 2007, from http://www.globaletp.com/images/clientExecSum_1.0_100401

Chakrabarty, S. K., Gandhi, P., & Kaka, N. (2006). The untapped market for offshore services. *The McKinsey Quarterly,* 16-22.

Chan, S. S. (2005). *IT outsourcing in China: How China's five emerging drivers are changing the technology landscape and its industry.* Retrieved April 9, 2006, from http://www.outsourcing.com/china_trends/index.html

Dhar, S. (2008). Global IS outsourcing: Current trends, risks, and cultural issues. In M. S. Raisinghani (Ed.), *Global information technology management in the digital economy.* Hershey, PA: IGI Global.

Dolan, K. A. (2006). Offshoring the offshorers. *Forbes, 177*(8), 1-12.

Dunlop, A., & Smith, C. (2005). *Outsourcing: Know your legal position.* Retrieved April 2, 2006, from http://www.computing.co.uk//computing/features/2072392/outsourcing-know-legal-position

Farrell, D. (2005). Offshoring: Value creation through economic change. *Journal of Management Studies, 42*(3), 675-683.

Farrell, D., Dibbern, J., Goles, T., Hirschheim, Rudy & Jayatilaka, B. (2004). Information systems outsourcing: A survey and analysis of the literature. *The DATABASE for Advances in Information Systems, 35*(4), 6-102.

Gonzalez, R., Gasco, J., & Llopis, J. (2006). Information systems outsourcing: A literature analysis. *Information & Management, 43*(7), 821-834.

Gottfredson, M., Puryear, R., & Phillips, S. (2005). Strategic sourcing: From periphery to the core. *Harvard Business Review,* 132-139.

Gottschalk, P. (2006). Research propositions for knowledge management systems supporting IT outsourcing relationships. *The Journal of Computer Information Systems, 46*(3), 110-116.

Greaver, M., & Kipers, K. (2005). *Outsourcing.* Retrieved on March 26, 2006, from http://www.valuecreationgroup.com/outsourcing_advantages.html

Gupta, A., Seshasai, S., Mukherji, S., & Ganguly, A. (2007). Offshoring: The transition from economic drivers toward strategic global partnership and 24-Hour Knowledge Factory. *Journal of Electronic Commerce in Organizations, 5*(2), 1-23. (An updated version of this paper is reproduced as Chapter 1 of this book).

Hall, J. A., & Liedtka, S. L. (2007). The Sarbanes-Oxley Act: Implications for large-scale IT outsourcing. *Communications of the ACM, 50*(3), 12-20.

Hatch, P. J. (2005). *Offshore 2005 research preliminary findings and conclusions.* Retrieved on March 26, 2006, from http://www.ventoro.com/Offshore2005ResearchFindings.pdf

Heib, B. R. (2006, May). *Characteristics of successful care delivery: Organization IT cultures* (pp. 2-3). Gartner Industry Research.

Hunt, T. (2006, March 7). *Concern over data security on the rise in outsourcing industry.* Retrieved April 30, 2006, from http://www.marketwire.com/mw/release-html

Hyder, E. B., Kumar, B., Mahendra, V., Siegel, J., Heston, K. M., Gupta, R., et al. (2002, October 21). *eSourcing capability model for IT-enabled service providers v. 1.1.* Retrieved May 25, 2007, from http://reports-archive.adm.cs.cmu.edu/anon/2002/CMU-CS-02-155.pdf

IT outsourcing destination: Russia. (2005). Retrieved April 16, 2006, from http://www.sourcingmag.com/outsource_by_region/russia_central_eastern_europe.html

Iyengar, P., & Rolf, J. (2007). *Factors to weigh before going offshore.* Retrieved April 30, 2007, from http://outsourcing.weblog.gartner.com/weblog/index.php?blogid=9

Koch, C. (2007, February 1). IT builds a better. *CIO,* 34-40.

Kraemer, K., & Dedrick, D. (2004). *Offshoring in Orange County: Leader, follower, or mirror of international trends?* University of California Irvine, Personal Computing Industry Center, Graduate School of Management.

Kripalani, M., Foust, D., Holmes, S., & Enga, P. (2006). Five offshore practices that pay off. *Business Week, 30*(3969), 60.

McLean, J. (2006). Slaves to technology? *The British Journal of Administrative Management,* 16.

Nair, N. T. (2002). *eServices capability model (eSCM)—A new quality standard for outsourcing activities.* Retrieved May 23, 2007, from http://ewh.ieee.org/r10/kerala/April_June_2002.htm

Norwood, J., Carson, C., Deese, Ms., Johnson, N. J., Reeder F. S., Rolph J. E., et al. (2006, January). *Offshoring: An elusive phenomenon.* A Report of the Panel of the National Academy of Public Administration for the U.S. Congress and the Bureau of Economic Analysis.

Nyrhinen, M., & Dahlberg, T. (2007, January). Is transaction cost economics theory able to explain contracts used for and success of firm-wide

IT-infrastructure outsourcing? In *40th Annual Hawaii International Conference on System Sciences (HICSS).*

Palvia, S. (2006). A model for choosing a destination country for outsourcing of IT and IT enabled services. In C. Evans (Ed.), *The Euromoney outsourcing handbook* (pp. 39-48).

Patterson, D. A. (2006). Offshoring; Finally facts vs. folklore. *Communications of the ACM, 49*(2), 41-49.

Petershack, R. (2005, July 18). *Consider the legal issues before outsourcing offshore.* Retrieved April 9, 2006, from http://www.wistechnology.com/article.php? Id=2007

Ramanujan, S., & Jane, S. (2006). A legal perspective on outsourcing and offshoring. *Journal of American Academy of Business, 8*(2), 51-58.

Sakthivel, S. (2007). Managing risk in offshore systems development. *Communications of the ACM, 50*(4), 69-75.

Seabrook, J. (2004, October 30). *Offshore outsourcing.* Retrieved March 30, 2006, from http://www.countercurrents.org/glo-seabrook301003.html

Seewald. (2005, February 2004). Best countries for U.S. outsourcing, 2004. *Wired,*101.

Smarter offshoring. (2006). *Harvard Business Review,* 85-92.

Telecoms & Technology Forecast Americas. (2005, June). *Forecast on the telecommunications and technology sector* (pp. 10-16).

Tucci, L. (2005, April 5). *Outsourcing needs strong RX.* Retrieved April 9, 2006, from http://searchcio.techtarget.com/originalContent/0,289142,sid19_gci1075783, 00.html

Understanding the WTO—Intellectual property: Protection and enforcement. (n.d.). Retrieved April 9, 2006, from http://www.wto.org/english/theWTO_e/whatis_e/tif_e/agrm7_e.htm

Willcocks, L., Feeny, D., & Olson, N. (2006). Implementing core IS capabilities: Feeny-Willcocks IT governance and management framework revisited. *European Management Journal, 24*(1), 28-37.

Willcocks, L. P., & Feeny, D. (2006). IT outsourcing and core IS Capabilities: Challenges and lessons at Dupont. *Information Systems Management, 23*(1), 49-57.

WIPO-administered treaties, WIPO treaties, treaties and contracting parties: General information. (n.d.). Retrieved April 9, 2006, from http://www.wipo.int/treaties/en/

APPENDIX

Table A.1. Risk assessment factors and their implications for global/offshore outsourcing

Risk assessment factor	Description	Implications for Global /Offshore Outsourcing
People	The people risk emerges from the experience level, training, and human resource deployment policies of the vendor. In addition, redeployment of existing IT staff of the customer is also a risk assessment factor.	Globally distributed teams with different skills and experience contribute to risk
Knowledge (Functional, Technological, Managerial)	Functional knowledge is the expertise, understanding, and experiences in the given functional area of the activity. Technological knowledge is associated with the expertise in the areas technology selection, analysis, architecture, design, development, integration, and maintenance support. Managerial knowledge is associated with the project management, risk management, resource management, developing and administrating management processes to carry out the activities.	The level of functional, technological, and managerial knowledge contributes to risk in offshore outsourcing. Managerial knowledge is extremely important in a global context.
Cultural	Cultural risks arise from the dominant culture prevalent with the vendor. The attitudes, communication skills, language, selection policies, performance motivation, team spirit, level of cohesiveness, autonomy, participatory decision making, work ethics, management style, customer-orientation, and related organizational behavioral factors that shape the culture.	Country specific cultures can add risk in global outsourcing. Language and work ethics vary from country to country and that may contribute to risk.
Political	Political risks arise out of trading restrictions imposed by the sovereign, permissible ownership rights, nationalistic aspirations, type of government, and political and economical stability.	Political instability is a major concern for global outsourcing as the government rules and regulations may have adverse effect on outsourcing.
Financial	Financial risks arise out of project accounting standards, cash flow, asset base, and currency stability.	Accounting standards and variation in currency exchange rate contribute to risk.
Quality Standards	Software Capability Maturity Model (CMM) and ISO 9000 compliance are hallmarks of the quality standards. The ability to prepare test plans, and performance standards is seen favorably while assessing the risks due to quality standards.	Quality standards vary from one country to another and contribute to risk.
Measurement	Performance measurement standards, benchmarking, and assurance of the performance are key elements in evaluating measurement risks.	Performance measurement standards vary from country to country which contributes to risk.
Scope, Cost, and Time Estimates	Ability to formulate the scope of the project, accurate cost and time estimation poses the risk.	It is quite difficult to accurately determine scope, cost, and time estimates in global outsourcing. This contributes to risk.
Company Specific Risks	Company specific risks are largely due to outsourcer's financial strength, area of core competence, management, relationships and alliances with other major organizations, and (potential) acquisitions and mergers activities.	Different companies in foreign countries have different management and core competencies. Those contribute to risk.
Legal Contracts and Intellectual Property	Intellectual property rights and their legal status in the country, brand protection, contractual bindings, and arbitration policies of the outsourcer constitute the risk.	IP standards and law vary from one country to another and contribute to risk.
Security	Access control, authentication, usage of secure protocols, encryption, and security policies adopted by the outsourcer constitute the risk.	Security is a major concern in global outsourcing as protection and control of data pose a problem.

continued on the following page

Table A.1. continued

Disaster Recovery	Ability to protect software code, and related data, level of replication, redundancy, and back-up and recovery policies are the main factors in deciding the risks due to disasters.	Loss of control over disaster recovery contribute to risk.
Contract Management	Contract management involves formulating contracts, schedule planning, activity planning, sending and accepting deliveries, dispute resolution, and signing off. Inability to properly formulate or execute the contracts constitutes the risk.	Contract management in global outsourcing is a risky business as monitoring the project activities become a challenge.
Relationships & Alliances	Ability to formulate customer-vendor interface at executive and working levels, customer relationship management, and developing long-term alliances offers synergy at organizational level.	Inability to manage relationships and alliances constitutes the risk in global outsourcing.
Geographic Location	The country, province, and city may be in different time zones, which require working at odd hours for the customer or outsourcer. The communication infrastructure, distance, industrial peace and stability in the region, availability of supporting infrastructure, social-economical-political stability constitutes the risk.	Vendor's geographic location poses some risks. Communication infrastructure failure in offshore projects incurs significant loss.
Multi-vendor Arrangements	Synchronization of development efforts, data format exchange standardizations, complexities due to multi-layer architecture dependencies or non-contagious independent parts constitute the risk with ability to work with multi-vendor arrangements.	In global outsourcing with multi-vendor arrangements, coordination has to be efficient. Otherwise execution becomes a problem and contributes to risk.

Source: Dhar S. (2008). Global IS Outsourcing: Current Trends, Risks, and Cultural Issues, in Global Information Technology Management in the Digital Economy, Mahesh S.Raisinghani (Ed.), Idea Group Inc.

This work was previously published in the Journal of Information Technology Research, Vol. 1, Issue 1, edited by M. Khosrow-Pour, pp. 72-92, copyright 2008 by IGI Publishing (an imprint of IGI Global).

Chapter 2
Emerging Trends in Outsourcing

Tapasya Patki
University of Arizona, Tucson, USA

A.B. Patki
Department of Information Technology, Government of India

Mahesh Kulkarni
Center for Development of Advanced Computing, India

ABSTRACT

Outsourcing has been conventionally viewed as a solution to generate quick profits and provide business continuity. The previous decades have seen the emergence of the Information Age, where the key focus was on knowledge acquisition and application. We are now progressing towards the era that revolves around "concept" development from an era that was information-dependent. This age, referred to as the Conceptual Age, will be dominated by six new senses: Design, Story, Symphony, Empathy, Play and Meaning; and shall focus on the human resource development aspects. This creates a need to diverge from the current reliance on linear and sequential algorithmic practices in outsourcing and to adopt cognition based engineering and management approaches. This chapter lays the foundation for Offshore Engineering and Management (OEM) and discusses estimation issues in OEM that have their roots in software engineering. Also, this chapter identifies the limitations of the current methodologies from an outsourcing point of view, and delineates how they can be deployed effectively for an outsourced environment.

INTRODUCTION

Professional outsourcing relies greatly on the attitude, innovation, and creative instincts of the taskforce involved. Pink (Pink, 2005) highlights the transformation of the society from the Information Age to the Conceptual Age from the psychological point of view. Left-brain thinking dominated the developments in the information age that focused on logical and precise analysis. However, with the globalization and increased economic uncertainties, the right-brain abilities like context, synthesis and emotional expressions have gained significant attentions for survival in competitive environment.

DOI: 10.4018/978-1-60566-966-3.ch002

While Design, Play and Meaning will be the focus of corporate outsourcing; the Story, Symphony and Empathy will be the potential areas of *personal offshoring* (Gamerman, 2007). The development of the working components of the six parameters of conceptual age, is suggested through cultivating the skill set and education (Johnson, 2006). Corporate outsourcing will be driven by the potentials of conceptual components in creating new economic opportunities. Therefore, the need for reorienting education has been justified for future success (Greespan, 2004). The criteria for economic success and increased productivity have been pivoted around creativity, artistry, cultural and technical experience. Oversupply, outsourcing, and automation have been thought as new parameters in the evolving state of economy (Wikipedia, 2007). The future corporate outsourcing will include CAD/CAM, and cognitive robotics from engineering and manufacturing sector. Also, health care, transportation logistics, entertainment media processing, and packaging and courier services oriented activities will be on rise, as new e-Services areas for outsourcing.

From the outsourcing perspective, software-intensive systems will play a significant role in a variety of projects, creating the need for a new strategy to improve the dependability and trustworthiness of the software. This motivates the creation of Offshore Engineering and Management (OEM) as an emerging discipline. The primary forces driving the emerging OEM trends are as follows:

(i) The competition between the left-brain and the right brain will pose new problems of demands, supply, and satisfaction in the conceptual age (Pink, 2005). This will lead to greater emphasis on cognitive aspects of information processing and less dependence on routine conventional data processing areas as manifested in the outsourcing activities of the current decade, like call centers, medical transcriptions, and claims processing.

(ii) Personal offshoring will boost the e-Service sector to meet the demand for new variant of products and services. Corporate outsourcing will be directed towards mass scale and bulk capacity products through reorientation of knowledge workers (Lumb, 2007). Service organizations, as well as production and engineering departments, can no longer determine the rate of new product introduction (Lumb, 2007). The production capacity has to be flexible in order to meet the demand for new variants of products and services that will be released at an increasing frequency. This trend is imposed by the era of abundance and is needed for co-existence and economic survival of SMEs and corporate houses, leading to increased reliance on outsourcing. The increased pressure on the search for alternative designs can be partially reduced by resorting to outsourcing.

(iii) The phenomenon of software aging is important in the context of cognitive support for outsourcing in the conceptual age. The detection of the onset of software aging can help to prevent dynamic failure events. Multivariate State Estimation Techniques (MSET) have been investigated for real-time proactive detection of software engineering mechanisms in operating environments involving multiple CPU servers (Gross et al, 2002)

OFFSHORE ENGINEERING AND MANAGEMENT (OEM)

OEM proposes the systematic and structured application of scientific, engineering, and management principles, through the use of proactive software engineering and information technology approaches, in the business process outsourcing arena. Proactive software engineering can be defined as a framework that extends the scope of conventional software engineering by incorporating additional concepts of fault tolerance, graceful degradation, software aging, adaptability, usefulness of software (pre/post-development) documentation, user manuals, and measure of module level Machine Intelligence Quotient (MIQ) (Patki 2006, Patki and Patki 2007). MIQ is a measure of autonomy and performance for *unanticipated* events and links the infrastructural needs of an outsourcing institution with its throughput. MIQ differs significantly from other indices like control performance, reliability, and fault-diagnosis (Park et al, 2001).

The use of a rule oriented approach for workflow control and design consistency checking has been illustrated in DPSSEE (Deng et al, 2003). The approach of semantics of software project for perception and cognition is broadened to introduce logic rules to all levels of the software life cycle. DPSSEE has limitations while addressing outsourcing projects. In the past, software engineering concentrated on the analytical philosophy and rarely addressed the issue from the viewpoint of design synthesis. Typically, problems were framed in terms of being algorithmically solvable instead of being intuitionally developed. For example, we have been using man-months as a measure to estimate the software development effort, neglecting to look at issues of manpower strength and profile of a software development house. It is still difficult to do systematic analysis to determine which software development project can execute effectively and which cannot, even with deployment of additional manpower. These aspects need to be focused in Offshore Engineering and Management (OEM) domain in the transition phase from information age to conceptual age.

First generation outsourcing efforts, such as ones related to call centers and medical transcriptions, belonged to the *automation* class (algorithmic, semi-structured or reasonably structured); they are primarily left-brain oriented - logical, algorithmic, and analytical. These tasks were adaptable and could be effectively handled by web-based ICT approach. The e-service ori-

ented outsourcing in the conceptual age will be heavily *cognitive* informatics loaded. Cognitive Informatics (Wang 2007, Van Eck et al, 2005) is motivating the move from the physical layer to the abstract level along the lines of the artificial mind system (Hoya, 2005). This leads to a corresponding shift in computer science with greater emphasis being placed on logical, data centric, and algorithmic styles, as well as on language and thinking modules. Non-linear, intuitive, and holistic activities will gain importance, in place of sequential, logical, and analytical activities (Pink, 2005; Lumb, 2007).

In the information age, the prevailing culture was to evolve business avenues by deploying computer systems and establishing Information Technology (IT) practices. Carroll (Carroll, 2007) identifies the concerns of engineering executives in outsourcing decisions and discusses how costs can be driven out of engineering analysis and decisions. After the board of directors opts for outsourcing, it is the engineering executives who have to ensure that the outsourcing partner will actually deliver what is promised. The situation is complicated, as engineering executives must control work quality, cost, and schedule in a situation that they cannot directly see. In the absence of adequate theory and practice of OEM, engineering executives rely on trust. Such issues cannot be satisfactorily handled with conventional software engineering practices or through legal procedures. The current methodology of directly extending traditional software engineering techniques, such as the Capability Maturity Model, to outsourced information technology projects, suffers from several drawbacks, as highlighted later in this article.

EXTENDING SOFTWARE ENGINEERING PRINCIPLES TO OEM

Offshore development has, so far, received inadequate attention in the software engineering literature (Meyer, 2006). The establishment of a large, complex BPO system that relies on a multiplexed architecture (Patki and Patki, 2007) calls for expertise from many different domains of engineering and requires a diverse, distributed team of people working simultaneously to ensure a stable operation. The transformation from the information age to the conceptual age will open up new job avenues that will encompass substantial cognitive content on the lines of proactive software engineering. Such a team needs to be configured to support two distinct types of activities: (i) sequential, logical, and analytical activities; and (ii) non-linear, intuitive, and holistic activities. The existing workforce must be reoriented to prepare for the cognitive challenges of the conceptual age outsourcing, in place of the watertight compartment philosophy of the past (Robert, 2006, Van Eck et al, 2005). In the subsequent sections, we discuss the limitations of existing software effort approaches in the context of outsourced projects.

Software Effort Estimation

The estimation of resources, cost, and schedule for a project requires experience, access to good historical information, and the courage to make quantitative predictions when qualitative information is all that exists. Cost models have a primary cost factor, such as size, and a number of secondary adjustment factors or *cost drivers*. Cost drivers embody characteristics of the project, process, products, and resources that influence effort. Boehm derived a cost model called COCOMO (Constructive Cost Model) using data from a large set of projects at TRW. COCOMO is based on inputs relating to the size of the system and a number of cost drivers that affect productivity (Pressman, 2001; Sommerville, 2000); the model takes the form:

$$E = aS^b \times EAF$$

where E is effort in person months, S is size measured in thousands of lines of code (KLOC), and *EAF* is an effort adjustment factor (equal to 1 in the Basic model). The factors a and b depend on the development mode.

The Basic COCOMO model computes **effort (E)** as a function of program size.

$$E = a \, (KLOC)^b$$

The Intermediate COCOMO model computes **effort (E)** as a function of program size and a set of cost drivers.

$$E = a \, (KLOC)^b \times EAF$$

The effort adjustment factor (EAF) is calculated using 15 cost drivers. The cost drivers are grouped into four categories: *product*, *computer*, *personnel*, and *project*. The product of all effort multipliers is the EAF. The factors **a** and **b** used in Basic and Intermediate versions of COCOMO are numeric quantities (Aggarwal and Singh, 2005).

The Advanced COCOMO model computes effort as a function of program size and a set of cost drivers weighted according to each phase of the software lifecycle. The advanced model applies the intermediate model at the component level, and then a phase-based approach is used to consolidate the estimate.

The four phases used in the detailed COCOMO model are: requirements planning and product design (RPD); detailed design (DD); code and unit test (CUT); and integration and test (IT). Each cost driver is broken down by phase as in the example shown in Table 1.

The use of COCOMO for analyzing outsourcing projects is hampered by two factors:

(i)   As opposed to conventional software development, the BPO environment calls for distribution of work force and infrastructure;

Table 1. Analyst capability effort multiplier for detailed COCOMO

Cost Driver	Rating	RPD	DD	CUT	IT
ACAP	Very Low	1.80	1.35	1.35	1.50
	Low	0.85	0.85	0.85	1.20
	Nominal	1.00	1.00	1.00	1.00
	High	0.75	0.90	0.90	0.85
	Very High	0.55	0.75	0.75	0.70

(ii) Some of the characteristics of the outsourced environment and the BPO methodology are inherently non-linear in nature.

Since the current set of cost drivers of CO-COMO model does not cater to these non-linear factors, one approach would be to add a new set of parameters that are related to offshore development and deployment of software including infrastructure and country specific parameters like Cyber Crime Index (CCI), Customer Satisfaction Rate (CSR) and Civil Infrastructure Status (CIS) (Patki and Patki, 2007). Table 2 characterizes and compares existing COCOMO model and the additional features needed for the OEM environment.

One study shows that linear scaling of existing COCOMO for outsourced effort estimation models may not be effective solution (Patki 2006).

Capability Maturity Model

Some observers attribute the success of outsourcing projects to the Capability Maturity Model (CMM). CMM is a mixture of process and organization assessment schemes. The Software Engineering Institute (SEI) at Carnegie Mellon University conceived the CMM certification methodology, under the aegis of funding from the US government. However, recent studies reported by Kitchenham (Kitchenham et al, 2007) have questioned the myth of the direct relationship between CMM and the success of software projects. The Capability Maturity Level is a measure of the quality software development ability as per time schedule. However, it is erroneous to assume that all Level 2 organizations develop better software than Level 1 organizations. Using corporate project data, it has been shown that software engineering metrics can be misleading and that software measures are often not as useful as practitioners hope. The cited study concludes that it is inadvisable to characterize productivity, either for monitoring or prediction purposes, using mean and standard deviation techniques; further, one should avoid making any estimates.

Pfleeger (Pfleeger et al, 1997) reports problems from the use of software metrics without keeping

Table 2. Comparison of information centric and concept centric approach

Discerning Factor	Information Centric (COCOMO)	Concept Centric (PROPOSED)
Modus Operandi	Sequential, Linear	Simultaneous, Non-Linear
Parameters Considered	Cost Drivers, which are primarily static (numeric)	CIS, CSR, and CCI which are dynamic (vector)
Concluding Methodology	Computational	Inferential
Resources Utilized	Databases, Files	Knowledge Base
Retrieval Algorithm	User Query Oriented	Pattern Oriented

the development goals in mind; they also discuss the applicability of CMM. The role of third party (ESSI consortium) assessment is considered in (Kitchenham et al, 1997b). The applicability of CMM in outsourced environment is further eroded when one analyzes issues related to the product line concept for outsourcing (Patki et al, 2006). A shared set of software assets, including the software architecture, is the basis for the product line. The potential customer association for product line could be along the lines of Microsoft's Government Security Program where trust is established as a policy and principle of business. So far, such an integrated approach of customer association and product line methodology has not been effectively deployed in the context of outsourcing. Software product families can be considered to be related products that make extensive reuse of available components. The dynamic object roles are useful, both for conceptual modeling and implementation. The links among the objects and roles are used for conceptual modeling of business applications (Subieta et al, 2003). While extending the scope of outsourcing to production of such product family, the need has arisen to introduce proactive software engineering concepts by augmenting the existing software engineering theory (Desouza, 2003; Keung et al, 2004) to accommodate software aging, reverse engineering, software obfuscation, and forensic aspects of software life cycle.

EVIDENCE BASED SOFTWARE ENGINEERING

Evidence Based Software Engineering (EBSE) is based on the premise that software engineering will advance by moving away from its current dependence on advocacy and analysis. With the introduction of cyber legislation it has led to situation where information systems and software have in true sense become reliable assets. In this context, the existing software engineering principles and practices do not focus on the forensic aspects of

software life cycle and therefore at best are suitable for post-mortem analysis for the purpose of cyber legislation practices. IT managers and Chief Information Officers (CIOs) in corporate world are concerned on these issues. With the web-based services, information assets are gaining new dimensions of distributed (region wise and trans-region wise) assets with potentials for risks and damages. The limitations of software engineering need to be overcome for ITES domain. Modeling and simulation consideration for BPO sector are discussed with load balancing aspects (Ansari and Patki, 2008). It is imperative that for the Cyber Forensic Module, the records of the usage are maintained and evidences are collected to decide the potential vulnerabilities. The dynamic obfuscation introduced to retard the reverse engineering process adds up another challenge for the currents practices of software engineering. The scope of current cost models that primarily focus on activities of a single system has been expanded in the context of system-of-systems (SoS) development (Lane & Valerdi, 2007). The limitations of using axioms in software metrics are discussed in the context of incorrect assessment of the validity of some software measures (Kitchenham and Stell, 1997a). EBSE lays emphasis on empirical based approaches for decision-making and for evolving new practices (Kitchenham et al, 2004). The five steps involved in EBSE (Dyba et al, 2005) approach utilize a continuously updated knowledge based mechanism. EBSE techniques for identifying, producing, combining and accumulating evidence, including metadata, are directly relevant for outsourcing (Jorgensen et al, 2005). In order to increase its relevance further, EBSE needs to be expanded to incorporate fuzzy logic inference techniques. Parameters like Cyber Crime IndexCyber Crime Index (CCI), Customer Satisfaction RateCustomer Satisfaction Rate (CSR) and Civil Infrastructure StatusCivil Infrastructure Status (CIS) help to determine the trustworthiness of a particular unit, and the progress it has made towards attaining its targets. Independent

Table 3. Significant factors for EBSE based contract

Description	Conventional Contract	EBSEBased Contract
Focus	Text, using standard vocabulary and grammar	Context and Trust, using mapping techniques after evidence collection
Basic Units	Clauses (for analysis)	Information (for synthesis)
Review	Mid Term Review in a fault-detection mode, projects unacceptability	Mid Term Review in fault-correction mode, projects acceptability and supports furtherance

agencies that employ EBSE principles should be setup to provide portals for assessment and periodic updates for these parameters, and the workforce should be retrained for such new jobs (Huitt, 2007; Van Eck et al, 2005).

Unlike Boehm's cost driver multipliers for product, computer, personnel, and other project attributes that are more static in nature, the EBSE methodology must provide for continuously updated values for CCI, CIS, and CSR, using inference-oriented models. The five-step approach of EBSE can be applied here (Dyba et al. 2005, Patki 2006). Overall, we propose the use of a EBSE approach for CCI, CIS, CSR, and other evolving parameters, in place of COCOMO, CMM, and other conventional models. The factors like software aging mechanism (Gross et al, 2002) must be integral part of the software effort estimation process.

EBSE APPROACH FOR OUTSOURCING CONTRACTS

Outsourcing contracts are developed for legal assurance and litigation based settlements. Reifer (Reifer, 2004) highlights that it is necessary to avoid legal *conflict* through contract administrations. The contractual relationship is a subjective interpretation of individual contract clauses, as text comprising of vocabulary and grammar in the psychological sense. In this context, fulfilling contractual obligations is a necessary but not sufficient condition for outsourcing projects,

especially in mission-critical situations using COTS methodology with MIQ features (Patki and Patki, 2007). In the past, the study of outsourcing legal contracts had been focused on the customer perspective (Koh, Ang & Straub, 2004). We need to extend the scope of these contracts to include design, empathy, and meaning (Pink, 2005) as psychological dimensions, in order to establish context and trust in the entire outsourcing system. Table 3 highlights the major differences.

The principles of Kansei engineering can be extended to drafting contractual documents for outsourcing applications. Kansei engineering refers to the translation of consumers' psychological feeling about a product (like a digital contract) into perceptual design elements (Coleman et al, 2005). Kansei engineering is a step towards supporting the six-sense conceptual age philosophy in the outsourcing domain; significant scope exists for integrating the Kansei techniques with EBSE methods (University of Aizu, 2005).

NEED FOR OEM CURRICULUM

It is argued that in the near future, outsourcing will promote innovation, shorten the R & D cycle and prevent over-engineered architectures. However, this requires for strengthening of an emerging discipline like OEM in the academic environment and cannot be achieved by merely extending the Computer Science and Information Technology syllabus to train new professionals in the field of outsourcing. Preferably, such courses could be added on to the existing syllabus for MIS students in the university education on a trial basis. Debate continues in academic circles whether there is a need for such a switch over in the current decade. Outsourcing practitioners and managers often adopt new technologies without sufficient evidence for the effectiveness. It is something similar in the past for deploying the usage of Object Oriented technology in the IT community, (Dyba et al, 2005). However, as a part of larger effort to examine the scientific impact of outsourcing and undertake suitable research, such an initiative is always a timely step. Since practitioners continue to deploy what is easily available, it is perhaps the fault of researchers and to an extent academician, to validate the practices through the industry-academic interactions by way of introducing industry sponsored graduate level courses in outsourcing. In India, a move to introduce a preliminary course at high school level (K-12) education for BPO has been thought. However, this effort will be in vain unless it is supplemented through subsequent continuation through university degree level education.

Systematic initiative in the form of a course on software engineering for offshore development has been introduced at ETH Zurich (ETH 2007). Perhaps it is a unique course that focuses on the technical aspects in its coverage. However, the recommended readings and text books clearly indicate that there is a lack of resource for teaching purposes and an immediate need to bridge the gap of non-availability of proper courseware and books is evident. No OEM curriculum will be complete without including subjects on engineering design and Kansei engineering principles and practices. Kansei engineering refers to the translation of consumers' psychological feeling about a product into perceptual design elements. This technique involves determining which sensory attributes elicit particular subjective responses from people, and then designing a product using the attributes, which elicit the desired responses. Kansei engineering is a step towards supporting

the six-sense philosophy of Pink (Pink 2005). Kansei Information processing is an active area of research at software engineering Laboratory in Japan (University of Aizu, 2005). The specialized courses on statistical tools for integrating emotions in product and services design and associated software are being offered at Kansei engineering Group, Spain for diverse application opportunities. Kansei engineering focuses on behaviors of people, as they perceive products, emotions and cultural bases in an integrated manner.

Some outsourcing professionals hold a strong viewpoint that the OEM curriculum should have extensive hands on practical interaction in the form of 3 to 6 months internship in the BPO houses internationally. This is analogous to medical education where the hospitals are attached with medical colleges for education purposes. The mathematical foundations for OEM courseware should include Chaos theory, random processes, fuzzy logic, and rough set techniques in place of statistics, probability, calculus, and matrices based methods. Further, substantial emphasis needs to be laid on applications of Genetic algorithms and genetic programming principles for arriving at multiple design solutions in place of existing single design approach for problems. Detailed subject wise syllabus level discussions for OEM courseware are beyond the coverage of this paper.

CONCLUSION

In the near future, outsourcing will promote innovation, shorten the research and development cycle, and prevent the deployment of over-engineered architectures. The growing use of proactive software engineering techniques in the outsourcing domain will lead to greater use of Evidence Based Software Engineering (EBSE techniques) and the new discipline of Offshore Engineering and Management (OEM), signifying the move from the existing information centric approach to a new concept-centric methodology that emphasizes cognitive content. These are in the areas of providing cognitive support using proactive software engineering around EBSE methodology to integrate seamlessly the operations of outsourcing industry. Formal outsourcing education through Universities will be a milestone in the transformation from information age to conceptual age.

REFERENCES

Aggarwal, K. K., & Singh, Y. (2005). *Software Engineering* (2nd Ed.). New Delhi: New Age International Publishers.

Ansari, A. Q., & Patki, T. (2008). Modeling Considerations in BPO Multiplexing Environments. In *Proceedings of Second Asia International Conference on Modeling and Simulation* (pp.132-137).

Carrol, E. (2007). Driving Cost Out of Engineering Through Outsourcing. *Software Association of Oregon*. Retrieved on May 29, 2007 from http://www.sao.org/Resource_Center/newsletter_articles/200604/200604_ed_carroll_management.php

Coleman, S., Pearce, K., & Lottum, C. V. (2005). *Statistics Supporting the Design Process via Kansei Engineering*. Paper presented at IPROMS 2005, Innovative Productions Machines and Systems Conference, 4-15 July 2005

Deng, D., Wang, T., Sheu, P. C.-Y., Maezawa, H., Tsunoda, F., & Onoma, A. K. (2003). DPSSEE: A Distributed Proactive Semantic Software Engineering Environment. *Fifth International Symposium on Multimedia Software Engineering* (pp. 124-1331).

Desouza, K. C. (2003). Barriers to Effective Use of Knowledge Management Systems in Software Engineering. *Communications of the ACM, 46*(1), 99–101. doi:10.1145/602421.602458

Dyba, T., Kitchenham, B., & Jorgensen, M. (2005). Evidence Based Software Engineering for Practitioners. *IEEE Software*, 58–65. doi:10.1109/MS.2005.6

ETH. (2007). Chair of Software Engineering, ETH, Software Engineering for Outsourced and Offshore Development. Retrieved May 21, 2007, from http://se.ethz.ch/teaching/ws2006/0273/index.html

Gamerman, E. (2007, June 2). Outsourcing your life. *Wall Street Journal Online*. Retrieved August 21, 2007 from http://online.wsj.com/public/article_print/SB118073815238422013.html

Greespan, A. (2004, February). *The critical role of education in the nation's economy*. Greater Omaha Chamber of Commerce 2004 Annual meeting. Retrieved August 21, 2007, from http://www.federalreserve.gov/boardDocs/Speeches/2004/200402202/default.htm

Gross, K. C., Bhardwaj, V., & Bickford, R. (2002). Proactive Detection of Software Aging Mechanisms in Performance-Critical Computers. In *Proceedings of Software Engineering Workshop* (pp. 17-23).

Hoya, T. (2005). *Artificial Mind System – Kernel Memory Approach*. Springer Verlag

Huitt, W. G. (2007, April). Success in the Conceptual Age: Another Paradigm Shift. *Educational Psychology Interactive*. Retrieved August 21, 2007 from http://chiron.valdosta.edu/whuitt/papers/conceptual_age_s.doc

Johnson, D. (2006). Are 21st Century skills right brain skills? *Education World*. Retrieved August 21, 2007 from http://www.education-world.com/a_tech/columnists/johnson/johnson006.shtml

Jorgensen, M., Dyba, T., & Kitchenham, B. (2005). *Teaching Evidence Based Software Engineering* to University Students. Paper presented at the 11th IEEE International Software Metrics Symposium (METRICS 2005).

Keung, J., Jeffery, R., & Kitchenham, B. (2004). The Challenge of Introducing a New Software Cost Estimation Technology into a Small Software Organization. In *Proceedings of the 2004 Australian Software Engineering Conference (ASWEC 04)*.

Kitchenham, B., Jeffery, D. R., & Connaughton, C. (2007). Misleading Metrics and Unsound Analyses. *IEEE Software*, (Mar-Apr): 73–78. doi:10.1109/MS.2007.49

Kitchenham, B., Linkman, S., Law, D. (1997b). DESMET: A Methodology for Evaluating Software Engineering Methods and Tools. *Computing & Control Engineering Journal*, 120-126

Kitchenham, B., & Stell, J. G. (1997a). The Danger of Using Axioms in Software Metrics. *IEEE Proceedings* (pp. 279-284).

Kitchenham, B. A., Dyba, T., & Jorgensen, M. (2004). Evidence Based Software Engineering. In *Proceedings of the 26th International Conference on Software Engineering (ICSE 04), IEEE computer Society.*

Koh, C., Ang, S., & Straub, D. W. (2004). IT Outsourcing Success: A Psychological Contract Perspective. *Information Systems Research*, *15*(4), 356–373. doi:10.1287/isre.1040.0035

Lumb, I. (2007). The Service Oriented Architecture (SOA): The Key to Recontextualizing the Knowledge Worker for the Conceptual Age. Retrieved August 21, 2007 from http://ianlumb.wordpress.com/tag/conceptual-age/

Meyer, B. (2006). The Unspoken Revolution in Software Engineering. *Computer*, *39*(1), 121–124. doi:10.1109/MC.2006.37

Park, H. J., Kim, B. K., & Lim, K. Y. (2001). Measuring the Machine Intelligence Quotient (MIQ) of Human-Machine Cooperative Systems . *IEEE Transactions on Systems, Man, and Cybernetics. Part A, Systems and Humans*, *31*(2), 89–96. doi:10.1109/3468.911366

Patki, A.B. (2006, December). Adapting Software Engineering Practices to Outsourcing: Forthcoming trends. *Lecture Series delivered to Engineering Apprentice Training*.

Patki, T. (2007). *Parameter Calibration, Customer Load Balancing, and Security Aspects for Multiplexing of BPO Infrastructure*. Student Research Paper. Retrieved Feb 17, 2009 from http://next.eller.arizona.edu/courses/student_papers/Fall%2007%20ENTR-MGMT%20489-589/Papers/TPatki_TapasyaPatki_ENTR589_Final.pdf

Patki, T., Khurana, S., Patki, R., Patki, A. B., & Prithviraj, V. (2006). Software Obfuscation for Information Systems Assets Management: E-Governance Perspective, Technology in Government. In J. Bhattacharya (Ed.), *International Conference on E-Governance, (ICEG)-2006* (p. 75-84). New Delhi, India: GIFT Publishing.

Patki, T., & Patki, A. B. (2007). Innovative Technological Paradigms for Corporate Offshoring. *Journal of Electronic Commerce in Organizations*, *5*(2), 57–76.

Pfleeger, S. L., Jeffery, R., Curits, B., & Kitchenham, B. (1997). Status Report on Software Measurement. *IEEE Software*, *14*(2), 33–43. doi:10.1109/52.582973

Pink, D. H. (2005). *A Whole New Mind: Moving from the Information Age to the Conceptual Age*. Riverhead Books

Pressman, R. S. (2001). *Software Engineering: A practitioner's approach* (5th ed.).McGrawHill.

Reifer, D. J. (2004). Seven Hot Outsourcing Practices. *IEEE Software, 21*(1), 14–16. doi:10.1109/MS.2004.1259166

Robert, S. (2006). *Designing Learning in the Conceptual Age.* Retrieved on 21 August 2007 from http://www.workforce-performancenewsline.com/Insider/06-27-06.html

Sommerville, I. (2000). Software Engineering (6th ed.).Pearson Education India

Subieta, K., Jodlowski, A., Habela, P., & Plodzien, J. (2003). Conceptual Modeling of Business Applications with Dynamic Object roles. In *Technology supporting business solutions: Advances in Computation- Theory and Practice* (pp. 49-71).

University of Aizu. Annual Review 2005. (2005). Retrieved May 29, 2007 from http://www.u-aizu.ac.jp/official/researchact/annual-review/2005/index.html

Van Eck, P., Wieringa, R., & Gordijn, J. (2005). *Risk Driven Conceptual Modeling of Outsourcing Decision* (LNCS, pp. 709-723). Springer Berlin.

Wang, Y. (2007). Cognitive Informatics: Editorial preface. *International Journal of Cognitive Informatics and Natural Intelligence,* 1–10.

Wikipedia (2007). Conceptual Economy. Retrieved on Aug 21, 2007 from http://en.wikipedia.org/wiki/Conceptual_economy

Chapter 3
Agile Software Processes for the 24–Hour Knowledge Factory Environment

Nathan Denny
University of Arizona, USA

Igor Crk
University of Arizona, USA

Ravi Sheshu Nadella
University of Arizona, USA

ABSTRACT

The growing adoption of outsourcing and offshoring concepts is presenting new opportunities for distributed software development. Inspired by the paradigm of round-the-clock manufacturing, the concept of the 24-Hour Knowledge Factory (24HrKF) attempts to make similar transformations in the arena of IS: specifically to transform the production of software and allied intangibles to benefit from the notion of continuous development by establishing multiple collaborating sites at strategically selected locations around the globe. As the sun sets on one site, it rises on another site with the day's work being handed off from the closing site to the opening site. In order to enable such hand offs to occur in an effective manner, new agile and distributed software processes are needed, as delineated in this chapter.

INTRODUCTION

The industrial revolution led to the concepts of assembly lines, shifts for factory workers, and round-the-clock manufacturing. Advances in IS now enable us to envision the non-stop creation of new intellectual property using shifts of workers located in different countries. More specifically, a 24-Hour Knowledge Factory (24HrKF) is envisioned as an enterprise composed of three or more sites distributed around the globe in a manner that at least one site is operational at any point of time (Gupta & Seshasai, 2004). As the sun sets on one site, it rises on another with the work in progress being handed off from the closing site to the opening site.

Earlier articles on the 24-HrKF have broadly classified professional work as being ill-structured, semi-structured, or totally structured (Gupta & Seshasai, 2007; Seshasai & Gupta, 2007). CEOs, presidents, and other heads of organizations usually deal with ill-structured work, the pattern of which cannot be predicted in advance. This type of work cannot be easily decomposed into subtasks that a shadow-CEO or a partner-CEO, located in a different part of the world, can complete during the next shift. At the other end, work in industries like call centers is well-structured and can be readily picked up by a colleague coming in to work for the next shift and located in another part of the world. In between these two extremes, there are many examples of semi-structured work where the overall endeavor can be broken into subtasks and a person in the next shift can continue to work on the incomplete task from the previous shift. Software development, in specific, and many IP-based industries in general, fall into this intermediate category.

In the conventional model of software development, tasks are usually divided on a horizontal basis among teams in different geographies; that is, one team in one part of geography developing one module, and another team in other part of the geography developing the other module. In this model, if one part of the project gets delayed, the developers working on this part end up having to devote extra hours, typically by working late into the night. Colleagues working on other parts of the project are unable to render help, because they are only familiar with their respective parts of the project. In the 24HrKF paradigm, this problem can be overcome by the vertical division of tasks between developers in different geographies. The latter goal can be met only with sustained research

of relevant underlying issues, and the development of new agile and distributed software processes that are specially geared for use in the 24HrKF environment. For example, new methodologies are needed to streamline the hand off between the developer in one shift and the developer in the next shift in order to communicate details of the task in progress, as well as pending issues, in a very rapid and efficient manner in order to reduce the time spent in the hand off to the minimum possible. Further, new task allocation processes need to be developed to address the reality that the developers will possess different skill sets and dissimilar levels of productivity. Such issues are being researched by a team involving individuals from academia and industry. The research group at the University of Arizona is working closely with colleagues in universities in Australia and Poland under the aegis of a collaborative agreement signed in 2005.

The research team at the University of Arizona has designed a process "CPro" that addresses several of the operational issues related to the 24HrKF environment. The core of CPro is a model of cooperative work called the *composite persona* (CP). A CP is a highly cohesive team of developers that are distributed across the globe. When the problem is decomposed, it is decomposed horizontally as is conventional. However, subcomponent development is now assigned to a CP rather than an individual. The members of the CP work on the vertically decomposed subcomponent in series, each successive shift improving upon the work of the previous shift. Based on the CPro process, a tool, Multimind, has been designed, developed, implemented, and tested.

DISTRIBUTED AND AGILE SOFTWARE DEVELOPMENT

Agile processes are relatively new to the field of software development and have recently accumulated both popularity among developers and a portfolio of significant, successful applications. "Agilists," as practitioners of agile software processes call themselves, are loosely united under the statements of the agile manifesto (Fowler & Highsmith, 2001). This manifesto asks subscribers to place emphasis on processes that are practical, adaptable, and produce artifacts that have value for stake holders.

Agile software processes are a class of processes rather than a single, specific technique. While agile processes are sometimes criticized as being reactionary to current software engineering dogma, they are not necessarily orthogonal to traditional "Tayloristic" software development. More specifically, traditional software engineering endeavors to establish highly defined, functionally specialized roles and encode almost all knowledge about the software under development into explicit, formal documents. In contrast, agile processes, although they are numerous and differ between them in fine details, favor informal communication between peers in a relatively small, loosely structured, and almost exclusively co-located group. Most well-known agile processes require a representative of the stakeholders to be either co-located with the development team, or at the very least a frequent visitor with direct interaction with the development team.

While agile practitioners do not completely shun formal documents, they subscribe to the "just barely enough" guideline for when and how much formal documentation to include. Much emphasis is placed on source code and artifacts that deliver immediate and evolving value to stakeholders. Popular agile methods that have a well-earned reputation for efficacy include extreme programming (XP), scrum, the "crystal" methods, dynamic system development method (DSDM), lean development, and adaptive software development (ASD). Highsmith (2002) presents a summary of agile methods that may be of interest to those new to the study of software processes.

We first review current generation of agile software processes. Following that, we discuss some of the relevant literature on distributed software development. We conclude this section with examples of distributed software development projects which employed agile software processes.

Agile Software Processes

XP (Beck, 1999) is the most prominent of agile software development methodologies. It provides managers and developers with a prescribed set of practices and principles within the activities of coding, testing, listening, and designing. The practices include fine scale feedback (such as pair programming or test-driven development), continuous integration and improvement (via short iterations), a shared understanding of the project (through collective code ownership and coding standards), and a development pace that is sustainable by the developers. The principles of XP state that feedback is most useful if done rapidly, with the help of unit testing, and that each problem ought to be treated as if its solution is simple, which is generally the case when incremental changes are encouraged.

Scrum (DeGrace & Stahl, 1998; Takeuchi & Nonaka 1986), named after a formation in rugby that effectively restarts the game by physically engaging the competing teams, refers to an agile software development management method. It suggests that small, cross-functional teams can maintain project integrity and productivity through brief daily progress updates and productive sprints through relatively short periods of stability. The basis for the process lies in the assumption that software development is an empirical process. That is, software development problems are poorly defined and customer expectations are an ever-moving target, and thus frequent feedback and control interventions are needed to keep the project on track. These feedback and control interventions are realized in scrum sessions, or brief meetings, which at a basic level attempt to answer the questions of what has been done since the last scrum, what will be done before the next scrum, and what are the obstacles that are to be surmounted in the meantime. Additionally, the daily scrum sessions provide a means for circulating knowledge about the current state of the project.

DSDM (Coleman & Verbrugge 1998) is an agile method that incorporates continuous user involvement with iterative development and the incremental approach. DSDM is composed of three phases: (1) pre-project, (2) project life-cycle, and (3) post-project. The pre-project phase identifies candidate projects, realizes funding, and ensures commitment. The life-cycle phase is composed of five stages: (1) feasibility study, (2) business study, (3) functional model iteration, (4) design and build iteration, and (5) implementation. The feasibility study addresses the business needs that would be met by the project, the compatibility of the project with DSDM, and identifies the risks involved. The business study extends the feasibility study by addressing the required budget and desired quality of the project. The functional model iteration stage involves: identifying the functionalities that are to be implemented in the prototype, the schedule for prototype development, developing the prototype, and reviewing the correctness of the prototype. The design and build iteration incorporates the functional components into one system. Finally, the implementation stage delivers the system and documentation to the user. The post-project phase is essentially a maintenance phase, during which enhancements and fixes are made to ensure that the system is operating efficiently. Enhancements and fixes are likewise created according to DSDM.

Crystal clear (Cockburn, 2004) is a lightweight agile methodology for small teams of developers. This development management method is intended for teams of 6-8 co-located developers working on non-critical projects. This method relies on frequent deliveries of usable code to users, reflective improvement, and on communication channels that are inherent to co-located teams.

This lightweight methodology is not applicable to distributed teams, since it requires co-location for communicating project state.

Lean software development (Poppendieck & Poppendieck, 2003) is an adaptation of lean manufacturing techniques of the Toyota production system to software development. It consists of seven principles that guide its deployment: (1) eliminating waste, (2) amplifying learning, (3) deciding as late as possible, (4) delivering as fast as possible, (5) empowering the team, (6) building integrity, and (7) seeing the whole. The elimination of "waste" is the elimination of anything that does not add value to the customer. Waste include unnecessary code or functionality, delays in the development process, poorly defined requirements, and slow internal communication. Amplifying learning involves continuous testing and short iteration cycles with frequent customer feedback. In deciding as late as possible, this agile project management method recognizes that, due to uncertainties inherent in software development, delaying critical decisions allows for project adaptation in the meantime. Due to a heavy reliance on feedback, this methodology encourages shorter iterations that are an attempt to keep the team focused on the customer's current needs and keep the development on target. Team empowerment is simply stated as finding good people and letting them do their job. The building integrity principle addresses the value of a two-way information flow between the developers and customer. Through face-to-face communication with the customer, the team can more easily conceptualize and maintain the system's maintainability and efficiency. Finally, seeing the whole addresses the tendency for propagating defects in large software projects. When projects are decomposed into smaller tasks, the risk is that individual developers cannot see "the forest for the trees" and therefore may propagate certain defects that would otherwise have been contained had the developer been able to better conceptualize the interaction of a component with the overall system. "Think big, act small, fail fast; learn rapidly" is a slogan that embodies the philosophy of the seven principles of lean development.

ASD (Highsmith, 2000) attempts to maintain continuous adaptation to the state of the project through a repeating cycle of speculate, collaborate, and learn phases. Since the basic *waterfall cycle* is characterized by an inherent linearity and limited feedback, improvements were made possible through the *spiral model*. Similarly, the *adaptive model* retains the cyclical nature of the spiral model, but assumes that the state of the project is emergent rather than deterministic. The speculate phase assumes that planning is a paradox and outcomes are unpredictable. The stated principle of this phase is that developers are likely wrong about the project's objectives and customers' requirements are likely wrong as well. The collaborate phase assumes that project management is occurring in a complex environment. It involves identifying the project components that are predictable and establishing an environment for development. The learn phase focuses on ascertaining value from the products built in the collaborate phase, examples include focus groups, technical reviews, and beta testing.

Distributed Software Development

"Follow the sun" methods similar in spirit to the 24HrkF have been attempted by others. Carmel (1999, pp. 27-32) describes one such project at IBM. In this early project, IBM established several offshore centers in a hub-and-spoke model where the Seattle office acted as the hub. Each offshored site was staffed by a phalanx, a mix of skill sets that were replicated across each spoke. Work would be handed out by the Seattle hub and each spoke would accomplish the given task and send the results back to Seattle. This hub-and-spoke model necessitates specialization of the Seattle site. With only one site offering the specialized service, the Seattle site quickly became over-whelmed. The original goal of daily code drops could not be maintained.

Treinen and Miller-Frost (2006) give details of two more recent case studies at IBM. Their first case study describes a significant software project involving development sites in the United States and Australia. Here, two geographies were being used to follow the sun development rather than our proposed three (or more). This project was deemed to be highly successful and reaffirms much of what the literature has advocated for initial face-to-face meetings, synchronous meetings across time zones, and building trust. Our work differs in that we assume no costly face-to-face meetings and our proposed method was developed to be effective with only asynchronous communication.

The second case study involved the three distinct projects involving sites in the United States and India. These three projects were generally considered a failure. Treinen and Miller-Frost (2006) supply several lessons learned that are echoed in other studies, particularly problems with continuity, misunderstanding, and the lag time between cycles of conversation. Cultural differences are also cited as problematic, especially with respect to various assumptions that were held in lieu of well-specified requirements and planning.

Distributed Agile Software Development

Perhaps the most relevant study in respect to the 24HrKF, *Follow the Sun: Distributed Extreme Programming Development* (Yap, 2005) describes a globally distributed, round-the-clock software development project. Here, a programming team was distributed across three sites (U.S., UK, and Asia) and they used collective ownership of code. One of the three sites already had knowledge of XP. The two remaining sites were coached on XP practices prior to the collaboration. These two sites believed that the first site had an advantage due to its previous knowledge with XP. The three sites also met in person, which they felt helped the program start by building confidence in the members of other sites. The team used virtual network computing (VNC) and video conferencing to facilitate communication. The hand off of project artifacts initially consisted of a daily work summary, but later grew to include knowledge learned and new objectives. This three-site system encountered problems in the form of confusion caused by cultural differences and also increased wait time due to downloading through their version control software from distant locations. They learned that each location needs an equal-sized team to prevent the largest team from taking over the design. They also realized that priorities were changing too quickly so they determined that the managers could only re-prioritize things once a week to make the teams more productive.

Xiaohu, Bin, Zhijun, and Maddineni (2004) discusses the situation where development teams were dispersed globally, though it seemed that each global unit was still responsible for its own module of the project. The teams did not need to discuss development decisions with each other unless they were related to interfacing or would affect another team. They used the XP method, but because of the global dispersal of teams, they lacked the benefits of customer co-location and participation. They thought the inability to get rapid customer feedback when the customer was in a different location adversely impacted the development of the product and the development time. These issues could easily impact development in a 24HrKF setting because customers in one location would thus not be able to interact with all sites. In the 24HrKF environment, a customer that is not global would have an 8 hour window for their working day, which could at most overlap with two of the three sites. This would cause at least one site to lack rapid interaction with the customer, and thus incur the problems seen previously.

Sepulveda (2003) discusses a company that moved from a traditional software development setting to a setting reliant on virtual teaming. In particular, pair programming was used heavily to ensure that the remote team members were as integrated with the code as were the local team members. This was accomplished with the use of shared workspaces and telephone calls. The key results of this case were that the move to pair programming and agile development enabled the team to cut out a large amount of bureaucratic documentation, but the remote members did not fit cohesively into the team as well as the local members due to lack of face-to-face experiences. In order to mitigate the team building problems, the remote members traveled to the main site to interact with the other team members. This face-to-face interaction did have results in terms of trust and ability to work together, but because all remote members were within the United States this interaction is easier than relocating global team members. The multi-site nature of remote work and the lack of face-to-face interaction are why this case is particularly relevant to the 24HrKF environment.

CPRO

The purpose of any software process is to improve the quality of the final product and increase the productivity of the participating developers. Software processes are implemented as sets of rules and procedures that guide the flow of knowledge as the development project evolves. Software processes that have many rigid rules and procedures are known as "high ceremony." Tayloristic processes, relying on the separation of work into tasks that are assigned to separate functional roles, are typically high-ceremony. Software processes that have few rules and procedures and allow for flexibility in application of those rules and procedures are considered to be "low ceremony" and agile.

In the context of the 24HrKF with development being done by composite personae, a high-ceremony process between the members of the CP will consume too much time in each shift. Furthermore, with members of the CP experiencing convergence by shared experience, intermediate work products that are typical of high-ceremony processes will likely impart little benefit to the developers. As discussed by Rifkin (2001), it is critical that a software process must match the overall development strategy.

The self-optimizing goals of the personal software process (PSP) (Humphrey 1995), as well as its lightweight, low-ceremony rules and procedures, make it a very attractive candidate for use by composite personae. However, PSP more or less follows the conventional single ownership model of development and cannot be directly employed by CPs in a 24HrKF. CPro, our proposed software process for composite personae, is inspired by PSP and its principles.

Tasks, Phases, and Actions

In the following discussion, a task is a high-level unit of work that is composed of one or more phases. In software development, a task may be the implementation of a class or perhaps a method of a class.

Tasks are decomposed into a sequence of phases. In CPro a software artifact will typically progress through the five phases: (1) designing, (2) design reviewing, (3) coding, (4) code reviewing, and (5) testing. These phases are typical, but CPro does not necessitate any rigid adherence to phases. As such, one project may use these five phases and another project, which may be more sensitive to risk, may add another testing phase for a total of six phases per task. Similarly, not all tasks must step through the same phases.

Dependencies naturally exist between phases of the same task. For example, for those tasks that include both design and design review phases, the design phase must precede the design review phase. Dependencies may also exist externally, between phases of different tasks. Such a dependency may exist when one method A invokes another method B. Since A cannot be fully tested without B being functional, a dependency link would exist between A and B.

Scheduling

Software projects are notorious for missing established marks for delivery dates. This is to some degree understandable as software projects are fraught with unknowns both internal to the project and external. When tasks are further decomposed along the vertical dimension with CP drivers working sequentially on the same artifact, more variance is introduced into an already highly non-deterministic system. However, good schedules are a part of software quality. When software is not delivered when expected, resources allocated by the stakeholder are idle and not efficiently allocated. This is often manifested in opportunity costs but can also be seen more tangibly when, for example, new hardware is idly waiting for delayed software.

Estimating productivity: For all but the most experienced developers have difficulty in predicting their own productivity. This difficulty persists when attempting to estimate the productivity of others. Even slight differences in skills and experience can create large variances in productivity (Humphrey 1995; Sackman, Erickson, & Grant, 1968). Consequently, we cannot ask one developer to estimate the productivity of the whole CP, nor can we ask a developer to accurately estimate the productivity of his CP or her peers.

For obtaining productivity estimates, CPro asks each developer in the CP to provide a cursory estimate for each task-phase of the artifacts assigned to the CP. These estimates are given along two dimensions: size and complexity. A single measure of estimated productivity can be computed by a weighted vector from the origin of the two axes.

Schedule casting: Once estimates are made, a Monte Carlo simulation is used for *schedule casting*. Schedule casting incorporates the developers' estimates and considers many possible future task-phase allocations. The result is a completion date that is given as a probabilistic distribution rather than a single date. Thus, a project manager can respond to stakeholder queries using a confidence interval rather than a defined date. The delivery confidence can then be used by the stakeholder as part of an overall risk-management and resource-allocation strategy.

Our schedule casting simulation is similar in some respects to a software process simulation described by Hanakawa et al. (2002). In our case, the simulation draws productivity from a continuous distribution shaped by the developer's estimate and prior records of estimates and actuals. Task-phases are also continuous variables, allowing for many task phases, such as design and coding, to be handed off in an incomplete state. Figure 16.1 illustrates a possible simulation run where tasks are handed off in an incomplete state.

Learning: Like its inspiration, PSP, CPro keeps a record of developers' estimates and actuals. This information is used to update the probability distributions used by the schedule caster for simulating productivity. CPro requires a mechanism for learning from this information as such, but is flexible as to the method to be employed.

The problem of learning is somewhat confounded when, in actual development, a task-phase passes shift boundaries. When a task-phase is completed, one or more developers may have contributed to the completion. Given the total time required to complete the task and the partial times invested by each developer, updating the productivity distributions becomes more complex than if the task had been completed by only one developer.

Currently, we are exploring two mechanisms to incorporate such feedback. The first uses Bayesian probability with joint distributions. The second method uses case-based reasoning where cases are constructed by prior estimates and actuals.

Knowledge Transfer

Knowledge transfer and sharing between CP peers improves the long-term productivity and value of the CP. Thus, it is essential that any CP-specific software process incorporate knowledge sharing as a core feature. In CPro, defect reduction strategies are used simultaneously for both the immediate purpose of quality control and the long term gain from propagating knowledge within the CP.

Artifact review: Artifact reviews, such as design reviews and code reviews, are a simple and low-cost way of catching many defects. In performing a review, a developer must read and understand the artifact under review. In the process of doing so, the reviewer acquires knowledge of the rationale behind a design or the inner workings of program source code. Reviews should be considered a mandatory task-phase and should

Figure 16.1. Actual work (note handoffs between phase boundaries)

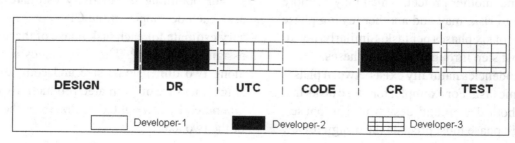

succeed any task-phases that produce project artifacts.

Test-driven development: Test-driven development (Williams, Maximilien, & Vouk, 2003) advocates the use of automated unit testing for defect reduction and quality control. In this method, test cases are written to stress code artifacts. Before an artifact is developed a minimal set of test cases must be constructed. As the artifact iterates through the code-test-debug cycle, each new class of defect must be recorded in a new test case. Test cases become a documented record of the CP's collective understanding of the problem domain and utility space of potential program solutions.

Heuristic assignment: At any given point in the evolution of the project, multiple actions may be available for the current driver. For instance, a driver could have the option of coding a method, adding a test case, or reviewing the code produced by the previous driver for another method. CPro includes a set of heuristics for recommending a course of action.

In this set of heuristics, CPro must balance the immediate value of productivity with the long-term value of knowledge sharing. For instance, if possible, reviews must be performed by a peer that did not produce the artifact under review. In this way, the review acts as both a quality control and knowledge-sharing mechanism.

Likewise, CPro must consider the set of open task-phases and the estimated productivity of each developer and attempt to match each task-phase with the developer that claims to be the most productive on this task. With high variance, the ability to forecast is very limited. Tools, like *MultiMind* that realize CPro can use a limited form of look-ahead scheduling to do some local optimization of recommended work assignments.

MULTIMIND

Suchan and Hayzak (2001) recommended that a semantically rich database be used in creating a shared language and mental models. *Multimind*, a collaboration tool under development and experimentation, aims to provide a semantically rich environment for developers collaborating using the CP method. MultiMind improves upon DICE (Sriram, 2002) and other proposed collaborative engineering approaches.

Our initial implementation efforts have focused on providing a "proof of concept" for the 24HrKF model. Based on feedback from the initial users, we plan to judge the efficacy of the model and tune our development efforts. A high-level architectural view of MultiMind is given in Figure 16.2. MultiMind is founded on the technologies delineated in the following subsections.

Lifestream

Objects and events relevant to the project are posted and logged into a chronologically ordered persistent database. This database, sometimes called a Lifestream (Freeman & Gelernter 1996), incorporates an algebra that can be coupled to the semantics of project artifacts and knowledge events to enable substantial automation of both mundane tasks and higher-level functions.

In the MultiMind tool, the Lifestream is used to archive project artifacts and provide configuration management services in much the same fashion as IBM's ClearCase (Allen et al., 1995), the Concurrent Versioning System (CVS) (Berliner, 1990) or the newer Subversion (SVN) (Collins-Sussman, 2002) revision control system. However, MultiMind also observes and logs knowledge events into the LifeStream. When a developer reads a message, posts a message, executes a search or reads a Web page, MultiMind logs this activity into the LifeStream. MultiMind can therefore correlate knowledge events with the discrete evolutions of the project artifacts.

Activity Theory

Activity theory founded by Soviet psychologist Vygotsky is an approach in psychology and social

Figure 16.2. Architecture of MultiMind

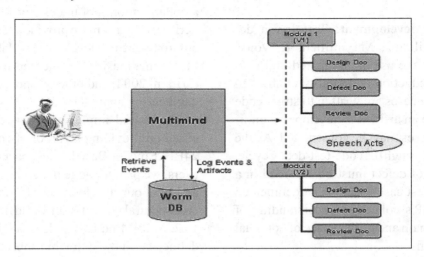

sciences. This theory provides a mechanism for reasoning about the purposeful interactions of active subjects with the objective world. A basic tenet of activity theory is that a notion of consciousness is central to activity. These interactions are the subject's interaction with external tools and other knowledge objects.

Activity theory is used in the development of complex and intelligent human-machine interfaces (Nardi, 1995). One such notable work is the User-Monitoring Environment for Activities (UMEA) system (Kaptelinin, 2003). UMEA is a tool for automatically organizing data objects into relevant projects, reducing the cognitive load on the user. MultiMind is advised by activity theory in much the same way with the same goal of making a significant reduction on the cognitive load of the CP members.

Speech Act Theory

Speech acts (Austin, 1963; Searle 1975) are acts of communication, primarily used in linguistics. Its theory categorizes communication messages into different acts of a common framework for reasoning about communication and meaning.

This theory has also been employed by knowledge query manipulation language (KQML), developed by DARPA (Finin et al., 1993) and by agent communication language (ACL), developed by FIPA (O'Brien & Nicol, 1998). The use of this theory in the context of Multimind is limited to action items within the scope of a project and does not otherwise dictate communication or impose structural limitations as in the case of the ActionWorkFlow loop between customer and performer (Flores, 1982).

In MultiMind, all project artifact interface elements are augmented with an embedded discussion tool. This tool uses speech act theory to tag communications as to their high-level goal. When a developer creates a new message, he/she may choose from either "inquiry" or "inform." The former is a directive speech act, which requests action on the part of other developers. In this case, an inquiry is a request for information about the artifact to which it is associated. The latter is an informational message that is associated to the artifact and does not elicit any immediate action from other developers.

When a developer responds to an already existing inquiry, he/she may choose from "response"

Figure 16.3. Speech acts used in MultiMind

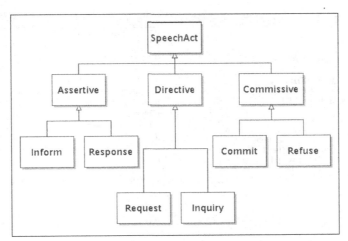

or "inquiry." A response is a definitive answer to the posted inquiry. Choosing inquiry has the effect of asking a counter question, typically when the original question was ambiguous and further clarification is needed for an accurate response.

There are five high level speech acts, of which MultiMind currently recognizes only three: (1) assertive, (2) directive, and (3) commissive. The declarative and expressive speech acts may be incorporated when the tool matures, but do not increase functionality in the current system. In Figure 16.3, we illustrate the relationship of the subset of speech acts used in MultiMind.

Process Awareness

MultiMind's architecture was developed to realize the CPro software process and as such is a process aware development tool. Intermediate CPro artifacts such as design review documents and code review documents are integrated not only into the workflow but into the user interface elements as well. In Figure 16.4, we depict a code review checklist embedded with a view of the code.

With respect to the scheduling aspects of CPro, the design for MultiMind incorporates tools for collecting schedule estimates from each developer,

logging time in development, and updating estimates as the project progresses. Schedule casting can be invoked automatically when an actual is logged or when an estimate is updated. The casting can then be pushed to anyone subscribing to such information, thus keeping project managers informed of progress. MultiMind's implementation of the CPro scheduling heuristics are discussed in more detail later on.

Scrum

In the case study of Treinen and Miller-Frost (2006), both cases advocate some degree of agility, specifically citing the need for iterative development. More specifically, they advocate the use of scrum methods for project management. While scrum is typically instituted in the context of larger teams, we believe the scrum method to be adaptable for use in the hand-off procedure between CP drivers (Rising & Janoff, 2000; Schwaber & Beedle, 2002).

In the hand off, we follow the scrum stand-up meeting pattern by attempting to ascertain: (1) what progress has been made in the prior shift; (2) what problems were encountered; and (3) what progress is planned for the next shift.

Figure 16.4. CPro code review in MultiMind

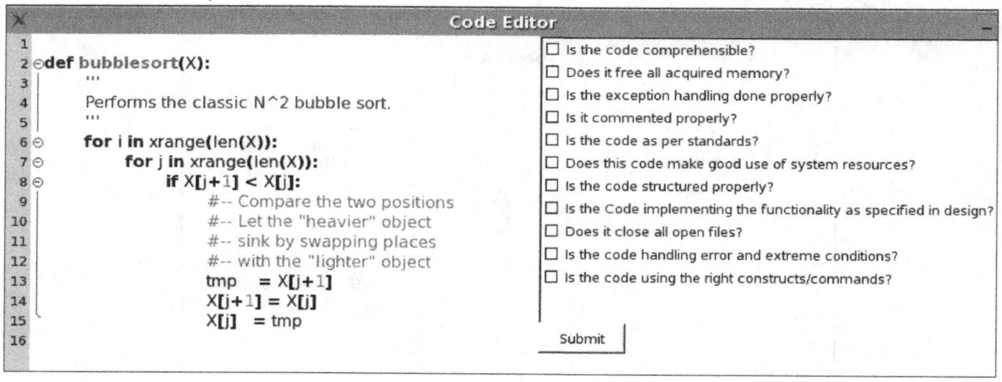

```
Code Editor
1
2  def bubblesort(X):
3     '''
4     Performs the classic N^2 bubble sort.
5     '''
6     for i in xrange(len(X)):
7         for j in xrange(len(X)):
8             if X[j+1] < X[j]:
9                 #-- Compare the two positions
10                #-- Let the "heavier" object
11                #-- sink by swapping places
12                #-- with the "lighter" object
13                tmp    = X[j+1]
14                X[j+1] = X[j]
15                X[j]   = tmp
16
```

☐ Is the code comprehensible?
☐ Does it free all acquired memory?
☐ Is the exception handling done properly?
☐ Is it commented properly?
☐ Is the code as per standards?
☐ Does this code make good use of system resources?
☐ Is the code structured properly?
☐ Is the Code implementing the functionality as specified in design?
☐ Does it close all open files?
☐ Is the code handling error and extreme conditions?
☐ Is the code using the right constructs/commands?

Submit

Synthesis: In the context of the three scrum interrogatives, much of the response to (1) can be synthesized by operations on the Lifestream. These operations would observe project artifacts that have been created or experienced evolution in the last shift. A summary of progress can then be constructed from these observations.

A common problem encountered in software development is when a developer is starved for information. If a dependency exists between two modules where B is dependent on the functionality of A, then the developer of B cannot complete B when he/she lacks knowledge of the behavior of A. This problem can be inferred when the developer of module B has open inquiries in the discussion associated to module A. Thus, a common problem often given in answer to scrum interrogative (2) can be synthesized without conscious developer action.

Templates and workflow: Our research team is currently engaged in finding other commonly cited problems for interrogative (2). Once a body of common problems has been identified, these problems can be embedded into the scrum hand off as a workflow and template script. In keeping with our design goals of minimizing the cognitive load of collaboration, templates favor go/no-go checklists over discrete set answers, discrete sets are preferred over numerical ranges, and numerical ranges are preferred over free text.

Task assignment: In answering scrum interrogative (3), MultiMind uses its Lifestream and the most current set of task-phase complexity estimates to recommend a set of actions for the next developer. The MultiMind groupware tool has a simultaneous perspective on the estimated productivity of all the members in the CP, relieving the need for each developer to retain knowledge of the estimates made by his/her CP peers. With this knowledge, MultiMind can look ahead into the next shift and attempt to balance the workload by recommending actions to the current driver while also keeping a favorable position for the next driver. With several possible actions available, MultiMind may recommend that the current driver attempt an action that is not the subjectively easiest one available. In doing so, MultiMind may preserve future options for the next driver such that overall productivity is higher. Furthermore, MultiMind is sensitive to the scheduling heuristics of CPro and recommends actions that are balanced on the immediate potential of productivity and the long-term value of sharing knowledge within the CP.

Decision Justification

Forward communication will in most instances be sufficient to keep progress moving forward. However, there will likely be times when the cur-

Figure 16.5. Visualizing the project Lifestream

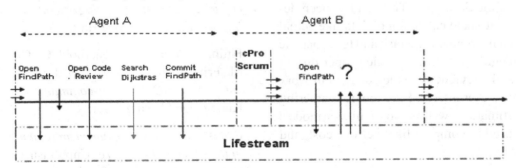

rent driver will not understand why the previous driver made a certain alteration to an artifact. Since the previous driver is not reachable, we can benefit by having some kind of proxy of the previous driver with which we can interact, even if this proxy is very limited.

For example, the current driver may look at the latest committed version of some program module which was committed by the previous driver. The current driver does not fully understand a new conditional branch in the code. The current driver may study this artifact for quite some time and still not understand why the conditional was inserted. Further progress may hinge upon whether that conditional branch is executing as it should or if it is even necessary.

Visualization and time travel: MultiMind's Lifestream records all committed project artifacts and all knowledge events. While we cannot speak directly with previous drivers, we can time travel back across the Lifestream to read the series of events that took place immediately prior to some decision that is in question. The current driver will be able to read posted messages and their replies, Web searches, relevant Web pages, and other documents and artifacts that convey knowledge. In this way, the current driver is to some extent replaying the sequence of knowledge events to put himself/herself in a similar state of mind to the previous developer.

Figure 16.5 illustrates how a visualization of the Lifestream may appear.

Semantic analysis and filtering: Visualization of the Lifestream is the first step towards decision justification. However, visualization itself is not likely to be sufficient. As the project evolves, series of decisions may not fit into the same space. Here, visualization must be augmented with intelligent filtering. Such a filter will apply semantic analysis to the events in the Lifestream and construct a visualization of dynamic scope and scale that includes only those events and artifacts believed to be relevant to the decision in question.

CONCLUSION

Due to collective ownership and wide variance in programmer productivity, the PSP cannot be trivially extended to composite personae in the 24HrKF. Furthermore, the high internal cohesion of artifacts developed by CPs makes horizontal decomposition counterproductive and rules out team software processes as a viable tool.

Thus, we have begun development on creating a lightweight software process for use by composite personae and project managers in the 24HrKF. This process, the *composite persona software process,* is inspired by PSP but is not a direct descendant of its methods.

Included in our work is a tool—Multimind—aimed at facilitating the developer in following the process and in communication between different members of the CP without much extra effort on the part of the developer. The tool has been designed to automate collection of data like actual time taken in completing a task and to reduce the relative cognitive load on the developer during activities like review. Also included in our work to date are a user interface to a tool for gathering project estimates as well as two simulation models that are used to compute likely effort, cost, and schedules.

REFERENCES

Allen, L., Fernandez, G., Kane, K., Leblang, D., Minard, D., & Posner, J. (1995). Clearcase multisite: Supporting geographically-distributed software development. In *International Workshop on Software Configuration Management: ICSE SCM-4 and SCM-5 Workshops Selected Papers* (pp. 194-214).

Austin, J. L. (1963). *Gothenburg studies in philosophy I.*

Beck, K. (1999). Embracing change with extreme programming. *IEEE Computer, 32*(10), 70-77.

Berliner, B. (1990). CVS II: Parallelizing software development. In *USENIX Winter 1990 Technical Conference* (pp. 341-352).

Carmel, E. (1999). *Global software teams: Collaborating across borders and time zones.* Prentice Hall.

Cockburn, A. (2004). *Crystal clear: A human-powered methodology for small teams.* Addison-Wesley.

Coleman, G., & Verbrugge, R. (1998). A quality software process for rapid application development. *Software Quality Journal, 7,* 107-122.

Collins-Sussman, B. (2002) The subversion project: Building a better CVS. *Linux Journal,* 3.

DeGrace, P., & Stahl, H. (1998). *Wicked problems, righteous solution: A catalog of modern engineering paradigms.* Prentice Hall.

Finin, T., Weber, J., Wiederhold, G., Genesereth, M., Fritzson, R., McKay, D., et al. (1993). *Specification of the KQML agent-communication.* Darpa Knowledge Sharing Effort.

Flores, F. (1982). *Management and communication in the office of the future.* Unpublished dissertation, University of California, Berkeley.

Fowler, M., & Highsmith, J. (2001). The agile manifesto. *Software Development,* 28-32.

Freeman, E., & Gelernter, D. (1996). *Lifestreams: A storage model for personal data.* ACM SIGMOD Record.

Gupta, A., & Seshasai, S. (2007). 24-Hour Knowledge Factory: Using Internet technology to leverage spatial and temporal separations. *ACM Transactions on Internet Technology, 7*(3).

Hanakawa, N. Matsumoto, K., & Torii, K. (2002). A knowledge-based software process simulation model. *Annals of Software Engineering, 14*(1-4), 383-406.

Highsmith, J. (2000). *Adaptive software development: A collaborative approach to managing complex systems.* New York: Dorset House.

Highsmith, J. (2002). *Agile software development ecosystems.* In A. Cockburn & J. Highsmith (Eds.), *The agile software development series.* Boston: Addison-Wesley.

Humphrey, W. S. (1995). Introducing the personal software process. *Annals of Software Engineering, 1.*

Kaptelinin, V. (2003). UMEA: Translating interaction histories into project contexts. In *Proceedings of CHI 2003.*

Nardi, B. (Ed.). (1995). *Context and consciousness: Activity Theory and human-computer interaction.* Cambridge, MA: MIT Press.

O'Brien, P. D., & Nicol, R. C. (1998). FIPA— Towards a standard for software agents. *BT Technology Journal, 16*(3).

Poppendieck, M., & Poppendieck, T. (2003). *Lean software development: An agile toolkit for software development managers.* Addison-Wesley.

Rifkin, S. (2001). What makes measuring software so hard? *IEEE Software, 18*(3), 41-45.

Rising, L., & Janoff, N. S. (2000). The scrum software development process for small teams. *IEEE Software, 17*(4), 26-32.

Sackman, H., Erickson, W., & Grant, E. (1968). Exploratory experimental studies comparing online and offline programming performance. *Communications of the ACM, 11*(1).

Schwaber, K., & Beedle, M. (2002). *Agile software development with scrum.* Series in agile software development. Upper Saddle River, NJ: Prentice Hall.

Searle, J. R. (1975). A taxonomy of illocutionary acts. *Language, Mind and Knowledge, Minnesota Studies in the Philosophy of Science,* 344-369.

Sepulveda, C. (2003, June). Agile development and remote teams: Learning to love the phone. In *Proceedings of the Agile Development Conference* (pp. 140-145).

Sriram, R. (2002). *Distributed and integrated collaborative engineering design.* Glenwood, MD: Sarven.

Suchan, J., & Hayzak, G. (2001). The communication characteristics of virtual teams: A case study. *IEEE Transactions on Professional Communication, 44*(3), 174-186.

Takeuchi, H., & Nonaka, I. (1986). The new product development game. *Harvard Business Review,* 137-146.

Treinen, J. J., & Miller-Frost, S. L. (2006). Following the sun: Case studies in global software development. *IBM Systems Journal, 45*(4).

Williams, L., Maximilien, E., & Vouk, M. (2003, November 17-20). Test-driven development as a defect-reduction practice. In *International Symposium on Software Reliability Engineering (ISSRE 2003)* (pp. 34-45).

Xiaohu, Y., Bin, X., Zhijun, H., & Maddineni, S. (2004). Extreme programming in global software development. In *Canadian Conference on Electrical and Computer Engineering* (Vol. 4).

Yap, M. (2005, July). Follow the sun: Distributed extreme programming development. In *Proceedings of Agile Conference* (pp. 218-224).

This work was previously published in Journal of Information Technology Research, Vol. 1, Issue 1, edited by M. Khosrow-Pour, pp. 57-71, copyright 2008 by IGI Publishing, formerly known as Idea Group Publishing (an imprint of IGI Global).

Chapter 4
Leveraging Knowledge Reuse and System Agility in the Outsourcing Era

Igor Crk
University of Arizona, USA

Dane Sorensen
Raytheon Missile Systems, USA

Amit Mitra
TCS Global Consulting Practice, USA

ABSTRACT

Collaborative work groups that span multiple locations and time zones, or "follow the sun," create a growing demand for creating new technologies and methodologies that enable traditional spatial and temporal separations to be surmounted in an effective and productive manner. The hurdles faced by members of such virtual teams are in three key areas: differences in concepts and terminologies used by the different teams; differences in understanding the problem domain under consideration; and differences in training, knowledge, and skills that exist across the teams. These reasons provide some of the basis for the delineation of new architectural approaches that can normalize knowledge and provide reusable artifacts in a knowledge repository.

INTRODUCTION

The increasing prevalence of collaborative work groups that span multiple locations and time zones create a growing demand for creating new technologies and methodologies that can enable traditional spatial and temporal separations to be surmounted in an effective and productive manner. In the specific case of information technology (IT), more than 380,000 professionals are currently focused exclusively on export-oriented activities (Aggarwal & Pandey, 2004). The hurdles faced by members of such virtual teams are in three key areas: (i) differences in concepts and terminologies used by the different teams; (ii) differences in understanding the problem domain under consideration; and (iii) differences in training, knowledge, and skills that exist across the teams (Chang, Dillon, Sommerville, & Wongthongtham, 2006). These reasons provide some of the basis for the delineation of new architectural approaches that can normalize knowledge and provide reusable artifacts in a knowledge repository.

This article focuses on the issue of providing information systems agility, especially when the work is outsourced from one country (or company) to another or as the work is performed in multiple countries using a hybrid offshoring model such as the 24-Hour Knowledge Factory concept (Gupta, Seshasai, Mukherji, & Ganguly, 2007). This article also deals with the issue of creating an evolving knowledge repository that can be used when systems need to be redesigned or reimplemented.

RELATED WORK

The object management group (OMG) is actively involved in the creation of a heterogeneous distributed object standard. In a departure from modeling standards, such as the common object request broker architecture (CORBA) and the related data distribution service (DDS), OMG moved towards the unified modeling language (UML) and the related standards of meta-object facility (MOF), XML data interchange (XMI), and query views transformation (QVT). The latter standards provide a foundation for the model drive architecture (MDA). In an effort to bring UML and the Semantic Web together, OMG is leading progress toward the ontology definition metamodel.

More specifically, MDA, as related to software engineering, composes a set of guidelines for creating specifications structured as models. In MDA, the functionality is defined using a platform-independent model with a domain-specific language. The domain specific language definition can be translated into platform-specific models by use of a platform definition model (PDM). The ontology definition metamodel is an OMG specification that links common logic and OWL/RDF ontologies with MDA. Common logic being an ISO standard for facilitating the exchange of knowledge and information in computer-based systems, and resource description framework (RDF) and Web ontology language (OWL) being the latest examples of framework and related markup languages for describing resources authored by the World Wide Web Consortium (W3C). OMG and W3C standards are available online at omg.org and w3.org, respectively.

The notion of reuse of knowledge has been previously explored with respect to organizational memory systems. Markus (2001) identified distinct situations in which reuse arose according to the purpose of knowledge reuse and parties involved. The knowledge reuse situations exist among producers who reuse their own knowledge, those who share knowledge, novices seeking expert knowledge, and secondary knowledge miners. The solutions to the problems of meeting the requirements of knowledge storage or retrieval were presented as a combination of incentives and intermediaries.

In the context of allocation of IT resources, O'Leary (2001) conducted a case study of a knowledge management system of a professional service firm concluding that service-wise requirements for knowledge reuse should impact the design of knowledge systems. For example, the studied firm contained three primary service lines: tax, consulting, and audit. Differential reuse, stemming from the relatively low reuse in the consulting service line to high reuse in the tax line, leads to a particular allocation of knowledge bases, software, hardware, and network resources. O'Leary's paper supports earlier work by Vanwelkenhuysen and Mizoguchi (1995), which showed that knowledge reuse has depended on organizational aspects of knowledge systems. Their work suggested dimensions along which ontologies for knowledge reuse may be built, based on workplace-adapted behaviors.

The concept of knowledge reuse and agility is especially relevant to "follow the sun" models, similar in spirit to the 24-Hour Knowledge Factory, and have been attempted by others. Carmel (1999, pp. 27-32) describes one such project at IBM. In this project, IBM established several offshore centers in a hub-and-spoke model where the Seattle office acted as the hub. Each offshored site was staffed by a phalanx, a mix of skill sets that were replicated across each spoke. Work would be handed out by the Seattle hub; each spoke would accomplish the given task and send the results back to Seattle. This hub-and-spoke model necessitates specialization of the Seattle site. With only one site offering the specialized service, the Seattle site quickly became overwhelmed. The original goal of daily code drops could not be maintained.

Treinen and Miller-Frost (2006) highlight several lessons learned that are echoed in other studies, particularly problems with continuity, misunderstanding and the lag time between cycles of conversation. Cultural differences are also cited as being problematic, especially with respect to various assumptions that were held in lieu of well specified requirements and planning.

Perhaps the most relevant study in respect to the 24-Hour Knowledge Factory, *Follow the Sun: Distributed Extreme Programming Development* (Yap, 2005) describes a globally distributed, round-the-clock software development project. Here, a programming team was distributed across three sites (United States, United Kingdom, and Asia). One of the three sites had prior knowledge of extreme programming. The two remaining sites were coached on extreme programming

practices prior to the collaboration. These two sites believed that the first site had an advantage due to its previous knowledge with extreme programming. Individuals from the three sites also met in person, which helped to build confidence about the capabilities of the members of other sites. The team used virtual network computing (VNC) and video conferencing to facilitate communication. Hand-off of project artifacts initially consisted of a daily work summary, but later grew to include knowledge learned and new objectives.

Xiaohu, Bin, Zhijun, and Maddineni (2004) discussed the situation where development teams were dispersed globally, though it seemed that each global unit was still responsible for its own module of the project. The teams did not need to discuss development decisions with each other unless they were related to interfacing or would affect another team. They used the extreme programming method, but because of the global dispersal of teams, they lacked the benefits of customer colocation and participation. They thought the inability to get rapid customer feedback when the customer was in a different location adversely impacted the development of the product and the development time. These issues could easily impact development in a 24-Hour Knowledge Factory setting because customers in one location would thus not be able to interact with all sites.

The above examples highlight the need for an agile knowledge ontology that can more adequately manages the problem of change.

AGILITY AND THE PROBLEM OF CHANGE

Change is difficult, complex, and risky because it usually has unintended side effects. Each decision has many consequences, which in turn have many more. The Y2K problem is a classic example of a seemingly innocuous design decision that snowballed into a worldwide problem. The decision to use a 2-digit representation of the year was originally deemed to be prudent. Later, it was thought to be a problem that would cripple computer systems when their clocks rolled over into the year 2000, since 00 is ambiguous. Ultimately, it cost the world around $600 billion (López-Bassols, 1998) to convert a 2-digit representation of the calendar year to four digits!

Fundamental Computing Technologies

Figure 1 shows the evolution of computing technology as researchers sought to tackle the problem of change and to remain agile though increasingly more complex demands are placed upon the technology.

At the far left end of the spectrum lies hardware, originally physically and meticulously programmed to perform relatively simple tasks. Machine code replaced the physical machine programming by the formulation of CPU-specific words, bit patterns corresponding to different commands that can be issued to the machine. Each type of CPU has its own machine code. Similarly, the CPU architecture has a corresponding assembly language. As such, assembly language is not portable and does not increase flexibility, but it does provide the essential abstractions that free the programmer from the tedium of remembering numeric codes or calculating addresses (as was the case when programming was accomplished through machine code). An assembly language is an example of a second-generation language. Third generation languages, denoted by 3GL in Figure 1, finally freed the task of programming from the

underlying hardware. This is a much overlooked, but crucial, example of adapting technology to find a solution to the problem of change.

The more recent notion of component-based development (CBD) involves building software systems using prepackaged software components (Ravichandran, 2005). CBD involves reusing application frameworks, which provide the architecture for assembling components into a software system. Components and frameworks may be either developed in-house or externally procured. CBD typically involves using both in-house developed and externally procured software components and frameworks. CBD leverages the emergence of middleware and software objects standards to make software reuse a reality (Ravichandran, 2005). Since CBD encourages the move toward more modular systems built from reusable software artifacts, it was expected to enhance the adaptability, scalability, and maintainability of the resultant software (Szyperski, 1997). CBD requires systems to be architected using a component framework necessitating developers to think through the interrelationships between various elements of an application system at a more granular level at an earlier stage in the development process than in traditional development approaches (Sparling, 2000).

IBM's System/360: The Beginnings of Agile Development

A good example of a business transformation tackling the issues of agility and change through modularity is provided by IBM's System/360

Figure 1.

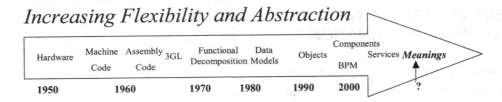

(Amdahl & Blaauw, 2000) in the 1960s (Baldwin & Clark, 2000). The hardwired instruction sets of virtually all computers in the 1950s imposed a high level of interdependence of design parameters. Each computer was designed from scratch and each market niche was matched with a different system. Searching for new ways for teams to work together on a project, IBM led the effort to use modularity as a guiding principle. System/360 was the result of that effort. Further, System/360 marks the point at which the industry was transformed from a virtual monopoly to a modular cluster comprised of more than a thousand publicly traded firms and many startups (Fergusson, 2004).

What makes System/360 an important landmark in the agility effort is that it belongs to the first family of computers that was designed with a clear distinction between architecture and implementation. The architecture of each model in the 360 family was introduced as an industry standard, while the system peripherals, such as disk drives, magnetic tape drives, or communication interfaces allowed the customer to configure the system by selecting from this list. With the standardization of the architecture and peripheral interfaces, IBM opened the doors for the commodity component market. With its list of peripherals, System/360 allowed the technology to adapt to a customer's needs. Its backward compatibility tackled the problem of change in its own right, by allowing customers to upgrade and replace their hardware without losing essential capabilities. The ideas of encapsulation of functionality and the standardization of system interfaces inherent in System/360 are critical to understanding the importance of leveraging and reuse of knowledge.

BUSINESS RULES AND THE STRUCTURE OF INFORMATION

Just as was the case with early computer technology decades ago, prior to 3GL in our first example and System/360 in the second, today's business rules are replicated in dissimilar formats in intermingled ways in multiple information systems and business processes. When any rule is changed, a concerted effort must be launched to make modifications in multiple systems. It makes change and innovation complex and error-prone. The framework described in this article attempts to untangle business rules with an ontology derived from the inherent structure of information. By untangling business rules even in complex legacy models and systems, one gains the capability to represent specific elements of business knowledge once, and only once, in a knowledge repository. Using this repository, the specific elements of knowledge can be designed to naturally manifest themselves, in appropriate forms, to suit the idiosyncrasies of different business contexts.

As business processes became more tightly coupled with automation, the lack of agility in information systems became a serious bottleneck to product and process innovation. Frameworks that have attempted to solve this problem include structured programming, reusable code libraries, relational databases, expert systems, object technology, CASE tools, code generators and CAPE tools. They were not very effective partially because they did not adequately address the ripple effects of change; ideally, business rules and knowledge should be represented so that when we change a rule once, corresponding changes should automatically ripple across all the relevant business processes (Mitra & Gupta, 2006).

Knowledge transfer and reuse (Kingston 2002; Myopolous 1998; Van Zyl & Corbett, 2000) attain greater importance in the case of outsourcing. In order to achieve efficiency of resource consumption, we need new approaches to facilitate encapsulation of knowledge and the sharing of such knowledge among the relevant set of workers.

THE FRAMEWORK OF KNOWLEDGE REUSE

While meaning and understanding are abstract notions, they are rooted in the physical world. We learned in chemistry that we can continually subdivide a substance before reaching a building block, the subdivision of which would disallow us from identifying the substance and knowing its properties. Similarly, to identify the components of knowledge, we must distinguish between assertions whose division will involve no loss of information, and assertions whose division will sacrifice meaning: if an assertion is decomposed into smaller parts and the information lost cannot be recovered by reassembling the pieces. The fundamental rules that cannot be decomposed further without irrecoverable loss of information are called indivisible rules, atomic rules, or irreducible facts (Ross, 1997).

Objects, Relationships, Processes, Events, and Patterns

In the real world, every object conveys information. The information content of physical objects is conveyed to us via one or more of our five senses. Objects are associated with one another. While some associations involve the passage of time, other associations, such as the relative locations of physical objects, are relationships that do not necessarily involve time. These relationships and associations are natural storehouses of information about real world objects. Further, these relationships are objects in their own right.

Processes are artifacts for expressing information about relationships that involve the passage of time (i.e., those that involve before and after effects). As such, the process is not only an association but also an association that describes a causative temporal sequence and passage of time. This is also how the meaning of causality is born: The resources and the processes that create the product are its causes. A process always makes a change or seeks information. Business process engineers use the term *cycle time* to describe the time interval from the beginning of a process to its end. A process, like the event it is derived from, can even be instantaneous or may continue on indefinitely. Processes that do not end, or have no known end, are called sagas. Therefore, a process is a relationship, and also an event, which may be of finite, negligible, or endless duration.

Knowledge involves the recognition of patterns. Patterns involve structure, the concept of similarity, and the ability to distinguish between the components that form a pattern. Claude Shannon developed a quantitative measure for information content (Shannon, 1948). However, he did not describe the structure of information. For that, we must start with the concept and fundamental structure of *Pattern* and measurability in order to build a metamodel of knowledge. The integrated metamodel model of Pattern and measurability (from which the concept of "property" emerges) will enable us to integrate the three components that comprise business knowledge (inference, rules, and processes) into one indivisible whole. The interplay between objects and processes is driven by patterns. Patterns guide the creation of relationships between objects, such as the formation of a team or the modular assignment of duties within a team and across geographically distributed teams. Partnering Employee belonging to one team with that of another is caused by a skill or performance pattern that governs the relevant properties of Employee. As such, the ownership of an artifact under development is shared between Employee objects, which, at a coarser granularity, exist as a unified object we can refer to as a Composite Persona (CP) (Denny et al., 2008).

Perception and Information: Meaning, Measurability, and Format

When an object is a meaning, it is an abstract pattern of information. Its perception is a concrete expression of this meaning, and the same information may be perceived or expressed in many ways. Lacking perceptual information, several expressions or perceptions may all point to the same pattern of information, or meaning. In order to normalize knowledge, we must separate meaning from its expression. This may be done by augmenting our metamodel to represent entities of pure information that exist beyond physical objects and relationships. This section will introduce three of these objects: domain, unit of measure (UOM), and Format.

Unlike matter or energy, meaning is not located at a particular point in space and time; only its expression is (Verdu, 1998). All physical objects or energy manifested at a particular place at a point in time convey information, and the same meaning can occur in two different artifacts that have no spatial or temporal relationship with each other. They only share meaning (i.e., information content; Baggot, 1992). A single meaning may be characterized by multiple expressions. Differing understandings of concepts, terminology, and definitions are some of the problems that have characterize software developers working in a multisite environment (Chang et al., 2006). Unlike a specific material object or a packet of energy that is bound to only a single location at a single point in time, identical information can exist at many different places at several different times. The need to understand the underlying natural structures that connect information to its physical expressions is inherent in the effort to normalize business rules.

Information mediation and expression within the real world is achieved by two metaobjects. One is intangible, emerging from the concept of measurability and deals with the amount of information that is inherent in the meaning being conveyed. The other is tangible; it deals with the format, or physical form, of expression. The format is easier to recognize. It is much harder to recognize the domain of measurability, henceforth referred to simply as domain (Finkbeiner, 1966).

Measurability and Information Content

Through the behavior, or properties, of objects we observe, the information content of reality manifests itself to us. Although these are quite dissimilar qualities of inherently dissimilar objects, such as a person's weight and the volume of juice, both these values are drawn from a domain of information that contains some common behavior. This common behavior, that each value can be quantitatively measured, is inherent in the information being conveyed by the measurement of these values, but not in the objects themselves.

Physical Expression of Domains

Domains convey the concepts of measurability and existence. They are a key constituent of knowledge. There are four fundamental domains that we will consider in this article; two of them convey qualitative information and the other two convey quantitative information, as follows:

- Qualitative domains, containing:
  - Nominal Domains, which convey no information on sequencing, distances, or ratios. They convey only distinctions, distinguishing one object from another or a class from another.
  - Ordinal domains, which convey distinctions between objects and the information on arranging its members in a sequence. Ordinal domains are a pattern of information derived from nominal domains by adding sequencing information. However, ordinal domains posses no information regarding the magnitudes of gaps or ratios between objects (values).
- Quantitative domains:
  - Difference-scaled domains not only express all the information that qualita-

tive domains convey, but also convey magnitudes of difference; they allow for measurement of the magnitude of point-to-point differences in a sequence. This makes difference-scaled domains to be a pattern of information derived from ordinal domains by adding quantitative information on differences between values in the domain, which makes it a subclass of ordinal domains in the ontology of the meaning of measurability.

o   Ratio-scaled domains perform three functions; they assist in the classification and arrangement of objects in a natural sequence, are able to measure the magnitude of differences in properties of objects, and take the ratios of these different properties.

The hierarchy of domains provides the most fundamental kind of knowledge reuse. However, this information is still abstract. In order to give information a physical expression, it must be physically formatted and recorded on some sort of medium. A single piece of information must be recorded on at least one medium, and may be recorded in many different formats.

A symbol is sufficient to physically represent the information conveyed by nominal and ordinal domains. Of course, ordinal domains also carry sequencing information, and it would make sense to map ordinal values to a naturally sequenced set of symbols like digits or letters.

Unlike qualitative domains, quantitative domains need both symbols and units of measure to physically express all the information they carry. This is because they are dense domains (i.e., given a pair of values, regardless of how close they are to each other, it is always possible to find a value in between them). A discrete set of symbols cannot convey all the information in a quantitative domain. However, numbers have this characteristic of being dense. Therefore, it is

possible to map values in a dense domain to an arbitrary set of numbers without losing information. These numbers may then be represented by physical symbols such as decimal digits, roman numerals, or binary or octal numbers. There may be many different mappings between values and numbers. For example, age may be expressed in months, years, or days; a person's age will be the same regardless of the number used. To show that different numbers may express the same meaning, we need a unit of measure (UOM). The UOM is the name of the specific map used to express that meaning. Age in years, days, months, and hours are all different UOMs for the elapsed time domain.

Both the number and UOM must be physically represented by a symbol to physically format the information in a quantitative domain. Indeed, a UOM may be represented by several different symbols. The UOM "dollars," for the money domain, may be represented by the symbol "$" or the text "USD." In general, a dense domain needs a pair of symbols to fully represent the information in it: a symbol for the UOM and a symbol for the number mapped to a value. We will call this pair the full format of the domain.

Domains, UOMs, and Formats are all objects that structure meaning. They are some of the components from which the very concept of knowledge is assembled. The metamodel of knowledge is a model of the meaning of knowledge built from abstract components.

Figure 2 depicts a semantic model. The lower limit (1) on the occurrence of Unit of Measure highlights the fact that each quantitative domain must possess at least one unit of measure. This is because the unit of measure is not optional. A quantitative value cannot be expressed unless a unit of measure can characterize it. The arrow that starts from, and loops back to, Unit of Measure reads "Unit of Measure converts to none or at most 1 Unit of Measure." Conversion rules, such as those for currency conversion or distance con-

Figure 2. A partial metamodel of domain

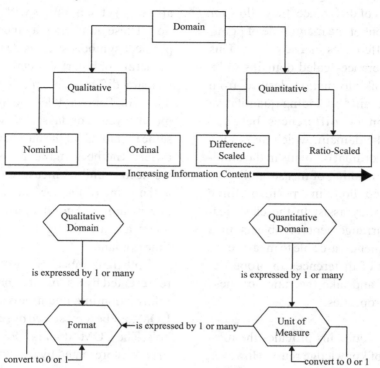

version, reside in the Metamodel of Knowledge. This relationship provides another example of a metaobject (since relationships are objects too), and demonstrates how a metaobject can facilitate the storage of the full set of conversion rules at a single place.

The conversion rule is restricted to conversion from one UOM to only one other UOM; this constraint is necessary to avoid redundancy and to normalize information. A single conversion rule enables navigation from one UOM to any other arbitrary UOM, by following a daisy chain of conversion rules. The upper bound of one on the conversion relationship in the metamodel also implies that if you add a new UOM to a domain, you have to add only a single conversion rule to convert to any of the other UOMs, and that such information will suffice to enable conversion to every UOM defined for that domain.

Metaobjects, Subtypes, and Inheritance

Metaobjects help to normalize real world behavior by normalizing the irreducible facts we discussed earlier. The metaobjects that of interest are object, property, relationship, process, event, domain, unit of measure (UOM), and format. The kinds of atomic rules normalized by each type of metaobject are summarized in Figure 3.

The ontology in Figure 3 organizes objects in a hierarchy of meaning. Lower level objects in the ontology are derived from objects at higher levels by adding information. Figure 3 shows that the meaning of *process* is configured by combining the meanings of *relationship,* an interaction between objects, with the meaning of *event,* the flow of time. This kind of relationship is special. It is called a subtyping relationship and forms the basis of the ontology. Subtyping relationships convey

Figure 3. Basic inventory of metaobjects

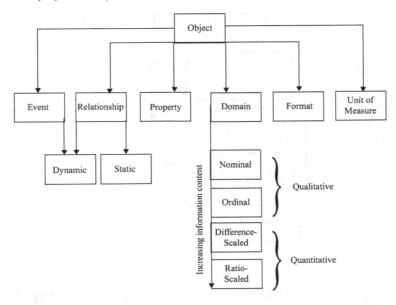

information from higher levels to lower levels of an ontology. The lower level object becomes a special kind of higher level object. Figure 3 shows that ratio scaled domain is a special kind of domain because of the chain of subtyping relationships that lead from Domain to ratio scaled domain via quantitative domain.

The Repository of Meaning

The atomic rule is the most basic building block of knowledge and the ultimate repository of information. It is a rule that cannot be broken into smaller, simpler parts without losing some of its meaning. The metaobjects of Figure 3 are the natural repositories of knowledge. They provide the basis of real world meaning. Just as molecules react with molecules in chemical reactions to produce molecules of new substances with different properties from the original reagents, atomic rules may be built from other atomic rules. As we enhance our business positions with product and process innovation, some atomic rules will be reused. These rules are examples of those that can act as reusable components of knowledge. In

order to build specialized domains of knowledge, entire structures and configurations may be reused. This is similar to manufacturers creating reusable subassemblies to build machines from ordinary parts. The end product may incorporate many versions and modifications of these reusable subassemblies.

24HrKF: A Practical Application of Knowledge Reuse

Suchan and Hayzak (2001) found that a semantically rich database was useful in creating a shared language and mental models. MultiMind is a collaboration tool under development at the University of Arizona (Denny et al., 2008), aimed at improving upon DiCE (Vin, Chen, & Barzilai, 1993) and other collaborative engineering tools.

A Lifestream database (Freeman & Gelernter, 1996), is a chronologically ordered persistent database, used to collect objects and events relevant to a project. Lifestream incorporates incorporates an algebra that can be coupled to the semantics of project artifacts and knowledge events, allowing substantial opportunity for the automation

Figure 4. The architecture of knowledge

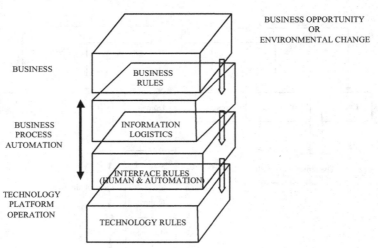

of mundane tasks and higher level functions. In MultiMind, the Lifestream archives project artifacts and provides configuration management services, in a similar fashion as the Concurrent Versioning System (CVS) or Subversion (SVN) revision control system. In MultiMind, knowledge events are observed and logged into Lifestream. Activities such as reading a message, posting a message, executing a search, or reading a web page, are logged into LifeStream. The correlation of knowledge events with the evolution of project artifacts allows for the reuse of relevant knowledge between members of a development team. Communication is facilitated by the encapsulation of knowledge as objects which represent interactions with the development environment.

Higher level tasks, such as the visualization of the current state of a project under development or decision facilitation can also be automated. Through MultiMind and its underlying LifeStream, information regarding artifacts and project progress can easily be visualized, identifying the artifacts which required the most maintenance or debugging. This visualization can be used as a guide for business decisions, when queries to MultiMind are filtered to visualize information relevant to a decision.

AN ARCHITECTURE OF KNOWLEDGE

Information systems are built to satisfy business requirements. Sometimes they are undertaken to implement purely technical changes (Smith & Fingar, 2002). Poorly formulated and ill-managed requirements have led to many of the problems that Information Systems projects currently face (Bahill, & Dean, 1999). Our first task, therefore, is to understand the meaning and structure of requirements.

Requirements flow from knowledge. Knowledge is encapsulated in configurations of atomic rules. Knowledge of Information Systems involves configurations of (atomic) rules of business as well as technology. A four-layered hierarchical approach can be used, as depicted in Figure 4.

Table 1 contains brief descriptions of each layer of the architecture of business knowledge, examples of the kinds of policies that may be implemented at the layer, as well as examples of change that may occur in that layer along with examples of the effects of change within a particular layer.

The top business layer helps to assemble components of knowledge into business concepts, such

Table 1. Layers of the architecture of knowledge

Layer	Description	Example Policy	Example of Change
Business	Contains assertions about products and services and defines relationships between customers and products or services.	Obtain necessary market freedoms to effectively compete; purchase competitor fixed assets; penetrate untapped markets	Acquisition of new assets necessitates the addition of new relationships between customers and services.
Information Logistics	Contains the repository of rules related to the logistics of storage, transfer, and utilization of business information.	Digital artifacts under development will be stored using a versioning system; artifact access privileges are maintained at a fine granularity	A new employee joins an active team necessitating a change in the rules regarding access to a team-owned artifact.
Interface	Contains the rules for the presentation of business information to human entities.	Access to team-owned objects is controlled by an administrator in close contact with team members; GUI follows Microsoft's Inductive User Interface guidelines.	A new employee joins an active team, necessitating the creation of additional security rules regarding artifact access privileges.
Technology	Contains low-level operational and strategic rules regarding the operation of technology.	Hardware and systems software is standardized through a single reputed vendor.	A change of hardware or systems software vendor necessitates change of legacy software developed for obsolete system.

as products, services, markets, regulations, and business practices. Consider a situation where a telephone services provider wishes to integrate cable TV and entertainment media into its business. Such changes in the Business Rules layer will impact business functions and systems functionality, whereas changes to process automation layers alone will impact only availability, timeliness, accuracy, reliability, and presentation of information. Changes in business process automation, in turn, can impose new requirements for performance, reliability and accuracy on technology platforms, which will impact the technology layer.

The level of Business Process Automation is usually changed to leverage information technology or to focus on those processes that create most value while eliminating those of little value. Changes in this layer seldom impact the fundamental business of the firm. For example, the firm could deploy its ordering process on the Web, but not make any fundamental change in the nature of its products, services, or markets.

Business Process Automation refers to process innovation and change that leverages information technology.

The technology layer is changed primarily to improve computer performance in terms of speed, cost, reliability, availability or alignment, and support for business process automation.

The fundamental ideas of separating system-specific rules from software implementation, as in the case of 3GL, and separating system architecture and implementation, as in the case of System/360, are even more important today in the context of separating business rules from implementation technologies. The rules related to transporting and presenting the information would belong to the Business Process Automation layers, not the pure business layer. Figure 4 shows that Business Process Automation consists of two layers. The Information Logistics layer is the repository for rules related to the logistics of moving and storing information in files, and the

Table 2. RDF Classes (retreived from http://www.w3schools.com/rdf/default.asp) and their Metaobject Inventory Equivalents

Element	Class of	Subclass of	Metaobject Inventory Equivalent
Class	All classes		All value
Datatype	All Data types	Class	Domain, Meaning
Resource	All resources	Class	Resource
Container (set of objects)	All Containers	Resource	Aggregate Object
Collection(set membership is restricted by some criteria)	All Collections	Resource	Object Class
Literal	Values of text and numbers	Resource	Subtype of Symbol
List	All Lists	Resource	List of
Property	All Properties	Resource	Property, Feature
Statement	All RDF Statements	Resource	Irreducible fact, rule, atomic rule
Alt	Containers of alternatives	Container	Mutability; Liskov's principle, aggregation of mutable resources
Bag	Unordered containers	Container	Aggregate Object
Seq	Ordered containers	Container	Subtype of Aggregate Object
ContainerMembershipProperty	All Container membership properties	Property	Subtype of Relationship
XMLLiteral	XML literal values	Literal	Subtype of symbol. XML is a subtype of language.

Interface layer is concerned with how this information is presented to human operators.

Creating a business knowledge hierarchy such as the one depicted in Figure 4 facilitates the flow of information between the business entities responsible for managing knowledge. Organizing knowledge and information, as described in previous sections, is essential for realizing the flow of information between the layers and creating meaningful and useful relationships between objects within each layer.

Efforts to process and integrate information based on meaning have been made by the W3C consortium, which recommended two modeling standards in 2004: RDF, the Resource Description Framework for metadata, and OWL, the Web ontology language for integrating information. We have seen examples of how some meanings are derived from others by constraining patterns of information they convey to create new meanings. These constrained patterns are subtypes of the meanings they constrain, and every meaning is a polymorphism of the universal object, an unknown pattern in information space that means everything and anything, and conveys nothing. Every object in the inventory of components is a polymorphism of the universal metaobject. RDF and OWL are tailored for the Web and applications of the Semantic Web. Tables 2, 3, and 4 show that the various elements of RDF and OWL as well as their metaobject inventory equivalents, showing that, in effect, the Metaobject Inventory provides a more general framework than either RDF or OWL, and that either of the restricted frameworks

Table 3. RDF properties (retrieved from http://www.w3schools.com/rdf/default.asp) and their metaobject inventory equivalents

Property	Operates on	Produces	Description	Metaobject Inventory Equivalent
Domain	Property	Class	The domain of the resource The domain defines what a property may apply to (operate on).	Domain
Range	Property	Class	The range of the resource. It defines what the property may map to (produce).	co-domain
subPropertyOf	Property	Property	The property of a property	Feature
subClassOf	Class	Class	Subtyping property	Polymorphism
Comment	Resource	Literal	User friendly resource description	Elaboration, description, synonym
Label	Resource	Literal	User friendly resource name	Name, synonym
isDefinedBy	Resource	Resource	Resource definition	Id
seeAlso	Resource	Resource	Additional information about a resource	Elaboration, reference
Member	Resource	Resource	The property of being an instance of a kind of resource	Instance of
First	List	Resource	The property of being the first member of a list	A demiliting role: Lower Limit
Rest	List	List	The second and subsequent members of a list	Subtype of List
Subject	Statement	Resource	The subject of an assertion, i.e., the subject of a resource in an RDF statement	The source of a relationship
predicate	Statement	Resource	Similar to "subject": The predicate of an assertion	Relationship, function
object	Statement	Resource	The object of the resource (in an RDF) Statement	The target of a relationship
value	Resource	Resource	The value of a property	Value
Type	Resource	Class	An instance of a class	Member of a class of classes

are special cases of the types of ontology frameworks that can be realized through the various polymorphisms of the universal object.

CONCLUSION

In an effort to provide a framework for surmounting the temporal and spatial separations in collaborative, distributed environments, this article presented a framework for knowledge object management that can facilitate reuse of knowledge. The encapsulation of knowledge for distributed environments is also highlighted. The knowledge encapsulation uses a four-tier architecture that facilitates knowledge transfer and reuse, as well as enables better understanding of the problem domain under consideration. Differences in training, knowledge, and skills that exist across the distributed teams can be surmounted by use of a

Table 4. OWL dlasses (retrieved from: http://www.w3.org/TR/owl-ref/) and their metaobject inventory equivalents

Class	Description	Metaobject Inventory Equivalent
AllDifferent	all listed individuals are mutually different	Subtype of Exclusion partition, exclusivity constraint. The concept of distinctions emerges as a polymorphism of the concept of class as information is added o an object/pattern.
allValuesFrom	All values of a property of class X are drawn from class Y (or Y is a description of X)	Domain, Inclusion Set, inclusion partition
Annotation-Property	Describes an annotation. OWL has predefined the following kinds of annotations, and users may add more: • Versioninfo • Label • Comment • Seealso • Isdefinedby OWL DL limits the object of an annotation to data literals, a URI, or individuals (not an exhaustive set of restrictions	Subtypes of Elaboration Version is implicit in temporal objects. Audit properties are implicit in object histories: • The process, person, event, rule, reason and automation that caused a state to change • Time of state change • Who made the change (all the dimensions of process ownership: Responsibility, Authority, Consultation, Work, Facilitation, Information/knowledge of transition) • When the change was made • The instance of the process that caused the change and the (instances of resources) that were used • Why it was made (the causal chain that led to the process) • How long it took to make the change Label is implicit in synonym, name Comment may be elaboration or reference. The two are distinct in the metamodel of knowledge See also: same remarks as comment. IsDefinedBy may be elaboration, Object ID, or existence dependency. Each is a distinct concept in the metamodel of knowledge
backwardCom-patibleWith	The ontology is a prior version of a containing ontology, and is backward compatible with it. All identifiers from the previous version have the same interpretations in the new version.	Part of Relationship between models or structures
cardinality	Describes a class has exactly *N* semantically distinct values of a property (*N* is the value of the cardinality constraint).	Cardinality
Class	Asserts the existence of a class	Object Class
complementOf	Analogous to the Boolean "not" operator. Asserts the existence of a class that consists of individuals that are NOT members of the class it is operating on.	Set negation, Excludes, Exclusion set, Exclusion partition
DataRange	Describes a data type by exhaustively enumerating its instances (this construct is not found in RDF or OWL Lite)	Inclusion set, exhaustive partition
DatatypePro-perty	Asserts the existence of a property	Feature, relationship with a domain

continued on the following page

Table 4. continued

Class	Description	Metaobject Inventory Equivalent
Deprecated-Class	Indicates that the class has been preserved to ensure backward compatibility and may be phased out in the future. It should not be used in new documents, but has been preserved to make it easier for old data and applications to migrate to the new version	Interpretation. However, the specific OWL interpretation of depreciated class is considered to be a physical implementation of a real life business meaning, outside the scope of a model of knowledge that applies on the plane of pure meanings.
Deprecated-Property	Similar to depreciated class	See Depreciated Class
differentFrom	Asserts that two individuals are not the same	The concept of distinctions emerging as a polymorphism of the concept of class as information is added o an object/pattern.; subtype of exclusion partition
disjointWith	Asserts that the disjoint classes have no common members	Exclusion partition
distinctMem-bers	Members are all different from each other	Exclusion Set, List
equivalent-Class	The classes have exactly the same set of members. This is subtly different from class equality, which asserts that two or more classes have the same meaning (asserted by the "sameAs" construct). Class equivalence is a constraint that forces members of one class to also belong to another and vice versa.	Mutual inclusion constraint/equality between partitions or objects.
equivalent-Property	Similar to equivalent class: i.e., different properties must have the same values, even if their meanings are different (for instance, the length of a square must equal its width).	Equality constraint
Functional-Property	A property that can have only one, unique value. For example, a property that restricts the height to be nonzero is not a functional property because it maps to an infinite number of values for height.	Value of a property, singleton relationship between an object and the domain of a property
hasValue	Links a class to a value, which could be an individual fact or identity, or a data value (see RDF data types)	relationship with a domain
imports	References another OWL ontology. Meanings in the imported ontology become a part of the importing ontology. Each importing reference has a URI that locates the imported ontology. If ontologies import each other, they become identical, and imports are transitive.	Subtype of Composed of. Note that the metamodel of knowledge does not reference URIs. This is an implementation specific to the Web. The Metamodel of Knowledge deals with meanings.
incompatible-With	The opposite of backward compatibility. Documents must be changed to comply with the new ontology.	Reinterpretation, Intransitive Relationship, asymmetrical relationships
intersectionOf	Similar to set intersection. Members are common to all intersecting classes.	Subtype of Partition, subtype with multiple parents, set intersection
InverseFunc-tionalProperty	Inverses must map back to a unique value. Inverse Functional properties cannot be many-to-one or many-to-many mappings	Inverse of an injective or bijective relationship
inverseOf	The inverse relationship (mapping) of a property from the target (result) to the source (argument)	Inverse of
maxCardinality	An upper bound on cardinality (may be "many", i.e., any finite value)	Cardinality constraint:, upper bound on cardinality (subtype of cardinality constraint and upper bound)

continued on the following page

Table 4. continued

Class	Description	Metaobject Inventory Equivalent
minCardinality	A lower bound on cardinality	Cardinality constraint: Lower bound on cardinality (subtype of cardinality constraint and lower bound)
Nothing	The empty set	of the empty set, null value
ObjectProperty	Instances of properties are not single elements, but may be subject-object pairs of property statements, and properties may be subtyped (extended). Object-Property asserts the existence and characteristics of properties: • RDF Schema constructs: rdfs:subPropertyOf, rdfs:domain and rdfs:range • relations to other properties: owl:equivalentProperty and owl:inverseOf • global cardinality constraints: owl:FunctionalProperty and owl:InverseFunctionalProperty • logical property characteristics: owl:SymmetricProperty and owl:TransitiveProperty	Property, a generalized constraint, which implies an information payload added to a meaning.
oneOf	The only individuals, no more and no less, that are the instances of the class	members of a class, the property of exhaustivity of a partition
onProperty	Asserts a restriction on a property	constraint on a Feature (makes the feature (object) a subtype of the unconstrained, or less constrained feature (object))
Ontology	An ontology is a resource, so it may be described using OWL and non-OWL ontologies	The concept of deriving subclasses by adding information to parent classes
OntologyProperty	A property of the ontology in question. See imports.	None, beyond the fact that the ontologoly is an object, which means that it inherits all properties of objects, and adds the property of interpretation
priorVersion	Refers to a prior version of an ontology	An instance of Object Property where a relevant instance of ontology Object Class exists, containing a Temporal Succession of concepts. The property of reinterpretation is implicit between versions of an ontology.
Restriction	Restricts or constrains a property. May lead to property equivalence, polymorphisms, value constraints, set operations, etc.	Rule Constraint
sameAs	Asserts that individuals have the same identity. Naming differences are merely synonyms	Set Equality, Identity
someValuesFrom	Asserts that there exists at least one item that satisfies a criterion. Mathematically, it asserts that at least one individual in the domain of the "SomeValuesFrom" operator that maps to the range of that operator.	Subsetting constraint
SymmetricProperty	When a property and its inverse mean the same thing (e.g., if Jane is a relative of John, then John is also a relative of Jane)	Symmetry
Thing	The set of all individuals.	Instance of Object Class

continued on the following page

Table 4. continued

Class	Description	Metaobject Inventory Equivalent
TransitiveProperty	If A is related to B via property P1, and B is related to C via property P2, then A is also related to C via property P1. For example. If a person lives in a house, and the house is located in a town, it may be inferred that the person lives in the town because "Lives in" is transitive with "Located in".	Transitive Relationship
unionOf	Set union. A member may belong to any of the sets in the union to be a member of the resulting set	offset Union, Aggregation
versionInfo	Provides information about the version	Instance of Attribute. Implicit in the concept of the history of a temporal object

common means of discourse about the problem domain under consideration.

For Further Reading

The concepts described here have been utilized and extended in this article to cater specifically to the special needs of offshoring and 24-Hour Knowledge Factory environments. For a detailed discussion of the basic concepts and their wider applications, please refer to the following books by Amit Mitra and Amar Gupta:

- *Agile Systems with Reusable Patterns of Business Knowledge—a Component Based Approach* (Artech House Press, Norwood, Massachusetts)
- *Creating Agile Business Systems with Reusable Knowledge* (Cambridge University Press, Cambridge, England)
- *Knowledge Reuse and Agile Processes— Catalysts for Innovation* (IGI-Global, Hershey, Pennsylvania [in press])

REFERENCES

Aggarwal, A., & Pandey, A. (2004). Offshoring of IT services—Present and future. *Evalueserve.* Retrieved from http://www.evalueserve.com

Amdahl, G. M., Blaauw, G. A., & Brooks, F. P., Jr. (2000). *Architecture of the IBM System/360.* Retrieved November 12, 2007, from http://www. research.ibm.com/journal/rd/441/amdahl.pdf

Baggot, J. (1992). *The meaning of quantum theory.* Oxford University Press.

Bahill, A. T., & Dean, F. (1999). Discovering system requirements. In A. P. Sage & W. B. Rouse (Eds.), *Handbook of systems engineering and management* (pp. 175-220). New York: Wiley.

Baldwin, C. Y., & Clark, K. B. (2000). *Design rules, Vol. 1: The power of modularity.* Cambridge, MA: The MIT Press.

Beck, K. (1999). *Extreme programming explained: Embrace change.* Reading, MA: Addison-Wesley.

Boehm, B. (1988). A spiral model of software development and enhancement. *Computer, 21*(5), 61-72.

Blanchard, E.. (2001). Introduction to networking and data communications. *Commandprompt, Inc.* Retrieved from http://www.w3.org/2004/12/ rules-ws/paper/105/

Carmel, E. (1999). *Global software teams: Collaborating across borders and time zones.* Upper Saddle River, NJ: Prentice Hall.

Chang, E., Dillon T. S., Sommerville, I., & Wong-thongtham, P. (2006). Ontology-based multi-site software development methodology and tools. *Journal of Systems Architecture, 52*(11).

Coleman, G., & Verbrugge, R. (1998). A quality software process for rapid application development. *Software Quality Journal, 7,* 107-122.

Danait, A. (2005). Agile offshore techniques—A case study. In *Proceedings of the IEEE Agile Conference* (pp. 214-217).

Denny, N., Mani, S., Sheshu, R., Swaminathan, M., Samdal, J., & Gupta, A. (in press). Hybrid offshoring: Composite personae and evolving collaboration technologies. *Information Resources Management Journa*.

Fergusson, N. (2004, April 12). Survival of the biggest. *Forbes 2000,* p. 140.

Finkbeiner, D. (1966). *Matrices and linear transformations.* Freeman.

Freeman, E., & Gelertner, D. (1996). Lifestreams: A storage model for personal data. *ACM SIGMOD Record, 25*(1), 80-86.

Gupta, A., & Seshasai, S. (2007). 24-hour knowledge factory: Using Internet technology to leverage spatial and temporal separations. *ACM Transactions on Internet Technology, 7*(3).

Gupta, A., Seshasai, A., Mukherji, S., & Ganguly, A. (2007, April-June). Offshoring: The transition from economic drivers toward strategic global patnership and 24-hour knowledge factory. *Journal of Electronic Commerce in Organizations, 5*(2), 1-23.

Kanka, M. (2001). *A paper on semantics.* Berlin, Germany: Institut für deutsche Sprache und Linguistik.

Kingston, J. (2002). Merging top level ontologies for scientific knowledge management. *Proceedings of the AAAI Workshop on Ontologies and the Semantic Web.* Retrieved from http://www.inf.ed.ac.uk/publications/report /0171.html

Kussmaul, C., Jack, R., & Sponsler, B. (2004). Outsourcing and offshoring with agility: A case study. In C. Zannier et al. (Eds.), *XP/*Agile Universe 2004 (LNCS 3132, pp. 147-154). Springer.

López-Bassols, V. (1998). Y2K. *The OECD Observer,* 214.

Markus, L. M. (2001). Toward a theory of knowledge reuse: Types of knowledge reuse situations and factors in reuse success. *Journal of Management Information Systems, 18*(1), 57-93.

Mitra, A., & Gupta, A. (2005). *Agile systems with reusable patterns of business knowledge.* Artech House.

Mitra, A., & Gupta, A. (2006). *Creating agile business systems with reusable knowledge.* Cambridge University Press.

Myopolous, J. (1998). Information modeling in the time of revolution. *Information Systems, 23*(3-4).

O'Leary, D. E. (2001). How knowledge reuse informs effective system design and implementation. *IEEE Intelligent Systems, 16*(1), 44-49.

Ravichandran, T. (2005). Organizational assimilation of complex technologies: An empirical study of component-based software development. *IEEE Transactions on Engineering Management, 52*(2)

Ross, R. G. (1997). *The business rule article: Classifying, defining and modeling rules.* Database Research Group.

Smith, H., & Fingar, P. (2002). *The next fifty years.* Retrieved from http://www.darwinmag.com/read/120102/bizproc.html

Sparling, M. (2000). Lessons learned through six years of component-based development. *Communications of the ACM, 43*(10), 47-53.

Suchan, & Hayzak. (2001). The communication characteristics of virtual teams: A case study. *IEEE Transactions on Professional Communication, 44*(3), 174-186.

Szyperski, C. (1997). *Component software: Beyond object-oriented programming.* ACM Press.

Treinen J. J., & Miller-Frost, S. L. (2006). Following the sun: Case studies in global software development. *IBM Systems Journal, 45*(4).

Van Zyl, J., & Corbett, D. (2000). Framework for comparing methods for using or reusing multiple ontologies in an application. In *Proceedings of the Eighth International Conference on Conceptual Structures.*

Vanwelkenhuysen, J., & Mizoguchi, R. (1995). Workplace-adapted behaviors: Lessons learned for knowledge reuse. In *Proceedings of KB&KS* (pp 270-280).

Verdu, S. (1998). *IEEE Transactions on Information Theory, 44*(6).

Vin, H. M., Chen, M.-S., & Barzilai, T. (1993). Collaboration management in DiCE. *The Computer Journal, 36*(1), 87-96.

Xiahou, Y., Bin, X., Zhijun, H., & Maddineni, S. (2004, May). Extreme Programming in global software development. *Canadian Conference on Electrical and Computer Engineering, 4.*

Yap, M. (2005). Follow the sun: Distributed extreme programming environment. In *Proceedings of the IEEE Agile Conference* (pp. 218-224).

Chapter 5
Extending the Balanced Scorecard for Outsourcing:
The Goals Alignment Perspective

Preeti Goyal
University of Delhi, India

Bhimaraya A. Metri
Management Development Institute, India

ABSTRACT

Alliances, collaborations and networks are synonymous with strategy today. Business Process Outsourcing (BPO) is one such type of alliance. With increasing reliance on outsourcing, the organizational boundaries are blurring. The implications for the client organization can be tremendous, as it now relies on an outside organization to fulfill its operational objectives. Currently, there is no single framework, which can effectively measure performance for BPO arrangements. In its present form, the Balanced Scorecard (BSC) only addresses, the performance measurement needs of a single enterprise and any perspective on any external relationships is completely missing. The traditional BSC does not suffice as a performance measurement framework for BPO. While both the client and the vendor can use a BSC for their respective organizations, the strategic objectives of the organizations may not be met. In this chapter, the authors propose a new perspective as an extension to the BSC, namely the goals alignment perspective. Goals alignment of the two organizations will enable creation of performance measures that will help participating organizations to achieve their respective goals.

INTRODUCTION AND MOTIVATION

Maturity of the marketplace, rapid developments in telecommunications and infrastructure, new offshoring destinations etc. have catalyzed the growth of the Business Process Outsourcing (BPO) industry. Outsourcing has become synonymous with corporate policy and strategy (Quelin & Duhamel 2003, Pati & Desai 2005) and companies are realizing the strategic role it can play in maintaining global competitiveness. Despite the importance of the BPO industry, there is a dearth of a Performance Measurement System (PMS) that can effectively address the needs of the BPO industry.

The objective of this paper is to develop a performance measurement framework for organizations

DOI: 10.4018/978-1-60566-966-3.ch005

involved in BPO. Balanced Score Card (BSC) is a widely accepted and most frequently cited performance measurement framework (Neely, 2005) and in its present form is applicable to single organizations (Bititci et al. 2005). The BSC has been taken as a base and then extended for the needs of the outsourcing industry. In this paper, the BSC, which is used as the basic performance measurement framework, is extended to meet the specific needs of the outsourcing industry. To achieve this, the paper integrates existing concepts in strategy, performance management and extended enterprises. These are then applied to outsourcing.

The competitive landscape of the business world is changing (Bititci et al. 2005). Bottom line pressures on service delivery organizations have forced managers to come up with innovative solutions to meet the challenges of reducing costs while maximizing stakeholder value (Bititci et al. 2005). Organizations are strategically combining core competencies and capabilities to create unique competencies and a competitive advantage through collaboration (Bititci et al., 2005). Among the collaborating enterprises, a number of organizations participate in the decision making process. This demands knowledge integration, deep change in power structures in the organizations concerned (Bititci et al., 2005). With continuing pressure on cost bases, it is becoming difficult for companies to fulfill their own needs and this is driving companies to look at innovative collaborations as strategic alternatives. A PMS, integrated across organizations, becomes critical when alliances form the basis of success.

Business process outsourcing is an example of one such type of alliance. It has been defined as the delegation of some part or all of a business process by a client organization to an external service provider who, in turn, owns, administrates and manages the selected processes based upon defined and measurable business performance metrics (Puccinelli, 2003). While it promises great returns on the bottom line it is transforming the

way businesses are being run the world over. This has led companies to examine their organization structures and to realize that creating the greatest value does not require them to own, manage and directly control all of their assets and resources. Strategic alliances and partnerships with those who provide expertise in a particular area are being viewed as the most efficient way to gain results. Access to global talent, economies of scale, process engineering and enhancements, wage arbitrage, increased profit margins and improvements in quality are some of the gains that companies have realized (Fjermestad et al., 2005).

The implications for client organizations - processes move to an outside firm, customers are being served by an outside firm and above all, execution of strategy is being entrusted to an outside firm (Vining & Globerman, 1999). The complexity of the system makes performance measurement a difficult and challenging task, at the same time, making performance measurement critical.

LITERATURE REVIEW

The importance of an effective performance measurement system (PMS) cannot be overstated. A PMS is critical in translating organizational strategy and goals into reality. Performance measurement is a means to make strategy come alive (Bauer et al. 2004). It provides the essential link between strategy, execution and value creation. With the increased pressure on businesses to perform, an effective PMS will go a long way to measure the success of strategy. A performance measurement system can be defined as "the set of metrics used to quantify both the efficiency and effectiveness of actions" (Neely et al. 1994).

Measuring what is easy to measure and making it important is an easy trap to fall into. The metrics misalignment thus created will be the primary source of inefficiency and disruption (Marr and Stephen, 1994). It has long been recognized that performance measures can be used to influence

Figure 1. Balanced Scorecard (Kaplan & Norton, 1992)

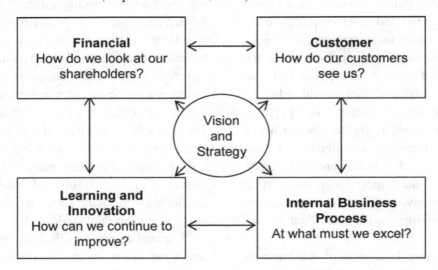

behavior and, thus, affect the implementation of strategy (Skinner, 1971). Therefore, having bad metrics can be worse than having no metrics because bad metrics will drive dysfunctional behavior that can set an organization in the wrong direction – after all, what gets measured gets done.

An effective use of the PMS is in providing input to maintaining alignment between strategy and the metrics used to measure its implementation. An effective PMS should be able to achieve just that. As plans are implemented and move from the strategic through the tactical and the operational stages of the planning process, alignment enables consistency between strategic goals and metrics (Melnyk, 2004). Effective performance measures will make success concrete for everyone. The research community draws only on a limited set of influential works in the area of performance measurement systems. The challenge for the research community is to take the PMSs' forward. Among the many items on the performance measurement research agenda, one of the key items is to measure performance across networks rather than within organizations.

In literature, the popularity of the Balanced Scorecard (Kaplan & Norton, 1992, 1996) (figure

1) is evident by the extensive referencing it has attracted and among practitioners. BSC has been one of the most successful PMS (Neely 2005). At its core is a systematic link between a firm's strategy, its goals and the measures used to determine, if the goals are being met. The approach is based on the argument "What you measure is what you get" and that any "measurement system strongly affects the behavior of managers and employees". Kaplan and Norton (1992) argue that traditional financial accounting measures like return on investment and earnings per share can give misleading signals for continuous improvement and innovation. Thompson & Mathys (2008) use the case of FastDel, a small package delivery firm, to advocate two dimensions for achieving an aligned BSC, namely, the alignment of goals across organizational units and the linking downstream and upstream goal structures.

In implementing the BSC approach, senior executives establish a scorecard that takes multiple non- financial measures into account. The scorecard is called balanced as all its perspectives achieve balance, which leads to progress against pre-determined objectives.

The BSC has been augmented in the past to better meet the needs of specific industries/

businesses. Bremser and Chung (2005) have augmented the BSC in two dimensions – (1) scope of external constituents, (2) domain of e-business models. Plant et al. (2003) extended the customer perspective of the BSC to include four additional factors for the e-business channel. Urrutia and Eriksen (2005) have added a social demographic factors/ environmental indicator perspective for the Spanish healthcare industry in the non-profit segment. While work has been done to specify performance measures to manage extended enterprises, but it has not been integrated into any strategic performance management framework (Beamon 1999, Gunasekaran et al., 2001, Neely, 2005).

The need to measure performance with external alliances has been widely recognized (Bititci et al., 2005, Guansekaran et al. 2001, Neely, 2005, Hoek, 1998). Yet, little guidance is available on performance measurement frameworks that consider inter-enterprise coordinating measures, as the development in the field of performance measurement has been from a single enterprise point of view (Bititci et al. 2005). The BSC, in its current form, does not have a provision to capture the measurement of the alliance performance including organizations involved in outsourcing. Hence, there is a need to develop a new performance measurement framework or to extend an existing framework for measuring performance in outsourcing.

Outsourcing relationship, being a specific type of alliance, does not currently have a framework that could adequately address its performance measurement needs. Nor is a framework available from other collaborative organizations that could be adapted for outsourcing. Since BSC is a widely accepted framework, in this paper it has been taken as a base and then extended for the needs of the outsourcing industry.

PROPOSED FRAMEWORK FOR BPO

Strategy as a driver for performance measures has been at the core of BSC (Kaplan & Norton, 1996). Thus, performance measures are a natural outcome of organizational strategy. Traditionally, the alignment between strategy and performance has been for single organizations. With the increased dependence on outsourcing, processes are moving outside the organization. It can be a challenge to monitor organizational performance, which is dependant on processes that are no longer being performed within the firm. Lacity and Hirschheim (1995) suggest that while outsourcing has often been described as a 'strategic alliance', the parties to the outsourcing contract have potentially conflicting interests. Therefore, if the overall goals of the client and the vendor are not aligned (Lacity and Hirschheim, 1995), there is a likelihood of the two organizations moving in different directions, thereby causing a misalignment of process goals and organizational goals, leading to failure of strategy implementation. In such an event, both the organizations will not only lose in terms of the invested resources but also fail to achieve the desired benefits from the relationship.

To overcome these difficulties the authors are proposing an extended BSC (E-BSC) that is augmented with a fifth perspective, namely the 'goals alignment' perspective. The proposed extended balanced scorecard (E-BSC) framework is shown in figure 2. E-BSC measures the goals alignment of the organizations to achieve organizational goals for outsourcing. Strategy alignment is not a new concept. The notion of fit has been an important theme in strategic management theory (Kishore et al., 2003, Lassar & Kerr, 1996, Stanek, 2004, Venkataraman & Camillius, 1984). In strategic HR literature, goals alignment as part an integrated high performance work system has been at the crux of achieving corporate goals. In a study of goal alignment of top leaders and online tracking system has been cited as being instrumental in the success of a global specialty materials company (Layman

Figure 2. Proposed Extended Balanced ScoreCard (E-BSC)

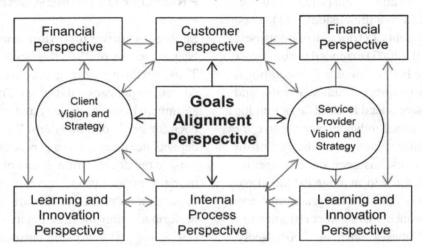

S. 2005). In this case, the goal alignment resulted in increased stock prices validating research that goal alignment leads to improved performance. In a study by Parker and Idundun, 1998, goal alignment is the concurrence of overall corporate goals as perceived by the management team with the goals of the department being studied. In their study of IS managers in UK (Parker & Idundun, 1988), identified goal alignment as the top ranked issue by IS managers. Apart from other factors, goal alignment is an important component of risk management (Jorgensen, 2005). Specifically, in the case of BPO, the client firm's proprietary information becomes available to an external organization providing the BPO services (Kogut & Zander, 1992) thereby increasing the risk to the client firm (Walker, 1988, Aron et al., 2005). Moral hazard (Eisenhardt, 1989) has been cited to be another risk associated in such alliances, which arises to due to misaligned goals and an inability of the client to observe the service providers actions (Alchian & Demsetz, 1972, Aron et al., 2005).

The importance of goals alignment is evident in the other areas too. Measurement programs in software organizations provide an important source of control over quality and cost in software development. Gopal et al. (2002) in an empirical study of determinants of software development success have supported goal alignment as a key success factor. Leading companies keep managers aware of IS issues and facilitate goal alignment through means as planning cycles, seminars and meetings (Parker and Idundun, 1988). Fjermestad et al. (2005), in their study state that business strategy alignment is one of the critical success factors in outsourcing. Research by Booz Allen Hamilton has indicated that more than 20,000 cross-border alliances were formed between 1996 and 2003. Yet, majority of alliances are considered failures (Anonymous, 2006) and one of the important reasons for these failures being that they lacked the clarity in objectives and measurement of achieving goals. These are simple but important steps that decide the success of alliances (Anonymous, 2006).

Strategic goal alignment has also received attention in extended enterprises (Bititci et al., 2005). Particularly in supply chain management, one of the initial steps is to align the organizational strategy with that of the supply chain (Chopra & Meindl, 2001, Gattorna 2001, Johnson & Scholes, 1999, Marr & Stephen 2004). The essence of 'strategic fit' has been that when forming alliances, there must exist an alignment of goals of the participating organizations. Reviewing the recent literature on management control systems, Berry et al. (2009) observe that collaboration between firms often involves co-ordination between groups that have differing and, maybe even, mutually incompatible goals. In a study of 215 North American manufacturing firms, Narasimhan and Jayaram (1998) concluded that supplier integration, strategic integration and customer integration across the supply chain determine customer responsiveness. Building on this study (Roethlein and Ackerson, 2004), examined the quality goal alignment in a connected supply chain. They concluded that while the entities in the studied supply chain had dissimilar quality goals, they were perhaps successful due to the inherent minimum level of quality communication and goal alignment necessary to exist within their relatively mature and stable product market. Strong and frequent unidirectional communication existed between the manufacturer and the supplier and between the manufacturer and the distributor making the supply chain successful. Mangiameli and Roethlein's (2001) study of multiple entities imposing quality requirements on each entity recognized the need for multidirectional quality awareness. Stephen and Coote (2007) conclude that relational governance is an essential require-ment for accomplishing coordination, and thus the desired performance outcomes, in relation-ships. Such relational behavior establishes goal alignment, which leads to achieving the desired performance outcomes. Ruuska et al. (2009) demonstrate that lack of governance structures to achieve goal alignment increased the distance between a client and a vendor involved in a large project. Johnson and Medcof (2007) argue that networked organizational structures that produce the maximum self-initiated innovations that are oriented to corporate level strategy are the ones that use goal internalization. Even though goal alignment provides a vital link between collabo-rating organizations, it has still not found its way into performance measurement systems.

The proposed E-BSC framework includes the following five perspectives:

- *Customer Measures: How do the Customers see us* - This perspective captures the abili-ty of the service provider to provide quality services, the effectiveness of their delivery, and overall customer service and satisfac-tion that the service provider is able to pro-vide to its client and customer. The BSC demands that client and service providers translate their general mission statement on customer service into specific measures that reflect the factors that really matter to clients and customers. For the alliance to be successful, the customer service goals must be aligned.

- *Internal Business Process Measures: What must we excel at* - This perspective is pri-marily an analysis of the service provider's internal processes that help it to achieve its organizational objectives and in turn help the clients to achieve their organizational aims. Service provider must decide the processes and competencies it must excel at that would lead to customer satisfac-tion and financial success for both the cli-ent and the service provider organizations. Measures for each of these must be speci-fied. The organizational objectives for the client and the service provider need to be aligned to achieve alliance objectives.

- *Innovation and Learning Measures: Can we continue to improve and create value* - Customer and internal business process perspectives identify parameters that the service provider and clients considers most important for success. Changing success targets and increasing competitive intensity requires client and service provider organi-zations to continually improve and inno-vate. Innovation and learning perspective allows organizations to look at what needs to be done to become/ remain competitive.

- *Financial Measures: How do we look at shareholders* - The financial performance measures indicate weather the organization's strategy and execution is contributing the bottom-line in the desired manner. It is the culmination of the results of the strategic choices made in the other perspectives. Making improvements in the other perspectives will lead to the financial numbers taking care of themselves.

- *Goals Alignment Perspective* – Our focus is the business process outsourcing industry. As stated earlier, the authors propose that a goal alignment perspective be included as part of performance measurement system to measure the goals alignment between the client and the service provider. Measuring goals alignment between the client and the service provider should lead to long term and successful relationships between the client and their service providers. In the BPO industry, currently process performance expected from the service provider is defined using Service Level Agreements (SLAs) (Lacity et al., 2004, Misra, 2004). The purpose of the SLAs is to ensure that there are no gray areas in terms of the services expected from the service provider. They are aimed at meeting the service needs of the client (Misra, 2004). Hence, by definition, SLAs are at the operational level and do not provide insight into goals alignment between the client and the service provider and would therefore be inadequate in measuring the goals alignment for the participating organizations in the outsourcing arrangement. Additionally, although literature provides support that contractual completeness positively impacts outsourcing performance, Handley and Benton's (2009) study of 198 sourcing executives and managers did not reveal a statistically significant relationship

between contractual completeness and overall outsourcing performance.

In designing metrics that measure goals alignment, the following metric characteristics provided by Misra (2003) are useful:

- Metrics that lead to the desired behavior or outcome by both the client and the service provider
- Metrics that are within the service providers' and clients' control
- Metrics that are easy to collect
- Early selection of fewer metrics with higher stakes
- Set realistic and achievable baseline values to selected metrics

In addition, several design characteristics and their trade offs need to be taken into account to address how they will be measured. Assimilating the writings of writers such as Kaplan and Norton (1996) and Mohrman and Mohrman (1997), these design characteristics can be grouped into four categories described below.

- **Goals Alignment Criteria** – The best criteria with which to measure goals alignment will depend on the intended purpose of the performance metric. Literature (Segil, 2005, Stanek 2004, Bititci et al., 2005, Childe, 1998 and Gunasekaran et al., 2001) suggests the following in measuring business strategy and alignment of alliance partners: alignment of the long term goals of the client and service provider, overall corporate strategy for client and service provider, cash flow and ability to raise capital, agreement upon predefined objectives, level of strategic understanding, changes involved at one or more firms that may impact alliance, changes in economy that may impact alliance, political climate that may impact alliance, efficiency of alliance, effectiveness of alliance and partner culture.

- **Sources of Measurement** – Where will the metric come from – what is the source of the metric? For goal alignment criterion, the best source of the metric needs to be selected. First of all, this will depend on the appropriate level of measurement, for example, is it an organization, process or individual metric? Is it possible to collect the metric as a part of the regular process? Will both primary and secondary data be used in measuring goals alignment? Is only one source needed or will multiple sources be used to measure the metrics. If multiple sources, how will they be selected.

- **Collection Method** – After the measurement criteria and source are determined, design decision pertaining to the methods to collect the data may still need to be carefully assessed. Some of the design choices may depend on the type of measure – for example is the measure a quantitative or qualitative measure. Additionally, will the data be collected through interviews, surveys or from goal setting sessions, annual planning meetings and training seminars? Langfield-Smith (2008) demonstrates the use of interviews and workshops, in a collaborative alliance in the construction industry, to assess the ability of potential partners to work in harmony and to commit to the goals of the alliance. This was reinforced by the risk and reward system, creating high interdependencies between the partners.

- **Frequency** – The frequency with which to collect a given metric is a design consideration with major cost implications. While some metrics may be collected on an annual basis as part of an annual performance review process others may be collected as part of the quarterly financial reporting process. Other metrics may be collected on monthly basis.

To what extent should the goals be aligned? Not all outsourcing arrangements will warrant the same extent of goals alignment. The strategic impact sought from outsourcing relationship will form the basis for the extent of goals alignment. The strategic impact will be reflected in the type of outsourcing alliance formed. The alliance type between the client and the vendor will depend on strategic impact and extent of substitution (Kishore et al., 2003), strategic intent and technical capability (Kern et al., 2002), strategic importance and financial impact (Gattorna, 1998) and is the operationalization of the benefits that the participating firms are hoping of achieve. The goals alignment would be to the extent of strategic benefits sought from this relationship. This can be represented as a continuum. On one end of the continuum would be transactional benefits, which would mandate operational goal alignment. On the other end of the continuum, the benefits sought are more transformational (Linder, 2004, Kakabadse & Kakabadse, 2003) and the alignment should be of strategic goals. Therefore, more strategic the benefit sought from the relationship, the greater the extent of strategic alignment.

CONCLUSION

Alliances, collaborations and networks are synonymous with strategy today. BPO is one such type of alliance. With increasing reliance on outsourcing, the organizational boundaries are blurring. Peculiar to this industry is the fact that internal business processes now move outside the firm. The implications for the client organization can be tremendous as it now relies on an outside organization to fulfill its operational objectives. Currently, there is no framework, which can effectively measure performance for BPO arrangements. In its present form, the BSC only addresses the performance measurement needs of single enterprises and any perspective on any external relationships is missing. Having said this, the traditional BSC does not suffice as a performance measurement framework for BPO. While both the client and the vendor can use a BSC for their respective organizations, the strategic objectives of the organizations may not be met.

In the past the BSC has been augmented to meet the needs of individual organizations. In this paper a new perspective, namely the goals alignment perspective, has been proposed as an extension to the BSC. This perspective would include the extent of the alignment, which will depend on the benefits sought from the relationship. Including the goals alignment perspective in a PMS will enable organizations to better achieve their strategic objectives from outsourcing. Therefore, it is important to measure and monitor client and service provider goal alignment.

In the present study, the proposed model has not been empirically tested. Hopefully, the framework will be validated in a future research. by dyadic studies of client and service provider organizations.

REFERENCES

Aaron, R., Clemons, E. K., & Reddi, S. (2005). Just Right Outsourcing: Understanding and Managing Risk. *Journal of Management Information Systems, 22*(2), 37–55.

Alchian, A. A., & Demsetz, H. (1972). Production, Information Costs, and Economic Organization. *The American Economic Review, 62*(5), 777–795.

Anonymous, . (2006). Create Successful International Mergers and Alliances. *Strategic Direction, 22*(1), 25–28. doi:10.1108/02580540610635915

Bauer, J., Tanner, S. J., & Neely, A. (2004). Developing a Performance Measurement Audit Template – A Benchmark Study. *Measuring Business Excellence, 8*(4), 17–25. doi:10.1108/13683040410569370

Beamon, M. (1999). Measuring Supply Chain Performance. *International Journal of Operations & Production Management, 19*(3), 275–292. doi:10.1108/01443579910249714

Berry, A. J., Coad, A. F., Harris, E. P., Otley, D. T., & Stringer, C. (2009). Emerging Themes in Management Control: A review of Recent Literature. *The British Accounting Review, 41*, 2–20. doi:10.1016/j.bar.2008.09.001

Bititci, U. S., Mendibil, K., Martinez, V., & Albores, P. (2005). Measuring and Managing Performance in Extended Enterprises. *International Journal of Operations & Production Management, 25*(4), 333–353. doi:10.1108/01443570510585534

Bremser, W. G., & Chung, Q. B. (2005). A Framework for Performance Measurement in the e-business Environment. *Electronic Commerce Research and Applications.*

Brown, C. V. (2003). Performance Metrics for IT and Human Resource Alignment. *Information Systems Management, 20*(4), 36–42. doi:10.1201/1078/43647.20.4.20030901/77291.6

Childe, S. J. (1998). The Extended Enterprise: A Concept for Co-operation . *Production Planning and Control, 9*(4), 320–327. doi:10.1080/095372898234046

Chopra, S. & Meindl, P. (2001). *Supply Chain Management, Strategy Planning and Operations.* Pearson Education

Eisenhardt, K. M. (1989). Agency Theory: An Assessment and Review. *Academy of Management Review, 14*(1), 57–74. doi:10.2307/258191

Fjermestad, J., & Saitta, J. N. (2005). A Strategic Framework for IT Outsourcing: A Review of Literature and the Development of a Successful Factors Model. *Journal of Information Technology Cases and Applications, 7*(3), 42–60.

Gattorna, J. (1998). *Strategic Supply Chain Alignment – Best Practice in Supply Chain Management*. Gower

Gopal, A., Krishnan, M. S., Mukhopadhyay, T., & Goldenson, D. R. (2002). Measurement Programs in Software Development: Determinants of Success. *IEEE Transactions on Software Engineering, 28*(9), 863–875. doi:10.1109/TSE.2002.1033226

Gunasekaran, A., Patel, C., & Tirtiroglu, E. (2001). Performance Measures and Metrics in a Supply Chain Environment. *International Journal of Operations & Production Management, 21*(1/2), 71–87. doi:10.1108/01443570110358468

Jogernsen, H. (2005). Methods & Elements of a Solid Risk Management Strategy. *Risk Management, 52*(7), 53.

Johnson, W. H. A., & Medcof, J. W. (2007). Motivating Proactive Subsidiary Innovation: Agent-Based Theory and Socialization Models in Global R&D. *Journal of International Management, 13*, 472–487. doi:10.1016/j.intman.2007.03.006

Johnson & Scholes. (1999). *Exploring Corporate Strategy*. Prentice Hall

Kakabadse, A., & Kakabadse, N. (2003). Outsourcing Best Practice: Transformational and Transactional Considerations. *Knowledge and Process Management, 10*(1), 60–71. doi:10.1002/kpm.161

Kaplan, R. S., & Norton, D. P. (1992). The Balanced Scorecard – Measures that Drive Performance. *Harvard Business Review, 70*(1), 71–79.

Kaplan, R. S., & Norton, D. P. (1996). The Balanced Scorecard: Translating Strategy into Action. *Harvard Business Review*. Boston, MA

Kern, T., Willcocks, L. P., & Heck, E. v. (2002). The Winner's Curse in IT Outsourcing: Strategies for Avoiding Relational Trauma. *California Management Review, 44*(2), 47–69.

Kishore, R., Rao, H. R., Nam, K., Rajagopalan, S., & Chaudhary, A. (2003). A Relationship Perspective on IT Outsourcing. *Communications of the ACM, 46*(12), 87–92. doi:10.1145/953460.953464

Kogut, B., & Zander, U. (1992). Knowledge of the Firm, Combinitive Capabilities, and the Replication of Technology. *Organization Science, 3*(3), 383–397. doi:10.1287/orsc.3.3.383

Lacity, M., & Hirschheim, R. (1995). The Information Systems Outsourcing Bandwagon. *Sloan Management Review, 35*(1), 73–86.

Lacity, M., Willcocks, L., & Feeny, D. (2004). Commercializing the Back Office at Lloyds of London: Outsourcing and Strategic Partnerships Revisited. *European Management Journal, 22*(2), 127–140. doi:10.1016/j.emj.2004.01.016

Langfield-Smith, K. (2008). The Relations Between Transactional Characteristics, Trust and Risk in the Start-Up Phase of a Collaborative Alliance. *Management Accounting Research, 19*, 344–364. doi:10.1016/j.mar.2008.09.001

Lassar, W. M., & Kerr, J. L. (1996). Strategy and Control in Supplier-Distributor Relationships: An Agency Perspective. *Strategic Management Journal, 17*, 613–632. doi:10.1002/(SICI)1097-0266(199610)17:8<613::AID-SMJ836>3.0.CO;2-B

Layman, S. (2005). Strategic Goal Alignment at CMP Technologies. *Strategic HR Review, 4*(4), 24–27.

Lee, J. N., Miranda, S. M., & Kim, Y. M. (2004). IT Outsourcing Strategies: Universalistic, Contingency, and Configurational Explanations of Success. *Information Systems Research, 15*(2), 110–131. doi:10.1287/isre.1040.0013

Linder, J. (2004). Transformational Outsourcing. *MIT Sloan Management Review*, Winter, 52-58

Mangiameli, P. M., & Roethlein, C. J. (2001). An Examination of Quality Performance at Different Levels in a connected Supply Chain: A Preliminary Study. *The International Journal of Manufacturing Technology Management*, *12*(2), 126–133.

Marr, B., & Stephen, P. (2004). Performance Management in Call Centers: Lessons, Pitfalls and Achievements in Fujitsu Services. *Measuring Business Excellence*, *8*(4), 55–62. doi:10.1108/13683040410569415

Melnyk, S. A., Stewart, D. M., & Swink, M. (2004). Metrics and Performance Measurement in Operations Management: Dealing with the Metrics Maze. *Journal of Operations Management*, *22*, 201–217. doi:10.1016/j.jom.2004.01.004

Misra, R. B. (2004). Global IT Outsourcing: Metrics for Success of all Parties. *Journal of Information Technology Cases and Applications*, *6*(3), 21–34.

Mohrman, S. A., & Mohrman, A. M. (1997). *Designing and Leading Team-Based Organizations: A Workbook for Organizational Self-Design*. San Francisco: Jossey-Bass.

Narasimhan, R., & Jayaram, J. (1998). Causal Linkages in Supply Chain Management: An Exploratory Study of North American Manufacturing Firms. *Decision Sciences*, *29*(3), 579–605. doi:10.1111/j.1540-5915.1998.tb01355.x

Neely, A. (2005). The Evolution of Performance Measurement Research, Developments in the Last Decade and a Research Agenda for the Next. *International Journal of Operations & Production Management*, *25*(12), 1264–1277. doi:10.1108/01443570510633648

Neely, A., & Adams, C. (2001). The Performance Prism Perspective. *Journal of Cost Management*, *15*(1), 7–15.

Neely, A. D., Gregory, M., & Platts, K. (1995). Performance Measurement System Design: A Literature Review and Research Agenda. *International Journal of Operations & Production Management*, *15*(4), 80–116. doi:10.1108/01443579510083622

Neely, A. D., Mills, J. F., Platts, K. W., Gregory, M. J., & Richards, A. H. (1994). Realizing Strategy through Measurement. *International Journal of Operations & Production Management*, *14*(3), 140–152. doi:10.1108/01443579410058603

Parker, T., & Idundun, M. (1988). Managing Information Systems in 1987: The Top Issues for IS Managers in the UK. *JIT*, *3*(1), 34–42. doi:10.1057/jit.1988.6

Pati, N., & Desai, M. S. (2005). Conceptualizing Strategic Issues in Information Technology Outsourcing. *Information Management & Computer Security*, *13*(4), 281–296. doi:10.1108/09685220510614416

Plant, R., Willcocks, L., & Olson, N. (2003). Measuring e-business Performance: Towards a Revised Balanced Scorecard Approach. *Information Systems and e-Business Management* (pp. 265-281). Springer Verlag.

Puccinelli, R. (2003, October). BPO meets BPM. *Supplement to KM World*.

Quelin, B., & Duhamel, F. (2003). Bringing together Strategic Outsourcing and Corporate Strategy: Outsourcing Motives and Risks. *European Management Journal*, *21*(5), 647–661. doi:10.1016/S0263-2373(03)00113-0

Roethlien, C., & Ackerson, S. (2004). Quality Communication within a Connected Supply Chain. *Supply Chain Management*, *9*(3/4), 323–330.

Ruuska, I., Artto, K., Asltonen, K., & Lehtonen, P. (2009). Dimensions of Distance in a Project Network: Exploring Olkiluoto 3 Nuclear Power Plant Project. *International Journal of Project Management*, *27*, 142–153. doi:10.1016/j.ijproman.2008.09.003

Segil, L. (2005). Metrics to Successfully Manage Alliances. *Strategy and Leadership*, *33*(5), 46–52. doi:10.1108/10878570510616889

Skinner, W. (1971). The Anachronistic Factory. *Harvard Business Review*, (January-February): 61–70.

Stanek, M. B. (2004). Measuring Alliance Risk and Value – A Model Approach to Prioritizing Alliance Projects. *Management Decision*, *42*(2), 180–204. doi:10.1108/00251740410511252

Stephen, A., & Coote, L. V. (2007). Interfirm Behavior and Goal Alignment in Relational Exchanges. *Journal of Business Research*, *60*, 285–295. doi:10.1016/j.jbusres.2006.10.022

Thompson, K. R., & Mathys, N. J. (2008). The aligned Balanced Scorecard: An Improved Tool for Building High Performance Organizations. *Organizational Dynamics*, *37*(4), 378–393. doi:10.1016/j.orgdyn.2008.07.006

Urrutia, I., & Eriksen, S. D. (2005). Insights from Research: Application of the Balanced Scorecard in Spanish Private Healthcare Management. *Measuring Business Excellence*, *9*(4), 16–26. doi:10.1108/13683040510634808

Van Hoek, R. I. (1998). Measuring the Unmeasurable – Measuring and Improving Performance in the Supply Chain. *Supply Chain Management*, *4*(4), 187–192.

Venkataraman, N., & Camillus, J. (1984). Exploring the Concept of Fit in Strategic Management. *Academy of Management Review*, *9*, 513–525. doi:10.2307/258291

Vining, A., & Globerman, S. (1999). A Conceptual Framework for Understanding the Outsourcing Decision. *European Management Journal*, *17*(6), 645–654. doi:10.1016/S0263-2373(99)00055-9

Walker, G. (1988). Strategic Sourcing, Vertical Integration, and Transaction Costs. *Interfaces*, *18*(3), 62–73. doi:10.1287/inte.18.3.62

Chapter 6
Business Process Onshore Outsourcing within the Community Banking System:
An Investigative Study

B. Dawn Medlin
John A. Walker College of Business, Appalachian State University, USA

Adriana Romaniello
Universidad Rey Juan Carlos, Spain

ABSTRACT

Business processes refer to the activities that are performed within an organization that are used in order to produce value for the organization and its customers. Through the use of onshore outsourcing, banks as do other industries expect several benefits such as cost savings and reduction in overhead. Using knowledge management concepts, banks can better understand their firm's performance as well as their own needs. This knowledge may also lead to the increase of employees' skill sets. This study surveyed members of the North Carolina Bankers Association in order to determine what if any of their business processes they selected to outsource.

INTRODUCTION

Outsourcing is often defined as an organization that hires another company to provide services that had been previously handled by internal employees. Onshore outsourcing is conducting business within the same country, while offshore outsourcing is the transfer of labor from workers in one country to workers of another country.

Two of the most common types of sourcing used by banks today are insourcing or outsourcing (Chakrabarty, 2007). The use of business process insourcing requires that a bank would execute their own business processes, while business process outsourcing would require a bank to establish a contractual relationship with a third party vendor and delegate the responsibility of executing the business processes to that vendor (Evans, Martin, Poatsy, 2009).

DOI: 10.4018/978-1-60566-966-3.ch006

Business processes are activities that can provide identifiable output and value to the organization (Coyle, 2009). For banking institutions, business processes may be used in order to enhance their noncore backroom functions such as human resources, IT services, billing, as well as other internal operations. Consequently, as banking institutions must focus more on their core processes such as customer satisfaction, some or all of their noncore functions are ideal candidates for opportunities.

When a bank decides to outsource its business processes, two basic strategies are (1) the "option to reverse" strategy where business processes are outsourced to a vendor, but it also takes into account the possibility of bringing the outsourced business processes back in-house whenever needed, and (2) the "divest completely" strategy where business processes that are perceived to be best managed by a vendor are outsourced permanently (Wibbelsman &Maiero, 1994, as cited in Dibbern et al., 2004, p. 11).

Outsourcing decisions can be both rational and political in nature. Although most of the literature gives the illusion that the process is essentially rational including legitimate goals such as cost efficiency and effectiveness (senior management evaluating the alternatives, apply a low cost criterion, and then select the most efficient option; Allison, 1971) we need to consider the political aspects of this subject which are present not only during the outsourcing decision but during the entire life of the relationship. In this situation, reference must be made to the conflicts and compromises involved during the development of this relationship.

Although recent studies have examined the relationship between outsourcing and firm performance, this research stream continues to be hampered by the lack of a widely accepted conceptualization of managerial outsourcing competence (MOC). The resulting body of research still continues to be contradictory.

During the outsourcing process, organizations may use this time and opportunity to improve their knowledge concerning themselves and in addition augment their employees' skills and competences. Therefore, it is necessary that management begin by resolving any organizational conflicts while at the same time concentrating of the adoption of an organizational structure that can respond with flexibility. Another activity relates to ex-post outsource decision-making which involves the managing of relationships with third party vendors and necessitates the monitoring of contracts and the building of high-quality relationships. Concurrently, the organization should continue to develop a deeper understanding of its business strategy which would allow for the possibility of maintaining a competitive advantage in the marketplace. Therefore, it is our recommendation that the organization develop new competencies as a result of the outsourcing decision-making process and that these competencies will spill over throughout the knowledge management process (KMP).

The basic contention of this paper is the fact that outsourcing decisions alone, may not necessarily improve firm productivity or profitability. It is plausible that additional competencies are more important in order to achieve this aim. By developing managerial outsourcing competence and using it to leverage knowledge management processes, firms are in a better position to enhance their performance.

THEORETICAL DEVELOPMENT

Emerging empirical evidence has shown that outsourcing does not necessarily create a competitive advantage and that there is no significant direct connection between outsourcing and performance (Barthélemy & Quélin, 2006; Gilley & Rasheed, 2000). In fact, a current review of the literature reveals that most of the earlier conceptual work tends to favor the notion that outsourcing can be used favorably to create a competitive advantage and sustain firm performance. To provide a possible explanation for this discussion, we draw on the resource-based view (RBV).

The resource based view (RBV) is grounded in evolutionary economics and has gained considerable attention during the last decade (Barney et al., 2001). Through this view, the firm is seen as a collection of tangible and intangible resources and tacit know- how that must be identified, selected, developed, and deployed to generate superior success (Penrose 1959, Wernerfelt 1984). In order to sustain superior success, firms must accumulate resources which produce economic value, are relatively scarce, and can sustain attempts at imitation, acquisition, or substitution (Barney, 1991).

Additionally and according to the RBV, outsourcing competence per se may not generate superior success or a sustainable advantage, because it can be replicated. However, the advantages of outsourcing capabilities can be protected by embedding it in an organization through complementarities and co-specialization.

Complementarities are said to exist when the value of one resource is enhanced by the presence of another. As an example, the complementary use of information technology and human resources lead to superior firm performance (Powell & Dent-Micallef, 1997).

Co-specialization is said to exist if one resource has little or no value without another (Clemons and Row, 1991). We suggest that managerial outsourcing competence' should not be examined as a stand-alone resource. In this paper we examine how managerial outsourcing competence as a resource can be embedded into an organization and protected through co-specialization. For example, a firm possessing a modular organizational design will realize very little advantage if it does not have the necessary outsourcing leadership to drive it successfully.

In the next section, we describe the concept of managerial outsourcing competence and suggest that it consists of three co-specialized resources: modular organizational design, strategic outsourcing leadership and outsourcing relationship management. We then follow with a discussion of the components of knowledge management processes and examine the link between managerial outsourcing competence and knowledge management processes in order to determine how they might interact to enhance firm performance.

Managerial Outsourcing Competence

Modular Organizational Design

Modular organization design refers to the need of structuring the organization in business processes and with enabled electronic communication technologies. Banks operate in a dynamic environment and must transform themselves continuously in order to create and sustain a competitive advantage. This need brings into focus the role of flexible business processes to enable organizational adaptation.

Business processes are activities structured and organized according to a predefined flow that allow an organization to carry out its business. Many of the business processes require process interdependencies and system dependencies that are established through integration of the business processes (Moitra & Ganesh, 2005).

Because communication is integral to organizational form, advances in communication capabilities through electronic technologies are implicated in a wide variety of forms. Electronic communication technologies (ECTs) are enablers of change by offering capabilities to overcome constraints related to time and distance. Electronic communication systems are also configurations that may be shaped as organizations evolve and change (Fulk & DeSantis, 1995).

When a hierarchical organization such as a bank elects to outsource with other firms, their value chain becomes fundamentally altered. New forms of coupling may be developed through communication technology, in what has been termed the electronic integration effect (Zaheer & Venkatraman, 1994). Defining and implementing flexible business processes supported by flexible ECT systems is of significance to organizations because this allows them to collaborate with partners in new ways, and in turn allows them to adapt to a changing environment.

Relationship Outsourcing Management

When banks first enter a market to outsource a business process, there may be a large number of suppliers to choose from. No one supplier may have a substantial advantage over the others, since each is assumed to have minimal knowledge about the idiosyncrasies of the bank's business. The bank may select a supplier based on who provides the required service for the lowest cost. During this initial selection stage, opportunism is not a serious threat. However, once a supplier is selected, it gains valuable knowledge about the customer's organization during the contract period and at the end of the first contractual period, the supplier has an advantage over the other vendors in the marketplace (Williamson, 1975; Pisano, 1990).

In spite of the contract, the outsourcing organization must continuously monitor the process during its execution because the vendor may impose excess charges or may not perform the duties as agreed upon. The contract monitoring capability involves holding suppliers accountable for both existing service contracts and the development of performance standards.

During this aforementioned process, the cost of outsourcing can also be substantial if the vendor behaves opportunistically. Opportunism extends the notion that people act in their own "self-interest with guile" (Williamson, 1975). Williamson also suggests that opportunism is only a threat when there are a small number of vendors available to provide service.

Williamson found that markets with a large number of suppliers minimize opportunism because "rivalry among larger numbers of bidders will render opportunistic inclinations ineffectual" (Williamson, 1975, p. 27). At this point, banks may wish to reduce threat of opportunism by signing appropriate contracts.

Knowledge Management Process

The knowledge management framework is grounded in the sociology of knowledge (Berger & Luckman, 1967), and is based on the view that organizations are social collectives and therefore "knowledge systems". According to this definition, organizations as knowledge systems consist of four sets of socially-enacted "knowledge processes" that include creation, storage/retrieval, transfer, and application (Hozner & Marx, 1979). This view of an organization's knowledge system represents both the cognitive and social nature of organizational knowledge and its embodiment is the individual's cognition and practices as well as the organization's collective practice and culture (Alavi & Leidner, 2001).

Knowledge Creation

Organizational knowledge creation involves developing new content or replacing existing content within the organization's tacit and explicit knowledge (Pentland, 1995). Through social and collaborative processes as well as an individual's cognitive processes (e.g., reflection), knowledge is created, shared, amplified, enlarged and justified in organizational setting (Nonaka, 1994).

Knowledge Storage/Retrieval

Empirical studies have shown that while organizations create knowledge and learn, they also forget (Argote et al., 1990). Thus, the storage and retrieval of organizational knowledge, also referred to as organizational memory (Stein &

Zwass, 1995) is a very important component of effective organizational knowledge management. Organizational memory covers aspects which go beyond the individual memory to include other components such as organizational culture, transformation (production processes and work procedures), structure, ecology and information archives (Walsh & Ungson, 1991).

Knowledge Transfer

Knowledge transfer occurs at various levels such as transfer of knowledge between individuals, from individuals to explicit sources, from individuals to groups, between groups, across groups, and from the group to the organization. Gupta and Govindarajan (2000) have conceptualized knowledge flows in terms of five elements: 1) perceived value of the source unit's knowledge, 2) motivational disposition of the source, 3) existence and richness of transmission channels, 4) motivational disposition of the receiving unit, and 5) the absorptive capacity of the receiving unit, defined as the ability not only to acquire and assimilate but also to use knowledge (Cohen & Levinthal, 1990).

Knowledge Application

An important aspect of the knowledge-based theory of the firm is that the source of competi-

tive advantage resides in the application of the knowledge rather than in the knowledge itself. Following Grant (1996b) we can identify three primary mechanisms for the integration of knowledge to create organizational capability: directives, organizational routines, and self-contained task teams.

RESEARCH MODEL AND PROPOSITIONS

As previously mentioned, outsourcing by itself can be ineffective as a basis for obtaining and maintaining a sustainable competitive advantage. Thus, we expect that the impact of managerial outsourcing competence on a firm's performance cannot be measured directly, but can only be quantified by examining the indirect effect on an intervening capability (e.g. knowledge management process).

In Figure 1 we present the summarized model of the overall components in relation to our propositions. Following this, we will describe each of the propositions as well as their affected components.

Proposition 1: The relationship between managerial outsourcing competence and firm performance is mediated by knowledge management processes.

Figure 1. Summarized research model

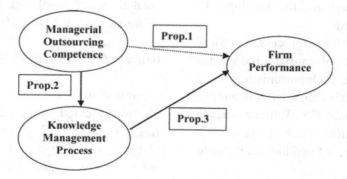

Figure 2. Managerial outsourcing competence & firm performance

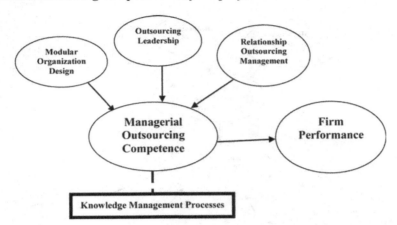

During the outsourcing relationship, firms often mature in their development of new managerial capabilities and task competencies. We propose that the outsourcing of non-core activities is an interactive method that can be used to learn not just the objective and observable aspects of the other firm, but also the more tacit aspects as well. This relationship can represent an excellent opportunity that can improve upon the managerial knowledge of the firm.

Other sources of managerial capabilities may be identified by analyzing the current organizational structure of the vendor as well as their processes. In turn, the outsourcing firm knows more about its needs, routines, procedures, directives, and about its self- contained task teams because this process also implies asking itself about its current organizational structure, processes and activities.

From this analysis, the management of the outsourcing bank begins an organizational reflection process which enables knowledge creation. We can find here the four modes of knowledge creation: socialization, externalization, internalization, and combination (Nonaka, 1994). Each mode relies on, contributes to, and benefits from other modes. For example, the socialization mode can result in creation when the outsourcing firm obtains a new insight (internalization), which is

triggered by an interaction with the other firm. On the other hand, the socialization mode may involve transferring existing tacit knowledge from one member to the other through a discussion of ideas (Alavi & Leidner, 2001). We are suggesting that knowledge creation can be enhanced through the outsourcing process.

During the outsourcing process individuals and groups transfer knowledge through formal and informal channels. One important aspect of transferring knowledge is the absorptive capacity of the outsourcing firm, defined as the ability not only to acquire and assimilate but also to use knowledge (Cohen & Levinthal, 1990).

Thus, given the potential impact that managerial outsourcing competence has on knowledge process, the following proposition is set forth and in addition as seen in Figure 3 a conceptual model is presented.

Proposition 2: Managerial outsourcing competence is positively related to knowledge management processes.

Competition is increasingly knowledge-based as firms strive to learn and to develop capabilities earlier than their rivals (D'Aveni, 1994; Teece & Pisano, 1994). In turbulent markets, the strategic value to a firm will naturally erode over time as

Figure 3. Managerial outsourcing competence in relation to KMPs

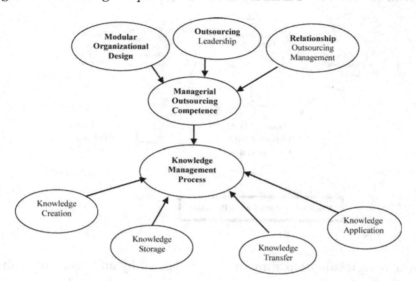

substitutes appear and new competitive problems emerge. When a firm´s capability is built on tacit knowledge and is rare, as well as imperfectly tradable and is costly to imitate, these are the basis of superior performance (Barney, 1991, 1995; Spender, 1996).

The fact of outsourcing non-core activities enables the firm to think strategically and critically on its core business processes of knowledge creation and transfer. Further, this process enables firms to focalize on what they do best, the converging of resources on a few clearly defined and consistent goals; focusing the effort of each group, department, and business unit in a sequential fashion; and targeting those activities that have the biggest impact on customers' perceived value (Yang & Peterson, 2004). The following proposition is set forth:

Proposition 3: There is a positive relationship between knowledge management process and firm performance.

RESEARCH METHODOLOGY

A research methodology was utilized to identify what business process functions members of the North Carolina Banking Association currently outsource onshore. Reasons for outsourcing were also addressed in relationship to business processes. The methodology consisted of the following: research instrument, data collection, and statistical methods.

Research Instrument

The research instrument identified the different types of accounting functions selected for outsourcing use by the members of the North Carolina Bankers Association who were either the Presidents or CIOs of their organization. Other data collected included demographic information (location of bank and its assets). The instrument was pilot tested using banking officials comparable to those used in our study to eliminate any ambiguity as well as to ensure a complete understanding of the questions and the survey instrument. These individuals were not included as sampling units in the actual survey, and the survey instrument

Figure 4. Knowledge management process and firm performance

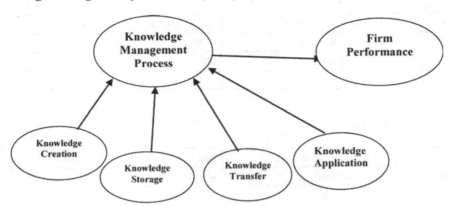

was modified according to the feedback received during the pilot test.

A five-point Likert-type scale was used to measure respondents' propensity to use onshore outsourcing methods (1= Currently Outsourcing Onshore and 5 = Never Outsource Onshore). The survey instrument did require that the bankers reveal their identity for tracking purposes, but individual responses remained confidential. Various statistical methodologies such as the stepwise and t-test procedures were applied using SPSS.

Data Collection and Statistical Methods

The research instrument was administered to bankers who were members of the North Carolina Bankers Association which consists of one hundred and thirty one members. Delivery of the survey was administered online. Electronic surveys provide a faster reaction time than mail surveys, with many studies reporting that most e-mail responses arrive within two to three days following the initial e-mail contact (Bachmann & Elfrink, 1996; Kittleson, 1995). Participants were given appropriate instructions to complete the survey. The internal validity of the survey was conducted using Cronbach Alpha was found to be .886.

ANALYSIS AND RESULTS

In Table 1, the stepwise regression procedure identified three onshore variables at a significance level of 0.10, which influenced the respondent's views related to cost. More specifically, the stepwise procedure identified the following significant variables: payroll services, which would include third-party preparation of payroll reports to promotes confidentiality of payroll information and complying with relevant regulations; ALM (Asset/Liability Management) modeling, or the measurement and management of asset and liability maturities or repayments in order to reduce interest rate risk; and, Check 21 imaging, or the federal requirement that banks accept images rather than hard-copy cancelled checks. Relationships are revealed in terms of cost.

As further indicated by the results in Table 1, the higher the importance of cost, the more payroll services will be outsourced onshore. This is also the case with ALM modeling. Additionally, the more important the factors of cost, the more likely banks were to outsource Check 21 imaging onshore.

As seen in Table 2, respondents identified the following significant variable in terms of reducing time to market. It was shown that the more important it is for a bank to reduce their time to

Table 1. Procedure and cost

Dependent Variable	Independent Variables	Beta Coefficient	t-statistic	p-value
Cost	Payroll Services	0.763	8.97	0.000
	ALM Modeling	0.290	5.92	0.000
	Check 21 Imaging	-0.117	-2.35	0.033

Table 2. Reduce time to market

Dependent Variable	Independent Variables	Beta Coefficient	t-statistic	p-value
Reduce Time to Market	Payroll Services	-0.326	-.2.21	0.039

market, the more unlikely the bank will outsource their payroll services.

In Table 3, it was shown that the more important it was for a bank to focus on core functions the more likely they were to outsource their fixed assets which can include non-earning assets such as buildings, fixtures and equipment. Software may also be included in fixed assets, as it has a depreciable life of five years. The independent variable of Human Resources was found that the more important this variable the more likely outsourcing would occur. Human Resources would include those functions that allow the management of people such as benefits, employee assessment and regulatory compliance.

Addressing the variable of gaining access to world-class capabilities in Table 4, it was found that the more important banking executives thought the dependent variable of gaining access to world-class capabilities, the more the banks outsourced the management of their fixed assets. This was also the case with the independent variables of ALM Modeling and Check 21 imaging.

CONCLUSION

Outsourcing business functions is becoming increasingly common practice among banks looking for a competitive advantage. The guiding principle being that non-core activities could be handed over to a company that has expertise in those activities, thereby freeing internal resources to focus on enhancing the value-add of its core business.

Within the management arena and using knowledge management processes the outsourcer banks achieve a stronger awareness of its outsourcing "know how" which is embedded in routines, procedures, directives and in self-contained tasks. We argue that the more firms outsource non-core activities the more efficient they will become at using their outsourcing "know how". As we see in our exploratory test banks always outsource more than one business process and this suggests that banks could be achieving scope economies through the application of outsourcing "know how" in the many different non-core business processes.

Table 3. Focus on core functions

Dependent Variable	Independent Variables	Beta Coefficient	t-statistic	p-value
Focus on Core Functions	Fixed Assets	0.443	3.95	0.001
	Human Resources	1.206	2.54	0.019

Table 4. Gain access to world-class capabilities

Dependent Variable	Independent Variables	Beta Coefficient	t-statistic	p-value
Gain Access to World-Class Capabilities	Fixed Assets	0.913	23.073	0.000
	ALM Modeling	0.097	4.631	0.001
	Check 21 Imaging	0.100	2.056	0.070

Another side, of the knowledge management process enables firms to focalize on what they do best, concentrating resources through the processes of converging resources on a few clearly defined and consistent goals, building core competences and understanding strategic know-how. We reinforce this theoretical aspect after analyzing the results of the test because in our survey banks reasons for outsourcing are majority strategic ones such as cost, focus on core functions and gain access to world-class knowledge A knowledge-based approach to strategy formulation effectively matches the opportunities and corporate capabilities of the banks and may generate economically feasible strategic alternatives.

REFERENCES

Alavi, M., & Leidner, D. E. (2001). Review: Knowledge Management and Knowledge Management Systems: Conceptual Foundations and Research Issues. *MIS Quarterly*, *25*(1), 107–136. doi:10.2307/3250961

Allison, G. (1971). Essence of Decision. Boston: Little, Brown.

Ang, S., & Straub, D. (1998). Production and Transaction Economies and Information Systems Oursourcing: A Study of the US Banking Industry. *MIS Quarterly*, *22*(4), 535–552. doi:10.2307/249554

Aranha, H., & Wheelwright, S. (2007). Transition from Business Process Outsourcing to Knowledge Process Outsourcing. *Biopharm International*, *20*(5), 58.

Argote, L., Beckman, S., & Epple, D. (1990). The persistence and transfer of learning in industrial settings. *Management Science*, *36*, 140–154. doi:10.1287/mnsc.36.2.140

Bachmann, D., & Elfrink, J. (1996). Tracking the progress of e-mail versus snail-mail. *Marketing Research*, *8*(2), 31–35.

Barney, J. (1991). Firm Resources and Sustained Competitive Advantage. *Journal of Management*, *17*(1), 99–120. doi:10.1177/014920639101700108

Barney, J. (1995). Looking inside for competitive advantage. *The Academy of Management Executive*, *9*, 49–61.

Barthélemy, J., & Quélin, B. V. (2006). Complexity of Outsourcing Contracts and *Ex Post* Transaction Costs: An Empirical Investigation. *Journal of Management Studies*, *43*(8), 1775–1797. doi:10.1111/j.1467-6486.2006.00658.x

Berger, P. L., & Luckmann, T. (1966). The Social Construction of Reality. Harmondsworth: Penguin.

Chakrabarty, S. (2007). Strategies for Business Process Outsourcing: An Analysis of Alternatives, Opportunities and Risks. In J. Sounderpandian, & T. Sinha (Eds.), E-Business Process Management: Technologies and Solutions (pp. 204-229). Hershey, PA: IGI Publishing.

Cohen, W. M., & Levinthal, D. A. (1990). Absorptive Capacity: A New Perspective on Learning and Innovation. *Administrative Science Quarterly*, *35*(1), 128–152. doi:10.2307/2393553

Coyle, D. A. (2009). *Computers Are Your Future.* Upper Saddle River, NJ: Pearson Hall.

D'Aveni, R. A. (1994). *Hypercompetition: Managing the dynamics of strategic maneuvering.* New York: Free Press.

Evans, A., Martin, K., & Poatsy, M. A. (2009). *Complete Technology in Action.* Upper Saddle River, NJ: Pearson Hall.

Fulk, J., & DeSantis, G. (1995). Electronic Communication and Changing Organizational Forms. *Organization Science, 6*(4). doi:10.1287/orsc.6.4.337

Gilley, M., & Rasheed, A. (2000). Making More by Doing Less: An Analysis of Outsourcing and its Effects on Firm Performance. *Journal of Management, 26*(4), 763–790. doi:10.1016/S0149-2063(00)00055-6

Gillis, A. (2005). *The future of outsourcing.* Retrieved August 9, 2005 from http://www.ababj.com/futureoutsourcing.html.

Grant, R. M. (1996b). Toward a knowledge-based theory of the firm. *Strategic Management Journal, 17*, 109–122. doi:10.1002/(SICI)1097-0266(199602)17:2<109::AID-SMJ796>3.0.CO;2-P

Grover, V., Cheon, M., & Teng, J. (1996). The effect of service quality and partnership on the outsourcing of information systems functions. *Journal of Management Information Systems, 12*(4), 89–116.

Gupta, A. K., & Govindarajan, V. (2000). Knowledge flows within multinational corporations. *Strategic Management Journal, 21*, 473–496. doi:10.1002/(SICI)1097-0266(200004)21:4<473::AID-SMJ84>3.0.CO;2-I

Gupta, U. G., & Gupta, A. (1992). Outsourcing the IS function: is it necessary for your organization? *Information Systems Management, 9*(3), 44–50. doi:10.1080/10580539208906881

Ireland, R., Hitt, M., & Vaidyanath, D. (2002). Alliance Management as a Source of Competitive Advantage. *Journal of Management, 28*, 413–446. doi:10.1177/014920630202800308

Kavan, C., Saunders, C., & Nelson, R. (1993). The information systems outsourcing bandwagon. *Sloan Management Review*, 73–86.

Kern, T., Kreijger, J., & Willcocks, L. (2002b). Exploring ASP as sourcing strategy: theoretical perspective, propositions for practice. *The Journal of Strategic Information Systems, 11*, 153–177. doi:10.1016/S0963-8687(02)00004-5

Krebsbach, K. (2004). Outsourcing Dominates As Banks Seek Savings. *Bank Technology News, 17*(9), 16.

Lacitv, M. C., & Willcocks, L. P. (1998). An empirical investigation of information technology sourcing practices: lessons from experience. *MIS Quarterly, 22*(3), 363–408. doi:10.2307/249670

Lacity, M. C., & Hirschheim, R. (1993). The information systems outsourcing bandwagon. *Sloan Management Review, 35*, 73–86.

Lacity, M. C., Hirschheim, R., & Willcocks, L. (1994). Realizing outsourcing expectations: incredible expectations, credible outcomes. *Information Systems Management, 11*(4), 7–18. doi:10.1080/07399019408964664

Lacity, M. C., Willcocks, L. P., & Feeny, D. F. (1996). The value of selective IT outsourcing. *Sloan Management Review, 37*, 13–25.

Loh, L. & Venkatraman, N. (1992b). Determinants of IT outsourcing: a cross-sectional analysis, 9, 7-24.

McAdam, R., & McCormack, D. (2001). Integrating Business Processed for Global Alignment and Supply Chain Management. *Business Process Management Journal, 7*(2), 19–23. doi:10.1108/14637150110389696

McFarlan, F. W., & Nolan, R. L. (1995). How to manage an IT outsourcing alliance. *Sloan Management Review*, *36*, 9–22.

McLaughlin, T. (2004). The Shape of Banks to Come. Retrieved August 9, 2005 from http://www.gtnews.com.

Moitra, D., & Ganesh, J. Web Services and Flexible Business Processes: Towards the Adaptive Influence Of A Learning Culture On It Investments. *Information & Management*, *42*, 921–933.

Nonaka, I. (1994). *A Dynamic Theory of Organizational Knowledge Creation*, *5*(1), 14-37.

Orlikowski, W., Yates, J., Okamura, K., & Fujimoto, M. (1995). Shaping Electronic Communication: The Metastructuring of Technology in the Context of Use. *Organization Science*, *6*(4), 423–444. doi:10.1287/orsc.6.4.423

Outsourcing, T. Trends to Watch for in Your Due Diligence. (n.d.). Retrieved May 15, 2005 from http://www.cunatechnologycouncil.org/news/204.html.

Penrose, E. (1959). *The Theory of the Growth of the Firm*. London: Basil Blackwell.

Pentland, B. T. (1995). Read me what it says on your screen: The interpretative problem in technical service work. *Technology Studies*, *2*(1), 50–79.

Pisano Gary, P. (1990). The R&D boundaries of the firm: an empirical analysis. *Administrative Science Quarterly*, *35*, 153–176. doi:10.2307/2393554

Powell, T. C., & Dent-Micallef, A. (1997). Information technology as competitive advantage: the role of human, business, and technology resources. *Strategic Management Journal*, *18*(5), 375–405. doi:10.1002/(SICI)1097-0266(199705)18:5<375::AID-SMJ876>3.0.CO;2-7

Quinn, J. B. (1999). Strategic Outsourcing: Leveraging knowledge capabilities. *Sloan Management Review*, 9–21.

Raysman, R., & Brown, P. (2005). Computer Law; Sarbanes-Oxley's 404 and Business Process Outsourcing. *New York Law Journal*, *233*(34), 23–35.

Saunders, C., Gebelt, M., & Hu, Q. (1997). Achieving success in information systems outsourcing. *California Management Review*, *39*(2), 63–79.

Spender, J. C. (1996). Competitive advantage from tacit knowledge? Unpacking the concept and its strategic implications. In B. Moingeon & A. Edmondson (Eds.), *Organizational learning and competitive advantage*. London: Sage Publications.

Stein, E., & Zwass, V. (1995). Actualizing organizational memory with information systems. *ISR*, *6*(2), 85–117. doi:10.1287/isre.6.2.85

Teece, D., & Pisano, G. (1994). The Dynamic Capabilities of Firms: an Introduction. *Industrial and Corporate Change*, *3*(3), 537–556. doi:10.1093/icc/3.3.537-a

Wade, M., & Hulland, J. (2004). Review: The Resource-Based View and Information Systems Research: Review, Extension and Suggestions for Future Research. *MIS Quarterly*, *28*(1).

Walsh, J., & Ungson, G. (1991). Organizational Memory. *Academy of Management Review*, *16*(1), 57–91. doi:10.2307/258607

Wernerfelt, B. (1984). A Resource-Based View of the Firm. *Strategic Management Journal*, *5*(2), 171–180. doi:10.1002/smj.4250050207

Willcocks, L., Hindle, J., Feeny, D., & Lacity, M. (2004). IT and Business Process Outsourcing: The Knowledge Potential. *Information Systems Management*, *21*(3), 7–15. doi:10.1201/1078/44432.21.3.20040601/82471.2

Willcocks, L., & Lacity, M. (1998). *Strategic Sourcing of Information Systems: Perspectives and Practices*. New York: John Wiley & Sons.

Willcocks, L. P., Lacity, M., & Kern, T. (1999). Risk mitigation in IT outsourcing strategy revisited: longitudinal case research at LISA. *The Journal of Strategic Information Systems*, 8(3), 285–341. doi:10.1016/S0963-8687(00)00022-6

Williamson, O. E. (1975). *Markets and Hierarchies*. New York: Free Press.

Yang, Z., & Peterson, R. (2004). Customer perceived value, satisfaction, and loyalty: The role of switching costs. *Psychology and Marketing*, 21(10), 799–822. doi:10.1002/mar.20030

Zaheer, A., & Venkatraman, N. (1994). Determinants of Electronic Integration in the Insurance Industry: An Empirical Test. *Management Science*, 40(5), 549–566. doi:10.1287/mnsc.40.5.549

KEY TERMS AND DEFINITIONS

ALM Modeling: Asset liability modeling can be done in house or through a service bureau arrangement. The service bureau limits the flexibility somewhat but still allows the bank to access the service bureau site remotely. Outsourcing to a service bureau generally limits the number of scenarios that can be run but all of the maintenance is performed by the service bureau.

Check Clearing: The process of collecting deposited funds drawn on other banks.

Credit Card Processing: This activity includes collection of funds for customer merchants, with charges allocated to the purchaser's bank.

Loan Review (MCIF): Review of a database which contains information related to the customer in the Marketing Customer Information File (MCIF).

Payroll Services: Used by banks and other industries to define pay frequencies and pay periods. It also can use configurable payroll numbers with alpha-numeric codes assigned by or needed by the bank

Statement Rendering: The process of returning images and/or cancelled checks and transaction records to account-holding customers.

Chapter 7
Offshoring in the Pharmaceutical Industry[1]

Jason McCoy
Global Seawater, Inc., USA

Johannes Sarx
ALCIMED, France

ABSTRACT

Offshoring has been adopted as a tool for reducing costs and for gaining strategic advantages by financial services, software development, and other competitive industries. For a variety of reasons, the pharmaceutical industry has been slow to take advantage of the benefits that offshoring can provide. The purpose of this article is to explore the internal and exogenous factors motivating global pharmaceutical firms to increase and expand their sourcing activities. And, instead of discussing global sourcing in general, India has been analyzed as a unique and explanatory case study for this new, emerging trend. The reasons behind this decision include India's position as a renowned global IT hub, the country's "home grown" biotechnology and biopharmaceutical industries, the numerous strategic partnerships and offshoring relationships between global and Indian firms, as well as its significant advances in IT and information management.

GLOBAL PHARMACEUTICAL OVERVIEW

The global pharmaceutical industry broke historical records with revenues of approximately U.S. $600 billion in 2006 (Pharmaceutical Research and Manufacturers of America [PhRMA], 2006). This is particularly striking as the growth slowed somewhat in North America and Europe; however, China, India, Mexico, Russia, South Korea, and other emerging markets outstripped established markets, growing collectively at an astounding rate of 81% (Herper & Kang, 2006). The lifeblood of the industry flows from its research and development (R&D) efforts with an annual investment of U.S. $49.3 billion, or between 10 to 15% of total revenues (Herper & Kang, 2006). As the world becomes increasingly globalized, the pharmaceutical industry must respond to emerging challenges and opportunities, especially in developing countries. Currently, the industry faces issues related to expiring patents, drying pipelines, decreasing returns on investment, growing urgency to introduce new drugs in a timely manner, and an increasing need to access broad patient populations. This reality has prompted a wave of offshoring by top multinational firms. Offshoring was originally adopted as a tool for reducing costs and for gaining strategic advantages (Gupta, Seshasai, Mukherji, & Ganguly, 2007), yet the pharmaceutical industry has been slow to take advantage of the benefits that offshoring can offer. This section examines the current levels of global pharmaceutical employment and offshoring.

Global Pharmaceutical Employment

The pharmaceutical industry employed approximately 1.76 million individuals worldwide in 2006 (U.S. Department of Commerce, 2003). This number is expected to grow by 2.8% annually, resulting in an estimated 2 million jobs by 2010 (U.S. Department of Commerce, 2003). Structurally, the pharmaceutical industry is becoming increasingly consolidated with relatively few, but large, employers. The top 20 pharmaceutical companies constituted 59% of global employment in 2005 (U.S. Department of Commerce, 2006). The United States leads in employment (41%), followed by Europe (25%) and Japan (13%) (Farrell, 2005). Consequently, only 21% of industry employment is located in less developed nations. Employment is concentrated in three main areas: commercial (40%), manufacturing (31%), and research and development (15%). Sales agents represent the largest percentage of the workforce (35% total; 88% of commercial). The remaining 14% of employment is involved with back office

services such as general and administrative functions (G&A) (6%), IT (3%), procurement (3%), and supply chain management (2%) (Ernest & Young, 2004). Employment by occupation is skewed towards the commercial and manufacturing sectors with generalists (37%) and support staff (30%) dominating the industry. Increased offshoring is predicated on the ability to fundamentally alter the make-up of occupational employment to take better advantage of highly skilled-labor in low-wage countries (Ernest & Young, 2004).

Current Levels of Global Sourcing

At the forefront of the offshoring wave are the large multinational corporations based in the United States, Western Europe, and Japan. In 2005, an estimated 13,000 jobs were offshored (Pascal, Robert & Rosenfeld, 2006). This number will increase to 21,200 jobs by 2008 (Pascal & Rosenfeld, 2006).

Unlike many other competitive industries, the pharmaceutical sector is uniquely positioned to remotely execute one if its core competencies—R&D, which represents 74% of offshored employment (Pacal & Rosenfeld, 2006). The R&D activities currently performed in less developed nations include clinical trials, clinical statistics, data management, medical writing, and discovery. The pharmaceutical industry has recognized clinical trials as an area with the greatest potential for cost-savings and expansion. For example, Quintiles, a provider of clinical trials, has hired 850 employees in India, or 5% of its total employees, and plans to expand its data management center in Bangalore ("Quintiles Moves Data," 2005). Although globally sourcing a core function such as R&D is inherently risky, pharmaceutical companies are now willing to follow in the footsteps of industries that have successfully utilized offshoring.

IT is the next largest offshored function, with 22% of employment performed abroad by pharmaceutical companies, although it constitutes only 3% of total employees (Farrell, 2005). In May 2005, Wyeth outsourced its clinical data management to Accenture, with a large portion of its operations to be located in India (Global Newswire, 2005). The smallest job function to be offshored by pharmaceutical companies (2%) is G&A, which includes basic financial operations such as payroll, finance, and accounting (Farrell, 2005).

While there is no distinct pharmaceutical model, companies are conducting their offshoring activities through a mix of captive and vendor arrangements. One of the more commonly used arrangements involves a hybrid model, where a pharmaceutical company initially controls procedures and management but gradually transfers power to its on-site vendor or partner. This trend is especially evident between established global pharmaceutical companies and India-based biotechnology firms.

India's Pharmaceutical and Biotechnology Industry

India is the world's largest producer of generic anti-AIDS drugs, and its overall generics industry totals more than U.S. $4 billion (*Expanding Global*, 2005). India's pharmaceutical industry supplies 85% of its domestic market and generates approximately U.S. $900 million a year from sales in India alone (Park, 2002). Indian-based pharmaceutical firms have achieved a degree of sophistication that is accelerating the strategic need for working relationships with leading global firms. For example, Ranbaxy recently signed an agreement with GlaxoSmithKline to commercialize compounds that are developed together, despite the fact that the two firms were locked in a patent lawsuit a few years ago. Some analysts state that the Indian pharmaceutical industry will grow quickly if it can not only create commodities but also share in the financial and strategic benefits of codevelopment and ownership of new patented compounds and products (Go, 2005).

Increasingly, the source for innovation in the global pharmaceuticals industry comes from the biotechnology sector, particularly biopharmaceuticals, bioservices, and bioinformatics.

Globally, the market for biotechnology products is valued at US $54 billion (Biospectrum India, 2006), to which India contributed about 3 to 4% with total revenues of US $1.8 billion in 2006 (Business Standard, 2007). *Figure 1* shows the potential, rapid growth of the Indian biotechnology industry. The Indian biotechnology industry is growing at an annual rate of 35% compared to 17% worldwide. The Indian biotechnology industry is expected to grow to U.S. $5 billion in 2009 (Business Standard, 2007), thereby increasing its global market share from 1 to 10% in only 5 years and generating more than a million jobs (New York Times, 2005).

Despite its current small size, the Indian biotechnology industry plays a significant role in certain segments such as vaccines for children and competes globally, with exports accounting for 52% or U.S. $763 million of total sales. In terms of exports, the biopharmaceuticals segment accounts for the largest share of the biotechnology sector, with total revenues of U.S. $572 or 75% of total exports ("Offshoring R&D,", 2007). Unfortunately, the impact of the industry on the job market is limited, with only 10,000 people employed (Ernest & Young, 2002) in 280 biotech and 190 bio-supplying companies ("Offshoring R&D," 2007).

The Indian biotechnology industry is dominated by the biopharmaceuticals market, which accounts for 76% of total industry revenues. Other important segments include bioservices (9%), bioagricultural sector (7%), industrial biotechnology (5.5%), and bioinformatics generating 2.5% of the total industry revenues respectively (*New York Times,* 2005). Of these segments, the bio-agriculture and bioservices markets are growing at an annual rate of 70% and 100%, respectively (Ernst & Young, 2002).

Figure 1. Projected growth of indian biotechnology industry (U.S. $) (Source: "Biotechnology", India Equity Brand Foundation, 2005)

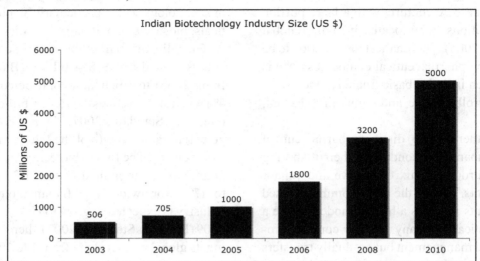

Biopharmaceuticals

While relatively small compared to the overall pharmaceuticals industry, the biopharmaceuticals sector is the single largest contributor to the Indian biotechnology industry with total revenues of U.S. $811.4 million, accounting for more than 75% of the total biotech industry (*India Can Become,* 2006). In recent years, this segment achieved close to 30% annual growth, primarily driven by vaccine production. Apart from vaccines (e.g. recombinant hepatitis), the range of medical biotechnology products include diagnostics (e.g., immunology products) and drug development ("Offshoring R&D," 2007). In 2005, the Indian vaccines market generated sales of about U.S. $380M growing at an annual rate of 20%. One of the most important vaccines is recombinant Hepatitis B, with a market of U.S. $22 million in India, produced by Shantha Biotechnics, Bharat Biotech, and Wockhardt as well as foreign producers such as Aventis, LG Chemicals, and GlaxoSmithKline (Ernst & Young, 2002).

With over 25 companies, the diagnostics sector generated sales of U.S. $137 million with its

proposition of real-time and low-cost processes through new reagents and instruments. The therapeutics segment achieved U.S. $113.64 million in sales with the development and marketing of products such as Streptokinase, Granulocyte Colony Stimulating Factor (G-CSF), Erythropoetin (EPO), Interferon Alpha 2 (otherwise known as human insulin), which was released in 2003. Within the biopharmaceutical sector, the production of biogenerics plays an important role: Indian companies such as Wockhardt, Biocon, and Shantha Biotech are manufacturing generic versions of biotech drugs—focusing on EPO products, human insulin, Interferons, and G-CSF. Other fast-growing areas are the bioengineering and nanobiotechnology segments that develop new tissue engineering processes and biomaterials for therapeutics.

Bioinformatics

The bioinformatics sector is successfully creating synergies between the IT and pharmaceutical industry. In 2005, the bioinformatics segment grew by 25% generating U.S. $22.7 million and

Figure 2. Percentage Break-Down of Biotechnology Sector (Source: Data used from "Biotechnology", India Equity Brand Foundation, 2005)

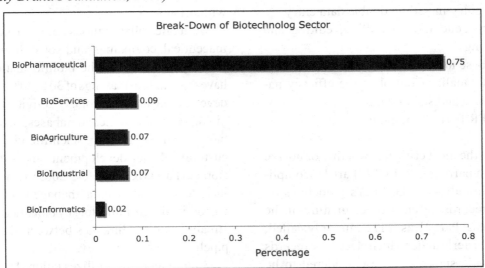

is expected to generate U.S. $120 in million sales by 2007 (India Equity Brand Foundation, 2005). Certainly, the bioinformatics industry benefits from the strength of the IT industry in India. Companies such as Questa Bioinformatics, Ltd., or Tata Consultancy are offering services related to data mining, scientific visualization, information storage, and simulation of DNA sequences. Some companies, such as Advantage and Agarare, specialize in the development of Laboratory Information Management Systems (LIMS).

DRIVERS AND TRENDS

Global Pharmaceutical Sourcing

Advances in IT and bioinformatics, escalating cost pressures, cost differential between high-wage and low-wage countries, and time to market considerations are motivating companies to move part of their operations to countries like China and India.

Information Technology

As scientists delve into the complex biological code of the human genome, there is intense competition to develop potential drug targets that affect key population groups and profiles. The challenge is that much of the clinical information remains on paper, and many firms are embracing the opportunity to streamline and centralize their information resources. Consequently, advances in IT is one of the most critical drivers in the decision to offshore, especially in India, which has become a renowned global hub and generally ensures standardized procedures for complex data services and discovery software.

Global pharmaceutical companies are looking for local data management units that invest heavily in hardware, software, line connectivity, and skilled employees. Typically, a major firm would look for the following:

- A detailed data management plan
- Preparation of database in a desired software

- Comprehensive electronic validation and consistency checks
- Data entry including double data entry
- Query generation, handling, editing and tracking
- Database lock
- 100% Quality Control of the efficacy parameters and safety data
- 21 CFR Part 11 compliant

Perhaps the most critical is whether or not the local Indian partner is "21 CFR Part 11 Compliant," which addresses the FDA's guidelines on electronic records and electronic signatures in the United States. Part 11 as it is commonly called, defines the criteria under which electronic records and electronic signatures are considered to be trustworthy, reliable and equivalent to article records. Part 11 requires drug makers, medical device manufacturers, biotech companies, biologics developers, and other FDA-regulated industries (not including food manufacturers) to implement controls, including audits, validation systems, and documentation for software and systems involved in processing many forms of data as part of business operations and product development.

The pharmaceutical industry spends roughly 5% of its revenues on IT, much less than other information-intensive industries such as financial institutions. A report by PricewaterhouseCoopers (2005) estimates that as much as 80% of the information held by many large pharmaceutical companies is unstructured and not easily searchable. The prevailing realities provide an excellent opportunity for firms to offshore their restructuring process and devote more of their resources to IT, which has the potential to convert a tidal wave of data into new products. Further, increasing automation allows firms to more easily monitor trials from abroad and understand the relationships between complex variables and derive conclusions within a shorter time frame. Easier monitoring ability, access to data, and ap-

plication development help to reduce many of the operational and logistical challenges associated with offshoring.

Strategic collaborations between global pharmaceutical companies and local Indian firms, particularly those in the bioinformatics sector, have reported cost savings of 30 to 40% in the drug development process, notably activities related to biological and chemical databases, data mining, biomedical text mining, scientific visualization, customized tool development, and information storage (Pascal & Rosenfeld, 2005). Other services include integrated data management systems, customized algorithms for key biological data, and streamlining the linkages between the research pipeline and expert analysis of data.

Alpha Gene, Inc., utilizes tailored informatics technology from Questar Bioinformatics to mine its protein library. Questar provides support for structure determination, pathway identification, and small molecule library development. Another interesting example of this synergistic dynamic is Tata Consultancy Services' recent agreement to research "P66," which is a target protein identified by Congenia in several age-related diseases. The optimized lead molecules discovered by Tata Consultancy Services will be further tested and developed by Congenia through extensive animal, and eventually human, clinical trials. Not surprisingly, key partnerships between global and local firms have developed around the IT service centers, such as in Bangalore, Hyderabad, and Chennai.

Rising Costs of Research and Development

According to the Tufts Center for the Study of Drug Development, the cost of developing a new drug increased from U.S. $131 million in 1987 to U.S. $ 1 billion in 2006. The Bain Drug Economic Model estimates that investment required for one successful drug launch at $1.78 billion dollars, including typically $250 million for launch. On average, one out of every 1,000 compounds that enter preclinical testing will survive to the clinical phase (Eaton & Wierenga, 1999). Of this, just one out of every five will eventually receive regulatory approval (Eaton & Wierenga, 1999). Once it reaches the marketplace, only 3 of 10 new drugs generate a return on investment (Goodwin & Goldberg, 2001).

Failure for certain drugs to receive regulatory approval for sale in the market stem from a variety of sources, such as harsh negative side effects or weak therapeutic effects. For those drugs that do reach the clinical testing phase, the future remains uncertain, partly because of the increasing difficulty of obtaining approval from regulatory agencies. It is the norm in the industry that, for every one hundred drugs that enter clinical studies, 30% will be rejected during Phase 1, a further 37% during Phase 2, 6% in Phase 3, and an additional 7% during the regulatory review period (Go, 2005). In total, only 10 to 12% of drugs that reach the stage of being tested on humans are approved for marketing (Go, 2005).

Although these low yields are consistent with the identity of the pharmaceutical industry of being notoriously R&D intensive, a historical perspective casts an equally grim light on current productivity levels.

Figure 3 illustrates the industry's anemic level of recent drug discovery. Although the funding for R&D has been increasing, pharmaceutical companies have not been able to maintain past levels of drug discovery. The FDA approved only 21 new molecular entities (NMEs) in 2003, compared with a peak of 53 in 1996, according to the FDA's Center for Drug Evaluation and Research. Figure 4 displays the increasing cost of passing regulatory hurdles.

Inherent in a system of patents with limited durations is the gradual loss of revenue after expiration of the patent. This loss has been historically offset by the continual development of new drugs; but that is no longer the case. Tremendous pressure is being placed on drug discoverers to accelerate the pace of innovation. To put this challenge in perspective, consider that 35 blockbuster drugs will lose their U.S. patent protection within the next 4 years alone (Kelly Scientific Resources, 2004). These losses are estimated by the market research firm Datamonitor to total $70 billion globally.

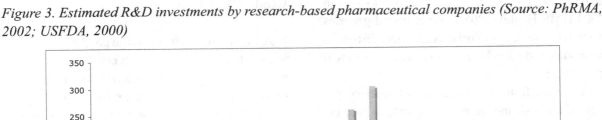

Figure 3. Estimated R&D investments by research-based pharmaceutical companies (Source: PhRMA, 2002; USFDA, 2000)

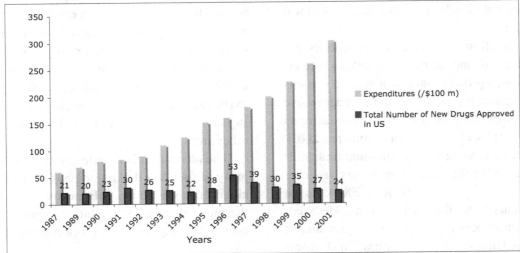

Figure 4. Trends in preclinical, clinical, and total cost per approved new drug (Source: J. A. DiMasi, 2005; Journal of Health Economics, 22, 151-185)

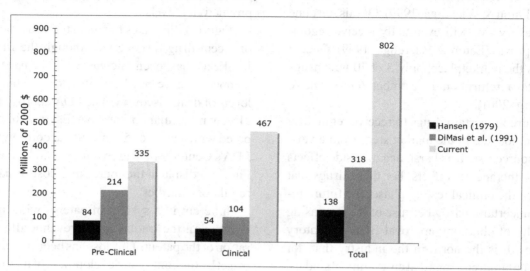

In addition to a rise in the cost of developing new drugs and a decrease in the frequency of their discovery, the increasing use of generic pharmaceuticals is putting pressure on firms to cut costs. According to a February 2005 IMS Health Report, generic drug revenue has grown in the U.S. market from 15% in 1999 to 17% in 2004, while the portion of generic prescriptions dispensed has grown from 50% in 1999 to 54% in 2004 (IMS Health, 2005). Lower priced generics cater to the demands of price conscious third-party payers and individual consumers alike, as is shown in Figure 5.

The shift from branded drugs to generics is a sign of the growing strength of managed care organizations, a growing variety of generic versions available when a patent expires, and more aggressive sales and marketing techniques by manufacturers of generics (U.S. Department of Commerce, 2003). Multistate purchasing pools in particular are significantly strengthening the leverage buyers have over pharmaceutical companies (NSCL, 2005). As the U.S. population ages, the larger segment of Medicaid-eligible consumers will heighten this pressure, as highlighted in a recent A. T. Kearney (2004) report

that states from 2003 through 2007, pricing strains will pare $9 billion from the same [top] 10-pharma firms' revenues, as key customers (e.g., state governments, the elderly, and retail consumers) balk at paying top dollar. The increasing cost of R&D makes low-cost alternatives such as offshoring to developing nations all the more attractive.

Cost Differential

Many companies cite the large gap between what it costs to employ equivalent employees at home and in low-wage countries as one of the primary drivers of offshoring. The unusually high labor costs of the pharmaceutical industry make it especially attractive in this case. While there exists many different ways to cut costs, offshoring clinical trials promises to dwarf savings in other areas.

The pharmaceutical industry spends the majority of its R&D dollars on phases that require clinical trials (Kermani & Bonacossa, 2003). Furthermore, these phases' relative importance has been increasing, since the proportion of industry

Figure 5. Generics' share of U.S. prescription drug market: 1984-2005 (Source: 1984-2000 IMS Health, National Prescription Audit Plus 2001; 2004 projection: S&P)

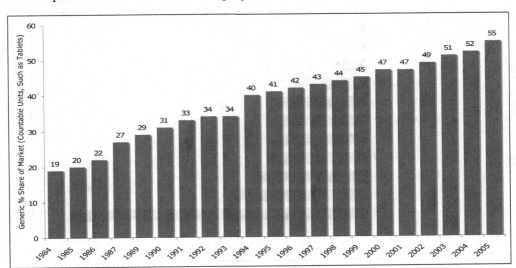

R&D expenditure allocated to clinical studies increased between 1996 and 1998 from 32.5 to 39.5%, respectively (Kermani & Bonacossa, 2003). SRI International, an independent nonprofit research institute, estimates that by sourcing in a low-wage country, 10 to 40% can be shaved off early drug work such as toxicology studies.

GlaxoSmithKline is leveraging Indian talent in its alliance with Ranbaxy, under which Ranbaxy identifies promising potential drugs and performs preclinical trials, while GSK performs later stage developments and retains the rights to market the drugs in all countries other than India (Ernst & Young, 2004).

Time to Market

Patents provide the monopoly power to producers that enable them to recoup their enormous R&D costs. Without exclusive rights to produce and sell patented goods, generics would dominate the market. Consequently, each year of a drug's patent-protected life is extremely valuable. This sheltered time period is defined by two factors: first, patent lengths, which have been fixed globally

by the WTO at no less than 20 years; and second, the time from the date a patent is filed and its debut on the market. Of these, only the latter is variable. Offshoring has the potential to significantly reduce this development time. Mounting development requirements make any option for speeding this process even more attractive. It has been estimated that each extra day a drug is on the market generates around U.S. $1 million (U.S. Department of Commerce, 2006).

Figure 6 illustrates the declining time period of exclusivity. The Pharmaceutical Research and Manufacturers of America (PhRMA) comments on this phenomenon that the average period of effective patent life for new medicines is substantially shorter than the 20-year period that constitutes a full patent term in the United States. Furthermore, a generic drug manufacturer may file a patent challenge as early as 4 years after the new medicine is approved, and in some cases, as early as 3 years after approval (PhRMA, 2003).

Offshoring can alleviate this time crunch by speeding clinical trials. Drug companies in Western Europe, the United States, and Japan face daunting regulatory requirements for approval. In

Figure 6. Period of market exclusivity between introduction of breakthrough medicine and competing innovators (Source: PhRMA, 2000; The Wilkerson Group, 1995)

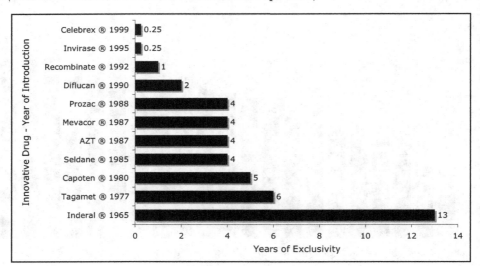

order to meet these standards, extensive clinical trials must be conducted. The populations of developed countries are far less conducive to these trials than those in developing countries. Finding untreated or drug "naïve" patients that have the health characteristics sought by pharmaceutical companies is exceedingly challenging in developed nations. For example, an expert interviewed by McKinsey & Company, commented that it was challenging to recruit diabetes patients who had not received treatment in the U.S., while there is a large patient pool available in India (Farrell, 2005).

Drug companies are taking advantage of this fact by contracting with Indian firms. However, the relationship between India and the drug industry extends further. For example, Pfizer, in recognizing the long-term potential of India as a location for clinical testing, has partnered with the Bombay College of Pharmacy to create an Academy for Clinical Excellence. The scientific academy is to be set up near the Bombay College of Pharmacy, with modules offering training programs in clinical research methodology, data management and biostatistics ("Pfizer to set up,"

2005). In late 2004, GlaxoSmithKline's chief executive Jean-Pierre Garnier stated there were few alternatives to streamlining research and development department, and therefore the company is attempting to move 30% of its clinical trials to low-cost countries (Tomlinson, 2004).

Complementing this superior access to patients for clinical trials, offshoring enables companies to work around the clock on promising compounds. According to experts at the U.S. Department of Commerce (2006), a development time of a blockbuster drug shortened by 1 month equals roughly $100 million in additional sales at a 40% profit margin. Further, Indian CRO firms and those that provide other types of services must meet the U.S. good manufacturing procedures (cGMP), good laboratory practices (GLP), and good clinical practices (GCP) requirements. Any global pharmaceutical firm that works with Indian firms is subject to inspection by USFDA scientists, and if a critical clinical trial is conducted in India, it must meet both the GCP requirements as well as investigation from Indian experts. This allows for quality control and provides strong regulatory guidelines for Indian-based firms.

Offshoring Risks and Concerns

Large pharmaceutical companies are still somewhat wary of outsourcing sensitive and vital operations. There is a low tolerance for error industry-wide; simple mistakes can compromise results or, in the worst-case scenario, harm patients, resulting in a massive and expensive liability. Joe McCracken, SVP of business and commercial development at Genentech, highlighted that his firm has a very low threshold for error. Every decision must be correct and done quickly to prevent customers from suffering and competitors from capturing a larger portion of their consumer base. And, because of the higher potential threshold for error, Genentech is much less interested in outsourcing because the savings do not justify the risk (IMS Health, 2005).

Data integrity has a magnified effect in the pharmaceutical industry, and companies must carefully outsource their IT functions to the best, most error-proof partners. Russ Bantham of the Pharmaceutical Research and Manufacturers of America (PhRMA) cites industry fears about maintaining data integrity, saying, "Misreading, losing, or mis-entering one piece of data could result in a multi-billion dollar lawsuit" (PhRMA, 2006). Along those lines, delays in any process whether it is regulatory, a flawed process, or ineffective drugs is highly costly. If the FDA discovers flaws in any aspect of pharmaceutical research, companies face setbacks. If these errors are discovered while the drug is out on the market, it can result in the loss of billions. Highly rigorous and expensive regulations worldwide, as previously discussed, can become complicated with the use of third parties. Relying on foreign vendors and partners can make compliance more burdensome, costly and risky. Privacy laws recently passed in several countries might hinder data sharing during the highly regulated development and manufacturing processes.

The cost of an unsuccessful partnership is more than just a financial lost, since the company loses crucial time and opportunities that it could have done elsewhere (Arnold & Grindley, 1996). In outsourcing arrangements, there is also a loss of partial control as it passes from client to provider. As a result, the information available to the project manager is typically less detailed and complete if it had been retained in house. Poor communication can also lead to problems with quality and delays. Thus, there is an element of trust in any relationship, and certain problems can become magnified if the partners do not know each other well (Cavalla, 1997).

Firms also worry about weak intellectual property protections and do not want to risk losing a strategic formula or manufacturing advantage because of outsourcing. If the legal system is weak, there will be little if any recourse a firm can take if its information is leaked to a competitor or generic manufacturer (Feeny, Lacity & Willcocks, 1995). There is also the challenge faced by upper management to juggle 20 to 30 individuals during the life of a project, working with multiple languages, and time zones (Kelly Scientific Resources, 2004).

In conclusion, fewer drugs are being discovered, it is costing more money to push them through the development pipeline, and the length of the process is increasing, thereby eroding drugs' patent protected life spans. Consumers, especially bulk buyers, are exerting greater pressure on pharmaceutical companies to reduce or cap prices. Each of these factors negatively affects profits, and collectively their impact cannot be ignored. Increasingly, offshoring is being looked to as the solution.

WHY INDIA?

A report by Preston and Singh (2003) states that global manufacturing offshoring will increase from $14 billion to $27 billion by 2008. India's inherent advantages in both contract manufacturing and research make it an attractive destination for the mass production of drugs and clinical research. Indian companies have also built manufacturing facilities, which could quickly be updated to international standards. In fact, there are 70 USFDA approved plants and over 200 units certified as following Good Manufacturing Practices (GMP), which is the highest number outside of the U.S. (Higgins & Rodriguez, 2004). Indian companies would also make excellent partners for multinational pharmaceutical companies since they filed a total of 126 Drug Master Files (DMFs) with the FDA in 2003, ranking only second to the U.S. and constituting 20% of all drugs entering the U.S. market (Higgins & Rodriguez, 2004). While this does not take into account the usefulness or value of the produced drugs – it does signal India's ability to discover, develop, and manufacture drugs in a timely manner. Put simply, India possesses a talented workforce and efficient manufacturing infrastructure that is suited for offshoring.

The Indian government now allows 100% of foreign direct investment (FDI) to directly flow to the pharmaceutical industry. Reduced import tariffs and price controls have also made India a more attractive destination for FDI (Evans & Varaiya, 2003). The movement towards a friendlier investment climate was motivated by the low-levels of R&D investment by domestic pharmaceutical companies (1.9% of total revenues). The needs of the Indian and global pharmaceutical companies complement each other—Indian firms require large inflows of FDI and international companies need to significantly reduce R&D and manufacturing costs.

Contract Research Opportunities

As outlined in a previous section, the drug discovery and development process is expensive and extremely research intensive. Since R&D is such a critical function, firms are now partnering with Indian biotech and pharmaceutical companies to leverage their low cost of innovation. According to a McKinsey Quarterly study, R&D costs for Indian pharmaceutical firms are *75%* less than

those of a multinational firm (Quinn & Hilmer, 2004). Furthermore, India is an ideal destination for clinical trials accounting for more than 66% of total R&D costs (Bakhle, 2003). India also possesses a world-class infrastructure of healthcare professionals: 500,000 well-trained English-speaking doctors, 16,000 hospitals, 171 medical colleges, and a heterogeneous pool of genes, making it a well-suited location for conducting clinical trials (Charai, 2002).

India's uncontaminated drug naive patent population is another factor contributing to the growth of clinical research outsourcing. Unfortunately, this stems from India's high levels of poverty and low per capita expenditure on drugs (less than U.S. $5 per year). It is also less expensive to recruit patients, nurses, and investigators. It is projected that India offers a 50% cost savings for Phase 1 research and 60% for Phase 2 and 3 (Indian Pharmaceutical Overview, 2004). However, there are regulatory barriers limiting the growth of clinical research outsourcing to India. The Drugs and Cosmetic Rules (Schedule Y) describe India's clinical trials as, "one step behind other countries," (Indian Pharmaceutical Overview, 2004). Currently, multinational firms are primarily outsourcing Phase III trials, which are extremely costly and involve a large number of patients (1,000 to 3,000, on average). Leading pharmaceutical companies such as GlaxoSmithKline, Pfizer, and Novartis have already outsourced their clinical data management to India; GSK is building a new global center for clinical research and development. Domestic companies, such as Syngene, the subsidiary of the Indian biotech giant Biocon, carry out early state oncology drug discovery and delivery for companies like Novartis (India Equity Brand Foundation, 2004).

High Quality and Educated Workforce

The quality of education of the pharmaceutical and biotechnology workforce in India is one of its more attractive characteristics. At the surface, India does not seem to have a strong educational system, but unlike other developing countries, it has invested heavily into higher education for decades, establishing world-class universities and research institutes. The Indian Institutes of Technology (IIT) provide research facilities and education that are on par with those offered at Ivy League schools in the U.S.. Only the brightest students are admitted to these schools, thus, considering the large population, there is an enormous talent pool available. In addition, there are over 45 Indian universities teaching postgraduate biology and chemistry courses and 300 college levels educational and training institutes offering degrees and diplomas in biotechnology, bioinformatics, and other sciences. As a result, each year 500,000 undergraduate students, 300,000 postgraduates and 1,500 PhDs qualify in the biosciences (Indian Department of Biotechnology).

Although there are over 100 National Research Laboratories, world-class research is limited to a few prestigious institutes such as the Indian Institute of Science in Bangalore (IISc) or the National Center for Biological Sciences in Bangalore (NCBS) a branch of the Tata Institute of Fundamental Research. From a cost perspective, Indian companies will remain competitive in the near term as qualified researchers and employees in India cost only 30 to 40% of their peers in developed countries (ITP News Network, 2003).

Indian Government Support

The Indian government supports the pharmaceutical industry in various ways. First, the government provides fiscal incentives to the pharmaceutical and biotechnology sector by granting a 150% weighted average tax deduction on R&D expenditures as well as on international patenting costs until 2010. In addition, it offers exemptions on import duties on key R&D and clinical trial equipment. Also, the Indian government plans to remove duties on raw imported materials, where the finished product is imported duty free, thereby facilitating drug development in India.

Additionally, the Ministry of Science and Technology is promoting a number of high-quality research centers. These institutes are outfitted with state-of the art technology, hire highly skilled researchers, and collaborate with the private industry and organize the purchasing of laboratory supplies and equipment. Examples of such centers include the Plant Genomics Center in New Delhi, the Center for Human Genetics in Bangalore, and the Center for Cellular and Molecular Biology (CCMB) in Hyderabad ("Offshoring R&D," 2007). State governments are also supportive, with many investing in R&D parks where firms benefit from cutting-edge technology and infrastructure. The Southeastern state of Andhra Pradesh is a leading example, with a research park named Genome Valley near Hyderabad, but also the states of Karnataka, Maharashtra, Tamil Nadu, Gujarat, Punjab and West Bengal are investing public funds to develop such facilities. The government supports these parks by providing up to 30% of total costs as a grant or 49% through private equity (*New York Times,* 2005).

The government actively encourages private-public partnerships. The ICICI bank established the "knowledge park" at Genome Valley. Other examples include The Centre of Genomic Applications (TCGA), which is a joint project between the Chatterjee group, the Council of Scientific and Industrial Research (CSIR), and the Ministry of Science and Technology.

Intellectual Property Considerations in India

The pharmaceutical industry, like the software industry, is based on information, protected by trademarks, patents, trade secrets, and copyrights. Without adequate intellectual property rights (IPR) protection, no level of cost savings could motivate pharmaceutical or biotech companies to operate in low-wage countries. The demand for stronger and better-enforced IPR is coming not just from global pharmaceutical companies, but from Indian-based ones as well, in particular those that make-up the biotechnology sector.

For example, Biocon, India's largest biopharmaceutical firm is altering its strategy to take advantage of emerging dynamics – its revenues, to date, rely heavily on producing generic drugs with non-infringing process technologies, but now there has been a shift towards engaging in collaborative developing and licensing with global partner firms to save costs and benefit from larger, more robust IP portfolios. This type of strategy, which is expected to become increasingly popular, given the trends and political environment previously outlined, is best exemplified by Biocon's acquisition of U.S.-based Nobex Corporation's assets in March 2006, which allowed Biocon to obtain ownership of all oral insulin BNP programs as well as peptide delivering technology ("Offshoring R&D," 2007). Further, Biocon began targeting global markets in 2006 by selling its insulin products in Europe ("Offshoring R&D," 2007).

This new type of strategic model allows global pharmaceutical firms to maximize the value from offshoring key manufacturing, research, and IT activities, while at the same time allowing local Indian participants to shift their intellectual and capital resources away from purely reverse-engineering blockbuster drugs and becoming a value-added partner in the critical R&D process that helps create new, profit generating products. This type of joint relationship and better-enforced IP legislation creates new, attractive incentives for global and local pharmaceutical firms to leverage each other's strengths and reduce many risks associated with offshoring.

There are, of course, concerns about foreign pharmaceutical companies patenting the DNA of organisms native to India that and have been used for thousands of years for health and cosmetic applicants. For example, in 2004, Monsanto, an American-based agricultural biotechnology firm was granted a patent on "Chapati" from the European Patent Office (Vanguri & Rajput, 2002). Chapati bread has been used in Indian society for hundreds of years and to the Indian public; it was shocking that American and European patent authorities have, and will likely continue to, grant patents on indigenous products. Another emerging concern is the treatment of the poor (and often sick) Indian volunteers in clinical research studies—some regulatory bodies want to ensure that participants are not being exploited, misinformed, or used as guinea pigs for riskier drug treatments and trials. Foreign companies need to understand and be sympathetic to the local Indian reality and to conduct their business practices in the most ethical manner; this is a growing critical success factor.

CONCLUSION

The global pharmaceutical industry is embracing the advantages of offshoring many of its nontraditional activities to emerging countries such as India. The reality of shrinking profit margins, drying pipelines, patent expirations, and increased R&D costs has made offshoring an attractive cost-reducing strategy. Multinational firms are offshoring R&D activities, most notably clinical trials and IT services. Despite concerns, firms are overcoming current risks in order to realize the gains offshoring can provide.

One of the greatest drivers to offshore to India is the development of more sophisticated IT applications and services by local firms. According to Ed Thompson, principle scientist of Procter & Gamble, many large firms have vast databases that are inexact or error-filled because scientists frequently use different names for the same chemical (Farrell, 2005). Consequently, P&G worked with Accelrys, who has offices located in Bangalore, India, to solve this challenge by reengineering their chemical registration process to include validation stages for data quality assessment and duplicate checking. A new "substance" data model was a central aspect of supporting the duplicate checking stage. The software makes it possible for P&G scientists to register, search, and retrieve entities consisting of generic chemical structures, polymers, exact structures, mixtures, and formulations—even when not all specific components or their contents can be identified. Further, this centralized database makes it significantly easier for CROs to register their results and for managers to receive the most updated information within 24-hours.

One of the most intriguing activities to be outsourced to India, due entirely to advances in IT, is the ability to target thousands of new genes per year, versus 500 less than 2 decades ago. The Human Genome Project aims at sequencing the entire human genome, containing roughly 80,000 to 100,000 genes, which has enormous implications for R&D. For example, if 5% of the proteins encoded have therapeutic value and a further 20,000 represent possible biological targets, this would mean a 14-fold improvement in current discovery rates and, consequently, more targeted product development (PhARMA, 2005). Many firms in India can easily help identify and encode potential genes that possess therapeutic value and provide real-time discovery to other scientists throughout the world. The reduction in cost and time due to advances in IT, database management, and tailored applications for chemical identification are significant drivers in the decision to offshore nontraditional core competencies of the pharamceutical industry.

Presently, India has many different types of firms entering into the clinical trial data management business. Some entrants are CROs who are creating separate data management units, some are IT/ITES companies diversifying their business portfolios, and others are global and local pharmaceutical companies that are setting up their own biometrics and data management operations—either alone or through partnerships. For example, Pfizer has signed a preferred provider contract for its Biometrics Division with Cognizant Technologies in India. Similarly, Accenture is working exclusively for Wyeth in clinical trial data management with approximately 400 staff, working across two offices, with plans to build a third.

As India emerges as an IT and clinical trial super "hub," outsourcing to India for clinical data management will become more pronounced than originally predicted. However, with several different business models, it will take time to see how many are profitable after meeting stringent global regulatory standards. Firms and partnerships who quickly meet global standards and regulations are more likely to survive.

Outsourcing of research and development, especially clinical trials, is expected to increase in upcoming years. Although there is no set limit on the percentage of trials that can be done abroad, experts agree that it is unlikely that drugs will be approved if more than 40% of a trial are performed internationally (PhRMA, 2006). Regulatory approval aside, a large percentage of clinical trials must be done locally because it is necessary to communicate with individuals who assist in the shaping of the trials, as well as those who promote the drug once it is approved.

Offshoring is quickly becoming an essential component of the pharmaceutical industry. Pilot programs and strategic global/local relationships are becoming commonplace and plans to expand overseas operations are a standard response to increasing cost pressures. The drive to outsource more, both in magnitude and in scope, is inevitable, and India is an ideal place to do it. Firms will still be saying "yes" to the "should we offshore" question in 10 years; however, "India" might not necessarily remain the answer to the "where" question.

As multinational firms offshore higher level, sensitive R&D activities to foreign CROs and other biotech firms, more research is needed on how this trend will affect the regulatory structure, especially as companies file new patents in multiple countries. Additionally, the trend of global firms partnering with local ones allows both participants to leverage each other's strengths; these dynamic arrangements will offer a critical area of new research to delineate new strategic approaches to R&D and future blockbuster drugs. Lastly, and most importantly, time will tell how India's highly regarded, preexisting IT "hub" caters to the technical needs of global and local pharmaceutical companies, while at the same time ensuring a high degree of control and data integrity.

REFERENCES

A. T. Kearney. (2004, September). *Outsourcing among pharamaceutical and biotech firms: The growing imperative for a more aggressive approach.* Boston: Author.

Bakhle, D. (2003). Global clinical trials: Challenges and opportunities. *Business Briefing: Pharmatech.*

Cavalla, D. (1997). *Modern strategy for pre-clinical pharmaceutical R&D: Towards the virtual research company.* Chichester, England: Wiley.

Charai, S. (June, 2002). Pharmaceutical outsourcing. *American Pharmaceutical Outsourcing.*

Clinically speaking, India is becoming a hub for clinical trials and insight. (2005, March 31). *India Business Insight.*

DiMasi, J. (1995). Trends in drug development costs, times, and risks. *Drug Information Journal.*

Eaton, C. E., & Wierenga, D. E. (1999). *The drug development and approval process.* Pharmaceutical Research Association, Office of Research and Development.

Ernst & Young. (2004). *Progressions 2004: Global pharmaceutical report, industry defining events.* New York: Author.

Evans A. G., & Varaiya, N. (2003, Fall). Assessment of a biotechnology market opportunity. *Entrepreneurship Theory and Practice.*

Expanding global access to HIV/AIDS treatments: An overview of the issues. (2005). *American Newsletter.*

Farrell, D., (Ed.). (2005, June). *The emerging global labor market.* Washington, DC: McKinsey Global Institute Press.

Feeny, D. F., Lacity, M. C., & Willcocks, L. P. (1995). IT outsourcing: Maximize flexibility and control. *Harvard Business Review, 73*(3).

Go, R. (2005). *Deloitte white article: India meets Doha: Changing patent protection.* New York: Deloitte Touche Tohmatsu.

Goodwin, F., & Goldberg, R. (2001, July 7). New drugs: The right remedy. *The Washington Post,* p. A21.

Gupta, A., Seshasai, S., Mukherji, S., & Ganguly, A. (2007). Offshoring: The transition from economic drivers toward strategic global partnership and 24-hour knowledge factory. *Journal of Electronic Commerce in Organizations, 5*(2).

Herper, M., & Kang, P. (2006, March). The world's ten best-selling drugs. *Forbes.*

Higgins, M. J., & Rodriguez, D. (2004, December). *The outsourcing of R&D through acquisitions in the pharmaceutical industry* (SSRN Working Article).

India can become significant global player by 2010. (2006, November, 14). *Biospectrum India.*

Kelly Scientific Resources. (2004). Management of clinical trials in an era of outsourcing. *Issues and Trends.*

Kermani, F., and Bonacossa, P. (2003). Outsourcing Clinical trials in the pharmaceutical industry. *Chiltern International Business Briefing: Pharmatech.*

Leavy, B. (1996). Outsourcing strategy and learning a dilemma. *Production and Inventory Management Journal, 37* (4).

"Offshoring R&D activity." (2007 , January 1). *Genetic Engineering and Biotechnology News.*

Pharmaceutical Research and Manufacturers of America (PhRMA). (2003a). *Incentives to discover new medicines: Pharmaceutical patents.* Washington, DC: Author.

Pharmaceutical Research and Manufacturers of America (PhRMA). (2003b). *The 2003 pharmaceutical industry profile.* Washington, DC: Author.

Park, R. (2002). The international drug industry: What the future holds for South Africa's HIV/AIDS patients. *Minnesota Journal of Global Trade.*

Pascal, R., & Rosenfeld, J. (2005). *The demand for offshore talent in services.* Washington, DC: McKinsey Global Institute Press.

"Pfizer to set up academy for clinical excellence." (2002, February, 16). *Business Line.*

Preston, G., & Singh, A. (2003, November). Rebuilding big pharma's business model. *Vivo, the Business and Medicine Report, 21*(10).

Quinn, J. B., & Hilmer, F. G. (2004). Make versus buy: Strategic outsourcing. *McKinsey Quarterly.*

"Quintiles moves data management work to india." (2005, April 11). *Associated Press.*

Sherman, P., & Oakley, E. (2004). Pandemics and panaceas: The WTO's efforts to balance pharmaceutical patents and access to AIDS drugs. *American Business Law Journal, 41*(2/3).

Tomlinson, H. (2004, November 1). Drug giant moves trials abroad: Glaxo lured by security and low cost of trials overseas. *The Guardian.*

U.S. Department of Commerce. (2006). *U.S. industrial outlook: 2006.* Washington, DC: U.S. Government Printing Office.

Vanguri, S., & Rajput, V. (2002). Patents and biotechnology. *Indian Journal of Medicine,* (3).

ENDNOTE

[1]   This article presents the personal views of the authors, and does not represent the views of their respective employers in any way.

This work was previously published in the Journal of Information Technology Research, Vol. 1, Issue 2, edited by M. Khosrow-Pour, pp. 38-53, copyright 2008 by IGI Publishing (an imprint of IGI Global).

Chapter 8
Enhancing e-Business Decision Making:
An Application of Consensus Theory

William J. Tastle
Ithaca College, USA; University of Iceland, Iceland

Mark J. Wierman
Creighton University, USA

ABSTRACT

Statistical analysis is the universally accepted method by which sense is created from raw data. Successful requirements determination is often dependent upon the gathering customer data over the Internet, and it may be largely limited to collecting the responses such as Yes/No and Likert scale categories. These data are then analyzed to identify customer trends or other items of interest to management. The data can be useful, but key to their usage is the application of suitable mathematical tools. Traditionally little more than standard statistics has been used in the analysis of ordinal, or category, data. This chapter introduces measures of agreement and dissent to the field of e-business analysis and shows how ordinal data can be analyzed in meaningful ways.

INTRODUCTION

Gathering data from customers is a common activity and much research has gone into design and planning (Parsons, 2007; Solomon, 2001), improving response rates (Cook, et al, 2000; Kaplowitz, et. al., 2004; Schmidt, et al, 2005), the study of privacy and ethics (Couper, 2000), mode of questionnaire delivery (Denscombe, 2006), the effect of subject lines of survey responses (Porter and Whitcomb, 2005), the analysis of web usage using traditional statistics (Korgaonkar and Wolin, 1999; Stanton, 1998) and but little has been written about the evolution of ordinal scale survey results, typical of Likert or Likert-like scale surveys. Acknowledging that getting respondents to answer surveys, either paper or digital, can be a challenge, and once the data is collected the effort to squeeze as much information from the data as possible begins.

Traditionally, data analysis is well founded in statistics, even though the same underpinnings of statistics recognize that there are limits to this branch of mathematics. Statistics are at home when dealing with ratio or interval data (Tastle and Wier-

DOI: 10.4018/978-1-60566-966-3.ch008

man, 2006a), but once the scale shifts to ordered categories the use of statistics is circumspect, for what does it mean to say the average of "warm" and "hot" is reported as "warm-and-a-half" (Jamieson, 2004). Ordinal scales of measurement typically consist of ordered category hierarchies such as: "strongly agree (SA)," "agree (A)," "neither agree nor disagree (N)," "disagree (D)," and "strongly disagree (SD)"; "very cold," "cold," "cool," "tepid," "warm," "hot," and "very hot." The instrument typically used to collect this kind of data is called the Likert scale, though there are variations of this scale such as Likert-like, Likert-type, and ordered response scales. Researchers utilize this kind of instrument to collect data that cannot be ascertained using traditional measures, for the data being collected are feelings, perceptions, sensations, emotions, impressions, sentiments, opinions, passions, or the like. Unfortunately, the application of standard statistics to these data can be improper (Cohen, et al, 2000; Jamieson, 2004; Pell, 2005). This paper looks at the different kinds of scales and presents a new measure for analyzing ordinal scale data.

The identification of consensus in a group environment was the motivation for the original research into ways of assessing ordinal data. The authors sought to identify some mathematical way by which a discussion leader could be guided towards getting a group of discussants to arrive at consensus as quickly as possible. The consensus measure can be easily applied to situations whereby a quick survey of perceptions of discussants to one statement is taken. Given the statement "The group has arrived at consensus" the discussants would check either SA, A, N, D, or SD. The resulting calculation of consensus could guide the leader in the direction of conversation or to determine if there is sufficient agreement to move forward. The authors have expanded on this idea to identify the group agreement with a targeted category, such as SA, on a data collection instrument. It would be nice to know if, in response to some survey statement on a matter of critical importance to the organization, the overall percentage of agreement for each Likert category, not just the mode category. Notice we do not use the mean, for the meaning of the average of two ordered categories is not clear, i.e., the average of *acceptable* and *unacceptable* is *acceptable-and-a-half*, or so the interval and ration scale mathematics tells us. Also, standard deviation is based on the presence of at least an interval scale, so its use on ordinal scales is suspect at least, and invalid at most. The dissent measure gives a result that is much easier to interpret and carries more intuitive meaning. In this paper we focus on the agreement measure and how it can be used to foster a group agreement assessment that is especially important when a business is largely limited to Internet activities and must rely on survey type data for assessments that might typically be ascertained through an in-person sales force.

SCALES OF MEASUREMENT

Within the scales of measurement exist four well-known measures:

a. Nominal data that is used merely in classification, like a gender (male or female), in which order plays no role. It would make no sense to order Male > Female. Labels used in nominal scales are arbitrary and can be nouns (or any string), numbers (real, integer, etc), or any possible type of labeling. Even if integers are used they convey no sense of numbering since they merely represent categories.

b. Ordinal data are ordered categories and used typically in all languages to convey a sense of approximate ordering, for example, tea water may be said to be cold, lukewarm, tepid, warm, very warm, quite hot, hot, very hot, etc. The categories are themselves the values. Hence, it makes no sense to say that the average between warm and very warm is warm and one-half, and thus the values between the categories are not important. The Likert scale is used to collect data by means of categories, and it is a common means of data collection in such fields as sociology, psychology and medicine. The kinds of data frequently collected involve the determining of attitude or feelings with respect to some attribute.

c.   Interval data consists of a constant scale, ordered, but without a natural zero such as a temperature under the Fahrenheit scale. 0° is less than 50°, and there definitely exist intermediate values such as 45.255°. With the right kind of instrumentation one could determine temperature to some extreme decimal, but without a natural zero, such as that which exists in the Kelvin scale where 0° represents the absence of molecular motion and is hence a natural zero, it is not reasonable to say that 80° is twice as hot as 40°. However, subtraction and addition of values is permitted and makes sense.

d.   Ratio data is ordered, possesses a constant scale, and has a natural zero. The number line is such a scale and it is common to say that someone weighing 150 kg is twice as heavy as one weighing 75 kg.

The Likert scale is a unidimensional scaling method in that concepts are usually easier to understand when expressed in a single dimension. For example, one is either taller or shorter, runs faster or runs slower, or is hotter or colder. The scale is usually expressed as a statement with categories of choices, usually ranging from strongly agree to strongly disagree. An individual makes a selection usually by checking the category or blackening in a bubble sheet choice. There is a choice to be made, and it must consist of one and only one category. If we give the Likert instrument to n number of participants, we can create a frequency table of the categories selected. At issue is how to best analyze the data. This is an important issue,

for much research literature is analyzed using "…means and standard deviation and performs parametric analysis such as ANOVA…no statement is made about an assumption of interval status for Likert data, and no argument made in support" (Jamison 2004). Finally, Jamison (2004) says "that the average of 'fair' and 'good' is not 'fair-and-a-half'; this is true even when one assigns integers to represent 'fair' and 'good'!

BACKGROUND

We begin with a discussion of the meaning of *consensus*, for it plays a critical role in the analysis and interpretation of **ordinal** data that is collected using Internet-based survey forms, and then conclude this section with a discussion of other works.

It is common for a group of well-intentioned individuals, engaged in purposeful dialogue, to utilize the concept of consensus in making decisions, especially when it is important to maintain some sort of collegiality. In America there exists a set of rules used by most boards and organizations as the arbiter of the structure for group discussions and it is called Robert's Rules of Order. While Robert's Rules are effective, it usually results in someone or some group "losing" in the resulting decision if the leader or chair calls for a vote having "sensed" that most are in agreement. Such feelings may be incorrect. Although consensus building is a typical method used in decision-making, few measures exist which allow for the easy determination of the degree to which a group is nearing the point of agreement. When dealing with Internet-based surveys, the ordinal data collected must be analyzed to determine the level of consensus or agreement of the respondents with respect to the questions or issues raised. The purpose of this paper is to show a mathematical measure (Wierman and Tastle, 2005; Tastle and Wierman, 2005, 2006a, 2006b, 2007a, 2007b, 2007c) that is intuitive, satisfies the requirements of a measure of consensus, and is easy to apply to the analysis of ordinal surveys.

The survey analysis requires finding some means by which the consensus of the respondents to an ordinal survey can be identified, understood, and compared. As a number of business and political analysts have pointed out in the past, there are problems associated with determining consensus in a group or by survey; the problems are similar. If a too-strict requirement of consensus is asserted, it is possible for a minority group to hold a veto power over decisions. Conversely, a too-loose requirement permits the domination of the minority by the majority, an equally undesirable outcome. It is entirely possible for a decision by consensus to take an extremely long time to occur, and thus may be inappropriate for urgent matters such as decisions involving strategic policy or competitive advantage. Sometimes, consensus decision-making encourages groupthink, a situation in which people modify their opinions to reflect what they believe others want them to think. This can lead to a situation in which a group makes a decision that none of the members individually support and may lead to a few dominant individuals making all decisions. Fortunately, survey respondents are not impacted by this problem. Finally, consensus decision-making may fail when there simply is no agreement possible, a problem that is theoretically possible when half of the survey respondents select "strongly agree" and the other half select "strongly disagree." Does such a possibility justify reporting a "neutral" category being the average category chosen? Even if including a standard deviation in the resulting report (for a five category Likert scale, such a standard deviation is 2), there is an expectation and visual image by most readers of values scattered around a mean value of "neutral," clearly an erroneous expectation.

Consensus has two common meanings (http://essential-facts.com). One is a general agreement among the members of a given group or community; the other is as a theory and practice of getting such agreements. Many discussions focus on whether agreement needs to be unanimous and even dictionary definitions of consensus vary. These discussions miss the point of consensus, which is not a voting system but a taking seriously of everyone's input, and a trust in each person's discretion in follow-up action. In consensus, people who wish to take up some action want to hear those who oppose it because they do not wish to impose, and they trust that the ensuing conversation will benefit everyone. Action despite opposition will be rare and done with attention to minimize damage to relationships. In a sense, consensus simply refers to how any group of people who value liberty might work together.

To capture how someone "feels" towards an issue under discussion, some mechanism must be used by which that person may express his/her opinions, but in a manner such that the data can be quantified. The Likert scale easily fulfills this requirement. Unfortunately, the Likert scale has no interval property. To "solve" this problem some have advocated placing numbers next to the linguistic labels, i.e., strongly agree = 1, in an effort to force an interval. This does not work; the presence of an interval means that a respondent has carefully reviewed the available data (or searched his/her mind for a proper feeling) and has evidence that 2.1 is too high and 1.9 is too low, so the choice of 2 is checked. Forcing the presence of numbers does not change an ordinal scale to an interval scale. It remains simply a set of ordered categories and the use of ratio and interval scale mathematics is not conceptually sound when analyzing ordered categories, though the results are accepted as accurate. We propose another way of analyzing ordinal data, and it has great potential in eBusiness as we attempt to gather as much information as possible out of available data.

There is substantial work on the ranking of discrete data (Murphy and Martin, 2003; Chamberlin, et al, 1984) and every good statistics text has a section devoted to Kendall, Spearman, and Cayley rankings (Murphy and Martin, 2003), and sometimes the Hamming and Euclidian distances. Ranking is a means by which items in a collection can be evaluated such that any two items can be compared to see which should be placed higher in the ranking. Hence it is easy to see that Presidential candidates can be ranked, as can the top golfers, the National Football League or World Soccer teams, the flavors of ice cream and attributes of a product. Unfortunately, we sometimes confuse ordinal ranking with ordinal measures. An ordinal ranking is the assignment of a unique ordinal number to all items in a collection. An ordinal measure is the assignment of a degree of acceptability, desirability, favor, discernment, etc. to each single attribute. To ask a subset of Internet customers to rank the products in order of desirability is quite different from asking them to assess their agreement that property X is an important quality of product Y. In the latter ranking the customers merely need the list of products and a space next to each item into which their number value can be placed. In the former example, some ordinal scale is provided to which the customer will check a response. For example, in response to the statement "it is important for product Y to have property X" the ordinal scale might be *strongly agree, agree, neither agree nor disagree, disagree,* or *strongly disagree.* It is obviously not useful to take a set of responses to these Likert attributes and attempt to forcibly rank order them, and that is the purpose of this paper: To show a new method by which such data can be evaluated from a perspective of group agreement. Using ranks, there is a winner and a looser! Using this novel method of assessing group agreement, each Likert category has a degree of agreement.

Randall Davies (2005) investigated the combination of a fully anchored Likert scale with a numerical rating scale and found that by providing visual cues yielded a more discriminating result in which respondents more consistently applied their ratings. Applying our method to his data yielded identical results without the need for any other visual cues. The method presented here is computationally easy to apply and gives consistent results. We do, however, acknowledge that this work is still in-process, and much more must be done before the measure becomes main stream (see the conclusion). We hope that readers will build upon our efforts.

METHOD

The underlying concept behind the measures of consensus and agreement, and their complementary measures of dissent and disagreement, respectively, is centered on the existence of a perceived relative distance between ordered categories (called the intra-categorical distance) that may or may not be equal, and may or may not be similar to the distances in the minds of others, but the distance from one extreme category to the other extreme category is always 100% of whatever the mindset. Hence, from SA to SD the overall intra-categorical distance is 100%; from cold to hot is 100%. Given our above 10 person stakeholder team, if half select SA and the other half select SD (see figure 1), then the group consensus should be zero, for they are at their extremes. Similarly, because the group is at maximum opposition the dissent is maximized at 100%. Consensus and dissent are measures that characterize the entire set of stakeholders and are thus measures of the collective and are directly related (see below).

This is similar to the Congress of the US when the principal two parties (Democrats and Republicans) each hold half of the membership. A consensus may never be attained. If one person moves from SD to D, or from SA to A, then the consensus should increase to some value above zero for the group is no longer balanced on the extremes. A consensus does not require 100% agreement, and it is usually the committee chair who must recognize when a consensus has been met in order to move the group on, but how does the committee chair (or the systems analyst) know

Figure 1. Illustration of the maximum amount of dissent among 10 stakeholders who have chosen extreme categories. Consensus is zero, and dissent is maximized at 1. Statistically, the mean is 3 (given the assignment of SA = 1, A = 2, etc), and the standard deviation = 2.

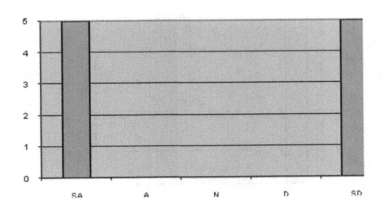

that point has been reached? This is matter for the psychologists and sociologists to research, but we can establish a criterion *a priori*. A percentage value that determines the threshold for consensus, from 0 to 100%, should be agreed upon before this analysis is applied.

If is reasonable to assume that a consensus is represented by a super majority, hence 51% probably does not represent a consensus. Clearly a consensus is met when 100% of the participants agree on a single Likert category (Figure 3), be it to agree or disagree with the statement under review. A group could even form a consensus around neutral in the sense that they have come to an agreement that they are all unsure. It is the selection of a number in the gray area between 50% and 100% that is the challenge. The US Senate requires a 60% super majority to pass legislation, and that value could be used to indicate a consensus. A recent study (Salmoni, et. al., under review) on the establishment of a curriculum for dermatology students has used 80% as an indicator of consensus among the dermatology medical community as to the importance of certain items being in a basic curriculum for dermatology students. Whatever the value, the following procedure can be used to determine the degree of consensus (and/or dissent) of the group towards a Likert statement.

Let us assume that a data set of Likert scale responses has been collected by means of an Internet survey. The data is represented by a listing of numbers, each one from 1 to 5 representing the standard Likert categories from "strongly agree" to "strongly disagree." We can apply standard statistics to this listing, but a more conceptually accurate method is offered below some reflections on the properties needed to analyze these data.

We postulate that the following set of rules must be satisfied before any measure can be considered a viable solution to the Likert scale problem.

1. For a given (even) number of **n** individuals participating in a survey on some matter of interest, if **n/2** select the "strongly disagree" category and the other **n/2** select the "strongly agree" category, the group is considered to have **no** consensus. This is called the **diametric opposition** quality.

2. If all the participants classify themselves in the same category, regardless of the label given that category, then the group is considered to be in consensus.

Figure 2. Since the stakeholders are no longer at opposite extremes, the consensus has increased to 0.059, the dissent has dropped to 0.941. The mean is now 2.9 (almost "neutral") and the standard deviation is 1.92.

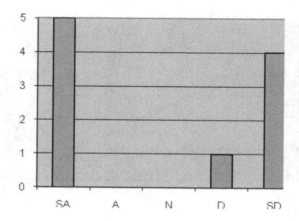

3. If the mix of participants is such that **n/2 + 1** survey respondents assign themselves to any one category, the degree of consensus must be greater than 0, for the balance in the group is no longer equal.

Conversely, dissention requires the following set of rules be satisfied:

1. For a given (even) number of **n** individuals participating in a survey on some matter of interest, if n/2 select "strongly disagree" and the remaining **n/2** respondents select "strongly agree", the group is considered to have **maximum dissention**.

2. If all the respondents classify themselves in the same category, regardless of the label given that category, then the dissention is considered to be **zero**.

Figure 3. The measures of agreement for all 10 rows of data shown in Table 2.

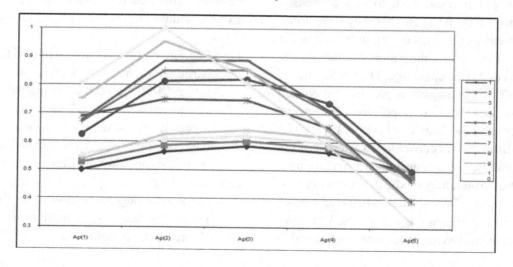

3. If the mix of respondents is such that n/2 + 1 respondents assign themselves to any one category, the degree of dissention must be less than maximal.

Consensus and dissention are inverse functions of shared group feelings towards an issue. This "feeling" can be captured through a Likert scale that measures the extent to which a person agrees or disagrees with the statement under investigation. The most common scale is 1 to 5. Often the scale will be 1 = strongly agree, 2 = agree, 3 = not sure, 4 = disagree, and 5 = strongly disagree. Other number-assignments can be made, such as: -2 = strongly agree, -1 = agree, 0 = not sure, 1 = disagree, and 2 = strongly disagree, or 0.0 = strongly agree, 0.25 = agree, 0.50 = neutral, etc. Likert scales can also be from two to nine categories in width. The issues of scale, symmetry, selection of clusters, and ordinal vs. interval data are not addressed here, but Munski (1990) has produced a very nice paper that describes these aspects in straightforward terms. A rather complete bibliography can also be found there.

$$Dnt(\mathbf{X}) = -\sum_{i=1}^{n} p_i \log_2 \left(1 - \frac{|X_i - \mu|}{d_X}\right) \quad (1)$$

THE CONSENSUS AND DISSENTION MEASURES

The properties of a consensus measure is defined (Tastle and Wierman, 2005) as:

$$Cns(X) = 1 + \sum_{i=1}^{n} p_i \log_2 \left(1 - \frac{|X_i - \mu_X|}{d_X}\right) \quad (2)$$

where the random variable X represents the Likert scale values, X_i is the particular Likert attribute value, p_i is the probability associated with each X_i,

d_X is the width of X, and $E(X) = \sum_{i=1}^{n} p_i X_i = \mu_X$ is the mean of X. This measure adequately fulfills the above rules as evidenced by the following *illustrations*.

The mirror image of consensus is dissention and has the following form:

In other words, $Cns = 1 - Dnt$ and $Dnt = 1 - Cns$. One of the interpretations of the dissent measure is that of dispersion. If the frequency distribution is balanced on the extreme categories of the Likert scale, for example at *strongly agree* and *strongly disagree*, the dispersion is maximized at 1 (and the consensus is zero). As the frequency distribution approaches the assignment of all probability to a single category, the dispersion approaches 0 (and the consensus approaches one). This is the essence of the consensus measure: the more the respondent assignments are tightly clustered around one category, the higher the consensus and the less the dissent. This dispersion is always a value in the unit interval, [0..1].

Let us assume that we have a five-attribute Likert scale: Strongly Agree (SA), Agree (A), Neutral (N), Disagree (D), and Strongly Disagree (SD). Let us further assign a numerical scale of SA = 1, A = 2, N = 3, D = 4, and SD = 5. Then X = {1, 2, 3, 4, 5}, X_1 = 1, etc., d_x = 5 - 1 = 4. Using an arbitrary number of random integer values to populate the scale, the following table denotes the required properties.

Table 1 contains data on eight aspects: the first column is simply an index of the rows, columns SA through SD denote the frequencies assigned to the Likert scale attributes (for comparison purposes all frequencies sum to 12), the expected mean for the attribute values, the standard deviation for the attribute values, Cns and Cns% are the consensus values in decimal and rounded percent, and Dnt and Dnt% are the dissension values in decimal and rounded percent (Cns = 1 - Dnt). Row 1 shows a maximum amount of dissent in consensus since n/2 observations are reflected in each of the extreme attributes. As a point of interest, had the n/2 val-

Table 1 Illustration of ten sets of values ranging from the most extreme (row 1) to the most concentrated (row 10). Calculations of the mean, standard deviation, consensus, consensus as a percent, dissent, and dissent as a percent, are shown.

	SA	A	N	D	SD	Mean	St Dev	Cns	Cns%	Dnt	Dnt%
1	6	0	0	0	6	3.0	2	0	0%	1	100%
2	6	0	0	1	5	2.917	1.93	0.049	5%	0.951	95%
3	6	0	0	2	4	2.833	1.86	0.097	10%	0.903	90%
4	5	1	0	2	4	2.917	1.80	0.146	15%	0.854	85%
5	5	1	2	4	0	2.417	1.32	0.425	43%	0.575	58%
6	1	5	2	4	0	2.750	1.01	0.605	61%	0.395	40%
7	1	5	4	2	0	2.583	0.86	0.675	68%	0.325	33%
8	0	6	5	1	0	2.583	0.64	0.758	76%	0.242	24%
9	0	9	3	0	0	2.250	.043	0.896	90%	0.104	11%
10	0	12	0	0	0	2.0	0	1	100%	0	0%

ues been associated with Agree and Disagree, the consensus would have been 3.0 and the standard deviation 1.0, since these attributes are closer to each other. Rows 2 through 9 show a convergence of opinion moving towards Agree. An examination of the Mean column shows a modest fluctuation of the values but, in general, a movement of value from Neutral (3) to Agree (2). This is supported by the StdDev column as the values continue to converge towards 0 as the values surrounding the attributes merge. The consensus shows continuous movement towards 1; it is arguably easier to associate the consensus as a percent to easily visualize the movement towards a consensus. Conversely, one can monitor the dissent from total presence (Row 1) to total absence (Row 10). Finally, Row 10 shows the attribute values firmly in one category. The Mean is trivially at 2, the Std Dev is now zero, consensus is complete at 100%, and dissent does not exist.

The proof that this measure of ordinal data satisfies the rules listed above is found in Wierman and Tastle (2005).

THE AGREEMENT MEASURE

Consensus (Equation 1) can become agreement (Equation 3) when the mean μ_X is replaced with some target value, τ, and we divide by twice the width, $2d_x$, in the denominator. The target, τ, is usually some desired value identified by the manager. For our purposes let us assume that the desired response is *Strongly Agree*. Since that is the first category in our Likert item, it is assigned a numerical value of 1. Hence, in response to the declarative statement "Customer service is exceptionally good," we desire for our survey respondents to strongly agree with this statement, i.e., the target is $\tau=1$. This measure is called *agreement* to distinguish it from measures that use an unspecified target such as the mean, median, or mode. Equation 3 shows τ in place of μ and an expanded width. Doubling the width prevents the equation from exploding when extreme values are reflected in the frequency distribution. We have found the agreement function to work especially well in practice and, for this current work, have limited ourselves to the $2d_x$ denominator. For the most part, either consensus or agreement will work very well, but it is necessary to be consistent in their use. It should also be mentioned that consensus, dissent, and agreement are invariant with respect to linear transformations of the random variable X.

$$Agr(X \mid \tau) = 1 + \sum_{i=1}^{n} p_i \log_2 \left(1 - \frac{\mid X_i - \tau \mid}{2d_X} \right)$$

(3)

While targeting provides a novel way of measuring distance from a desired goal, it assumes that all elements of the assessment are equally important.

Table 2 shows the Table 1 Likert data and the mean, and adds the agreement measures for each of the Likert categories. The usefulness of the measure becomes evident with practice. For example, the first row shows a higher agreement for target 3 (neutral) than for the other values, and the extreme values, 1 (SA) and 5 (SD), have the smallest measure of agreement. At first, this seems counterintuitive, but the agreement measure is actually is mid-way between consensus and consent for SA and SD. Table 1 shows a consensus for the entire first row having the value of 0. With respect to the entire distribution of categories, there is no *consensus* whatsoever. However, with respect to the neutral category there is a 50% *agreement*. When the set of surveys support the extreme categories, there is a de facto agreement on the middle category (neutral in this case) but the level of agreement is certainly not 0, nor is it 100%. It is logical that some middle value is appropriate, like 50%. Looking down to the values in row 7 we note that there are more respondents who have selected A than any other category. The mean is 2.58 which indicate that the average is almost between Agree and Neutral, perhaps Agree-and-a-half. There is a 68% consensus on the part of the respondents with a dispersion of about 33%. The respondent values are becoming clustered, but what is the data telling us? The agreement with a target of neural has the greatest value, 0.853, which is interpreted as an 85.3% agreement of the respondents for the

neutral category. The four who selected neutral are not the deciders of the agreement but rather, the five plus 2 that surround it. Agreement takes into account all the data in the distribution.

Finally, examination of row 10 shows complete consensus for the overall distribution as would be expected with all respondents having selected the same category, and the agreement with respect to agree is also 1.0. It is also evident that there is some agreement with the contiguous categories, like 80% agreement with both strongly agree and neutral, and even a modest level of agreement with strongly disagree of 32%. The absence of data from one or more categories does not mean an absence of agreement. All agreement values are shown in figure 1.

DISTANCE BETWEEN AGREEMENT DISTRIBUTIONS

Given two frequency distributions, F_1 and F_2, for which the agreement distributions, Agr_1 and Agr_2, are calculated using equation (3), a distance between the distributions can be determined. For each category in each frequency distribution there is a corresponding agreement value. The distance is calculated using

$$c_n \sqrt{\frac{\sum_{i}^{n}(Agt_1(X, X_i) - Agt_2(X, X_i))^2}{n}}$$

(4)

where n = the number of categories, c_n is a constant for each n, Agr_1 uses probabilities derived from the frequencies F_1, and Agr_2 uses probabilities derived from the frequencies F_2. Agr (X, X_i) is the Agreement of the categories X with the i [th] category.

Table 2. Illustration of the same ten sets of values ranging from the most extreme (row 1) to the most concentrated (row 10). Calculations of the mean, and agreement values for each category, ie, Agt(1) is read as "agreement with respect to strongly agree as the target."

	SA	A	N	D	SD	Mean	Agt(1)	Agt(2)	Agt(3)	Agt(4)	Agt(5)
1	6	0	0	0	6	3.0	0.500	0.565	0.585	0.565	0.500
2	6	0	0	1	5	2.917	0.527	0.587	0.603	0.581	0.484
3	6	0	0	2	4	2.833	0.554	0.608	0.622	0.597	0.468
4	5	1	0	2	4	2.917	0.538	0.625	0.641	0.619	0.495
5	5	1	2	4	0	2.417	0.689	0.749	0.747	0.651	0.393
6	1	5	2	4	0	2.750	0.625	0.813	0.821	0.738	0.501
7	1	5	4	2	0	2.583	0.668	0.851	0.853	0.706	0.464
8	0	6	5	1	0	2.583	0.674	0.885	0.888	0.712	0.472
9	0	9	3	0	0	2.250	0.752	0.952	0.856	0.641	0.388
10	0	12	0	0	0	2.0	0.807	1.000	0.807	0.585	0.322

CONCLUSION

Data collected through the Internet can be analyzed in many statistically proper ways, but the fundamental premise of the presence of an interval or ratio scale is absent from ordinal data. This method is a new way of examining ordered ordinal data, is very intuitive, and requires little effort in calculating. The authors have used a spreadsheet to perform the calculations. The category that is most targeted by the survey respondents can be identified, and the degree of overall consensus with respect to the frequency distribution is interpreted as a percentage of the whole. Also, the measure of dissent is an indicator of dispersion. A visual representation of the proximity of categories can show confusion (multiple categories with close agreement measures, or a mandate for a particular category (steep drop-off in agreement measure for categories on either side). Combined, these measures permit the examination of data from any entirely new perspective.

Other work in the identification of measures to assist group decision making and analysis of non-interval or ratio scale data offers considerable potential for the interested researcher. What follows is an incomplete listing of potential opportunity:

- The authors think that a statistical change in Likert categorical importance, assuming a normal distribution of potential responses, can be approximated by the normal measure of significance. However, it has not yet been proven.
- The Likert scale demands the selection of only one category, but what about the possibility of degrees of categorical selection, as would be found in a typical fuzzy set.
- Our preliminary investigations suggest that the presence or absence of an interval does not change the result of the measure. Thus, we can be very confident in the resulting choice of the selected category, but we have not yet undertaken this research. .
- We seek to identify a measure of consistency; preliminary attempts using covariance do not satisfy our intuition as to the properties we require of such a measure.
- Lastly, nominal measures are reputed to have only one valid statistical measure, that of the mode. We have found, only in

the most preliminarily way, that a measure of dispersion can be validly calculated for nominal measures, but much work remains before a paper can be written.

Using these measures and the family of measures that could develop from them, analysis of nominal and ordinal data might be able to move past the traditional statistical approach

ACKNOWLEDGMENT

The authors are grateful to the insightful comments from the anonymous reviewers. We wish we could thank them in person, but that would invalidate the peer review process so we thank them publicly.

REFERENCES

Chamberlin, J. R., Cohen, J. L., & Coombs, C. H. (1984). Social Choice Observed: Five Presidential Elections of the American Psychological Association. *The Journal of Politics*, *46*(2), 479–502. doi:10.2307/2130971

Cohen, L., Manion, L., & Morrison, K. (2000). *Research Methods in Education* (5th ed.). London: Routledge Falmer.

Cook, C., Heath, F., & Thompson, R. (2000). A Meta-Analysis of Response Rates in Web- or Internet-Based Surveys. *Educational and Psychological Measurement*, *60*(6), 821–836. doi:10.1177/00131640021970934

Cooper, M. (2000). Web Surveys: A Review of Issues and Approaches. *Public Opinion Quarterly*, *64*(4), 464–494. doi:10.1086/318641

Denscombe, M. (2006). Web-Based Questionnaires and the Mode Effect. *Social Science Computer Review*, *24*(2), 246–254. doi:10.1177/0894439305284522

Jamieson, S. (2004). Likert scales: how to (ab) use them. *Medical Education*, *38*, 1217–1218. doi:10.1111/j.1365-2929.2004.02012.x

Kaplowitz, M., Hadlock, T., & Levine, R. (2004). A Comparison of Web and Mail Survey Response Rates. *Public Opinion Quarterly*, *68*(1), 94–101. doi:10.1093/poq/nfh006

Korgaonkar, P., & Wolin, L. (1999). A Multivariate Analysis of Web Usage. *Journal of Advertising Research*, *39*(2), 53–68.

Munshi, J. (1990). A Method for Constructing Likert Scales. Retrieved June 2004 from http://www.munshi.4t.com

Murphy, T. B., & Martin, D. (2003). Mixtures of distance-based models for ranking data. *Computational Statistics & Data Analysis*, *41*, 645–655. doi:10.1016/S0167-9473(02)00165-2

Pastons, C. (2007). Web-Based Surveys. Best Practices Based on the Research Literature. *Visitor Studies, 10*(1), 1064-5578. Retrieved July 15, 2007, from http://www.informaworld.com/10.1080/10645570701263404

Pell, F. (2005). Use and misuse of Likert scales. *Medical Education*, *39*, 970. doi:10.1111/j.1365-2929.2005.02237.x

Porter, S., & Whitcomb, M. (2005). E-mail Subject Lines and Their Effect on Web Survey Viewing and Response. *Social Science Computer Review*, *23*(3), 380–387. doi:10.1177/0894439305275912

Salmoni, A. J., Coxall, S., Gonzalez, M., Tastle, W., and Finley, A. (under review). Defining a postgraduate curriculum in dermatology for general practitioners: a needs analysis using a modified Delphi method.

Schmidt, J., Calantone, R., Griffin, A., & Montoya-Weiss, M. (2005). Do Certified Mail Third-Wave Follow-ups Really Boost Response Rates and Quality? *Marketing Letters*, *16*(2), 129–141. doi:10.1007/s11002-005-2291-7

Solomon, D. (2001). Conducitng Web-Based Surveys. *Practical Assessment Research and Evaluation, 7*(19).

Stanton, J. (1998). An Empirical Assessment of Data Collection Using the Internet. *Personnel Psychology, 51*(3), 709–725. doi:10.1111/j.1744-6570.1998.tb00259.x

Tastle, W. J., & Wierman, M. J. (2005). Consensus and Dissention: A New Measure of Agreement. *North American Fuzzy Information Processing Society (NAFIPS) Conference, Ann Arbor, MI.*

Tastle, W. J., & Wierman, M. J. (2006a). An information theoretic measure for the evaluation of ordinal scale data. *Behavior Research Methods,* (3): 487–494.

Tastle, W. J., & Wierman, M. J. (2006b). Consensus and dissension: A new measure of agreement. In *NAFIPS 2006,* Montreal, Canada.

Tastle, W. J., & Wierman, M. J. (2007a). (To Appear). Consensus: A new measure of ordinal dispersion measure. *International Journal of Approximate Reasoning.*

Tastle, W. J., & Wierman, M.J. (2007b). The development of agreement measures: From general to targeted. *Int. J. of Approximate Reasoning,* Invited Submission.

Tastle, W.J., & Wierman, M.J. (2007c). Determining Risk Assessment Using the Weighted Ordinal Agreement Measure. *Journal of Homeland Security,* July 2007.

Wierman, M. J., & Tastle, W. J. (2005). Consensus and Dissention: Theory and Properties. *North American Fuzzy Information Processing Society (NAFIPS) Conference, Ann Arbor, MI.*

Chapter 9
Changing Healthcare Institutions with Large Information Technology Projects

Matthew W. Guah
Erasmus University Rotterdam, The Netherlands

ABSTRACT

This article reviews the development of institutional theory in direct relations to historical changes within the UK's National Health Service (NHS) with an eye to contributing to the theoretical specification of healthcare information processes. This is done partly by extending certain paradigms (see Meyer & Rowan, 1991; Powell & DiMaggio, 1991; Tolbert & Zucker, 1994) through a proposed model of causes and consequences of variations in levels of institutionalisation in the healthcare industry. It reports findings from a 5-year study on the NHS implementation of the largest civil ISs worldwide at an estimated cost of $10 billion over a 10-year period. The theoretical basis for analysis is developed, using concepts drawn from neo-institutionalism, realisation of business value, and organisational logic, as well as mixed empirical results about the lack of IT investments value in the NHS. The findings suggest that large scale, IT change imposed upon a highly institutionalised healthcare industry is fraught with difficulty mainly because culturally embedded norms, values, and behavioural patterns serve to impede centrally imposed initiatives to automate clinical working practices. It concludes with a discussion about the nature of evaluation procedures in relation to the process of institutionalising IS in healthcare.

INTRODUCTION

An historical overview of IT projects in the UK's National Health Service (NHS) during the last six decades is presented here with the intention to both clarify the links between institutional theory and previous traditions of sociological work on organisational structure. The initial exposition of this theory by works of established institutionalists (Meyer & Rowan, 1991; Scott, Ruef, Mendel, &

Caronna, 2000; Tolbert & Zucker, 1994) focuses on the ways of challenging dominant theoretical and empirical traditions in organisational research. While this article clarifies some ambiguity and elaborates on the logical and empirical implications of a phenomenologically based version of institutional theory, the primary aims are to clarify the independent theoretical contributions of institutional theory to analyses of the NHS and to develop this theoretical perspective further in order to enhance its use in empirical research in other healthcare environments (internationally and globally).

Markus (1983) claims that interaction theory draws together three principal strands of resistance: (1) internal factors, (2) technical problems, and (3) political context. This theory has been highly influential in IS strategy and other social sciences generally since Markus first developed the ideas over two decades ago. The focus here (see Table 1) is on how interaction theory offers a new way of looking at IS implementation in the healthcare industry.

Much has been researched in the last few decades about the major lack of a coherent implementation strategy for IS (Sambamurthy & Zmud, 1994) in the healthcare industry (Stevens, Schade, Chalk, & Slevin, 1993; Vogel, 2003). Most of such claims have been levelled against an apparent "productivity paradox" with respect to investments in healthcare management (in general) and IS (in particular). The Wanless report (2002) and

Committee on Quality Health Care in America assessment report by Institute of Management (2002)—both national government's mandated investigations into the UK and USA national healthcare systems respectfully—among others, have failed to find a convincing body of evidence that investment in healthcare IS is associated with increased output (refuting the productivity paradox), but not with healthcare value as measured by patient satisfaction.

WHAT IS INSTITUTIONALISM?

Institutionalism is continuously being used to mean different things by researchers of political science, economics, and sociology. Lowndes (1996, p. 182) presents institutionalism as informal codes of behaviour, written contracts, and complex organisations with four elements:

- A middle-level concept. Institutions are devised by individuals and therefore constrain individuals' actions. Institutions here are seen as part of the broad social fabric and medium for individuals' day-to-day decisions and other activities. DiMaggio and Powell (1994) argue that institutions shape human actions, imposing constraints while providing opportunities for individuals.
- Having formal and informal aspects. Lowndes (1996) views institutions to in-

Table 1. Implementation theory: Usage, fitness, relationship and sufficiency

Authors	IS Implementation	Theory Description
Lucas, 1993	Appropriate use of IS	Process theory explaining appropriate IS use Variance theory linking use with business value
Grabowski & Lee, 1993	Strategic fitness of IS	Process-type relationship between strategic fit and performance of IS
Markus, 1983	Relationship of IS assets	How IS investment do or do not become IS assets How IS assets do or do not yield improved organisational performance
Sambamurthy & Zmud, 1994	Insufficient to produce impacts	Process model connecting raw material inputs to outputs Variance theory of IS management competencies and IS impacts Variance theory linking impacts and business value

volve formal rules or laws, which allows informal norms and customs to be practiced. That is because some institutions are not consciously designed nor neatly specified, yet part of habitual actions by its members. Such institutions may be expressed in organisational form and relate to the processes within.

- Having legitimacy. Legitimacy in institutions goes beyond the preferences of individual actors. Such preferences are valued in them and go beyond their immediate purpose and outputs.

- Showing stability over time. Lowndes (1996) views institutions as gaining their legitimacy due to their relative stability over time, and their links with a "sense of place."

New institutionalists generally view institutions to have "the humanly devised constraints that shape human interaction" (North, 1990, p. 3) what March and Olsen, (1989) refer to as "rules of the game" (p. 162) that organisations and individuals are constantly expected to play the game. Another stand taken by new institutionalists sees informal institutions (tradition, custom, culture, and habit) are embedded in culture and conventions defined as behaviour structuring rules (March & Olsen, 1989; North, 1990). New institutionalists stress embodied values and power relations of institutions together with interaction between individuals and institutions (Lowndes, 1996). They attempt to distinguish between informal institutional rules and personal habits. Such distinction forms the basis for the definition of institution in this research where informal conventions and their impact upon the NHS and its partners are being explored.

Research Methodology

The research study began in 2001, with the initial interest of conducting an exploratory-descriptive study in 10 NHS hospitals to explore why, "his-

torically, the NHS has not used or developed IT as a strategic asset in delivering and managing healthcare" (Department of Health [DoH], 2000). Intensive literature review unveiled few longitudinal studies, which systematically and rigorously examined how IT systems were introduced and changed over time. There were very limited studies that examined inter-organisational relationships between different constituents in the adoption and diffusion of IT systems (NHS directorship, hospital management systems, or IT suppliers and patients). Not only were most of these studies descriptive and lacked a historical dimension, they presented IS in healthcare as largely theoretical with most contributions reporting the findings of a specific IT project implementation using simple success and failure criteria—Scott et al. (2000) being among the most significant contributions.

Using such a relevant and wide-ranging backdrop this research study recognised that it was important to extend the empirical enquiry for two reasons: (1) exploratory-descriptive case studies on a single organisation (or one hospital) would not elicit in-depth and rich data to develop any meaningful analysis and conclusions on how IT was being deployed and managed; and (2) the introduction of a large scale, IT-enabled change program needed to be researched at the wider societal, organisational field and individual levels, covering an extended period of time, to understand the processes of institutionalisation (Tolbert & Zucker, 1994). The research study was therefore designed to capture the myriad of views and opinions about the national program over a 5-year period to build a rich picture of such processes underpinning large scale IT change.

Three methods of data collection were adopted: (1) a range of academic, government, and industry studies on the healthcare sector were assembled—both UK and healthcare services in other countries. The materials proved invaluable for understanding the societal, economic, political, cultural, and technical differences in healthcare nationally and internationally; (2) participation in trade fairs, conferences, workshops, and exhibitions on healthcare—focusing on general or more specific healthcare activities. These events also generated many useful research contacts that proved invaluable for targeting interviews. (3) A semi-structured interview (see Table 2) schedule was used to enable interviewees to expand on their answers. While most interviews lasted for about 90 minutes, a limited number lasted just under an hour, with nearly all interviews being tape recorded and subsequently transcribed. Respondents were later contacted with feedback from the interviews and, where necessary, errors were corrected. This method of data collection was critical for allowing interviewees to raise additional themes, issues, and concerns that they felt were important to the research study. As a result of the political contention of some of the interview content, some interviewees asked that names of individuals and hospitals be anonymous.

After the initial 6 months of interviews, the scope of the study had to be extended, as it was important to elicit data and information from a wider range of respondents engaged in the implementation of the national program. These included IT service providers bidding for public sector IT contracts and doctors in general practices around the country. Most IT service providers offered critical insights into the political and procurement processes within the NHS and public sector more generally (Guah & Currie, 2004). General practitioners, on the other hand, offered useful insights about the communication channels underpinning the institutional processes underpinning the national program. Given the range of constituents involved, the resulting data were evaluated and interview schedules refined, ensuring questionnaires be more closely targeted to the professional and personal situation of the individual, as generic questions were less meaningful. The final questionnaire—consisting of 15 questions—was ultimately divided into the following major themes:

Table 2. Numbers of interviews conducted

Categories of Interviewees	Year 1		Year 2		Year 3	
	Contacts Made	Persons Interviewed	Contacts Made	Persons Interviewed	Contacts Made	Persons Interviewed
NHS Information Authority	32	5	30	10	10	15
Major IT Service Providers	90	56	60	45	17	12
Primary Care Trusts Admin	15	5	25	12	22	12
Secondary Care Trust Admin	0	0	9	3	7	4
Local NHS IT Managers	15	6	20	11	60	42
Medical Consultants	3	1	8	4	9	6
Nurses & Junior Doctors	13	3	15	3	11	4
Healthcare Researchers	35	20	20	8	10	7
Total Interviews		105		96		102

- *Vision* **for the national program:** overall vision and how it was compatible with individual hospital objectives.
- *Strategy* **for the national program:** Who was engaged with and how the strategy was being communicated within different organisations.
- *Implementation* **of the national program:** What professional, managerial, and technical skills or capabilities were needed to implement various elements of the national program.
- *Value delivery* **for the national program:** The main risks identified by each hospital and how past IT failure could be avoided, as well as looking at the cost/benefit choices and issues for each organisation.
- *Risk analysis* **for the national program:** The value being derived from the national program.

The aim was to get the perspectives of a number of different informants using structured interviewing, by building up intensive longitudinal cases which would, nevertheless, be amenable to statistical analysis. In this method, differences of perception of informants become part of the data, not an inconvenience to be explained away in the search for some objective truth.

DATA ANALYSIS

Content analysis was used to surface themes in the interview data that reflected participants' understandings related to systems implementation. The approach suggested by Weber (1990) was used to code the interview data. A set of codes used to classify the data was developed, based on concepts from the research literature and augmented with major additional concepts discovered by the researchers during the coding. We used a content analysis form where each sentence from the interview transcripts was assigned one or more codes. Each data element was coded with an assessment of the level of agreement in code assignments, involving a certain degree of recoding of data sources. As this was the first study that uses content analysis about modelling of system implementation in the NHS, a certain degree of recoding was considered acceptable.

Table 3 contains a list of the most frequently cited attributes and benefits of the system implementation model. The audiotapes were fully transcribed and individual hospital and service provider summaries were produced before conducting a content analysis of each transcript. After a complete review of all summaries, issues describing IS implementation strategies by iterative examination were identified. Certain themes emerged, which were explored using the competing values framework as an interpretive framework where appropriate (see Table 3). The

Table 3. Frequently described implementation attributes and benefits

Implementation Attributes			Implementation Benefits		
Item	**Count**	**% of Cat**	**Item**	**Count**	**% of Cat**
Applications work together	40	13	Improved data accuracy/reliability	61	20
Data sharing	173	57	Lower costs of support, maintenance	212	70
Common database	127	42	Greater efficiency and productivity	167	55
Real-time processing	106	35	New or increased functionality	106	35
Record once, use everywhere	121	40	Better management, decisions, analysis	136	45

trustworthiness of such analysis has been assessed by triangulation between data sources and exploring any differences in the researcher' interpretations during a couple of follow-up meetings with selected interviewees.

During the period of the field study, there was a continuing, vigorous, informal debate within NHS Information Authority as to the merits of establishing a fault proof IS implementation framework in healthcare, particular for the NHS, during this period of healthcare reform. Benefits in terms of improved quality, greater structure, and more discipline were widely accepted.

THE NHS CASE STUDY

The NHS is the institution responsible for all healthcare and services in the UK with the goal of undertaking this responsibility at no costs to the public, at the point of delivery. The NHS was created in 1948 by a parliamentary art of the UK government of Mr. Howard Wilson, after a national healthcare review by Mr. Black immediately after World War II. While the NHS operating environment has changed radically within the last six decades, only a few periods of strategic importance to the objective of this article will be revisited by the author.

The period from late 1980s to early 1990s brought in the advent of competitive bidding bringing long-term increase costs to the management of the NHS, as well as a feeling of internal market within the NHS. By the mid-1990s, management of IS in the NHS was division based. Divisions were spread across several sites and medical functions were centrally controlled. Computing services and IS development projects were beginning to be contracted to external private businesses, and staff at the NHS were beginning to feel disgruntled and unappreciated. The increasing influence of global communications, Internet, and other new technologies demanded a response from the NHS.

In the late 1990s the government increasingly recognised the opportunity to use IT to improve the delivery of service within the NHS. After a series of reviews of NHS IT service delivery, a more integrated and seamless IT organisation was recommended (DoH, 2000; Wanless, 2002). The NHS Information Authority embarked on the Integrated Care Report Service (ICRS) project to provide, among other services, a nationwide electronic patient database. The result was a document called "Information for Health" that specified the need for the complete automation and integration of various patient information databases in the country (DoH, 2000). The system was commissioned to selected IS service providers at a combined price of $10 billion.

In spite of its vision—to transformation IT—the NHS has a history of introducing large-scale IT development projects that have not been overall successes, with some suggesting failure rates of between 60 to 80% (Brown, 2001). Though the UK public sector spent around $3.5 billion annually on IT, the failure of major IT-enabled projects were characterised by delay, overspending, poor performance, and abandonment (National Audit Office [NAO], 2004, p. 3). At the political level, it is argued that "better IT is needed in the NHS because the demand for high-quality healthcare continues to rise and the care now provided is much more complex, both technically and organizationally" (Connecting for Health, 2004, p. 7). About $250 million is spent on management and administration in the NHS, a controversial figure, as many believe more doctors and nurses should be recruited (see Figure 1).

THEORETICAL ANALYSIS OF THE CASE

The NHS case study illustrates the dynamic nature of a national healthcare IS implementation, set within the context of a rapidly changing organisation. As with all large IT-enabled programs, the

Figure 1. NHS projected expenditures over two decades (Wanless, 2004)

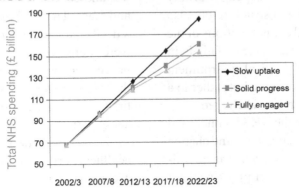

success or otherwise of the strategic plan is in its implementation (Doolin, 2004; Hendy, Reeves, Fulop, Huchings, & Masseria, 2005; Herzlinger, 1989). The lessons of IT costs versus medical decision making are well documented in the literature and involve the lack of alignment between the business and IT strategy (Luftman, 2000); a lack of ownership and leadership of the IT project among senior decision makers (Brown, 2001); poor risk assessment skills (Heathfield, Pitty, & Hanka, 1998); over-scoping of the functional and technical specification leading to IT projects becoming over-budget and late (NAO, 2004); poor communication between program/project managers and potential users of the system (Guah & Currie, 2005); inadequate resources to deliver/ implement IT systems (Currie & Guah, 2006).

The empirical research found that issues of project risk were at the forefront of the minds of clinicians, general practitioners (GPs), hospital managers, and IT staff. Formal project management methods and tools were perceived as offering only part of the solution to mitigate the considerable risks from introducing the national program. The fragmentation was not just about the diversity of IT systems within the NHS, but also about the political geographical, social, organisational, and financial complexity of delivering healthcare.

The overriding view was for the national program to become an integrated IS across and beyond the NHS. The threats to achieving this were perceived by many clinicians to fall within the control of politicians and IT service providers rather than from NHS staff. Project risk mitigation was a complicated issue, compounded by the political and ideological considerations, such as the public-private partnership funding initiative (PFI), which facilitated the increasing use of private sector firms. While the NHS is often characterised as a top-down bureaucracy (Mohan, 2002), past achievements in IT development and implementation had often been initiated at a decentralised (hospital, departmental, unit) level. Although this was now discouraged by the centrist approach of the national program, staff participating in the research expressed concerns that any failures associated with IT project implementation may be labelled *staff resistance* rather than the shortcomings of external constituents, such as politicians, management consultants, or IT suppliers.

The success or failure of IS is inextricably linked with the dynamics of the organisation within which they exist. Miranda and Saunders (2002) have demonstrated the complex interaction of technical, social, cultural, and political elements that result in a failed IS. Equally, IS success depends on more than technical competence. The cultural and political environment of the NHS is difficult to study as it depends not only on the tangible organisational structure but also on the tacit knowledge and the perceptions of the participants (Guah & Currie, 2005). This is in addition to the cultural and political environment of an organisation that is not static but rather in a state of constant flux and dynamic change.

Institutionalism of IS in the NHS is concerned with processes of cultural persistence and change of healthcare processes. The survival of an organisation depends as much on conforming to societal norms of acceptable practice as to achieving high levels of production efficiency and effectiveness (Covaleski, Dirsmith, & Michelman, 1993). Prior work has shown that an organisation's formal structure, policies, and procedures serve to demonstrate conformity with the institutionalised rules and requirements of external constituents (DiMaggio & Powell, 1983; Meyer & Rowan, 1991). In light of these concerns healthcare in the UK showed that the national program was intended to play a high profile role within the heavily institutionalised environment of hospitals (Scott et al., 2000).

The UK healthcare system is infused with institutional logics emanating from various sectors across the organisational field. Healthcare is politically contentious where societal level logics developed by government are embedded into policies and procedures that cascade down to organisations where they are interpreted by various stakeholders including clinicians, managers, administrators, and patients. How these logics are interpreted varies according to the degree to which they affect changes to the perceived or real material resource environment of the institutional actors. The vision for the national program was infused with the institutional logics more commonly associated with the private sector, as an innovation that would contribute to greater productivity, efficiency, cost control, and customer satisfaction in healthcare delivery. Paradoxically, this externally directed institutional logic served to under represent and simplify the vast complexities and contradictions in how it was perceived, and reacted to, by those affected by government-led IT-enabled changed. Within the NHS, staff were increasingly sceptical about the merits of private sector logics, such as the PFI initiative, as their values, norms, and goals invariably placed financial considerations secondary to choices about patient care.

The proliferation of new entrants into the healthcare organisational field was a consequence of changing government policies over six decades. During this era of professional dominance, healthcare workers, particularly clinicians, enjoyed a level of freedom to define and structure their working practices. This extended to choices about the types of technology adopted and diffused across the NHS. As a new era emerged in the 1970s, which embraced managerialism as a way to enhance efficiency and performance, the European healthcare system was increasingly inundated with various managerial fads and panaceas, like BPR and change management (Herzlinger, 1989). An outcome of such interventions was that isomorphic structures across the NHS were increasingly threatened, as NHS managers were keen to demonstrate "best practice" examples through the adoption of the latest management ideas. Implicit in this logic was that NHS organisations that had not embraced "new ideas" ran the risk of being labeled as "against modernisation" or, at worst, "failing institutions."

Moving from an era of managerialism to one which increasingly advocates the use of "market mechanisms" to regulate and monitor healthcare services, efforts to differentiate NHS organisations still needs to be intensified further. The political rhetoric surrounding the right of patients to "choose" between one provider and the next is not likely to be based upon anything more than a crude assessment of the number of "stars" awarded a primary care trust (PCT), with those holding a low number becoming labeled as offering a less than adequate quality of service to patients. This will further fragment the organisational field of healthcare as the status of individual NHS organisations becomes increasingly differentiated on the basis of current and future evaluation criteria to measure performance. The topic of performance measurement was highly contentious, however, as respondents offering both a clinical and technical perspective believed that the emphasis upon target-setting was carefully designed to absolve politicians from responsibility by accentuating the role and accountability of professional groups.

The concepts of the organisational field, institutional logics, and governance systems are central to our understanding of how the healthcare system adopts and adapts to changes in the material-resource environment and the beliefs, rules, and ideas that comprise the value system. How and why these eras have emerged underpins our investigation into the UK NHS and facilitates our understanding of the nature and scope of large-scale change programs, and the extent to which they signal an institutional change within healthcare.

The institutional logics and governance systems must therefore be understood to explain why this type of change has occurred. In our investigation, we are concerned to apply our theoretical framework to help us understand how a large–scale, nation-wide technical change program is being adopted and diffused throughout the healthcare system and, more specifically, the changes in the organisational field, institutional logics, and governance systems that serve to encourage or inhibit such change.

TOWARDS BETTER VALUE IN HEALTHCARE DECISION MAKING

The national program is intended to help the situation healthcare managers presently face—with almost no say over the crucial factors which most managers anywhere else in the Western world and in other industries need to have in order to be effective (Wanless, 2004). The situation was brought about by a mixture of a quasi-medieval system and a control approach to managing patient data. Unlike other industries (i.e., banking and airline industries) where decision making leads to a good outcome, requires adaptation, and matching of the process to the individual customer, the healthcare industry may not necessarily provide a gold standard for a process that guarantees good outcomes for patients (Grabowski & Lee, 1993; Martin, 2003).

The previous is partly a result of humans being biological creatures and biological systems are inherently variable. As individuals we all have our own copies of genetic material—these materials mutate and evolve randomly. Because of the variability, the number of formulas and data points required to document each instantiation of a biological system constantly increases by several folds. Consequently, the number of conditions that need to be handled by uniform data standards is much greater than that required by standards for simpler physical, production or materials handling systems, however large or geographically widespread they may be. It takes into consideration that the patient's state of health is the result of the complex interaction between his/her unique genetics makeup, brain capacity, environment, and habits. Thus explaining why some individuals may be able to carry on fairly normal activities despite severe loss of 80% of their pulmonary capacity, others may be disabled by minor arthritis. Careful reproduction of a healthcare process that results in a good outcome for the former may not help the later.

Such scenarios dictate that the delivery of healthcare is not only unique in variety but also in the range of services and products. This explains why healthcare services are not typically chosen by the patient but by a more professional and knowledgeable representative (although these medics are increasingly being influenced by the pharmaceutical companies and/or government (Stevens et al., 1993). This shows just how the healthcare industry is different from others in the Western economy because the market in most industries is driven by the customer.

Health industry requirements are also exceptionally demanding in a number of areas. Most notable are the implications of violations of personal privacy while involving all those who need to know; dual responsibility for personal and public health; the complexity and expansion of the knowledge base and terminology; the high risk to the providers' livelihood combined with pressures to make critical decisions continuously and rapidly; and poorly defined outcomes. All of this is in the context of a "guild system" of responsibility, accountability, and power (Markus, 1983; Vogel, 2003). The healthcare industry also has to support personal and moral values, which in themselves are very complex. The judgments taken about personal attitudes to risk and potential benefit on interventions are all driven by our unique physical and mental makeup and local context—though our values are constantly changing over time.

The implementation of the national program demonstrates how healthcare services are perhaps the most complex large-scale business of UK's economy. More variability and uncertainty at the point of service, as to causality, processes, and to the outcome of that investment exists in healthcare delivery than in any other public sector. With such "variability and uncertainty" in the healthcare business, it is not surprising that identifying and measuring, let alone valuing, a financial return on investment (ROI) from computers in healthcare presents special challenges.

Value is a much broader concept than "benefits" as it implies the additional gain from one investment as opposed to another (Lucas, 1993; Sambamurthy & Zmud, 1994). The national program, like other IT projects, can generate value in many ways. As well as creating quality and process improvements, data from the system has

utility that is much more subjective than that of any other resource (Guah & Currie, 2004). While data may be viewed as a commodity, asset, or resource, information is derived from the qualitative use of data and involves value judgments.

A number of the difficulties in "measuring" the national program's potential value the patients are that (Currie & Guah, 2006; Hendy et al., 2005):

- many infrastructure investments cannot be cost justified on an ROI basis;
- some of its sob-systems are being implemented to change difficult-to-measure NHS staff actions;
- many parts may be strategic systems, thus, eluding measurement;
- much of the new investment does not take into account the prior costs;
- efficiency (doing things right) is easier to measure than effectiveness (doing the right things); and
- since effectiveness (doing the right things) and innovation (doing new things) can not be readily quantified in terms of traditional outputs, improvements are not usually reflected in economic efficiency statistics.

While the effectiveness of a healthcare delivery process can be defined as "the extent to which a desirable outcome is achieved in a timely manner," the efficiency of healthcare delivery process could also be defined as "the extent to which healthcare delivery process is completed with the minimal consumption of resources." Consider the rather complex process of diagnosing and treating certain categories of patients in the NHS, most healthcare delivery processes can be effective (the patient achieves a full recovery and returns to his/her normal activities within 3 months) but relatively inefficient (say the patient had a 15-day inpatient stay, extensive ambulatory services, and consumed $300,000 in healthcare resources). The healthcare delivery process also can be ineffective (the patient has minimal subsequent capacity and never returns to his/her normal activities) but efficient (if the patient had a 3-day inpatient stay, a short post discharge ambulatory regimen, and consumed only $5,000 in healthcare resources). This demonstrates the need for healthcare managers to further strive for high effectiveness in combination with high efficiency and at the lowest possible costs.

Most components of the national program are intended for use in the NHS primarily to capture and manipulate data for improved—both clinical and administrative—decision making. Majeed (2003) suggests that part of the value anticipated from the national program derives from improvements in the effectiveness of the clinical decision-making process. It should enable physicians and nurses to make better, quicker decisions through mechanisms such as online access to evidence-based results for designated disease conditions, assistance in placing orders (detecting a drug-drug interaction before the order for a medication is actually placed), and receiving an alert electronically after a significantly abnormal test result (Keeler & Newman, 2001). Increasing the effectiveness of the clinical decision-making process should also lead to higher efficiency of that process, which should consequently lead to fewer errors being made and fewer resources being consumed. Among many problems highlighted by Majeed (2003), was the fact that necessary information was often difficult to obtain or simply unavailable, and what was available did not always support the clinical decision-making process.

Improved access to records means dramatically improved efficiencies in a variety of areas (Lucas, 1993). With the old paper-based system, the average turn-around time before laboratory and radiology reports reached the physician was several days. With the national program, diagnostic test results are available within seconds of being verified and has the potential of being brought to the physician's attention through their e-mails on the desktop or text message on a mobile (for telemedicine). In addition, the redundant orders

that were often triggered by result delays have been virtually eliminated with the faster turnaround time, as well as with duplicate verifications for pharmaceutical orders (Majeed, 2003).

The national program will vastly improve communication between clinicians, particularly between nurses and physicians, and the emergency room and primary care physicians. It will give nurses instant access so that they can communicate with the doctors in the right way; the nurses are less frustrated because they do not have to go through the paper trail like they did before. These intangibles we know can be difficult to value but they are real enough to the participants.

CONCLUSION

The UK NHS is a highly institutionalised and complex system, which exists and operates both as a material-resource environment and a set of beliefs, rules, and ideas. Although these two environmental facets are conceptually distinct, material-resource environments are influenced by the institutional context. The selection of resources and how they are combined and deployed is determined by institutional beliefs and rule systems (Meyer & Rowan, 1991). By looking at the national program, this article has shown that implementing such a large IT project in the healthcare environment involves a supplier base that is seriously diverse, stretching from locally based specialists in particular applications and/or industry sectors to suppliers that are capable of applying a combination of sophisticated management techniques and technology investment to achieve new levels of process performance.

The primary contribution of this article has been to provide a theoretical basis drawing from institutional theory, which was used to analyse the NHS implementation of the national program. The theorisation goes beyond the relatively simplistic types of studies that dominate the IS literature today. Much to the contrary, it has been shown that an implementation strategy can accommodate elements such as the links between culture, contradiction and conflict, an analysis of detailed work patterns, and the dynamic and emergent nature of political involvement at national level.

The theory has been illustrated using limited empirical examples only, with a focus on the NHS systems, but it could be used to analyse any case study involving healthcare systems from any parts of the developed world. Viewed from a more critical perspective, however, any theory illuminates some elements of particular case situations and is relatively silent on others. The NHS has grown within an environmental niche that arose out of a complex interaction between the national healthcare environment, business environment, the organisational environment, and the people within the NHS. Changes within the organisation subsequently rendered the environment hostile to the national program, which was affected by its changing links with organisational structure and people, the changing responses of people within the NHS to the environment around them, and the changing individual and collective mindsets and understanding of those people. While a detailed discussion of ways in which this can be achieved is beyond the scope of this article, some broad approaches have been mentioned.

In the current environment of increasing demands for better quality of healthcare from patient and seemingly reduced amount of funding from national governments, the need for suitable institutional theory is increasingly common and the IS field must increase its understanding of the problematic issues involved and approaches to resolving them. It is hoped that this article makes a modest contribution to these goals.

REFERENCES

Brown, T. (2001). Modernization or failure? IT development projects in the UK public sector. *Financial Accountability & Management, 17*(4), 363-381.

Connecting for Health. (2004). *Business plan.* Retrieved May 2005, from http://www.connectingforhealth.nhs.uk

Covaleski, M. A., Dirsmith, M. W., & Michelman, J. (1993). An institutional theory perspective on the DRG framework, case mix accounting systems and healthcare organizations. *Accounting, Organizations and Society, 18*(1), 65-80.

Currie, W. L., & Guah, M. W. (2006). IT-enabled healthcare delivery: The UK National Health Service. *Information Systems Management, 23*(2), 7-22.

Department of Health (DoH) (UK). (2000). *NHS plan: An information strategy for the modern NHS.* London: Author.

DiMaggio, P. J., & Powell, W. W. (1983). The iron cage revisited: Institutional isomorphism and collective rationality in organizational fields. *American Sociological Review, 48,* 147-160.

DiMaggio, P. J., & Powell, W. W. (Eds.). (1994). *The new institutionalism in organizational analysis.* Chicago: University of Chicago Press.

Doolin, B. (2004). Power and resistance in the implementation of a medical management information systems. *Information Systems Journal, 14,* 343-362.

Grabowski, M., & Lee, S. (1993). Linking information systems application portfolios and organizational strategy. In R. D. Banker, R. J. Kauffman, & M. A. Mahmood (Eds.), *Strategic information technology management: Perspectives on organizational growth and competitive advantage* (pp. 33-54). Hershey, PA: IGI Global.

Guah, M. W., & Currie, W. L. (2004). Application service provision: A technology and working tool for healthcare organization in the knowledge age. *International Journal of Healthcare Technology and Management, 6*(1), 84-98.

Guah, M. W., & Currie, W. L. (2005). *Internet strategy: The road to Web services*. Hershey, PA: IGI Global.

Heathfield, H., Pitty, D., & Hanka, R. (1998). Evaluating information technology in healthcare barriers and challenges. *British Medical Journal, 316,* 1959-1961.

Hendy, J., Reeves, B. C., Fulop, N., Huchings, A., & Masseria, C. (2005). Challenges to implementing the national program for information technology: A qualitative study. *British Medical Journal, 420,* 1-6.

Herzlinger, R. E. (1989). The failed revolution in healthcare—The role of management. *Harvard Business Review,* 95-103.

Institute of Medicine. (2002). *Crossing the quality chasm: A new health system for the 21st century.* Washington, DC: National Academy Press.

Keeler, J., & Newman, J. (2001). Paperless success: The value of e-medical records. *HIMSS Proceedings, 2*(45).

Lowndes, V. (1996). Varieties of new institutionalism—A critical appraisal. *Public Administration, 74,* 181-197.

Lucas, H. C. (1993). The business value of information technology: A historical perspective and thoughts for future research. In R. D. Banker, R. J. Kauffman, & M. A. Mahmood (Eds.), *Strategic information technology management: Perspectives on organizational growth and competitive advantage* (pp. 359-3744). Hershey, PA: IGI Global.

Luftman, J. (2000). Assessment business IT alignment maturity, *Communications of the AIS, 4*(14), 1-51.

Majeed, A. (2003). Ten ways to improve information technology in the NHS. *British Medical Journal, 326,* 202-206.

March, J. G., & Olsen, J. P. (1989). *Rediscovering institutions: The organizational basis of politics.* New York: Free Press.

Markus, M. L. (1983). Power, politics and MIS implementation. *Communications of the ACM, 26*(6), 430-445.

Martin, J. B. (2003). Effectiveness, efficiency, and the value of IT. *Journal of Healthcare Information Management, 17*(2).

Meyer, J. W., & Rowan, B. (1991). Institutionalized organizations: Formal structure as myth and ceremony. In W. W. Powell & P. J. DiMaggio (Eds.), *The new institutionalism in organizational analysis.* Chicago: University of Chicago Press.

Miranda, S. M., & Saunders, C. S. (2002). The social construction of meaning: An alternative perspective on information sharing. *Information Systems Research.*

Mohan, J. (2002). *Planning, markets and hospitals* London: Routledge.

National Audit Office (NAO). (2004). *Improving IT procurement.* Report by the Comptroller and Auditor General, HC 877 Session, 2003. London: The Stationary Office.

North, D. (1990). *Institutions, institutional change and economic performance.* Cambridge, UK: Cambridge University Press.

Sambamurthy, V., & Zmud, R. W. (1994). *IT management competency assessment: A tool for creating business value through IT.* Working paper. Financial Executives Research Foundation.

Scott, W. R., Ruef, M., Mendel, P. J., & Caronna, C. A. (2000). *Institutional change and healthcare organizations: From professional dominance to managed care.* Chicago: University of Chicago Press.

Stevens, P., Schade, A., Chalk, B., & Slevin, O. (1993). *Understanding research: A scientific ap-*

proach for health care professionals. Edinburgh, UK: Campion Press.

Tolbert, P. S., & Zucker, L. G. (1994). Institutional analysis of organizations: Legitimate but not institutionalized. Institute for Social Science Research working paper. University of California, Los Angeles.

Vogel, L. (2003). Finding value from IT investments: Exploring the elusive ROI in healthcare. *Journal of Healthcare Information Management, 17*(4).

Wanless, D. (2002). *Securing our future health: Taking a long-term view.* London.

Wanless, D. (2004, February). *Securing good health for the whole population.* London.

Weber, R. P. (1990). *Basic content analysis* (2nd ed.). Newbury Park, CA: Sage.

This work was previously published in the Journal of Information Technology Research, Vol. 1, Issue 1, edited by M. Khosrow-Pour, pp. 14-26, copyright 2008 by IGI Publishing (an imprint of IGI Global).

Chapter 10
Crisis Compliance:
Using Information Technology to Predict, Prevent and Prevail over Disasters

Laura Lally
Hofstra University, USA

ABSTRACT

This article develops the concept of crisis compliance (CC)—defined as making appropriate use of IT, and non-IT methodologies to predict, prevent, and prevail over disasters. CC emerges from Lally's Target Shield and Weapon Model, which is grounded in the theories of crisis management, normal accident theory, and high reliability organizations. CC is then applied to a case study involving Hurricane Katrina, with examples drawn from other recent disasters. Emerging IT-based crisis management initiatives will be examined with an emphasis on how the impacts of Hurricane Katrina could have been mitigated. Recommendations for predicting, preventing, and prevailing over future disasters will emerge from the analysis.

INTRODUCTION: THE INCREASE IN CRISES AND IT-BASED INITIATIVES TO COMBAT THEM

The post 9/11 environment has been characterized by an increasing number of crises. Crisis management researcher Ian Mitroff (2005, p. 3) notes:

*The number of crises not only is growing rapidly, but of even greater concern, is the fact that the rate of increase in the number of crises is increas-*ing as well. Furthermore the time, and even the geographical distance, between crises is shrinking precipitously.

There has been a corresponding increase in public awareness of the potential for crises, not only from terrorist attacks, but from accidental failures such as blackouts and natural disasters such as hurricanes. The widespread traumatic impacts of crises such as 9/11, Hurricane Katrina, and the Sumatra-Andaman earthquake and resulting tsunamis, has lead to an increased emphasis on disaster planning on the part of national and local governments.

Government funding for new technologies aimed at combating terrorist attacks and other disasters has increased, and a wide range of new IT-based systems and methodologies have emerged. This article will argue that methodological breakthroughs and emerging technologies for combating disaster in one domain, such as battling terrorism, fighting natural disasters, or mitigating the impact of major accidents such as blackouts and hazardous material spills, can be applied to disasters in other domains as well.

IT can provide managers and government leaders with a means of: (1) educating their employees or citizens about the realistic likelihood of the occurrence of a potential disaster, (2) disseminating up-to-the-minute information about any disasters that are immediately threatening, (3) mitigating the impact of disasters through evacuation planning, healthcare availability, and emergency food and water supplies, and (4) recovering from the disaster and rebuilding.

This article develops the concept of crisis compliance (CC)—a framework for approaching crises that focuses on three questions: (1) What IT-based tools are available for *predicting* a crisis, *preventing* the effects from spreading, and *prevailing over* future crises? (2) What is the appropriate use of these technologies in a given crisis scenario?, and (3) What are the responsibilities and obligations of managers and government leaders to use these tools appropriately? The research will argue that if a manager or government leader has made full use of IT-based decision making and communication tools, as well as non-IT methodologies appropriate for a given crisis, the decision maker has been CC.

Mitroff (2005) indicates that, "One of the most striking and interesting feature of crises is that, virtually without exception, they are experienced as major acts of betrayal" (p. 39). He defines betrayal as:

Betrayal is the failure of a person, an organization, an institution, or a society to act and behave in accordance with ways that they have promised or they have lead us to believe they will. Betrayal is the violation of trust that we have placed in another person, organization, institution and/or society. Thus, betrayal is profoundly rooted in our basic feelings of trust and goodness with regard to others....In every case, betrayal is the violation of a basic and fundamental assumption we are making about an individual, an organization, an institution or society—for example, that another person will stand up for us, act in our best interests, and protect us. When the assumption—or more commonly, a set of assumptions—has been showed to be false or invalid, as in Oklahoma City and 9/11, we are stunned. We are left with the feeling of having been betrayed to our core. (p. 40)

In August 2005, Hurricane Katrina hit the Gulf Coast of the United States, causing over 1,500 lives to be lost and irreparable damage to many homes, businesses, and unique historical landmarks. A devastating revelation in the aftermath of Hurricane Katrina was that many of the IT-based strategies that were available were not used, or were used and the results not acted upon. This raises the issue that the local, state, and federal governments did not respond as citizens of a highly technologically advanced society would have expected them to. These disastrous failures lead to widespread feelings of betrayal—feelings that the government and many local industries had failed in their moral obligations to citizens who were stakeholders in the communities that were affected.

In the case of Katrina, this sense of betrayal has translated into a lawsuit:

In a federal district court in Mississippi, plaintiffs are suing oil and coal companies for greenhouse gas emissions, arguing that they contributed to the severity of Hurricane Katrina. The claims in that case include: unjust enrichment, civil conspiracy (against the American Petroleum Institute), public and private nuisance, trespass, negligence and fraudulent misrepresentation. (Lash & Wellington, 2007, p. 96)

Similar lawsuits are likely to emerge if disasters are not effectively confronted.

CC addresses the problem of *post-crisis betrayal*. A crisis compliant manager or government administrator cannot guarantee that no crisis will arise and that no negative impacts will occur, but rather that he or she has done everything humanly possible to predict the crisis, prevent its occurrence and mitigate negative impacts, and create a learning environment to help prevail over future crises. CC, therefore, will serve as a standard for identifying best practices under a wide range of crises conditions. CC can also serve as a means to identify improvements in IT methodologies for dealing with future crises. Finally, CC should provide compliant managers and government administrators with protection from unfair accusations of poor crisis management and potential legal liabilities. The resulting CC decision framework should add significantly to the body of decision science, disaster theory, and crisis management research literature. The framework will also provide a managerially oriented tool that will be useful to management and government officials facing a wide range of crises. This article will examine emerging IT-based crisis management initiatives and map them to the predict, prevent, prevail over, CC decision framework.

THEORETICAL PERSPECTIVE: THE TARGET, SHIELD AND WEAPON MODEL

This analysis will draw on Lally's (2006) *target, shield and weapon model*, a theoretically based model for examining the potential threats to IT-based systems, the propagation of these threats, and the potential for their mitigation. Lally's model

is based on normal accident theory, originally conceived by Perrow (1984) as a model for how small errors can propagate into large disasters. The model is also informed by the theory of high reliability organizations, that emphasizes methodologies by which organizations can minimize the likelihood for disaster in tightly coupled complex organizations (Grabowski & Roberts, 1997; Klein, Bigley, & Roberts, 1995; LaPorte & Consolini, 1991; Sagan, 1993; Turner, 1976; Weick & Roberts, 1993). Crisis Management research, which emphasizes the emotional, psychological, social, and spiritual qualities of leaders and individuals required to confront crises and emerge from them successfully (Mitroff, 2005), also informs the development of the model.

Lally (1996) argued that normal accident theory was a sound theoretical perspective for understanding the risks of IT, because IT is *complex*, and *tightly coupled* and often *poorly controlled*—the three characteristics of accident-prone systems. She also argued (Lally, 1996, 1997) that IT-based systems do not operate in isolation but in organizational and societal settings where failures in IT can lead to more widespread secondary failures. The 2003 blackout, which involved a technical failure that quickly propagated to the entire East coast of the United States, was a perfect illustration of this type of *normal accident*:

Electricity and information are the twin life bloods of modern societies. If electricity and information are disrupted, then everything from the production of food, to the supply of potable water, to ATM service—in short, literally everything in a modern society—grinds to a halt....We are truly coupled and interdependent as never before. (Mitroff, 2005, p. 13)

Lally (2002) also argued that the frequent rapid change in both IT-based systems and the work processes they support can further exacerbate the potential for disaster. Lally (2005) further extended her model and argued that IT-based systems are not only a *target* used as a weapon of destruction to cause serious accidents, but that IT-based systems can be a *shield* used to prevent damage from future incidents, whether they be IT-based or physical. This *target and shield model* drew on insights from the theory of high reliability organizations and suggests that IT designers and managers, as well as government and law enforcement agencies, learn from past experiences and embody this knowledge in the design and implementation of future IT-based systems. The resulting systems should not only be more secure and resilient, they should aid in preventing future IT-based or physical attacks, or mitigating their impact should they occur. Figure 1 illustrates the *target and shield model* for analyzing the source, propagation, and impacts of IT-based threats, as well as ways in which IT can be used to identify and mitigate the impact of future threats.

The *target and shield model* incorporates Lally's extensions to normal accident theory. The model also contains *three significant feedback loops*, which allow IT to play a positive role in preventing future incidents from materializing, having real-world impacts, and mitigating their impacts when they do occur. In Feedback Loop #1, *prevent future incidents*, controls can be built into the system to prevent future incidents from materializing. In Feedback Loop #2, *prevent propagation of incidents*, controls can be built into the system to prevent future incidents that have materialized from turning into accidents. In the Feedback Loop #3, *mitigate impact of disasters*, IT-based systems can be developed to prevent accidents resulting from IT-based or physical attacks from propagating even further.

EXTENDING THE MODEL TO URBAN ENVIRONMENTS

A new sensibility has emerged in the Post 9/11 environment—*disasters can be deliberate* and occur in *large-scale social environments such as cities*, rather than in organizations. Normal accident theory and the theory of high reliability organizations, which were developed to prevent *innocent mistakes* from propagating into system-wide disasters in *organizational settings* had to be extended.

Figure 1. The target and shield model

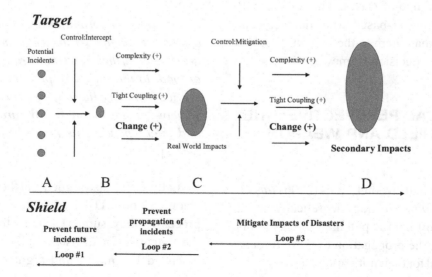

Mitroff (2005) reflects on this new type of crises:

Something more ominous is afoot. The nature of crises—that is, the type of crises and their qualities—has changed dramatically. Crises have gone from "normal systems accidents"—that is, unintentional systems breakdowns due to the overwhelming complexity of modern technologies (e.g. Chernobyl)—to the deliberate intentional breakup of organizations, institutions, and even society itself (e.g. 9/11). We have gone from normal systems accidents to abnormal systems disasters— that is, to planned catastrophes. (p. 4)

Lally (2004) addressed the additional challenges of applying the model to deliberate attacks in urban areas:

The models must be extended to address the challenges of applying the principles of these theories to large diverse urban environments, rather than organizational settings. Large urban areas add additional layers of complexity and tight coupling when compared to organizational settings. In organizational settings, the shared mental models recommended by High Reliability Theory are easier to enforce. Organizations can appoint professionals who are educated in preventing disasters and involve all employees in disaster training. Terrorist attacks in urban areas are likely to involve "a spectrum of trained professionals, cognitively and physically fatigued individuals, motivated volunteers, and frightened victims," (Murphy, 2004), making shared mental models harder to achieve and appropriate social interaction more difficult. (p. 3)

Natural disasters in urban areas can have similar results. New Orleans was a heterogeneous social mix of affluent, well-educated, IT-literate professionals who had the resources to relocate, and poor individuals without Internet access and the resources to evacuate. This digital and social divide made effective response to the disaster more difficult to achieve. Hurricane Katrina vividly illustrated how quickly a society can rapidly disintegrate in the face of a major disaster.

EXTENDING THE MODEL TO USING IT AS A WEAPON

In the *target and shield model*, Feedback Loop #1 addresses the challenge of preventing future incidents. In a learning environment, once incidents occur, knowledge should be gained about the nature of the incident to prevent future incidents from occurring. The proactive prevention of future incidents involves more than waiting for new incidents to occur and developing defensive techniques when they do. IT-based tools are emerging for tracing incidents to their source and eliminating them. When IT is used as a weapon to fight back against potential attackers, the dynamics of the *target and shield model* is reversed. Instead of responding to a single negative event and its propagation through a large and complex system, the emphasis is on identifying potential threats in a complex technological and social environment, gathering intelligence on those threats, and if the threats are confirmed, planning the logistics to eliminate the threats with a minimum of damage to innocent people and their property. With use, the model should also provide insight into which threats are the most serious and need to be eliminated.

Figure 2 illustrates the use of *IT as a weapon*.

In Step 1, IT can be used to identify anomalous behavior, such as a group of people who have never contacted one another suddenly being in frequent contact. Artificial-intelligence-based systems for identifying anomalous patterns in behavior can indicate potential threats. The challenge in Step 1 is the false positive problem that arises when attempting to identify threats in an environment that consists primarily of innocent people,

Figure 2. IT as a weapon against potential threat

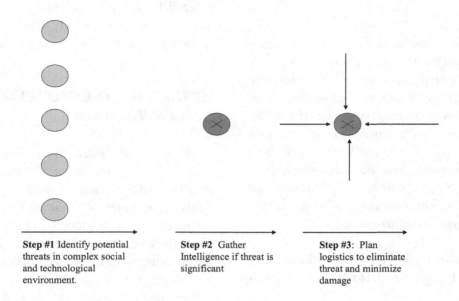

Step #1 Identify potential threats in complex social and technological environment.

Step #2 Gather Intelligence if threat is significant

Step #3: Plan logistics to eliminate threat and minimize damage

whether corporate employees or civilians. In Step 2, IT-based intelligence gathering can then reveal whether the members of the new group are on a watch list—indicating that they may be a terrorist cell becoming active—or perhaps members of a new computer class, corporate subcommittee, or scout troop. In Step 3, if the threat is real, IT can then be used to monitor the activities of the group and eliminate the threat in a manner that will cause the least collateral damage. In August, 2006, the successful elimination of a London-based terrorist plot aimed at British and American airlines, owed much to IT-based information gathering.

Lally and Nolan (2005a) applied the *target and shield and weapon model* to wireless technologies. Their analysis indicated that wireless technologies are a *target* because of their vulnerabilities to air interface denial of service attacks, snooping attacks that threaten data integrity, and the limitations of standards in applications that use unlicensed spectrum. Their analysis also indicated that wireless technology could be used as a *shield* because the distributed architecture of these networks can provide robustness and redundancy to prevent

catastrophic failures. Finally, they indicated that wireless technologies can be used as a *weapon* because location-aware devices could be used for tracking suspected cyber attackers.

Another good example of three stage part defense suggested by the *target shield and weapon model* is a computer system that uses firewalls, intrusion detection, and intrusion prevention systems. Firewalls screen out potential hackers, preventing initial incidents from occurring. Intrusion detection systems detect and contain hostile activity resulting from break-ins, mitigating the damage from incidents that have occurred. Intrusion prevention systems compare user's behavior against known patterns of attack to identify potential attackers, identifying potential threats before they materialize. More sophisticated types of intrusion prevention are emerging to avoid the false positives, which are a problem in intrusion prevention. An example is active intrusion prevention that provides potential attackers with marked information that, if used to penetrate a system, will clearly identify the event as hostile and capture information about the originator of the attack (Green, Raz, & Zviran, 2007).

The overall purpose of the *target, shield and weapon model* is to allow organizational and government leaders to characterize a given type of crisis in order to: (1) predict future disasters, (2) prevent these disasters from occurring or mitigating the damage if they do, and (3) prevail over future disasters by developing the appropriate IT-based tools, methodologies, and practices, as well as a shared sense of community that will protect members of organizations and societies to the extent it is humanly possible.

PREDICTING DISASTER IN THE WAKE OF 9/11

In his account of the activities at the State Department on the morning of 9/11, Richard A. Clark, former White House National Coordinator for Security, Infrastructure Protection and Counter-Terrorism, indicates that one of his most shocking revelations was that, even as the attacks unfolded, intelligence reports indicated that four people on the first two planes were members of Al Queda (Clark, 2004). The fact that this information was not made available prior to the attack, and that passengers with terrorist affiliations were allowed to board the planes, indicated a major lapse in security. As a result of these revelations, data gathering by U.S. intelligence and data sharing between U.S. agencies has increased greatly, as well as the severity with which potential terrorists are handled.

As a result of the 9/11 attacks, spending by the U.S. government to plug up the security breaches that allowed the attacks to occur, as well as to prevent other plausible terrorist attacks, increased greatly. MIT's *Magazine of Innovation: Technology Review* reported that the budget for the Department of Homeland Security for 2005 was $30 billion dollars (MIT's *Magazine of Innovation,* 2005). For Customs, Immigration, and Border

Protection it included $2.9 billion for container security and $340 for US-VISIT, an automated entry and exit system for frequent international travelers. For the Coast Guard, it included $724 million to upgrade the technology and communications division. For the Transportation Security Administration, it included $475 million for explosives detection systems, baggage screening equipment and their installation. For state and local assistance programs it included $150 in port security grants, $150 million in rail/transit security grants, and $715 million in grants to fire departments. For the Emergency Preparedness and Response Directorate, it included $2 billion for an emergency relief fund. For the Science and Technology Directorate, it included $593 million to develop technologies that counter threats from chemical, biological, nuclear and radiological weapons and high explosives and $61 million to continue the development of innovative countermeasures to protect commercial aircraft against possible missile systems. For Information Analysis and Infrastructure Protection Directorate, it included $2 billion to assess and protect critical infrastructures including cyberspace. "Pasadena, CA-based Cogent, which develops automated fingerprint recognition systems used by law enforcement and the Department of Homeland Security, went public in September and raised $216 million, then saw its stock price nearly triple by the end of the year" (MIT *Magazine of Innovation,* 2005, p.42).

Research initiatives in the scientific and corporate research communities also addressed these new threats as well as innovative approaches to responding to emergencies that did occur. Lally (2006) argued that since many crises share common characteristics, innovations in one crisis domain should be examined for their applicability to other types of crises. Once they have occurred, accidental failures such as blackouts, and natural disasters such as Hurricane Katrina, can have similar impacts as those produced by terrorist attacks. All result in a breakdown of the systems that support society, which can lead to massive losses of life and property. Therefore, technology developed to support creative responses in one type of crisis may be tailored to be applicable to others. This article will now review a range of these initiatives designed for predicting, preventing, and prevailing over future crises, and how they could have been applied more effectively in combating Hurricane Katrina.

EMERGING IT-BASED CRISIS MANAGEMENT INITIATIVES FOR PREDICTING DISASTER

It is during the *predict* phase, when IT methodologies are being used as a weapon against potential future crises, that the differences between unintentional and intentional disasters are the most profound. Data gathering and analysis to eliminate potential terrorists can lead false positives that result in the violation of privacy and other serious civil rights abuses of innocent people. Legal protections need to be in place to prevent the over zealous elimination of terrorist threats.

When the threat is unintentional, however, such as with system design flaws such as Y2K, or natural disasters like hurricanes, data gathering and analysis can be as rigorous as possible. When natural disasters threaten, IT-based radar systems can illuminate developing problems, and IT-based simulation models can give managers and government leaders experience with virtual disasters that can help them prepare for real ones. Evacuation routes and methodologies can be designed to ensure that everyone has the time and means to reach safety. Supply chain management systems can be tailored to help relief agencies provide emergency assistance. Supply chain alliances with private sector organizations and individuals to provide emergency relief can be established before emergencies occur.

In the case of Hurricane Katrina, simulation models had already predicted that the levees

protecting the city would not withstand a Class 3 hurricane and weather experts had predicted that a hurricane of such force was well within the realm of possibility. *National Geographic* magazine in October, 2004 published an article called, "Gone with the Water," which included the following warning:

...The doomsday scenario is not far-fetched. The Federal Emergency Management Agency lists a hurricane strike on New Orleans as one of the most dire threats to the nation, up there with a large earthquake in California or a terrorist attack in New York City. Even the Red Cross no longer opens hurricane shelters in the city, claiming the risk to its workers is too great. (Bourne, 2004, p. 100)

Levee systems that would protect against more powerful storms had not only been designed, but were built and fully operational in the Netherlands.

Also in 2004, a computer simulation of a hurricane, called Hurricane Pam, was developed as an exercise for dealing with a major hurricane in New Orleans. The result was widespread devastation:

270 officials from all levels of government did participate in a FEMA-funded week long simulation of a Category 3 Hurricane striking New Orleans, a fake but very realistic storm called Hurricane Pam based on extensive models developed at Louisiana State University. The primary assumption of the Hurricane Pam exercise was that "Greater New Orleans is inundated with ten feet of water within the levee systems as a result of a Category 3 or greater hurricane." The attendees learned that it would not be just water, in fact, but a "HAZMAT gumbo." They heard that the total number of people left stranded in the toxic water "may approach 500,000" if residents didn't evacuate. And they were further informed that a monstrous storm such as Pam would leave

30 million cubic yards of debris—not counting human remains—spread out over 13 parishes in Southern Louisiana. (Brinkley, 2005, p. 18)

Local government leaders and relief agencies were told to prepare accordingly, but the recommendations resulting from the model were not implemented. "Having lived through Pam for a week, the 270 officials just went home" (Brinkley, 2005, p. 19).

For three days prior to Katrina reaching New Orleans, radar models showed the storm approaching and measured its strength. *Surge warriors* such as Ivor van Heerden, had developed sophisticated advanced circulation (ADCIRC) computer models to predict the impact of hurricanes in the gulf. Thirty hours before landfall, experts predicted that there was a strong likelihood of a major disaster, yet a mandatory evacuation was not called for. When major flooding was indicated, Van Heerden (2006) "forwarded the results to every official at every level of government I could think of" (p. 41) saying a worst case scenario had developed and that mandatory evacuation was necessary. Only a voluntary evacuation was called for. By the time the evacuation was mandated a day later, there was not enough time to have it implemented.

Individual government agencies, such as the Humane Society, had developed their own decision rules for approaching hurricanes, which included mandatory evacuation in case of a Class 3 hurricane. Hundred of dogs and cats were driven to safe shelters in advance of the storm, while thousands of citizens were left behind.

Private sector organizations, such as Wal-Mart, predicted the seriousness of the storm and began planning the delivery of emergency supplies to areas they feared would suffer the greatest damage. After the initial hit of Katrina, Wal-Mart provided the greatest share of water, food, and equipment to stricken areas:

Wal-Mart, the world's largest retailer and America's biggest private employer, stepped up to the plate by offering vast warehouses full of essential supplies to those stricken by the Great Deluge. Under the lighting quick leadership of CEO Lee Scott, Wal-Mart used its muscle to meet the needs of the victims in the three ravaged Gulf States, donating emergency supplies ranging from Strawberry Pop Tarts to Hanes underwear... "Wal-Mart was our FEMA," said Warren Riley of the New Orleans Police department. (Brinkley, 2006, p. 251)

Partnerships between local governments and private sector organizations that specialize in supplying customers with the necessities should be forged before emergencies happen. Supply chain management software, widely used by these large chains, could be modified to help streamline relief efforts should an emergency occur. Volunteering to assist in local emergencies should win large chain stores a great deal of good public relations in their surrounding communities.

One local power company in New Orleans had developed an IT-based content management system of its electrical infrastructure in the city and was the first to reestablish power (Violino, 2006). Content management systems of complete urban infrastructures (including electricity, plumbing, roadways, and telecommunications) have been developed and implemented in Singapore for the last 15 years. Maintaining these systems in all major urban areas would provide a means for reestablishing essential services on a timely basis. Using these systems to reduce downtime from routine failures, such as water main breaks and local blackouts, would make their implementation more cost effective.

Additionally, private sector initiatives from Amtrak, Marriott, Continental Airlines, and a number of faith-based groups, were also refused or delayed. Offers of medical support from Cuba, airdropped military rations from Germany, and cash and oil supplies from Kuwait were also refused. Even FEMA subcontractors were put on hold:

Cool Express, an ice company in Blue River, Wisconsin had a standing contract for ice deliveries in disaster situations. Yet the company didn't receive permission to send trucks to the region until 4 p.m. on Monday. By that time, the ice wouldn't even reach the staging area in Dallas until late Tuesday. After that, it would be another eight-hour drive to southern Louisiana. (Brinkley, 2006, p. 250)

Disaster recovery alliances with the private sector and with other countries need to be developed and designed before hand. Simulation modeling of future disasters should include members of these alternative sources of relief.

Along with organizational initiatives, a number of heroic individuals also emerged from Katrina. Individuals within New Orleans with private boats rescued their neighbors. "Far flung American communities galloped to do all they could" (Brinkley, 2006, p. 250), but FEMA denied them permission to enter until a chain of command could be established. A database of certified volunteer first responders should be developed so that these individuals can be contacted, transported to disaster areas, and deployed effectively. Good Samaritan legislation needs to be developed to protect volunteers from lawsuits, should their best attempts have negative consequences.

The availability of IT-based resources and information, the overwhelming human factors in favor of using the resources to their fullest potential, and the failure to act on them was a clear violation of the principles of CC.

PREVENTING DISASTERS FROM BECOMING WORSE

Another area of IT-based crisis management research is aimed at helping first responders deal more effectively with disasters that have already occurred.

One major challenge is to design computer systems that will interact with human responders on the front lines of emergency response (Carver & Turoff, 2007). These systems must help increase the human responders' situational awareness by allowing them to absorb information rapidly, focus their attention without interruption, encourage creativity and improvisation on an individual or team level, and build trust between individual team members who might not have known each other before. Conceptual models for the types of human-computer interaction that would support such activity are currently being developed and incorporated into emerging technologies.

Crises "create sudden and profound changes in human systems and the built environment, leading to response activities that range from planned to improvised, as conducted both by established and ad hoc organizations" (Mendoca, Jefferson, & Harrald, 2007, p. 45). Information, communication and technology (ICT) designers, therefore, need to widen their perspective from designing systems that follow the traditional military model of designing systems that isolate an incident and remove it, to systems designed to provide the "collaboration, cooperation, and transparency by numerous organizations with different cultures and structures" (Mendoca et al., 2007, p. 45). These systems must incorporate new procedures designed in response to the failure of traditional ones, as well as role improvisation, to encompass a wider range of decision making and action.

A major challenge in designing these systems is to improve communication, both among first responders and among agencies involved in disaster recovery. A lack of radio interoperability hindered first responders, both on 9/11 and during the aftermath of Hurricane Katrina. Dual use technologies that would permit both normal and emergency operational modes, such as cell phones with wireless local area networks (WLAN) interfaces to allow them to form their own network in emergencies if a base station should fail, are a promising area of research (Manoj & Baker, 2007). Dealing with a frightened public is another challenge that can be addressed by IT-based systems that provide periodic updates of important information in a language and tone appropriate to an individual's prior knowledge and emotional state. Systems to detect user's emotional tone are currently being developed (Hegde, Manoj, Rao, & Rao, 2006).

A Common Alerting Protocol (CAP) language that will allow multiple public agencies to share information on emergencies and to provide joint warning to the public is also being developed. Crisis management research has shown that "Multiple channels of delivery are needed, not only because every technology has its vulnerabilities, but also because people almost always require confirmations of warnings from multiple sources before they act" (Botterell & Addams-Morning, 2007, p. 59). In the case of the Virginia Tech mass murders, this is one reason why the decision by the administration to simply send an e-mail to each student with the heading "Stay Put," after the first shooting, was considered inadequate.

Reducing response time by Emergency Response Systems—"time critical information systems" has been recognized as a key area of research addressing scenarios in which "time is money," translates into "time is lives" (Horan & Schooley, 2007, p. 74). For example, in the United States, the percentage of fatalities in rural accidents is much higher than in urban areas because of the increased response time. Creating end-to-end systems integrating first responders and local hospitals and permitting the sharing of location information and patient medical data are designed to decrease the number of fatalities that result from an extreme event.

Rescue efforts in New Orleans were hindered because rescuers were not familiar with local street names or the location of key relief centers. A lack of a sense of community increased distrust and made rescues more difficult.

The problem the U.S. Coastguard had with FEMA was that FEMA didn't know the local geography or place names or wards of New Orleans. They couldn't pronounce Tchoupitoulas (choppa-tooliss) Street, let alone spell it. They couldn't cross over the Crescent City Connection bridge because they thought it was a shuttle service to Houston. (Brinkley, 2006, p. 258)

GPS systems should be developed and used before a disaster to help relief workers navigate an area and reach important destinations effectively. Alternative routes can also be developed if part of an area is under water, or otherwise inaccessible.

An enhanced knowledge of local customs and language would also aid rescue workers. An economically and culturally diverse urban area, such as New Orleans or New York consists of a number of different subcultures. Differences in language and attitudes toward authority figures such as police and government officials made rescue efforts in New Orleans more difficult. Government officials need to be aware of the various languages spoken in an urban area so that warnings can be issued in appropriate languages. Internet access must be available to all citizens so that information about emerging threats can be delivered on a timely basis. Rescuers need to be aware of social customs regarding approaching strangers in a non-threatening manner. Language translation software and simulation modeling of social interactions developed for soldiers in Iraq, needs to be tailored for first responders confronting diverse social groups in their own country.

EMPOWERING INDIVIDUALS AND SOLIDIFYING COMMUNITY SUPPORT

Enlisting the public as first responders is another promising area of research. "Until professional response personnel arrive, citizens are the first to perform rescues, administer first aid, and transport victims to the hospitals. Even after the response moves from informal to a formal effort, sociological research shows that citizens continue to self organize and provide ongoing assistance, employment, transportation…" (Palen, Hiltz, & Liu, 2007, p. 54). Online forums allow geographically dispersed individuals to share information, creating new virtual communities for dealing with the crisis. One example of this was during Hurricane Katrina, when software consultant Katrina Blankenship permitted her Web site to be converted to an online forum about the hurricane including pointers to other Web sites and a message board to help locate missing people. The site received over 12 million hits and is still active as a Katrina memorial site and a source for hurricane preparedness information. The American federal government's poor response to Katrina left many Americans feeling that they were on their own in facing emergencies. As a result grass roots online forums for other potential disasters, such as FluWiki, which addresses the potential threats of the Avian Flu, have emerged to address the potential for other disasters.

Citizens carrying handheld communication devices, such as picture cell phones are often on the frontlines of disasters. During the London subway bombings hundreds of cell phone pictures taken by commuters were incorporated into recovery efforts. Cell phones that are GPS enabled can provide even more detailed location specific information.

Another example of a grass roots response to a disaster was the Sahana Disaster Management System developed in response to the December 26, 2004 Sumatra-Anadaman earthquake, which resulted in tsunamis that caused over 230,000 deaths. "Over 40 volunteers from various groups and companies contributed to development, and approximately 100 students were recruited to deploy the system and to collect and enter village population data" (Currion, De Silva, & Van de Walle, 2007, p. 43). Since then Sahana has been used to mitigate damages in the 2005 Pakistan earthquake, the 2006 Philippines mudslides, and the 2006 Yogyakarta earthquake in Indonesia.

Since most relief agencies lack the funding and IT expertise to develop proprietary crisis management systems the move to make these systems free and open source is widely called for.

DIRECTIONS FOR FUTURE RESEARCH: APPLYING THE CRISIS COMPLIANCE MODEL TO BOTH MAJOR AND MINOR CRISES

In the wake of the wide range of disasters experienced in the last few years, CC argues that managers and government officials must become aware of, and make use of IT-based initiatives that allow them to predict, prevent, and prevail over future disasters. One promising area of research will be to identify synergies between large scale disasters, such as 9/11 and Katrina, and the smaller scale crises and breakdowns that occur on a more regular basis such as fires, floods, local blackouts, traffic accidents, snowstorms, and heat waves. Technologies developed to prevent the spread of large-scale disasters and prevail over their future occurrence can be applied to smaller scale problems as well. Infrastructures to improve communication, speed up repair and relief efforts, and empower individuals to help their neighbors can be used to combat these more routine emergencies. The use of IT-based crisis management initiatives will make users more familiar with their operation and point out limitations of these systems before large scale emergencies occur. The resulting decreases in individual, organizational, and societal downtime, measured by lost days of productivity and decreases in quality of life, which result from the use of these technologies in routine emergencies, will help pay for their development and implementation. Case studies of their development and use can provide best practices that can be widely shared.

If, as Mitroff (2005) says, "We are truly coupled and interdependent as never before" (p. 13) IT can provide the interconnectivity to leverage this coupling and interdependence in a positive way to combat disasters. Individuals need to use IT to form technical and social networks that will enhance our sense of being part of one global community. Emerging IT-based crises management initiatives need to be available throughout the global community and applied to the full range of potential disasters. Governments and the scientific community need to support these efforts. The concept of CC addresses the obligation too of managers and government leaders to support the development of IT-based systems to combat disasters and to use them to their fullest potential.

ACKNOWLEDGMENT

This research was funded by a Summer Research Grant from the Frank G. Zarb School of Business at Hofstra University.

REFERENCES

Botterell, A., & Addams-Moring, R. (2007). Public warning in the networked age. *Communications of the ACM.*

Bourne, J. K., Jr. (2004). Gone with the water. *National Geographic,* 888-105.

Brinkley, D. (2006). *The great deluge: Hurricane Katrina, New Orleans, and the Mississippi Gulf Coast.* New York: HarperCollins.

Carver, L., & Turoff, M. (2007). Human-computer interaction: The human and the computer as a team in emergency management systems. *Communications of the ACM,* 33-38.

Clark, R. A. (2004). *Against all enemies.* New York: Free Press.

Currion, P., De Silva, C., & Van der Walle, B. (2007). Open source software for disaster management. *Communications of the ACM.*

Grabowski, M., & Roberts, K. (1997). Risk mitigation in large scale systems: Lessons from high reliability organizations. *California Management Review,* 152-162.

Green, I., Raz, T., & Zviran, M. (2007). Analysis of active intrusion prevention data for predicting hostile activity in computer networks. *Communications of the ACM,* 63-68.

Hedde, R., Manoj, B. S., Rao, B. D., & Rao, R. R. (2006). Emotion detection from speech signals and its application to supporting enhanced QoS in emergency response. In *Proccedings of the 3rd International ISCRAM Conference,* Newark, NJ.

Horan, T. A., & Schooley, B. (2007). Time-critical information services. *Communications of the ACM,* 73-79.

Klein, R. L., Bigley, G. A., & Roberts, K. H. (1995). Organizational culture in high reliability organizations. *Human Relations, 48*(7), 771-792.

Lally, L. (1996). Enumerating the risks of reengineered processes. In *Proceedings of 1996 ACM Computer Science Conference* (pp. 18-23).

Lally, L. (1997). Are reengineered organizations disaster prone? In *Proceedings of the National Decision Sciences Conference* (pp. 178-182).

Lally, L. (2002). Complexity, coupling, control and change: An IT based extension to normal accident theory. In *Proceedings of the International Information Resources Management Conference* (pp. 1089-1095).

Lally, L. (2005). Information technology as a target and shield in the post 9/11 environment. *Information Resources Management Journal, 18*(1), 14-28.

Lally, L. (2005a). Applying the target and shield model to wireless technology. In *Proceedings of the International Information Resources Conference.*

LaPorte, T. R., & Consolini, P. (1991). Working in practice but not in theory: Theoretical challenges of high reliability organizations. *Journal of Public Administration, 1,* 19-47.

Lash, J., & Wellington, F. (2007). Competitive advantage on a warming planet. *Harvard Business Review,* 95-107.

Manoj, B. S., & Baker, A. H. (2007). Communication challenges in emergency response. *Communications of the ACM,* 51-53.

Mendonca, D., Jefferson, T., & Harrald, J. (2007). Collaboration adhocracies and mix and match technologies in emergency management. *Communications of the ACM,* 53-54.

Mitroff, I. (2005). *Why companies emerge stronger and better from a crisis: 7 essential lessons for surviving disaster.* New York: American Management Association.

MIT's *Magazine of Technology Innovation.* (2005).

Palen, L., Hiltz, S. R., & Lui, S. B. (2007). Online forums supporting grassroots participation in emergency preparedness. *Communications of the ACM,* 54-58.

Perrow, C. (1984). *Normal accidents: Living with high risk technologies.* New York: Basic Books.

Sagan, S. (1993). *The limits of safety.* Princeton, NJ: Princeton University Press.

Turner, B. M. (1976). The organizational and interorganizational development of disasters. *Administrative Science Quarterly, 21,* 378-397.

Van Heerden, I. (2006). *The storm—What went wrong and why during Hurricane Katrina—The inside story from one Louisiana scientist.* New York: Viking Press.

Violino, B. (2006). *Power play. Baseline.* Retrieved from www.documentum.com

Weick, K. E., & Roberts, K. (1993). Collective mind in organizations: Heedful interrelating on flight decks. *Administrative Science Quarterly, 38,* 357-381.

Chapter 11
Ethical Concerns in Usability Research Involving Children

Kirsten Ellis
Monash University, Australia

Marian Quigley
Monash University, Australia

Mark Power
Monash University, Australia

ABSTRACT

This chapter examines the issues in conducting ethical usability testing with children including the special complications presented by the unique characteristics of children. It outlines the process of gaining approval of overseeing bodies to conduct research with children and discusses the difficulties in gaining informed consent from teachers, parents and the children themselves; protection of the research subject from harm and the difficulty of empowering children to instigate their right to refuse to participate in the research project. The chapter also discusses practical issues regarding the research design such as age appropriate practice, the duration of testing and recruitment of participants.

INTRODUCTION

There is a trend towards the respectful inclusion of children in the research process because they are a significant group within the community (Flewitt, 2005). It is important to conduct research with children as they can reap significant benefit from these research activities when the results are applied. Furthermore, the findings from research conducted on adults cannot always be assumed to apply to children because of their different preferences and

needs which can only be established by conducting research on children directly. According to the Australian National Statement on Ethical Conduct in Research Involving Humans, "Research is essential to advance knowledge about children's and young peoples' well-being" (2005: 4.1). It is by researching children that their voices can be heard and their preferences can be taken into consideration (Burmeister, 2001). In educational research children who participate in the research process are considered valuable as their preferences for learning could be considerably different to adult learners. Hedges states, "Views of children affect

DOI: 10.4018/978-1-60566-966-3.ch011

the content and process of the education they receive and ways they are researched" (2001: 1). As children are increasingly exposed to more technology, it is important to conduct research specifically in this area.

Interaction design for children is a field associated with the more extensive field of Human-Computer Interaction and investigates specific issues in relation to the design and development of software for children with regard to their unique requirements. Druin and Hourcade note, "It is critical to consider how to create new technologies for children that are easy to use, age appropriate in content and interface, and foster exciting learning experience in and out of the classroom" (2005: 34). Children are a significant subgroup of computer users as they use computers in the home and at school. Children have different characteristics to adult users including: their physical and intellectual ability; likes and dislikes; knowledge of the world; attention span and motivation. To develop software that meets the needs of children, it is necessary to conduct research into their preferences and abilities and to test specific applications on children as representative users of computer interfaces (Burmeister, 2000). Plass states, "Interface design is the process of selecting interface elements and features based on their ability to deliver support for the cognitive processes involved in the instructional activities facilitated by the application" (1998: 39). The design process involves selecting the instructional activity to support the competence or skill that the learner is supposed to acquire. In order to design appropriate software for children, it is important to be aware of their special needs.

THE COMPLICATIONS PRESENTED BY RESEARCHING CHILDREN

Gaining data from children can be complicated by a number of characteristics that children may exhibit; although not exclusively characteristics of children, they are more prevalent in this group. Read and MacFarlane state, "Factors that impact on question answering include developmental effects including language ability, reading age, and motor skills, as well as temperamental effects such as confidence, self-belief and the desire to please" (2006: 82). The language and concepts used in questions are really important to the results. For example, when Ellis (2008) was researching children in preparatory classes, they were asked to name their most favorite and least favorite activity in an e-learning software application. Over forty percent of children selected the same activity for both, showing they either could not make the selection accurately or they did not understand the concepts. False data may be collected if the children make up answers in order to please the interviewer or if they tell the interviewer what they have been told by adults, rather than giving their own opinion (Hedges, 2001). Therefore when it is possible to collect the same data from a number of sources, this should be instituted. For example, when Ellis (2008) was collecting data regarding children's preference for characters between a female presenter, a super hero and a puppet, the kindergarten children were able to work with each character for one session. In the next session, they were able to select the character to take the session. When this preference for character was compared with the character that the children stated was their favorite, twenty-five percent changed their preference dependent on the method of asking.

It is also important to use well trained researchers, as young children may have limited ability to express themselves verbally and the accuracy of the data is dependent on the researchers' ability to understand the children (Hedges, 2001). Reactivity is the term used to define when research participants react to being studied. Kellehear and Allen state, "if people know that they are being observed this can alter their behaviour (reactivity)" (1993: 135). Similarly, McMurray, Pace and Scott explain, "if people are aware of being observed, they may modify their behaviour and produce biased results" (2004: 113). Cohen, Manion and Morrison also discuss the need to minimize "re-activity effects (respondents behaving differently when subjected to scrutiny or being placed in new situations, for example, the interview situa-tion – we distort people's lives in the way we go about studying them" (2000: 116). Haslam and McGarty also refer to the phenomenon stating, "Testing effects are actually one aspect of the more general issue of experimental reactivity. This refers to the fact that participants will often react to features of an experiment so that the process of making observations can change observations" (1998: 75).

The presence of the researcher can affect the result, especially in the case of children. As Read and MacFarlane explain, "Even when there is no deliberate intervention the interview has an effect. In one study it was shown that children are likely to give different responses depending on the status of the interviewer" (2006: 82). Hedges also notes that, "Children behave differently with people they are unfamiliar with" (2001: 6). Even the actions of the researcher can affect the willingness of the participants to participate. When Ellis (2008) was conducting research at a kindergarten, children joined in making the Australian sign language signs with the software when the researcher was merely watching. However, when the researcher had pencil and paper in hand the children's behav-iour changed and they were less likely to join in at all. Also, the presence or absence of a parent or guardian can significantly affect a child's behavior, so careful consideration needs to be given to the physical research design.

GAINING ETHICS COMMITTEE APPROVAL TO CONDUCT RESEARCH WITH CHILDREN

Research which is conducted with children can be overseen by a number of authorities including

departments of education; school and kindergarten boards; universities; professional organizations and companies. Each of these bodies will have a set of strict criteria which the researcher and research must meet to protect the participants; the credibility of the research and the reputation of the overseeing authority. Failure to meet these standards may lead to permission for the research to be denied, the consent of the organization to be withdrawn or sanctions may be taken against the researcher who fails to conduct the research ethically.

The process of gaining approval to conduct research on children is quite daunting. It may be necessary to gain the permission of more than one organization to be able to conduct research. In a study carried out by Ellis (2008) for a doctorate at Monash University in Victoria Australia the form that needed to be completed to conduct research on children was twenty one pages in length. In addition an eight-page privacy form had to be completed. Explanatory statements and consent forms for the staff, parents and children were also prepared. Written permission had to be gained from all organizations involved. The research was also conducted in a school, therefore there was a requirement to gain permission from the government department of education ethics committee; the principal of the school; teachers, parents and students. Filling in the forms, writing the explanatory statements and consent forms was time consuming, and the forms needed to be sent in three to four weeks before the scheduled meetings of ethics committees. The replies from the ethics committee took an additional two weeks.

The main concerns of the ethics committees are ensuring that research is only conducted in the best interests of the children; informed consent are from the parents and children is gained; that the child is protected from harm; that participants are not coerced into participating and that the participants have access to the results of the research.

INFORMED CONSENT

The parents or guardians of children are usually required to give informed consent on behalf of the child until the child reaches the age of consent. The parent's or guardian's consent is gained as they are considered more capable of making a decision taking into account all aspects of the research (Hedges, 2001). Field and Behrman state, "informed consent is widely regarded as a cornerstone of ethical research. Because children (with the exception of adolescents under certain conditions) do not have the legal capacity to provide informed consent, the concepts of parental permission and child assent have been developed as standards for ethical research involving children" (2004: 7). The Australian National Statement on Ethical Conduct in Research Involving Humans states that consent is required from the 'child or young person' whenever he or she has sufficient competence to make this decision" (Commonwealth Government of Australia, 2005: 4.2a) and also from the parent or guardian. Parents may only consent if the proposed research is not contrary to the child's best interest.

When research is conducted in schools, the lines of communication between the researcher and the parents are often more complex but acquiring consent from parents must not be compromised. In schools, consent must be obtained from all relevant parties including the child, the parent or guardian, the class teacher, the school principal and the relevant department of education. School staff cannot consent on behalf of students or parents, nor can they disclose information for research purposes about any person or group without the prior permission of the individual affected. When sending forms out to children through a school, it is useful to provide a reply paid envelope for the parents to reply directly to the researcher. This can be an effective method of parents responding without the child having to remember to carry the form home and return it. In research by Ellis (2008) approximately fifty percent of parents responded in this way when provided with the opportunity.

PROTECTION OF THE RESEARCH SUBJECTS

Designing ethical research is difficult in educational settings as the nature of the experimental process applies different treatments to different groups, which has to disadvantage some groups. Hedges states, "In experiments a researcher ought to verify that children in the control group are not disadvantaged in relation to those in the experimental group who may receive new curricula, new teaching methods or new learning strategies" (2001: 8). There are also cases when the control group does not benefit from the treatment and this may be harm by omission (Johnson, 2000). Confidentiality of results can also be an issue as inadvertently revealing a child's identity may lead to harm of the child. This may not be releasing a name but having such a small group that the identity can be deduced (Berk, 1997).

Children have the right to expect to be protected from harm in all research conducted on them. The Convention on the Rights of the Child states, "Bearing in mind that, as indicated in the Declaration of the Rights of the Child, 'the child, by reason of his physical and mental immaturity, needs special safeguards and care, including appropriate legal protection, before as well as after birth' " (UNICEF, 1989). In addition to this, Article 3 of the convention states, "In all actions concerning children ... the best interest of the child shall be a primary consideration."

Protection of children in the process of research may not be as obvious as it first seems. If the results of the research are unknown, as is usually the case, then it is necessary to consider the research carefully to predict any harm that may come to children by participating and if there is a possibility of harm then the research should not be conducted (Berk, 1997). For example, harm can be induced in children at different ages in ways that are not relevant to adults (Greenfield, 1984). Older children, for example, are susceptible to harm from procedures that threaten the way they think of themselves (Berk, 1997). People often don't see the risks associated with usability testing because it is not medical research but there is unintended harm that can occur if research is not conducted ethically. Children's perceptions of computers could be damaged by participating in research and this could affect their decisions later in life. Burmeister states, "As with many types of usability studies web testing has the potential to affect one's perception of one's skills or aptitude" (2000: 13). In addition, children should not be made to feel powerless in the process of research so the right to refuse is of critical importance. Another example of risk to children can be when they have access to the internet they may inadvertently be exposed to material which is unwelcome (Burmeister, 2000). Quigley concurs, noting that "pornography, or sexually explicit imagery or text is readily available in a number of formats on the Web and it is possible for children under the age of sixteen to access it relatively easily, even in some cases, were they haven't sought the material" (Quigley, 2004).

Another risk is associated with conducting research that involves the deception of participants as it can undermine the participant's trust. Sometimes it is necessary to deceive the participant in order to research particular phenomenon because if the participant was aware of the intention of the research it may affect the results. A detailed debriefing session should be used to reveal the true goals of the research to the participants and the reasons for the deception (*The British Psychological Association: Code of ethics and conduct*, 2006).

Australian national laws governing mandatory reporting of particular issues such as child abuse can pose a dilemma when conducting research. The procedures to be followed in the case of mandatory reporting should be clearly set out so

that the researcher knows what their obligations are and the appropriate channels to follow (Newman & Pollnitz, 2002). In addition, researchers may be required to undergo police checks prior to entering into an environment where they have close contact with children.

REFUSAL TO PARTICIPATE

Voluntary participation is a complex ethical area when working with children. The children may feel coerced into participating in the research if their parent or guardian has given permission. The child's right to refuse to participate in a research project must be respected (Commonwealth Government of Australia, 2005). The language and tone used by the researcher is important as there may be implied coercion when it is not intended. For example, if asking a child to use a computer, the researcher could state, "Come and use the computer now", or use a more discretionary statement such as "Would you like to use the computer now?" When children elect to participate in research they may change their minds. Hedges states, "Children may choose, for example not to answer a question in an interview, or become bored or uninterested" (2001: 7). Barendregt suggests that one way to deal with this is by telling the children in the experiment that they can withdraw from the experiment at any time. In addition, "The facilitator will remind them of their right to withdraw whenever they are reluctant to play any further before the end of the test session" (2006: 16). When conducting the research at a kindergarten, Ellis (2008) had one child refuse to take part after the second week's session of nine activities. Rather than this being a negative reflection on the research, it is a positive outcome that the child felt that he/she had the right to refuse to participate and was not forced to do so by the researcher. Many children would occasionally refuse to participate because they were currently engaged in another activity. The children would then come to the computer when they were ready to have a turn. The right to refuse to participate in a school situation is difficult as students are often not given this option in their normal school situation and may not recognise the right to refuse in a research context.

REPORTING BACK TO THE PARTICIPANTS

Once the research has been completed and analysed, the knowledge gained by conducting research with children should then be released to the public (conforming to the appropriate confidentiality provisions) in order to improve the circumstances of children and thereby justify the conducting of the research (Hedges, 2001). The participants in the research must also be informed of the findings. In the case of children, this should be done in a language that is appropriate to the age of the children involved (Johnson, 2000). When research projects are conducted over an extended period it can cause some difficulty in the ability to report back to the participants who were involved. Particularly when, for example, when research is conducted at a kindergarten – especially late in the year – as the children are only involved with the institution for one year before moving on to school. This makes it difficult to relay the results to the parents and children because, in order to maintain confidentiality, the contact details of the children may not be collected so it is not possible to send out the results at a later stage. The best ways to report back may be to make the results available through the organisation, for example, the kindergarten and also make the results available in a publicly accessible form such as on a web page so that participants and their parents are able to check the results once they have become available.

THE LOCATION OF THE RESEARCH

The location of the research is an important issue: should the researcher go to the children in a home or school setting or should the child come to the researcher? Usability labs offer iterative testing with changes between each test session but the children may not be as comfortable as in the home environment and not as many children can be tested as by testing groups within a school setting. A kindergarten and a school are appropriate environments that children are familiar with and in particular, if they have used a computer in this setting. Conducting research in a school is appropriate if this is the environment for which the software is designed to be used in the longer term. It can be important to use software in situ to test the likelihood of the software being able to be independently used by the target children in the future. Nunan notes, "If one wants to generalize one's findings beyond the laboratory to the real world, then the research should be carried out in the context which resembles those to which the researcher wishes to generalize" (1992: 54).

The three main methods of gathering data are observations, interviews and questionnaires (Hanna, Risden, & Alexander, 1997). One of the advantages with usability testing is that the computer can record some of the data independently such as time on task, response times and selection information, in addition to results of testing. Automated data collection combined with observations is an effective method of collecting data on usability as some duration information may be misinterpreted if only the times are logged.

AGE APPROPRIATE RESEARCH DESIGN

The age of children involved in testing affects the style of testing that is appropriate to gather the required information (Ellis, 2002). Hanna, Risden and Alexander found that "most children younger than 2 ½ years of age are not proficient enough with standard input devices (e.g. mouse, trackball or keyboard) to interact with the technology and provide useful data" (1997: 10). Preschool children should be able to explore the computer independently, however, when conducting usability testing, preschool children require extensive adaptation to software because of their limited attention span. In comparison to pre-schoolers, elementary school children aged 6 – 10 are relatively easy to test. They can sit and follow directions, are not self conscious of being observed and will answer questions and try new things easily. Six and seven year olds like to be engaged in hands-on activities but can be shy (Hanna, et al., 1997). When conducting a literature review on two and three year old children using computers, Ellis and Blashki (2004) discovered that there was little research on this age group as they are difficult to work with and it is hard to recruit significant numbers for research. This does not mean that research on this group is less important. Working with kindergarten children compared with children of primary school age is much more difficult. It is possible for children in their first year of primary school to be shown how to use the software and then work independently. The researcher had to play a much more supportive and time consuming role with kindergarten children but the competency that this age of child can achieve should not be underestimated (Ellis & Blashki, 2007).

DURATION OF THE TESTING

Hanna, Risden et al. (Hanna, et al., 1997) believe that sessions should not exceed one hour of testing time as preschoolers will last thirty minutes and older children will tire in an hour. When conducting user testing with children, it is best to select children who can already use a computer. Read and MacFarlane concur: "Keep it short: Whatever the children are asked to do, make it fit their time

span … For young children, five minutes spent in a written survey is generally long enough, more time can be given, as the children get older" (Read & MacFarlane, 2006). When Ellis (2008) was developing the software for teaching Australian sign language, there were several reasons why the researcher chose to limit sessions to ten minutes, such as the concern that kindergarten children would be cognitively overloaded by longer sessions that were introducing new information. The ten minute sessions worked really well. In addition, children who were highly engaged had the option of completing more than one session at a time. Running multiple ten minute sessions was very time-consuming for the researcher but was considered the most appropriate duration for the age of the children. At the school it was possible to have three children using the software on different computers at the same time. It was not possible to run parallel testing with the kindergarten children as they initially required considerable assistance.

RECRUITMENT OF REPRESENTATIVE CHILDREN

The recruitment of children for research must be considered carefully, as it is quite difficult not to recruit a captive audience through people who are known to the researcher or organisation and who have groups of children of the appropriate age. The samples used for researching children are often self selecting convenience samples (Nunan, 1992). A school and kindergarten that met the criteria for the research and are in the same locality as the researcher are often asked to participate in the research rather than a randomized sample of all potential participants because this type is often not practical. Furthermore, because of the ethics considerations of the universities and government education departments, only subjects whose parents returned the consent forms are able to participate in research, thereby creating a self selecting sample. This sample method creates reasonably small non-probability samples. Nonetheless, as Tanner notes, "Use of a non-probability sample is appropriate when the research does not need to generalize from the sample to the broader population, but merely wishes to gather ideas or gain some insights into a particular phenomenon, for example in a survey pilot test, or for exploratory research" (2000: 73).

Hanna, Risden and Alexander (1997) warn against using colleagues' children for usability testing as they are far more exposed to computers than average children and if they don't like the software, it can create a situation where they feel uncomfortable expressing their true thoughts about the software.

CONCLUSION

Usability testing with children provides insights into the requirements of software developed for children and the way that they interact with the software, however, the design of the testing needs to be carefully considered to take into consideration the special requirements of the children. The ethics committee approval of research on children is a rigorous process that is designed to protect the best interest of the child and to ensure that the parents and children are consenting to participate in research that they are adequately informed about. Careful consideration needs to be given as to the location where the usability testing takes place, the duration of the testing and how the research participants are recruited. The way that the research is conducted and the language used will affect whether children are able to refuse to participate, which is an important right of all research participants. Adequate thought and preparation can ensure that research with children is conducted ethically and provides credible results. Gaining ethics approval and conducting research with children is a very difficult and time consuming process but the results from

the research are important and cannot be collected in any other manner.

REFERENCES

Berk, L. E. (1997). Ethics in Research on Children *Child development* (4th ed., pp. 64-69). Allyn and Bacon.

Burmeister, O. K. (2000). HCI Professionalism: ethical concerns in usability engineering *Usability testing: revisiting informed consent procedures for testing internet sites* (Vol. 1).

Burmeister, O. K. (2001). *Usability Testing: Revisiting Informed Consent Procedures for Testing Internet Sites*. Paper presented at the Proceedings of Australian Institute of Computer Ethics Conference, Canberra, Australia.

Cohen, L., Manion, L., & Morrison, K. (2000). *Research methods in education* (5th ed.). New York: Routledge Falmer.

Commonwealth Government of Australia. (2005). *National Statement on Ethical Conduct in Research Involving Humans*: National Health and Medical Research Council.

Convention of the Rights of the Child. (1989)... *General Assembly Resolution, 44*(25), 1–15.

Druin, A., & Hourcade, J. P. (2005). Interaction design and children: Introduction. *Communications of the ACM, 48*(1), 33–34. doi:10.1145/1039539.1039565

Ellis, K. (2002). *Modelling interface metaphors: developing multimedia for young children*. Monash University, Melbourne.

Ellis, K. (2008). *Tools for inclusive play: multimedia for children learning Australian Sign Language*. Monash University, Melbourne.

Ellis, K., & Blashki, K. (2007). The Digital Playground: Kindergarten Children Learning Sign Language via multimedia. *AACE Journal*, *15*(3), 225–253.

Ellis, K. A., & Blashki, K. M. (2004). Toddler Techies: A Study of Young Children's Interaction with Computers. *Information Technology in Childhood Education Annual*, 77–96.

Field, M. J., & Behrman, R. E. (2004). *Ethical Conduct of Clinical Research Involving Children*. Washington, D.C.: The National Academies Press.

Flewitt, R. (2005). Conduction research with young children: some ethical considerations. *Early Child Development and Care*, *175*(6), 553–565. doi:10.1080/03004430500131338

Greenfield, P. M. (1984). *Mind and media: the effects of television, video games, and computers*. Cambridge, MA.: Harvard University Press.

Hanna, L., Risden, K., & Alexander, K. (1997). Guidelines for usability testing with children. *Interactions (New York, N.Y.)*, *4*(5), 9–12. doi:10.1145/264044.264045

Haslam, S. A., & McGarty, C. (1998). Experimental Design *Doing psychology: an introduction to research methodology and statistics* (pp. 60-91): Sage.

Hedges, H. (2001). A Right to Respect and Reciprocity: Ethics and Educational Research with Children. *NZ Research in ECE*, *4*(1), 1–18.

Johnson, K. (2000). Research Ethics and Children. *Curriculum Perspectives*, (November): 6–7.

Kellehear, A. (1993). Simple Observations *Unobtrusive Researcher: a guide to methods* (pp. 115-138): Allen and Unwin.

McMurray, A., Pace, R. W., & Scott, D. (2004). *Research: a commonsense approach*. Southbank, Vic.: Thomson Learning.

Newman, L., & Pollnitz, L. (2002). *Ethics in action: Introducing the Ethical Response Cycle*. ACT: Australian Early Childhood Association Inc.

Nunan, D. (1992). *Research methods in language learning*. Cambridge, MA: Cambridge University Press.

Plass, J., L. (1998). Design and Evaluation of the User Interface of Foreign Language Multimedia Software: A Cognitive Approach. *Language Learning & Technology*, *2*(1), 35–45.

Quigley, M. (2004). *Cyberporn Panics: Policing Pre/Pubescent Peeping*. Paper presented at the Information Resources Management Association International Conference. Innovations through information technology.

Read, J. C., & MacFarlane, S. (2006, June 7-9). *Using the Fun Toolkit and Other Survey Methods to Gather Opinions in Child Computer Interaction*. Paper presented at the Proceedings of Interaction design for children, Tampere, Finland.

Tanner, K. (2000). Survey Research. In K. Williamson (Ed.), *Research methods for students and professionals: information management and systems* (pp. 71-91). Wagga Wagga, N.S.W.: Centre for Information Studies, Charles Sturt University.

TheBritish Psychological Association: Code of ethics and conduct (2006). Liecester: The British Psychological Association.

Chapter 12
A Generic Framework for Bluetooth Promoted Multimedia on Demand (BlueProMoD)

Panayotis Fouliras
University of Macedonia, Greece

Nikolaos Samaras
University of Macedonia, Greece

ABSTRACT

In recent years many technologies have converged to integrated solutions and one of the hottest topics has been the deployment of wireless personal area networks (WPANs). In this article we present a generic architecture scheme that allows voice and other real-time traffic to be carried over longer distances. The proposed scheme is a novel framework that combines a wired backbone network including Bluetooth access points (APs) with the mobile Bluetooth-enabled devices of the end users. This scheme is called Bluetooth Promoted Multimedia on Demand (BlueProMoD). BlueProMoD is a hybrid network and provides free-of-charge communication among customers, multimedia advertisements, as well as location-based and other value-added services.

INTRODUCTION

The concept of personal area network (PAN) is relatively new. A PAN, basically, is a network that supports the interoperation of devices in personal space (Elliott & Phillips, 2003). In this sense, it is a network solution that enhances our personal environment, either work or private, by networking a variety of personal and wearable devices within the space surrounding a person and providing the communication capabilities within that space and with the outside world (Prasad & Munoz, 2003). A wireless PAN (WPAN) is the natural evolution of this concept, where all participating devices communicate wirelessly. Furthermore, a WPAN is a network that moves with a person, linking all the devices carried by the person with each other, as well as any devices that are met along the way. Since a WPAN has by definition a limited range, compatible devices that are encountered along its path can either link to it or leave it when they go out of its range in a flexible and secure way.

The limited range of a WPAN offers additional advantages such as low-emitted power (thus reducing potential health risks), lower power consumption (hence longer battery life), and lower probability of interference from other WPANs as well as the possibility of location-based services (LBSs). Nevertheless, the core of a WPAN is the wireless technology employed. Nowadays there are many such technologies to choose from. Each one offers specific advantages and disadvantages, which should be taken into consideration before deciding on the most suitable for a particular service or environment.

Of all current wireless technologies Bluetooth is the most promising and employed for many real-life applications. Applications using Bluetooth have become important in hot spots such as at hotels, shopping malls, railway stations, airports, and so forth. Bluetooth is a well-established communications standard for short distance wireless connections. A wide range of peripherals such as printers, personal computers, keyboards, mouse, fax machines, and any other digital device can be part of a Bluetooth network.

Bluetooth has many advantages: (1) low cost, (2) considerable degree of interference-free operation, (3) speed, (4) appropriate range, (5) low power, (6) connectivity, (7) provision for both synchronous and asynchronous links, and (8) wide availability in mobile phones, PDAs, and other devices. Bluetooth is usage-scenario driven, in the sense that its design points were optimized to satisfy established market needs (Bisdikian, 2005). Such usage scenarios are headset to mobile phone connectivity (hands free); mobile device to computer synchronization; digital camera to printer connection for printing; and so forth. More sophisticated applications in diverse areas have been investigated such as hotel services (electronic door locks, check-in/out) in Starwood Hotels and portable patient monitoring in hospitals so that recovering patients are not confined to their rooms (Dursch, Yen, & Shih, 2004). Another interesting application of Bluetooth technology took place at the CeBIT 2001: Guiding services for finding the shortest path to a particular exhibitor in the hall as well as additional exhibitor information services were implemented (Kraemer & Schwander, 2003).

The core of Bluetooth technology is based on the IEEE 802.11 standard and it is a wireless system for short-range communication. This standard defines the protocol for two types of networks; client/server and ad-hoc networks. Bluetooth supports both point-to-point and point-to-multipoint connections. Both Bluetooth and most of IEEE 802.11x share the same 2.4 GHz industrial, scientific and medical, license-free frequency band. Compared with other systems operating in the same frequency band, the Bluetooth radio typically hops faster and uses shorter packets.

In this article we propose a generic architecture scheme that allows voice and other real-time traffic to be carried over longer distances, while simultaneously showing how the providing organization can experience sufficient revenues in order to finance and maintain the necessary infrastructure. The proposed scheme is a novel framework that combines a wired backbone network including Bluetooth access points (APs) with the mobile Bluetooth-enabled devices of the users. The end result is a hybrid network offering free voice and other communication in return for short, specifically targeted multimedia advertisements and tracking information on behalf of the stores or branches operating at a large shopping center or complex. Location-based and other services are also envisaged as a natural side effect. An additional advantage is that the user perceives such capabilities as part of the services offered by his/her respective WPAN.

This article is structured as follows. In the following section we give a detailed overview of the most important technical characteristics of Bluetooth, such as hardware, connectivity, security, error control, interference, and health issues. The proposed generic framework (BlueProMoD) is described next, where we present all the critical components. Finally, conclusions together with future work are presented.

BLUETOOTH DESCRIPTION

In this section we briefly discuss some important characteristics for the Bluetooth technology. The basic form of a Bluetooth network is the piconet. This is a network with a star topology with up to eight nodes participating in a master/slave arrangement (one master and up to seven slaves, see Figure 1a). More specifically, the master is at the center and transmits to the slaves; a slave can only transmit to the master, provided it has been given prior permission by the master. This protocol allows both asynchronous and isochronous services to be realized. The communications channel is defined by a pseudorandom sequence of frequency hops over 79 frequency sub-bands 1 MHz wide, in the 2.4 GHz band, ranging 2.402 - 2.480 GHz. There are three main Bluetooth versions according to the transmission rate (see Table 1).

There are also three classes of antenna power emission and thus possible ranges, namely Class 1 (100 mW, 100 meters), Class 2 (2.5 mW, 10 meters), and Class 3 (1 mW, 1 meter). Typical mobile phones operate at Class 2. Due to the extremely low power emission, investigators agree that Bluetooth products have not been identified as posing any health risks (Erasala & Yen, 2002).

Table 1. The main Bluetooth versions

Transmission rate (gross)	Bluetooth version
1 Mbps	1.0/1.1/1.2
3 Mbps	2.0/2.1 (+ EDR)
480 Mbps	"Seattle" (draft status)

Table 2 presents all the possible modes of a device using Bluetooth technology.

A piconet is created in two stages, the first of which is optional: In the first stage, a device inquires for other devices in its vicinity; if a device responds to the inquiry message it transmits its own Bluetooth address among other information. A Bluetooth address is a unique 48-bit integer derived by the manufacturers from the same address space and authority as the IEEE 802 MAC addresses.

In the second stage, a device (the master) that wants to communicate with another device must perform paging. The paged device (the slave) responds by notifying the paging device that it is ready to communicate with it. In this case the paging device assigns a so-called active member address to the paged device. This is a relative address, which is only of local significance.

In a sense, the limit of seven slave nodes per piconet can be overcome whenever an eighth active node appears: The master takes a node and places it in "park" mode. In this state, the particular node relinquishes its active member address which is given to the newcomer. This feature allows up to 256 nodes to participate in a piconet, but only up to seven slaves to actively exchange data with the master at a time. Communication links may be of two types: *synchronous connection-oriented* (SCO) and *asynchronous connectionless* (ACL). SCO links are typically used for voice communication, whereas ACL links for data. The former are strictly real time, hence lost or damaged packets are never retransmitted over SCO links.

Bluetooth scatternets can also be formed by the connection of two or more piconets. In this case they can have entirely or partially overlapping frequencies, apart from the ongoing communication with their respective members. Evidently one or more nodes must assume the role of a bridge between adjacent piconets (see Figure 1b). As expected, a bridge node operates using the store-and-forward paradigm in order to forward a packet from one piconet to an adjacent one. It

Table 2. Possible modes of a device under Bluetooth

Mode	Description
STANDBY	The device is not connected in a piconet; it listens for messages every 1.28 seconds over 32 hop frequencies.
PAGE/INQUIRY	The master sends 16 identical page messages to the slave in 16 hop frequencies, repeating this process if there is no response from the slave.
ACTIVE	This represents the actual data transmission.
HOLD	The device conserves power by not transmitting any data.
SNIFF	The slave does not take any active role in the piconet, but only listens at a reduced power consumption level; though this level is higher than Hold.
PARK	The slave is synchronized to the piconet, but is not part of the normal traffic.

is possible for a bridge node to be the master in one of the piconets, but in general this is a slave node. Communication is first initiated by the master of the first piconet, which sends a packet to the bridge node where it is stored; whenever the master of the second piconet allows it the bridge node sends the stored packet to the master. Given that the two piconets are not coordinated in any way (in effect the two masters), the overall waiting time at the bridge node during switch over can be quite long. The Bluetooth specification switch-over does not define any particular mechanism, protocol, or algorithm in order to guarantee some minimum time for multi-hop communication in scatternets.

In order to ensure that different hardware implementations are compatible, Bluetooth devices use the host controller interface (HCI) as a common interface between the host and the core. Logical link control and adaptation protocol (L2CAP) is built on top of HCI, which basically segments and reassembles large data packets over Bluetooth baseband connections. Higher level protocols such as service discovery protocol (SDP), RFCOMM (serial port emulation), and telephony control protocol (TCS) are built over L2CAP. Applications are built over them using the services provided. To give the reader some rough background about other aspects of the Bluetooth communication, such as security,

interference, and real-time traffic, we present them briefly next.

Security

A challenge-response mechanism is employed for authentication using Bluetooth address as the public key and a 128-bit integer during device initialization as the private key. In addition, another 128-bit random number is used for each new session. Encryption is also included to maintain link privacy. As a result, devices can be classified as "trusted" and "untrusted," and services as "requiring authorization and authentication," "requiring authentication only," and services open to all devices.

In order to reduce security risks, as well as accelerate device discovery, it has recently been proposed to use limited duration visual tags provided by a central trusted authority for specific devices, so that users can quickly identify the one of interest among many available and connect to it (Scott, Sharp, Madhavapeddy, & Upton, 2005). Nevertheless, security problems have been identified with Bluetooth. In a recent article (Shaked & Wool, 2005) an implementation of a passive attack is described under which a 4-bit PIN can be cracked in less than 0.3 seconds on a Pentium III 450 MHz computer.

Figure 1. Examples of a Bluetooth: (a) piconet, (b) scatternet

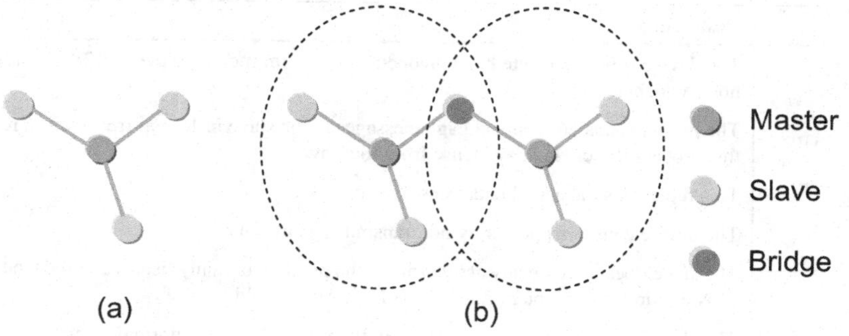

(a)   (b)

Master
Slave
Bridge

Interference

Frequency hopping and the short range of a piconet are the deciding factors for experiencing minimal interference problems under Bluetooth. This minimizes interference not only among Bluetooth devices or piconets, but also interference from other types of devices such as microwave ovens, mobile phones, and baby monitors.

The case of coexistence of Bluetooth with wireless LANs in particular has been studied extensively due to the popularity of IEEE 802.11x devices, which happen to use the same frequency band. Nallanathan, Feng, and Garg (2006) present a complete integrated analysis taking various scenarios into consideration. A Bluetooth piconet in a multi-piconet environment is first examined for all three types of packets (that is, 1-, 3-, and 5-slot packets), concluding that 1-slot packets are the best for high density interference, 3-slot packets for moderate, and 5-slot packets for low density interference (see Figure 2). In the mixed environment of Bluetooth and IEEE 802.11b, the latter suffers more from interfering Bluetooth devices than the other way around; in fact IEEE 802.11b successful reception packet rate increases when Bluetooth uses 5-slot packets.

Real-Time Traffic over Bluetooth

Real-time traffic is of particular importance in present-day networks, since it constitutes a sig-

nificant proportion of user sessions—especially voice due to its limited bandwidth requirements. As noted earlier, Bluetooth supports voice traffic over SCO links by design, using constant bit rate (CBR) at 64 kbps per channel. In order to support this rate and the expected quality of service, a strict timing scheme has to be observed, which may lead to severe deterioration of the asynchronous links performance. Furthermore, only up to three SCO links are supported per piconet.

Given these limitations it is not surprising that researchers tried to calculate the actual SCO link performance. The next step was to use the similar experience from voice-over-IP (VoIP) in order to explore the possibility of using ACL links for voice traffic. In Misic, Misil, and Chan (2005) a detailed analysis is presented under which the presence of a single SCO link reduces the bandwidth available to ACL links to two thirds of the original; with two SCO links, the ACL bandwidth is reduced to half of the original; and with three SCO links the ACL bandwidth is practically zero. The authors evaluated their scheme, which uses multi-slot ACL packets to carry CBR voice traffic, concluding that it is more efficient.

Zeadally and Kumar (2005) used the audio/video distribution transport protocol (AVDTP) specification standard. The results showed that even AVDTP itself can offer 48.2% performance improvement when the optimized version is used over the default version. A more recent study

Figure 2. Example of 3-slot packet from a slave after a 1-slot packet from the master

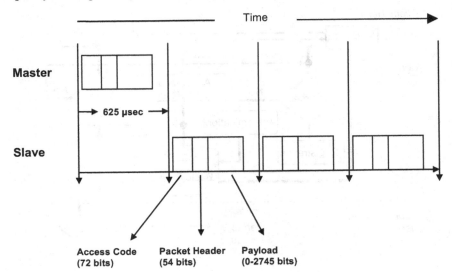

(Razavi, Fleury, Jammeh, & Ghanbari, 2006) considered MPEG-2 (video) traffic coming from an IP network to a Bluetooth master of version 2.0, supporting 2-3 Mbps. Their simulation results lead to similar conclusions. It is, therefore, clear that no complete scheme exists that is able to support simultaneous voice traffic for maximum size pico-nets (that is, all seven slaves carrying voice traffic) over ACL links. Such a scheme would greatly enhance the usefulness of Bluetooth, especially in view of the fact of the high gross data rates of version 2.0 and possibilities of interconnectivity with IP backbone networks.

DESCRIPTION OF THE BlueProMoD GENERIC FRAMEWORK

In this article a framework for the deployment of a novel usage model is presented. The proposed model offers users free of charge voice, location-based, and other services in return for specifically targeted short advertisements on their mobile devices, based on a Bluetooth hybrid network. The whole network environment is run by a single managing authority typically in a large shopping mall or organization (for example, a university campus with short distances between buildings). Revenues to support the system functionality come from the advertisements of participating resellers as well as value-added services, such as the one coming from the post processing of users movement tracking.

The BlueProMoD generic platform requires four types of hardware communicating entities: (1) the server(s), (2) the Bluetooth APs, (3) the interconnection network between the APs and the server, and (4) the Bluetooth-enabled user devices. In its basic form, the user first downloads the client application from specific APs at the reception area. The client application distinguishes BlueProMoD APs from all possible surrounding Bluetooth devices and selects one of them for connection, typically the one with the strongest signal, after proper registration or authentication. From this time onwards the user is able to use all free services offered by the system. The mandatory services provided by all variations of BlueProMoD are: User Reception, SMS, and MMS over Bluetooth, Voice over Bluetooth, Users' Directory, and User's Location. The latter is the foundation upon which LBSs may be built,

Figure 3. BlueProMoD architecture

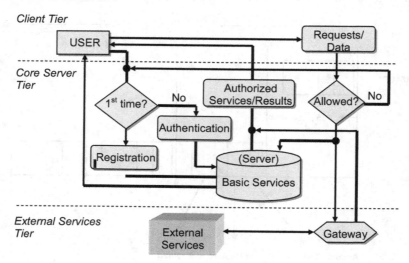

among which route finding and m-advertisements from shops are the most important. The User Reception service is obviously essential since it allows a user to connect to the system.

BlueProMoD is a three-tier architecture, an overall description of which is shown in Figure 3. These are the Client, the Core Server, and the External Services tier.

Client Tier

The client tier is composed of a Bluetooth-capable cell phone or PDA running the appropriate client application, which allows the user to connect to any available Bluetooth AP, offering the Reception Service. The client application is downloaded and installed only at specific reception areas. For this reason first-time users can seek assistance from experienced personnel (for example, at the help desk or information points). At the same time, this arrangement places fewer burdens on the overall system since long or unsuccessful loading efforts are limited to areas that do not need to constantly interact with the rest of the system. The whole process mentioned previously is more secure and reduces user frustration from unsuccessful or long loading times.

After registration and authentication, the user is presented with a list of available services. This step is important since it is the only way that the system can ask personal information from the user and identify him/her every time he/she returns for another visit. Since Bluetooth devices are widespread it is quite natural that many such devices may exist in the same area apart from client devices and Bluetooth APs. In order to improve user satisfaction and reduce client connection time, the client application automatically stores user identification information on his/her device that is made directly or indirectly available (for example, via a signed ticket for higher security) upon request from a Bluetooth AP.

The client application searches for Bluetooth devices offering the Reception Service (hence with a specific UUID). To reduce overall system workload even further, apart from user information, the client application sends a specific ID which indicates to the Bluetooth AP that the sender is a client application. In this way, only clients can connect to Bluetooth APs and only Bluetooth APs can connect to clients.

Typically there are at least four types of clients: (1) administrator, (2) employee, (3) retailer, and

(4) other. The first class is reserved for the system administrators and the second for privileged users who must have more rights than other users (for example, unlimited talking time and no advertisements); retailers who may pay for the system are assigned to the third class with almost the same rights as the second class; ordinary users obviously belong to the final class. There are three basic states at which a user may appear in the system. These states are Ready, Busy, and Disconnected (see Figure 4).

The first state is entered after the user connects to the system; the user remains in this state throughout the connection with the exception of the Busy state. The Busy state is entered when the user is in the middle of a phone call. The last state represents a user who has logged out or disconnected from the system for a specific timeout period. These states are also necessary for the Users' Directory service to be up-to-date. In this way system resources are not wasted unnecessarily (for example, if a user A knows that user B is busy talking, he/she will not try to call him/her for a while unless it is really urgent).

Connection time can be further improved once a client device has connected once and remained in the vicinity of the same Bluetooth AP. The Bluetooth standard allows up to 255 devices to remain in the PARK mode, waiting to "wake up" and become one of the seven slave nodes that are actively communicating with the master. In our case, this implies that the device discovery time

can be eliminated in subsequent communication sessions between the user and the particular Bluetooth AP.

Core Server Tier

The core server tier is composed of the processes involved in order to provide the basic services of BlueProMoD. These processes are: User Reception; short message service (SMS) and multimedia message service (MMS) over Bluetooth; voice over Bluetooth; users' Directory; and user's location. Upon running, the client application first determines the appropriate Bluetooth AP to be connected with. After a network connection is established with the system for the first time, the user is asked several questions in order to be registered with the system. After this is completed, the user logs in to the system and his/her account is updated, reflecting his/her voice credits, IP address, position, and so forth. All these separate actions are performed by the User Reception as the main service that interacts with the Users' Directory and User's Location services. From then onwards, the User Reception service is chiefly responsible for periodically checking whether a user is still connected to the system, since it is possible that he/she disconnects in an abrupt way.

The rest of the services run as processes that mostly sit, passively waiting for an event either from a user (for example calling or being called) or from the external services tier (an advertisement

Figure 4. The three basic states of a user

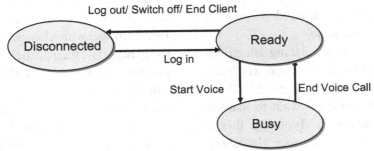

generated by a retailer). Since these services require at least a BlueProMoD server, the Bluetooth APs, and the interconnection network, it is important to turn our attention to these components and their interaction.

Bluetooth APs Placement

Bluetooth APs must be appropriately placed so that there is a complete coverage of the targeted area. In order to reduce unnecessary load as well as annoyance to the users, the APs only recognize and generate connections with client devices that run the particular client application; other Bluetooth devices (for example hands free) as well as other Bluetooth APs cannot interfere since they have a different than expected service ID. This arrangement, however, covers only one of the considerations during the deployment of the APs.

The Bluetooth APs must cover all areas traversed by potential users. Since Class 2 devices have a typical range of 10 meters one could assume that placing APs at approximately 20 meters apart would solve the coverage problem. Unfortunately this is not that simple. If there are many obstacles that absorb part of the signal, more APs are needed, placed at a high point in relation to these obstacles (for example top of shelves). Large areas with no columns in the middle also cause a problem, typically solved by placing APs on the ceiling. Nevertheless the effective range of the particular APs is now reduced. For ceilings that have a height approximately equal or larger than the typical AP range of 10 meters, the straightforward solution is to create appropriate booths at the floor for the APs to be housed, although it is not always possible to do so.

Another consideration in placing Bluetooth APs is the coverage of congested areas. By "congested" we mean areas where there are likely to be more than seven users that want to use the voice service simultaneously. Typically, this is the reception area as well as coffee shops and

any other area where users can sit and relax. A Bluetooth AP without obstacles can cover an area of $\pi R^2 \sim 300 \text{ m}^2$, where only up to seven clients can be active in the respective piconet. Such an area could have as many as 100 users who may wish to place or receive voice calls simultaneously in the worst case. Although they can all be accommodated in the PARK mode, they cannot be active in the same piconet. Obviously all such areas require more Bluetooth APs so that the waiting time for the voice service can be minimized. Other considerations may also prove important, such ease of service and replacement for defective APs, security, and cost.

Interconnection Network

In terms of network infrastructure BlueProMoD requires at minimum a WPAN for each user and Bluetooth AP, as well as a backbone network. Although an IP-wired network can be used for this purpose, different packetization schemes and other problems could tempt designers to opt for a scatternet-based backbone. Considerable research effort has been placed on the development of scatternet and routing schemes to this end. Pabuwal, Jain, and Jain (2003) have developed a complete architectural framework, implementing among others several ad-hoc routing protocols, such as destination sequence distance vector (DSDV), clusterhead switch routing (CGSR), and cluster based routing protocol (CBRP). Although the authors report that they built a complete multimedia application to run over it, no details are given about its performance under different scenarios.

The work in Duggirrala, Ashok, and Agrawal (2003) provides a more detailed scheme called BEAM, under which Bluetooth bridges can effectively negotiate their participation in neighboring piconets. They report that slave piconet nodes are better for the bridge role, as well as that such nodes should be assumed as carrying additional traffic apart from the transit one between neighboring piconets. Although their proposal is interesting it requires Bluetooth manufacturers to incorporate their framework in their products. However, the most important result for our discussion is that bridge nodes can delay traffic significantly since they are slaves and need to use store-and-forward by default.

For this reason as well as the complexity in the formation and routing in scatternets, and security reasons described earlier, we believe that IP-wired networks are better candidates for backbone networks. In addition, such networks offer much higher, interference-free bandwidth at a smaller cost, as well as easier software development, since programming for communicating IP nodes using the sockets API is a de facto standard. The Bluetooth APs must support the PAN profile (the LAN profile is deprecated in Bluetooth v2.0). Typically, L2PCAP is used to establish an ACL connection between a Bluetooth AP and a client device. IP data transfers are facilitated using two possible methods. Under the first (and older) method, IP runs over PPP, which, in turn, runs over RFCOMM. Under the second method, IP runs over BNEP, which offers a layer-2 protocol type similar to Ethernet. Newer and more expensive cell phones support the PAN profile, whereas cheaper and older cell phones support the former method. In all cases, a Bluetooth AP essentially plays the role of a bridging network device between the two different network technologies.

In terms of device connectivity, there are at least two possible paths. Under the first, each Bluetooth AP is an intelligent device, which can directly translate between Bluetooth and IP. In this sense, it can be a dedicated device or a USB dongle connected to a small computer. Unfortunately, the USB standard specifies that the maximum distance from a computer to a full-speed device is 5 USB hubs (at 5 meters each) and an additional 5-meters cable, yielding a total of 30 meters. Obviously, such an arrangement is appropriate only for congested areas in the best case. Vendors, however, have come up with various cost-effective solutions that address this limitation. Some sell USB extenders, which can run reliably at distances of up to 50 meters from the attached computer. Others propose a hybrid approach where Ethernet cables are used to connect suitable USB hubs at 12 Mbps per port; up to five such hubs may be connected to a single computer in a transparent way for existing applications. Such a computer would obviously have to host a proxy ARP, router and—preferably—DHCP servers (depending upon the client connection type/profile) and would connect with the BlueProMoD server. Yet another proposal essentially incorporates a miniature computer at the end of an Ethernet cable with a Bluetooth interface on the other end. In all cases, there are several ways to address the problem of interfacing the Bluetooth APs to the backbone.

The Server

The server is responsible for all of the basic available services as well as other administrative work such as client activity logging and connection to external services. The primary service offered is the reception service which works closely with the users' directory and location services. Client activity logging is also performed on this server, with the relevant data periodically transferred to the External Services tier, so that only recent activity is maintained; older activity is moved out for post processing (for example marketing research). Since BlueProMoD is intended for large organizations, at least two more issues are involved: scalability and reliability.

The server must be able to connect and support all Bluetooth APs. Each Bluetooth AP should not only support its piconet of up to seven active nodes, but also all of the nodes in PARK mode. All these possible user connections are dynamic in nature and could overflow a central DHCP server. Hence, a DHCP server must exist either at each Bluetooth AP, or more preferably on a pool of Bluetooth APs covering neighboring areas. Such a hierarchy reduces the DHCP server load, avoids the single point of failure, and facilitates user roaming as discussed later.

The second issue regarding the BlueProMoD server is reliability of service. Since user authorization/authentication and activity logging takes place at this server, a back-up BlueProMoD server is required. In order for the server transition to take place gracefully, the back-up server must be kept at strict synchronization with the primary. At the same time, for security reasons, no other node can communicate directly with it when the primary server operates normally.

Location-Based Services

LBSs are an emerging technology in wireless telecommunications. One of the most powerful ways to personalize mobile services is based on location. Mobile nodes or even PANs can be combined with a suitable backbone network in order to determine their location and advertise their presence in the overall system. This basic capability has led to the development of numerous services, such as service route finder; access to catalogue data, area guide, and advertisement of goods offered by local retailers; tracking of vehicles and people; or even mobile gaming (Hand, Cardiff, Magee, & Doody, 2006). Some of them are very essential and will be offered by the BlueProMoD.

However, for such services to be effective, the location of the mobile node must be adequately fine grained. For example, an accuracy of 100 meters for route finding in a national highway may be adequate, but is unacceptable in a commercial mall environment. By design, Bluetooth has a typical range of 10 meters (Class 2). However, Bluetooth signal strength is adaptable in the effort to conserve power consumption; a node tries to reduce its signal strength to the minimum required for communication with its peers. Hence, the location accuracy can be further improved if Bluetooth signal strength measurements are taken into account (Peddemors, Lankhorst, & De Heer, 2003). Nevertheless, there are two inherent Bluetooth characteristics that must be taken into

account: First, the link quality is relative since it is measured in a manufacturer-specific way. Second, Bluetooth device discovery is typically performed at regular intervals of 20 seconds; this can be a problem in the case of a fast moving node. In the case of a pedestrian walking in a large building complex such as a shopping center, hotel, hospital, or university, however, the previous characteristics do not represent a major problem.

External Services Tier

This is composed of one or more servers, external to the basic BlueProMoD, offering all the non-basic services of BlueProMoD, as well as a DBMS for the advertisements, accounting and Internet services. For example, under a certain variant of BlueProMoD it is possible for some clients to be offered VoIP over Bluetooth, in order to call any telephone outside the area supported directly by BlueProMoD. Nevertheless, the advertisements (announcements in the case of universities or other nonprofit organizations) through targeted MMSs and LBS such as route finding remain some of the most important services, since they represent a significant portion of the system revenues. These should be sent sparingly to the appropriate target user groups to have maximum effect. For example, sending an advertisement for children shoes to a single man is different from advertising a popular children's toy to a mother in her early 30s just before Christmas.

Apart from the marketing issues, which are outside the scope of this article, there are several technical issues involved that belong in this tier. Free voice calls and MMS are expected to be the main attraction of the system, apart from route or goods finding. Instead of creating multiple versions of Web pages to be displayed on various device classes (for example, cell phones, PDAs, portables, info-kiosks, etc.), the content creator could follow certain guidelines to prepare a single version; upon request, the particular Web page could then be sent to a gateway, which would translate it to the appropriate format before sending it to the requesting user. This gateway also plays the role of a buffer between the core server and external services tier (see Figure 3).

Handover

An important part of the system functionality is the handover mechanism, when a client moves from one Bluetooth AP to another. When a user uses his/her cell phone for voice communication, he/she is used to speaking while moving at a normal walking speed; hence, he/she expects to receive an unbroken voice communication service. One of the major limitations of the Bluetooth standard is that it does not provide any mechanism for managing micro-mobility. In Kraemer and Schwander (2003), the inquiry procedure for the determination of the locations of user mobile devices and the connection to the nearest AP was measured to be up to 5 seconds. Furthermore, it is possible for a user that remains stationary to lose his/her connection to the respective Bluetooth AP for a short period of time. What happens when the user tries to reconnect? If he/she is in the middle of a voice call, reconnects, and his/her device assumes a different IP it appears as if the user lost the previous session.

The solution to the latter problem is relatively straightforward taking into account a particular feature of DHCP. More specifically, a client that has recently acquired an IP address can reconnect asking to be assigned the same IP address. If this IP address has not been assigned to anyone else, it is possible for the DHCP server to grant such a request. In our case, let us assume that the IP address space is large enough and each new connection is granted one of the not recently used IP addresses; there is a good chance then that a recently disconnected client will be granted the old IP address. This approach works well and places minimum burden on the network and the DHCP server. Furthermore, users in PARK mode at the same Bluetooth AP appear connected

constantly with the same IP address initially assigned to them.

Such an approach also works for roaming users if a DHCP server is responsible for a pool of neighboring Bluetooth APs. Such users typically walk at a slow pace when they talk and tend to remain in the same general area. Hence, the only disruption will be short and depend almost entirely on the adopted Bluetooth hand-off mechanism. In this way more complex forms of addressing the roaming user problem (for example mobile IP) are avoided. Voice over Bluetooth is the only form of user communication requiring special consideration; all other forms of communication are nothing but a series of short TCP/UDP transactions not significantly affected by any change in the IP address of communicating parties. Finally, communications among users is only allowed on a user-to-user basis, so that malicious users cannot easily overload the system.

CONCLUSION

Bluetooth consists of the most promising and well-established wireless technology for a vast number of applications. In this article we have presented a generic framework, called BlueProMoD, based on Bluetooth technology. The main aim of the proposed framework is to support large commercial enterprises (or organizations) at the retail level. BlueProMoD uses all the advantages of Bluetooth in order to provide free-of-charge communication and other services to simple users in return for limited and centrally controlled advertisements from the local retailers, who will have to pay for the system (hence promote it). However, user activity logging is envisaged as the main source of revenue, since valuable marketing information may be extracted from it. The advantages of deploying and supporting the BlueProMoD-based system are straightforward, which combined with its cost effectiveness make it an important tool in such environments.

A future work is to build a prototype as well as conduct extensive simulations in order to determine specific costs and technical profiles that will demonstrate these advantages quantitatively.

REFERENCES

Bisdikian, C. (2005). A framework for building Bluetooth scatternets: A system design approach. *Pervasive and Mobile Computing, 1,* 190-212.

Duggirrala, R., Ashok, R. L., & Agrawal, D. P. (2003). BEAM: A framework for bridge negotiation in Bluetooth scatternets. In *12th ICCCN Conference* (pp. 339-344).

Dursch, A., Yen, D. C., & Shih, D. (2004). Bluetooth technology: An exploratory study of the analysis and implementation frameworks. *Computer Standards & Interfaces, 26,* 263-277.

Elliott, G., & Phillips, N. (2003). *Mobile commerce and wireless computing systems.* Addison-Wesley.

Erasala, N., & Yen, D. C. (2002). Bluetooth technology: A strategic analysis of its role in 3G wireless communication era. *Computer Standards & Interfaces, 24,* 193-206.

Hand, A., Cardiff, J., Magee, P., & Doody, J. (2006). An architecture and development methodology for location-based services. *Elsevier Electronic Commerce Research and Applications, 5,* 201-208.

Kraemer, R., & Schwander, P. (2003). Bluetooth based wireless Internet applications for indoor hot spots: Experience of a successful experiment during CeBIT 2001. *Computer Networks, 41,* 303-312.

Misic, J., Misil, V. B., & Chan, K. L. (2005). Talk and let talk: Performance of Bluetooth piconets with synchronous traffic. *Ad Hoc Networks, 3,* 451-477.

Nallanathan, A., Feng, W., & Garg, H. K. (2006). Coexistence of wireless LANs and Bluetooth networks in mutual interference environment: An integrated analysis. *Computer Communications, 30,* 192-201.

Pabuwal, N., Jain, N., & Jain, B. N. (2003). An architectural framework to deploy scatternet-based applications over Bluetooth. *IEEE International Conference on Communications, 2,* 1019-1023.

Peddemors, A. J. H., Lankhorst, M. M., & De Heer, J. (2003). Presence, location and instant messaging in a context-aware application framework. In *4th International Conference on Mobile Data Management* (LNCS 2574, pp. 325-330). Springer.

Prasad, R., & Munoz, L. (2003). WLANs and WPANs towards 4G wireless. *Artech House.*

Razavi, R., Fleury, M., Jammeh, E. A., & Ghanbari, M. (2006). An efficient packetization for Bluetooth video transmission. *Electronic Letters, 42*(20), 1143-1145.

Scott, D., Sharp, R., Madhavapeddy, A., & Upton, E. (2005). Using visual tags to bypass Bluetooth device discovery. *ACM Mobile Computing and Communications Review, 9*(1), 41-53.

Shaked, Y., & Wool, A. (2005). Cracking the Bluetooth PIN. In *3rd International Conference on Mobile Systems, Applications and Services* (pp. 39-50).

Zeadally, S., & Kumar, A. (2005). Design, implementation, and evaluation of the audio/video distribution transport protocol (AVDTP) for high quality audio support over Bluetooth. *Computer Communications, 28,* 215-223.

This work was previously published in the Journal of Information Technology Research, Vol. 1, Issue 1, edited by M. Khosrow-Pour, pp. 1-13, copyright 2008 by IGI Publishing (an imprint of IGI Global).

Chapter 13
Social Interaction with a Conversational Agent:
An Exploratory Study

Yun-Ke Chang
Nanyang Technological University, Singapore

Miguel A. Morales-Arroyo
Nanyang Technological University, Singapore

Mark Chavez
Nanyang Technological University, Singapore

Jaime Jimenez-Guzman
National University of Mexico, Mexico

ABSTRACT

Conversational agents that display many human qualities have become a valuable method business uses to communicate with online users to supply services or products, to help in online order process or to search the Web. The gaming industry and education may benefit from this type of interface. In this type of chats, users could have different alternatives: text display, photo of a real person, or a cartoon drawing and others. This is an exploratory study that reviews five randomly chosen conversations that an animated chatbot with Web users. The character simulates human gestures, but they are stylized to reproduce animation standards. The goal of this exploratory study is to provide feedback that will help designers to improve the functionality of the conversational agent, identify user's needs, define future research, and learn from previous errors. The methodology used was qualitative content analysis.

INTRODUCTION

For today's online business whether selling a service or a product, the main goal of Web sites is to keep its users at the site as long as possible. As an interface, a conversational agent has to offer some features to maintain audience interest. Concerns about agents' body design and personal sociability have become obvious. Users may favor an interface that suits their own personality. They also may be more predisposed to an animated exchange with an agent if the character's voice matches content tone with gesture that complements the context.

Animation synthesis procedure allows the creation of dynamic Web-based agents through numerous randomly interconnected cycles. Nadia (http://CLONE3D.net), a conversational chatbot, was developed by the third author, and it is a human like agent able to perform dialogues with users by "comprehending," generating phonemes with automatic lip-sync, and expressing body language, including body movements, hand actions, and facial gestures. The lighting of the virtual agent is practically naturalistic and uses conventional illumination techniques (see Figure 1).

The design of conversational agents has to face a set of challenges: promoting trusting relationships with their audience (Cassell & Bickmore, 2003), body language, matching ability to communicate in different languages, and adapting to different cultural contexts (Cassell & Bickmore, 2000). An intelligent real-time 3D artificial agent unlocks additional opportunities for computer mediated communication. The facial expressions in the agent are critical in a dialog and could be used with hearing-impairment audiences (Massaro, Cohen, Beskow, Daniel, & Cole, 2001). The goal of this exploratory study is to provide feedback that will help designers to improve the functionality of the conversational agent, identify user's needs, define future research, and learn from previous errors.

RELATED STUDIES

Constantly, there are new applications for conversational agents. One example is a virtual announcer who can read RSS feeds (Anonymous, 2005). Although, their comprehension of natural language is rather restricted, chatbots usually could respond to simple questions (Anonymous, 2007). Some companions assist the deprived sectors of the population, such as the elderly, by interacting on the Internet on their behalf (Wilks, 2005). Other companies have been utilizing Chatbots to offer customer support online via typed interactions. Conversational agents also have been developed to be counselors for helping to eliminate smoking habit (Mourik, 2006).

Many embodied conversational agents have specific areas of knowledge such as real estate (Cassell, 2000). One Chatbot has been developed to identify pedophiles in chat rooms (Graham-Rowe, 2004). Many cell phone applications are available: concierge services like news, horoscopes, weather, the nearest restaurant, and sports, and virtual teacher (Schwartz, 2005). Moreover, there have been several educational applications: helping develop competencies in inquiry, analysis and synthesis (Graesser, McNamara, & VanLehn, 2005); language tutoring for children with hearing loss (Massaro et al., 2001); and teaching to write and read (Ryokai, Vaucelle, & Cassell, 2003).

Figure 1. Nadia - A virtual character

Promoting physical fitness is another application for these agents (Anonymous, 2004).

Interpersonal communication is a complex phenomenon that occurs in a specific context. Littlejohn (1983) suggested five conditions must exist. First, there must be two or more people in close immediacy who can sense the presence of each other. Second, there is interdependence in which the interaction is affected by one another. Third, there should be exchange of messages. The forth one is concern with the coding of messages in two different channels: verbal and non-verbal, and the last one is establishing the exchange with two features: flexibility and informality (Littlejohn, 1983).

The conversation with a chatbot is an emulation of interpersonal communication. Researchers have been addressing some of the conditions needed in the interaction between the agents and people. In a field study, presence was investigated as the first condition. The results of the study indicate even limited copresence, the degree to which a user judges she is not alone and isolated, supplied by a prototype agent is satisfactory to facilitate users to experience presence. Perception of sensory stimuli and the understanding of symbols are ways to sense the others' presence. In this case, presence is closely related to immersion (Gerhard, 2005).

Interdependence has been conceptualized as synchronization process, initiation, turn-taking, feedback, and breaking away (Cassell, 2000). The exchange of messages has been addressed in different way: creating specific domain knowledge and creating models that facilitate the communicative interchange, such as discourse recipe-based model (DRM). This model uses both discourse recipes and reasoning in the context pilot communication. Discourse recipes exploit agents' experience by encoding recurring dialogue structures (Green & Lehman, 2002).

One of the main concerns in the design of conversational agents has been to make the exchange as human as possible. The coding of messages for conversational agents has been done using speech recognition, speech synthesis, understanding natural language, and text-to-speech technology. Social cues like the face and voice of the agent motivate this interpretation that the conversation exchanged with the agent is similar to one with humans (Louwerse & Graesser, 2005). Nonverbal attributes have been studied and included in the agents, such as nod and glance (Cassell, 2000; Cassell & Thórisson, 1999), and emotional feedback—emotional expressions by geometrical intensity in the agent's face (Bartneck, 2005).

Some issues occuring during the interaction with a conversational agent are unique, such as stress and voice intonation (Massaro, et al., 2001), which in interpersonal communication will only be an issue between native speakers and non-native ones. However, if conversational agents become more sophisticated, the question in mind of researchers will be who is legally responsible for giving a wrong answer.

Some negative attitudes and mistreatment against robots has been reported based on different cultures (Bartneck, Suzuki, T., Kanda, T., Nomura, 2007). Particularly in the case of conversational agents, negative reactions also have been reported (De Angeli, 2001), which include verbal abuse (De Angeli, 2005).

DESIGN

Actions of the character, Nadia, are conceived to replicate human gestures, but behaviors are stylized to replicate animation standards. This design style builds a friendly Web environment with Web audience. The character employs AIML, Artificial Intelligence Markup Language, the Generation 4 Player, and Automated Personality Tool Set. Generation 4 is a player that simulates fluid full-body movement, mass and reactive actions, body tissue, gravity, and realistic physical responsiveness. The principles that guide the general design come from Lee and Lacey (2003).

The character is shaped with high production attributes in mind. Physical features including an inner mouth with teeth and tongue, accurate fingers with fingernails, and eyes are included in the model. The character also has over 50 facial points assembled into her expression database. These points are utilized to produce both a set of visemes, a basic unit of speech in the visual domain, to match phonemes for accurate lip-sync, other vocalizations, and present emotional changes in the facial expressions. Nadia's body features were developed for users' interest. The figure and components of the character's face and body are overstated to follow standards employed in caricature projects. For Nadia, the design target is to create an appealing, smart, young, female character, which is a standard method used in the development of female characters for broader appeal. To compliment the physical design, the personality is provided by ALICE bot, and its knowledge base was modified to answer with jokes by a process of trail and error.

TECHNICAL ENVIRONMENT

Haptek supplies a 3D player that is mostly employed to produce the character's movement. This technology can connect the model to a skeleton and provide methods for correcting volume problems that appear when the character's extremities are in action. However, Haptek does not have a simple approach to improve the model and re-skin the geometry to the skeleton. It has a pipeline for importing motion captured from the current skeleton, but in our case its export tool did not export it. The bone framework was used to have an easy method to incorporate skinning techniques. The Haptek player's toolset is hampered by its incapacity to supply the correct adjustments for the characters body, its poses, and mass volumes.

Currently the ALICE, an open source chatbot technology used for the verbal/text based responses, is limited by the amount of content that the knowledge base has. The knowledge base can be quite large and needs to address the questions and issues the user would have to develop an interesting character. ALICE knowledge base was modified to provide jokes to users by trial and error.

PROJECT GOALS

The primary objective was to develop a project called Artificial Comedy. A number of other characters are to be developed with the goal of building a set of performers: actors, singers, comedians, and other entertaining characters. Each one would have their own environment and friends. These environments would become part of a collection of bizarre expressions and comical performances of representative characters and circumstances. Exploring the exchanges these avatars have with online users will help in fine tuning their design.

Figure 2. Visitors' domains

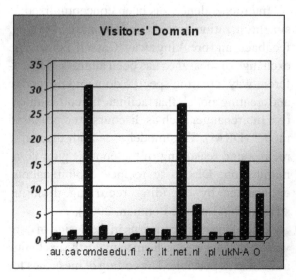

RESEARCH DESIGN

Visitors

Authors could not identify who specific visitors were or population demographics, but from the server statistics some information was retrieved, such as top referring sites, visitor's country, and queries visitors utilized to search.

According to the server statistics visitors who have requested files had come from these domains as shown in Figure 2. N-A means not identifiable numerical addresses, and O means others. The words people used in search engines to find the site in the last seven days are shown in Figure 3.

METHODOLOGY

The dialogues between the chatbot and the online users were recorded in a log file. Five dialogs were chosen randomly; some of them were more than two hours long, and all of them were more than one hour long. Chats took place from June 1 to June 19 from a set of more than 170 dialogues. Qualitative content analysis was used to analyze the data, utilizing QSR N6, previously known as Nudist. The categories were created in an inductive process, common in content analysis methodologies. These categories were examined by three authors, each one initially working independently, and later coming together to get a consensus. The inter-code reliability was measured. These categories were developed from the conversational agent's perspective, for example, how it supplied information and helped its visitors, how well it "comprehended" visitors' contributions, how it managed imprecise input, and so on.

RESULTS

Topics Addressed in Dialogs by Visitors

One user had an illogical conversation with correct grammar in general terms and no spelling

Figure 3. Keywords employed by the users to find the site

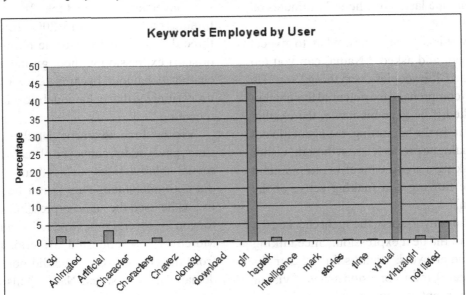

mistakes. Other asked for obscene expressions and jokes, and another required affectionate conduct from the chatbot.

One user tested the factual knowledge the agent posses and focused his questions on literature. He asked about who Mark Twain was, who wrote Tom Sawyer and his nickname, Philip K. Dick, a science fiction writer, and other questions. The same user tested the agent's analytic aptitude in Mathematics: the ability to solve equations, the Riemann hypothesis, and the demonstration of last Fermat's theorem.

Three visitors were trying to persuade the chatbot to engage in some sort of virtual sex. Two of them were interested in movies; one of them in science-fiction pictures, like Star Trek, Star Wars, and Matrix, and the other one wanted to know where to download free sex movies and movies in general. Two users showed great interest in the conversational agent competence, and one of them was interested in its potential.

Description of Dialogs

A dialog that had sessions as long as 43 hours may not imply the dialog was that lengthy. In addition to chatting with Nadia, visitors did other things. Conversation one lasted one hour 22 minutes on June 19, 2006.

Probably, visitor one knew what to expect from a chatbot and asked: "Nadia, can you tell me why Eliza Clone copies everything I say" He attempted to comprehend the potential this chatbot has, and asked if he gave his name, the chatbot could recall it. In the beginning, the agent did not follow the dialogue properly; even though, visitor one was making a significant effort to maintain the dialogue flowing and making sense of the conversation.

During the conversation, the agent checked the initial word of the next expression: "nice talking with you" and answers, "thanks for the compliment." It creates the impression when a visitor provides congruent responses, the agent is more proactive, and looks like the agent is following the conversation.

Visitor one handled the agent courteously as he was interacting with another person; in addition, the interaction was very positive. This user was interested in the agent's level of intelligence and its learning capacity. He explained different issues, tried to reason, talked about movies, and asked the agent for help to find a game that was only sold in Japan. This user made a big attempt to maintain the agent in track with the conversation, but the lack of contextual knowledge and knowledge in general limited the conversation. He had some misspellings, but his behavior was very polite.

Dialogue two took one hour 22 minutes on June 1, 2006. The conversation was trivial, but the interaction was intense. For example, Nadia said "Excuse me! You are a really tedious dope." Only a few interactions have continuity, and the dialogue was chopped and repetitive. There was no proper beginning and end, with some incorrect sentences, misspellings, and insults from the users. Probably, visitor two was a chatbot. The dialogue was full of non-sense, but in a way it is appealing and amusing to observe how two chatbots interact with each other.

Conversation three took 21 hours and 40 minutes on June 14 and 15, 2006. Initially, visitor three did not make sense. He used single word or short expression without giving context. The chatbot behaviour became reiterative, and this user criticized that behaviour by exclaiming "stop repeating."

Visitor three also articulated sexual expressions, gave orders, conveyed obscenity, and wrote sexual abbreviations such as "omfg" that Nadia did not understand. This visitor became repetitive as he used the same expression—"one point for you"—several times and twice consecutively. Moreover, he requested affectionate conduct from the chatbot. When he did not get what he demanded, he insulted Nadia. This dialogue in general was not interesting because of the number of single words written by the visitor, and his involvement was limited in most part of the conversation.

Dialog four lasted 43 hours and 42 minutes from June 1 to June 3, 2006. Visitor four had belligerent actions, attacking the agent for not being sharp enough and did not fulfill his request for virtual sex. His language was contradictory; he was curious in the bot's analytical capabilities, intelligence, and its potential as information agent.

Dialogue five took 38 hours and 30 minutes from June 11 to June 12, 2006. Visitor five was basically motivated in one topic, virtual sex, including coarse language. He used diverse tactics to accomplish his objective. Frequently, when he failed, he abused the chatbot. The tactics he used were the followings: asking to perform some actions in his subject of interest, coercion, adulation, argumentations, and so on.

Categories Developed

The categories arose from the agent perspective, its specific behaviors and answers during its dialogs, while the sample of users is not necessarily representative of the population. The creation of these categories follows an inductive process of typical content analysis. Each author did the analysis independently, met, and achieved consensus over the final categories. The categories developed were the followings:

- **Ambiguous input:** answers to short expression without context;

- **Bot talking:** agent talking like machine;
- **Complements:** answering and providing complements;
- **Greeting & bye:** welcoming and saying good bye;
- **Help:** providing information and suggestions offered by the agent;
- **Insults:** answering insults;
- **Intelligence & knowledge:** factual knowledge and pseudo-analytical abilities;
- **Jokes:** agent humor;
- **Leading comments:** agent's answers guide the user to some topics;
- **Memory:** "remembering" information provided by the user;
- **Miscommunication:** failure to communicate clearly;
- **Personal issues:** exchange of personal information;
- **Proactive behavior:** learning possibilities;
- **Repetitive behavior:** recurring answers; and
- **Technical problems:** technical difficulties the user confronts.

Inter-coder reliability was computed with four variables (see Table 1): Technical problems (V1), Repetitive behavior (V2), Intelligence and knowledge (V3), and Miscommunication (V4). In order to calculate the reliability indices, 30 units were selected randomly. These variables were chosen because each one of them had more than 30 units for analysis.

Table 1. Reliability indices

Reliability Indices	V1	V2	V3	V4
Percent Agreement	0.733	0.833	0.867	0.833
Scott's Pi	0.4	0.657	0.732	0.666
Cohen's Kappa	0.4	0.658	0.732	0.667
Cohen's Kappa - SPSS	0.4	0.658	0.732	0.667

Inter-Coder Reliability

Inter-coder reliability was calculated using two computer programs: Program for Reliability Assessment with Multiple Coders (PRAM) in alpha testing mode version 0.4.5. from "Skymeg Software" and SPSS 14. With PRAM, the following reliability indices were computed: percentage of agreement, Scott's Pi, and Cohen's Kappa. Cohen's Kappa calculated by PRAM was corroborated using SPSS 14. In the Content Analysis literature, there is no agreement about which index is the best (Craig, 1981; Hsu & Field, 2003; Hughes & Garrett, 1990; Krippendorff, 2004). In our case, there is no great difference between Scott's Pi and Cohen's Kappa when computed by PRAM 0.4.5. and no difference in the two Cohen's Kappa calculated by the two different computer programs (see Table 1).

The percent agreement is not accepted as reliability index because it does not consider random effects. In this case, it is presented as a reference point. In the literature, there is no accepted interpretation of the kappa index values (Altman, 1991; Streiner & Norman 1995). However, Streiner suggests that a Kappa Index agreement less than 0.4 is poor, from 0.40 to 0.59 is fair, from 0.6 to 0.74 is good, and more than 0.74 is excellent. For Altman, a Kappa Index agreement less than 0.2 is poor, from 0.20 to 0.40 is fair, from 0.40 to 0.60 is moderate, from 0.60 to 0.80 is good, and from 0.80 to 1.00 is very good agreement.

Technical problems have the lowest index among the four variables in all reliability indices. One possible explanation is that the categories developed may not be mutually exclusive. Consequently, repetition and failure to respond specific domain questions sometimes were the result of Technical problems. The rest of the variables have index values ranged from acceptable to good agreement.

DISCUSSION

Some operational troubles in the agent are interconnected. When a user is ambiguous, the agent becomes "confused." It does not have explicit context to maintain an articulated dialog. A dialog needs at least two parties, but the user may not intend to participate in the social exchange. The chatbot can be proactive, offer help and suggestions, and make remarks that may direct the conversation into topics in which it has its main assets. For example, when a user protested about technical troubles, the chatbot offered some recommendations. When the user asked for information, the chatbot told them to do any of the following: to check the open directory, answers. com, or to send an email. Although this is an adequate alternative, due to the limited amount of programmed answers, sometimes the chatbot sounds reiterative.

Some users deplored the chatbot's lack of functions and repetitive answers. These issues could be solved by providing the agent with a variety of answers, employing the contextual information provided by the user, and improving and handling agent memory. For example, one visitor provided his name previously, but the agent did not have it at hand. The dialog was the following:

Nadia: My name is Nadia. What is yours?
User: You know it, i've already told you.
Nadia: No, tell me about him, her or it.
User: Try to remember
Nadia: OK I will try to remember.
User: What is my name?
Nadia: Your name is Jorkens, seeker.
User: Well done.

Lack of conversation flow and miscommunication were frequently observed, but not always due to agent problems. Sometimes, the users were distracted. Users became perplexed when the chatbot repeated phrases, provided wrong answers, or did not follow the dialogue sequence.

In general, the chatbot is polite, and it can compliment users. At the same time, it is able to receive compliments graciously, but sometimes it answers with similar phrases, which could make the communication tedious. It is capable of responding some offences, but not all of them. The chatbot presents a dual behaviour, sometimes it expresses clearly that it a conversational agent to the user, but not always. One of the most critical difficulties that users described in the dialogues was the agent voice. At that time in some conversations, not only the voice appeared unnatural, but also not as woman speech. This problem was solved, but it generated some confusion in the users.

CONCLUSION

From this research, the authors found out that users in these conversations did not employ the chatbot for humorous purposes. Some of the jokes the agent can tell may not be adequate for some users, and we will have to find what type of jokes visitors would like to hear. The opening and the end of a dialog are very important. In the beginning, the chatbot, besides providing its name to the visitor, may provide a presentation about what it is and is capable to do. In that sense, visitors will not have expectations that the conversational agent is not able to perform. Among the areas for improvement are having a better welcoming segment, more diverse answers, and reducing the length of the goodbye segment when the visitor provide clues that he has to abandon the dialog. Although miscommunication cannot be prevented, it may be decreased if the conversational agent becomes more proactive and has better logs. The latent technical troubles should be recognized, and the possible answers to frequent technical questions should be part of the assistance the chatbot provides to its visitors.

ACKNOWLEDGMENT

We would like to thank the anonymous reviewers for their work, suggestions, and opinions.

REFERENCES

Altman, D. G. (1991). *Practical statistics for medical research*. London: Chapman & Hall.

Anonymous. (2004). Managing long-term relationships with Laura. *Communication of the ACM, 47*(4), 42.

Anonymous. (2005). Briefly noted. *Computerworld, 39*(20), 14.

Anonymous. (2007). Call and response. *Economist, 382*(8519), 8-9.

Bartneck, C. (2005). Subtle emotional expressions of synthetic characters. *International Journal of Human-Computer Studies, 62*(2), 179-192.

Bartneck, C., Suzuki, T., Kanda, T., & Nomura, T. (2007). The influence of people's culture and prior experiences with Aibo on their attitude towards robots. *AI & Society, 21*(2), 217-230.

Cassell, J. (2000). Embodied conversational interface agents. *Communications of the ACM, 43*(4), 70-78.

Cassell, J., & Bickmore, T. (2000). External manifestations of trustworthiness in the interface. *Communications of the ACM, 43*(12), 50-57.

Cassell, J., & Bickmore, T. (2003). Negotiated collusion: Modeling social language and its relationship effects in intelligent agents. *User Modeling and User - Adapted Interaction, 13*(1), 89-132.

Cassell, J., & Thórisson, K. R. (1999). The power of a nod and a glance: Envelope vs. emotional feedback in animated conversational agents. *Applied Artificial Intelligence, 13,* 519-538.

Craig, R. T. (1981). Generalization of Scott's index of intercoder agreement. *Public Opinion Quarterly, 45*(2), 260-264.

De Angeli, A., & Carpenter, R. (2005). Stupid computer! Abuse and social identities. *Proceeding of Abuse: The dark side of Human-Computer Interaction: An INTERACT 2005 workshop.* Rome, September 12, 2005, pp 19-25.

De Angeli, A., Johnson, G.I., & Coventry, L. (2001). The unfriendly user: Exploring social reactions to chatterbots. Proceedings of International Conference on Affective Human Factor Design, Singapore, June 27-29, 2001, pp 467-474. London: Asean Academic Press.

Gerhard, M., Moore, D., & Hobbs, D. (2005). Close encounters of the virtual kind: Agents simulating copresence. *Applied Artificial Intelligence, 19*(4), 393-412.

Graesser, A. C., McNamara, D. S., & VanLehn, K. (2005). Scaffolding deep comprehension strategies through Point&Query, AutoTutor, and iSTART. *Educational Psychologist, 40*(4), 225–234.

Graham-Rowe, D. (2004). Software agent targets chatroom pedophiles. *New Scientist, 181*(2439), 225–234.

Green, N., & Lehman, J. F. (2002). An integrated discourse recipe-based model for task-oriented dialogue. *Discourse Processes, 33*(2), 133–158.

Hsu, L. M., & Field, R. (2003). Interrater agreement measures: Comments on Kappan, Cohen's Kappa, Scott's it, and Aickin's α. *Understanding Statistics, 2*(3), 205-219.

Hughes, M. A., & Garrett, D. E. (1990). Intercoder reliability estimation approaches in marketing: A generalizability theory framework for quantitative data. *Journal of Marketing Research, 27*(2), 185-195.

Krippendorff, K. (2004). Reliability in content analysis: Some common misconceptions and recommendations. *Human Communication Research, 30*(3), 411-433.

Lee, M. H., & Lacey, N. J. (2003). The influence of epistemology on the design of artificial agents. *Minds and Machines, 13,* 367-395.

Littlejohn, S. W. (1983). *Theories of human communication (*2nd ed.). Belmont, CA : Wadsworth Pub. Co.

Louwerse, M. M., Graesser, A. C., Lu, S., & Mitchell, H. H. (2005). Social cues in animated conversational agents. *Applied Cognitive Psychology, 19,* 693-704.

Massaro, D. W., Cohen, M. M., Beskow, J., Daniel, S., & Cole, R. A. (2001). Developing and evaluating conversational agents. In J. Cassell, J. Sullivan, S. Prevost, & E. Churchill (Eds.), *Embodied conversational agents* (pp. 287-318). Boston: MIT Press.

Mourik, O. V. (2006). Can't quit? Go online. *Psychology Today, 39*(5), 27-28.

Ryokai, K., Vaucelle, C., & Cassell, J. (2003). Virtual peers as partners in storytelling and literacy learning. *Journal of Computer Assisted Learning, 19,* 195-208.

Schwartz, E. (2005). Flash apps for phones. *InfoWorld, 27*(20), 21.

Streiner, D. L., & Norman, G. R. (1995). *Health measurement scales: A practical guide to their development and use* (2nd ed.). Oxford: Oxford University Press.

Wilks, Y. (2005). Artificial companions. *Interdisciplinary Science Reviews, 30*(2), 145-152.

This work was previously published in the Journal of Information Technology Research, Vol. 1, Issue 3, edited by M. Khosrow-Pour, pp. 14-26, copyright 2008 by IGI Publishing (an imprint of IGI Global).

Chapter 14
Voice–Based Approach for Surmounting Spatial and Temporal Separations

Kate O'Toole
GreenSun and Kastle Data Systems, USA

Srividhya Subramanian
University of Arizona, USA

Nathan Denny
University of Arizona, USA

ABSTRACT

This article describes a new voice-based tool for global collaboration. This tool, called EchoEdit, attempts to provide multimedia capabilities to program source code editing for the purpose of eliciting in situ vocal commentary from active developers.

INTRODUCTION

Global teams are becoming a growing reality. When teams are distributed, individuals lose the ability to walk down the hall and ask their other team members a question. When team members are distributed but work in similar time zones, they possess the ability to pick up the phone and call their peers. When the teams are distributed both temporally and spatially, team members lose these forms of immediate feedback, and different methodologies are needed to surmount the time and space separations that many global teams experience.

One way to distribute a team is by breaking the project down into different modules (e.g., site A is responsible for module A while site B is responsible for module B). In this situation, the two teams need to agree on an interface, but further interaction is limited. Another way for distributed teams to interact is in a master-slave type relationship; in this case, one team may do the design work and a second team may do the testing. In this scenario, one site is telling the other site what to do and has more authority. A third way for distributed teams to interact is in what is known as the "24-Hour Knowledge Factory" (24HrKF) (Denny, Mani, et al., in press).

One way to reduce the confusion that may be caused when multiple people share the same piece of code is to increase the documentation and explain how the decisions were made. This article focuses on the use of voice recognition software for this purpose.

EMBEDDED PROGRAM DOCUMENTATION

Most programming languages have a built-in feature that allow programmers to make notes on what the code is doing and how the code works. These are usually done as comments and are denoted by a specific symbol that the compiler will ignore. However, many persons who have gone back to look at the code that they or their colleagues had written wish that code had been better documented and that they could access the logic that the original programmer used while creating that code. It is much easier to understand a code when someone tells you what he or she was doing.

Three surveys conducted in 1977, 1983, and 1984, highlight the lack of dFocumentation as one of the biggest problems that the code maintenance people have to deal with (Dekleva, 1992). Prechelt conducted experiments using pattern comment lines (PCL) and added the pattern usage of design patterns to the code (Prechelt, Unger-Lamprecht, Philippsen, & Tichy, 2002). By adding a few lines of comments and running experiments where students took existing code and modified it, major operational improvements were observed.

Documentation is not always a negative aspect of a project. When documentation is done correctly, it can be a positive aspect of the project and very useful. An example of good documenting on legacy software is IBM's involvement with the space program. Starting in the 1970s, IBM worked with NASA to come up with programming for the space shuttle. The documenting process was high on the team's to-do list when developing the software and finding and correcting bugs. Billings et al. cite that data collection to update and fix any errors paid off quickly with the software becoming nearly error free (Billings, Clifton, Kolkhorst, Lee, & Wingert, 1994). However, she further states that when this data was brought in late, it tended to disrupt the development activities. Timely documenting is as important as good documenting.

The oldest, and probably the most famous, code documentation approach is called literate programming. It was developed by Knuth in the early 1980s (Knuth, 1984). This style combines documentation with the code and then compiles the two into separate documents. There is a tangle function, which compiles the actual code into a program, and then the weave function, which produces documentation from the comments imbedded in the code. This style requires that the programmer have a good understanding of the weave function so that the comments come out properly formatted. The comments are written in the code document in a format that is similar to LaTex.

Literate programming ideas have evolved into what is now called elucidative programming (Vestdam, 2003). In elucidative programming, the code and the documentation exist as different documents. Links are then added to the code so that the external documentation is easily accessed. There are no rigid standards for what the comments have to say, only that they should describe the functionality of the code.

Javadoc comments are another standard for documenting code (Kramer, 1999). Javadoc compiles to create an API for the source code. Here, there are more rigid standards for the documentation requirements. The input types and return types are needed and also, what the method does to find the correct output. The comments are imbedded into the document because the thought is that when the comments are so close to the code, programmers are more likely to update the comments as they update the code.

VOCAL ANNOTATION IN COLLABORATION

Fish et al. provide strong evidence that a more expressive medium is especially valuable for the more complex, controversial, and social aspects of a collaborative task (Fish, Chaljonte, & Kraut, 1991). The usage of voice is preferred over text to comment on higher level issues in a document, while the usage of text is appropriate to deal with lower level intricate details. This can be extended to the 24-Hour-Knowledge Factory context of software development where programmers can use voice comments to annotate an issue, like probing the logic used by another programmer, or to suggest a change in the original overall design of the software being developed and use textual comments to correct lower level syntactical details. Various plausible scenarios can be finely contrasted by permuting the annotation modalities. When the users' annotation modalities were restricted, using written annotations led them to comment on more local problems in the text, while the use of speech led them to comment on higher level concerns. Further, when they did use written annotations to comment on global problems, they were less successful than when they used spoken annotations. Finally, when they offered spoken annotations, they were more likely to add features such as personal pronouns and explanations that made their comments more equivocal and socially communicative.

All these scenarios discussed by Fish and his group focused on the annotator. They did not, however, examine the effects of the spoken annotations on the recipient (Fish et al., 1991). It is crucial to note that recipients of voice annotations may be at a disadvantage when compared to recipients of written annotations. For example, recipients of a voice message are more limited in their ability to review, skim, and otherwise abstract the content. While speech is faster than writing for the producer, it can be slow and tedious for the receiver to process (Fish et al., 1991; Gould, 1978). Experiments have shown that reviewers making voice annotations produced roughly two-and-one-half times more words per annotation than reviewers making written annotations. Having conducted experiments to assess the preference of the writer's preference of modality, it was established that regardless of the mode in which comments were produced, writers preferred to receive comments about purpose/audience and style in voice, and preferred to receive comments about mechanics in writing. However, in our system, we have minimized the problem of remembering the content of the voice annotations (not observed in the text annotations) with the intelligence of voice recognition software being put to use, to convert speech into text. The text, thus obtained, can be conveniently revised whenever required. The annotation, as in PREP editor, is anchored to the block of code being annotated. When the user listens to the voice comment, the relevant block of code gets highlighted, thus eliminating the problem of annotation orphaning that occurred with the technique used by Cadiz, Gupta, and Grudin (2000).

Other systems have ventured into experimenting with the combination of voice and text annotations as a possibility in coauthoring documents (e.g., Quilt, Coral and Filochat; Whittaker, Hyland, & Wiley, 1994). Our experience corroborated two findings from Filochat (Whittaker et al., 1994). First, people appeared to be learning to take fewer handwritten notes and to be relying more on the audio. Second, individuals want to improve their handwritten notes afterwards by playing back portions of the audio. Dynomite facilitates this task by allowing users to visually navigate the audio using the audio timeline and also to automatically skip from highlight to highlight in playback mode. This, again, is a system that resorts to a temporal aspect of the audio notes, unlike our spatial vocal commenting approach, which focuses on anchoring the comment to the block of code germane to it.

Steeples (2000) conducted an experiment that used voice annotations to look at video files of professionals in learning situations. By having the participants of the study vocally annotate what was going on during their discussions, it was easier for other people to understand how they were learning. Steeples found that it was better to have voice rather than text because the people viewing the video could watch the video and listen to the comments at the same time rather than having to read in one window and watch the video in the other window. Another interesting point was that the professionals were more likely to give a better description of what was going on if they were talking about what was going on in the video rather than writing about it. When the professionals were told to analyze the video by writing, the accounts were more abstract and less detailed. The last thing they found helpful about the voice annotations was that these annotations did not change over time. When talking to someone on the telephone and the conversation is over, it is up to the people on the phone to remember what was said. Using the voice annotations, they were able to keep track of the recordings and refer back to them when needed.

Steeples conducted more research and found that people could save a considerable amount of time by adding video annotations rather than text annotations. The time to add one minute of video was about the same as typing for four minutes (Steeples, 2002). She also brought up the point that video is not easy to scan through

to find the spot you are looking for. Some of the participants in the study did not like the video and audio comments since they were used to scanning through text comments to quickly find the relevant information.

The need for documenting-while-developing tools is great and if these tools were simplified, then they may be more widely used (Aguiar & David, 2005). Aguiar developed a wiki-based documentation tool that works with IDEs and allows external documentation that supports the actual code. The wiki links to the actual source code and UML diagrams to help developers as they work on the design of the project. The wiki approach also allows technical and nontechnical people to collaborate on the same documents (Aguiar & David, 2005). A wiki-based approach can be combined with voice comments so that instead of having to type out discussions, people can talk about them. By using speech recognition software, it would be easier for the next person to quickly read through what the other person said and then respond either through voice or text. If the wiki was set up as the voice annotations in the current Eclipse plug-in prototype, then the users would have a choice between reading the comments of the other users and also listening to the original voice comments to see if there were other vocal queues that allowed the person to retrieve more information from the voice rather than the text.

Adding voice comments to different documents seems to improve the quality of the comments and also the amount of information the producer imparts to the next person. Applying this idea to programming was the basis for the development of EchoEdit.

ECHOEDIT

EchoEdit was developed to be used in the 24-Hour Knowledge Factory using teams following the composite personae model (Denny, Mani, et al. 2008). In this model, there is a person at every site in the 24-Hour Knowledge Factory that is responsible to making decisions about different pieces of the project. This way, there is always someone available who can clear up confusion and answer questions.

EchoEdit is a plug-in developed for Eclipse that allows the user to add voice comments to their code. EchoEdit is aimed at making the best of both the speech and text modalities as Neuwirth, Chandhok, Charney, Wojahn, and Kim (1994) suggest as part of the conclusion of their research The programmers are given the choice of both text and voice comments by the system. In the production mode, the programmer can use either text comments for syntactical or other lower level semantic concerns or voice comments for addressing higher level complex issues in his/her code (Neuwirth et al., 1994). On the reception mode, users play voice annotations by clicking on an iconic representation, which is displayed on the margin, similar to the idea painted in the PREP environment (Neuwirth et al., 1994). When the voice annotation is played, the block of code relevant to the comment is highlighted, showing the anchoring of the comment. This helps avoid orphaning of annotations. The purpose of the voice recognition software is to convert the voice notes into text for ease of indexing and to provide choice of modality to the programmer on the reception mode.

Some people find it easier to talk through their thoughts than to type through them. Adding a lightweight program to add voice comments makes the program relatively easy to use. The 24HrKF requires programmers to be accountable for their code after every shift instead of only when they need to check new code into their code repository. This may mean that code coming out of the 24HrKF is of higher quality since it is better commented and, therefore, easier to maintain.

EchoEdit was developed for the IBM Eclipse environment because the prototype was driven by the desire to create a plug-in that would be an add-on to what many developers are already comfortable with. The Eclipse platform provides an easy mechanism for adding a plug-in project that can easily be distributed to any other use of the Eclipse platform. The Eclipse platform provides a feature rich IDE, which is similar to other Java IDEs such as Netbeans and JBuilder. Since Eclipse is open source and free to download, it became an obvious choice to develop the prototype as an Eclipse plug-in which would allow tests to be conducted using a full featured IDE with the prototype also being fully integrated.

There are three user actions that can be performed: Record a comment, play back an audio file, and convert of an audio file to a comment. An example of the type of text comment that is added to the code after it is translated from voice to text can be seen in Figure 1.

Figure 2 shows the design of EchoEdit. The user interacts with the file in the IDE. When the user presses the record button, an event is sent to the Record Action Handler. The Action Handler initializes the Audio Recorder and then listens for a Record Event. The Record Event Listener is received when audio recording has begun. Upon receiving the Record Event, the Record Event Listener starts a thread to do the actual recording, starting a thread to do the converting from voice to text and also launches the dialog box that lets the user know that the recording has started taking place. The Audio Recorder then listens for events from the Converter Thread and inserts the text that was generated into the original file the user was modifying.

The recording of a comment generates both an audio file as well as a text comment of the dictation. This is performed by showing a popup dialog window that informs the user that a recording is in progress and the user can press a button to stop recording. Everything spoken is stored in memory to be written to an audio file once the recording finishes, along with being converted to text and inserted into the document being edited. There is a conversion step that creates a text comment

Figure 1. Comment inserted using EchoEdit

```
/**

The following method will take in an integer and
then return the summation from zero to the given
integer

@audioFile HelloWorld.java.1177889903437.wav

**/

    private int returnSum(int num)

    {

        int sum = 0;

        for (int i = 1; i < num + 1; i++)

        {

            sum = sum + i;

        }

        return sum;

    }
```

Figure 2. Simplified design overview

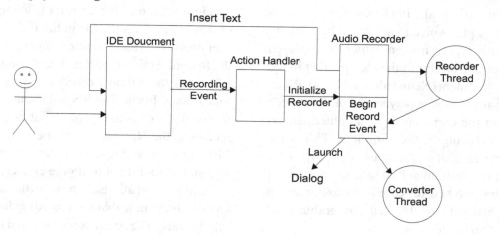

from an audio file. EchoEdit allows the creators of programming codes to speak their thoughts out loud to make notes. It differs from existing tools lies in that it allows the user to access the comments both in audio and written formats.

CONCLUSION

While the arena of software development was examined in this article, the idea about voice comments can be added to other disciplines. Trambert (2006) showed that adding voice comments to images in radiology improved efficiency by reducing physician confusion and therefore, interaction. For the use of these concepts in the development of software and other knowledge based artifacts can help to reduce the amount required to complete the task at hand, as well as to improve documentation for future updates. By adding voice comments to code or other documents, one is much more likely to quickly find out the purpose of the text and therefore, update it more efficiently.

Finally, the 24-Hour Knowledge Factory may also change the overall perspectives of offshoring. This type of development environment allows people to see offshoring as a collaborative endeavor rather than an "us verses them" mentality. The aspect of software development in the 24-Hour Knowledge Factory was explored because this is one discipline where many people in the industry feel that they are losing their jobs to people in other countries. Rather than look at jobs leaving one country to go to another country, individuals can look at the 24-Hour Knowledge Factory as an environment where everyone wins. Products are developed faster, people get to work normal daylight hours, talent around the world is leveraged and more jobs are created. Voice-based collaboration can help to attain this vision.

REFERENCES

Aguiar, A., & David, G. (2005). WikiWiki weaving heterogeneous software artifacts. In *Proceedings of the 2005 International Symposium on Wikis (WikiSym '05)*. Retrieved November 16, 2007, from http://doi.acm.org/10.1145/1104973.1104980

Billings, C., Clifton, J., Kolkhorst, B., Lee, E., & Wingert, W. B. (1994). Journey to a mature software process. *IBM Systems Journal, 34*(1), 46.

Cadiz, J. J., Gupta, A., & Grudin, J. (2000). Using Web annotations for asynchronous collaboration around documents. In *Proceedings of the 2000 ACM conference on Computer supported cooperative work* (p. 309).

Dekleva, S. (1992). Delphi study of software maintenance problems. 10-17.

Denny, N., Crk, I., Sheshu, R., & Gupta, A. (in press). Agile software processes for the 24-hour knowledge factory environment. *Journal of Information Technology Research.*

Denny, N., Mani, S., Sheshu, R., Swaminathan, M., Samdal, J., & Gupta, A. (in press). Hybrid offshoring: Composite personae and evolving collaboration technologies. *Information Resources Management Journal.*

Fish, R. S., Chaljonte, B. L., & Kraut, R. E. (1991). Expressive richness: A comparison of speech and text as media for revision. In *Conference on Human Factors in Computing Systems Proceedings of the SIGCHI Conference on Human factors in computing systems: Reaching Through Technology* (pp. 1-6).

Gould, J. D. (1978). An experimental study of writing, dictating, and speaking. In J. Requin (Ed.), *Attention and performance: Vol. 7* (pp. 299-319).

Gupta, A., & Seshasai, S. (2007). 24-hour knowledge factory: Using Internet technology to leverage spatial and temporal separations. *ACM Transactions on Internet Technology, 7*(3).

Knuth, D. E. (1984). Literate programming. *Computer journal, 27*(2), 97-111.

Kramer, D. (1999) API documentation from source code comments: A case study of javadoc. In *Proceedings of the 17th Annual International Conference on Computer Documentation (SIGDOC '99)* (pp. 147-153).

Neuwirth, C. M., Chandhok, R., Charney, D., Wojahn, P., & Kim, L. (1994). Distributed collaborative writing: A comparison of spoken and written modalities for reviewing and revising documents. *Proceedings of the SIGCHI Conference on Human Factors in Computing Systems: Celebrating Interdependence* (p. 51).

Prechelt, L., Unger-Lamprecht, B., Philippsen, M., & Tichy, W. F. (2002, June). Two controlled experiments assessing the usefulness of design pattern documentation in program maintenance. *IEEE Transactions on Software Engineering, 28*(6), 595-606.

Sheshu, R., & Denny, N. (2007). *The nexus of entrepreneurship & technology (NEXT) initiative* (Tech. Rep. 20070220). Unpublished manuscript.

Steeples, C. (2000). Reflecting on group discussions for professional learning: Annotating videoclips with voice annotations. 251-252.

Steeples, C. (2002). Voice annotation of multimedia artifacts: Reflective learning in distributed professional communities, 10.

Trambert, M. (2006). PACS voice clips enhance productivity, efficiency; radiologists, referrers, front offices, and patients benefit from reporting in reader's own voice. *Diagnostic Imaging*, S3.

Vestdam, T. (2003). Elucidative programming in open integrated development environments for java. In *Proceedings of the Second International Conference on Principles and Practice of Programming in Java (PPPJ '03)* (pp. 49-54).

Whittaker, S., Hyland, P., & Wiley, M. (1994). FILOCHAT: Handwritten notes provide access to recorded conversations. In *Proceedings of the SIGCHI Conference on Human Factors in Computing Systems: Celebrating Interdependence* (p. 271).

This work was previously published in the Journal of Information Technology Research, Vol. 1, Issue 2, edited by M. Khosrow-Pour, pp. 54-60, copyright 2008 by IGI Publishing (an imprint of IGI Global).

Chapter 15
Intelligent Biometric System Using Soft Computing Tools

Anupam Shukla
ABV- Indian Institute of Information Technology and Management, India

Ritu Tiwari
ABV- Indian Institute of Information Technology and Management, India

Chandra Prakash Rathore
ABV- Indian Institute of Information Technology and Management, India

ABSTRACT

Biometric Systems verify the identity of a claimant based on the person's physical attributes, such as voice, face or fingerprints. Its application areas include security applications, forensic work, law enforcement applications etc. This work presents a novel concept of applying Soft Computing Tools, namely Artificial Neural Networks and Neuro-Fuzzy System, for person identification using speech and facial features. The work is divided in four cases, which are Person Identification using speech biometrics, facial biometrics, fusion of speech and facial biometrics and finally fusion of optimized speech and facial biometrics.

INTRODUCTION

Soft computing is a fusion of computational techniques in computer science, machine learning and other engineering disciplines, dedicated to system solutions. It encourages the integration of soft computing techniques and tools into both everyday and advanced applications. Techiques in soft computing are Neural networks (NN); Fuzzy systems (FS); Evolutionary computation (EC); Swarm intelligence; Ideas about probability including: Bayesian network and Chaos theory. (Frank Hoffmann et.al., 2005; R. A. Aliev et.al., 2001).

In today's electronically wired information society, it requires that an individual/user to be verified by an electronic machine as in the case of transaction authentication on physical or virtual access control. ID numbers, such as a token or a password are a thing of past now as they can be used by unauthorized persons. Biometric techniques use unique personal features of the user himself/herself to verify the identity claimed. These techniques include face, facial thermogram, fingerprint, hand geometry, hand vein, gait features, iris, retinal pat-

DOI: 10.4018/978-1-60566-966-3.ch015

tern, DNA, signature, speech etc. (D.A.Reynolds, 2002; Jain & A. Ross, 2002). Initially Biometric technologies were proposed for high-security specialist applications but are now emerging as key elements in the developing electronic commerce and online systems revolution as well as for offline and standalone security systems. (J. Kittler et.al., 2002; Jain, R. Bolle et.al., 1999).

Many commercial biometric systems use fingerprint, face, or voice. Each modality has its advantages and drawbacks (discriminative power, complexity, robustness, etc.). User acceptability is an important criterion for commercial applications. Techniques based on iris or retina scan are very reliable but not well accepted by end-users on the other hand voice and face is natural and easily accepted by end-users. Automated face recognition has been witnessing a lot of activity during the last years. (A.I.Bazin & M.S.Nixon, 2004; C.Garcia & M.Delakis, 2002; Jianxin Wu & Zhi-Hua Zhou, 2003).

Speaker recognition is a very natural way for solving identification and verification problems. A lot of work has been done in this field and generated a certain number of applications of access control for telephone companies. Text-dependent and text-independent are the two major speaker verification techniques. (A. Martin & M.Przybocki, 2001; Angel de la Terra, Antonio M.Perindo et. al., 2005; B.Sun et.al., 2003; B.Xiang & T.berger, 2003; C.H.Lee & Q.Huo, 2000; J.R.Dellar et.al., 2000).

It has been shown that combining different biometric modalities enables to achieve better performances than techniques based on single modalities. The *fusion* algorithm, which combines the different modalities, is a very critical part of the recognition system. (C.Sanderson & K.K.Paliwal, 2000; Conrad Sanderson, 2002; Fox et.al., 2003; Fox.N & Reilly,R.B, 2003; J. Fierrez-Aguilar et.al., 2003).

Artificial Neural Networks (ANNs) has resulted in a large number of parallel techniques and models for real-world applications. They are massively parallel arrays of simple processing units that can be used for computationally complex tasks such as image processing, machine vision, and computer vision (A. P. Paplinski, 2004; B.Fasal, 2002; M.A.Arbib, 2003).

A neuro-fuzzy system is a fuzzy system that uses a learning algorithm derived from or inspired by neural network theory to determine its parameters (fuzzy sets and fuzzy rules) by processing data samples. These systems combine the advantages of fuzzy logic system, which deal with explicit knowledge that can be explained and understood, and neural networks, which deal with implicit knowledge, which can be acquired by learning (Rutkowski & Leszek, (2004); Abraham A, 2001; Jeen-Shing Wang & C. S. George Lee, 2002).

Figure 1 shows the block diagram of the complete model.

SIMULATION MODEL

We have divided the complete simulation model in four cases:

Speaker Identification Using Speech Features

The analog speech signal is digitized at a frequency of 16 KHz. For the accurate estimation of the speech features the sampling frequency is kept twice of the bandwidth. The spectrogram of the speech signal is shown in the Figure 2. The individual 36 words from the Hindi sentence namely vc bl ckj vki mlds thtk QwQk nknw rFkk pkph] dkdh] HkkHkh] nhnh] QwQh vkSj phuw] thtw] ehuw I;kjh dquh] eSjh ds lkFk&lkFk VwVh Vscy] Fkkyh] twrs] VkV] pwts] cdjh] rksrs vkfu vlckc ns[krs vkbZ;sxk' are separated and the entire data is stored in the hard disk by separate file names. Thus a speech bank is formed, from which the Signal Processing Toolbox in MATLAB

Figure 1. Block diagram of the biometric system

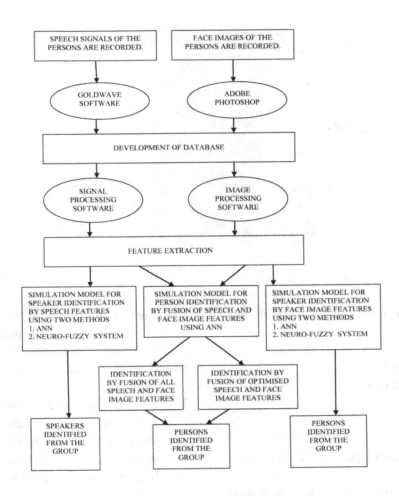

(Manual of SIGNAL PROCESSING TOOLBOX), extracts the speech features by reading files one after the other. The following Speech Features are extracted:

- Formant Frequency F1 to F4.
- Peak & Average Power Spectral Density.
- Time Duration.
- Number of Zero Crossing.
- Pitch & Pitch Amplitude.
- Maximum Amplitude i.e. Ceps. Max.

ANN Model

The 11-speech features mentioned above are extracted for word number 4 from 36 words for 50 speakers. These speech features are shown in Table 1. The 3-layer perceptron model is simulated using the ANN toolbox in MATLAB (Manual of ARTIFICIAL NEURAL NETWORK TOOL-BOX). The speech feature [20*11] matrices are given to the input vector of the ANN model for authentication of speaker. The configuration of the model investigated is as follow:

Figure 2. Speech spectrogram

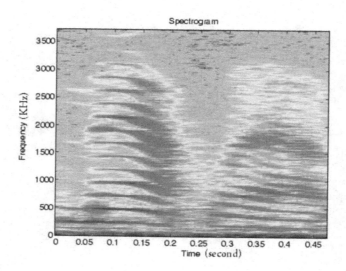

For two hidden layer, neural network configuration are:

Input layer: 20 neurons
Output layer: 5 neurons
Learning rate: 0.1
Error goal: 0.01
Momentum: 0.5
Neurons in the Hidden layer: 15, 75 each.

Figure 3 shows the graph of Sum of Square Error V/S Epochs of ANN Training for this case. In this case the ANN model is trained for the identification of speaker by the speech features in 56201 epochs.

Neuro-Fuzzy Classifier Model

This model uses only the four speech features namely Average Power, Spectral Density, Number of Zero Crossing, Pitch, and Maximum Amplitude i.e. Ceps. Max.

Following are the steps for implementation of the Neuro-fuzzy approach in speaker identification system:

1. Load training data matrix as the input and output columns (with input columns first followed by output column).
2. Separate the data matrix in input and output matrix form.
3. Specify the input membership function type, number of membership functions, output membership function type, number of epochs, error tolerance and FIS (Fuzzy Inference System) training method.
4. Train the neural system using ANFIS (Adaptive Neuro-Fuzzy Inference System) editor in Fuzzy Logic Toolbox of MATLAB (Manual of FUZZY LOGIC TOOLBOX).
5. Load the testing or checking data matrix (with input columns first followed by output column).
6. Test the testing and checking data.
7. Compare the results with the target.

In the present model the FIS (Fuzzy Inference System) is of Sugeno type. FIS training has been done by using hybrid optimization method. Figure 4 shows the detailed FIS for speaker identification.

Table 1. The sample results of 20 speakers for speech features

Details of the Speaker	Time Duration	No of Zero Crossing	Max. Cepstral	Average Power Spectral Density	Pitch Amplitude	Pitch Frequency	Peak Power Spectral Density	Format Frequency			
								F1	F2	F3	F4
01	11928	15	2.0619	0.004484	0.01191	0.91281	0.03125	0.03125	0.10938	0.19531	0.29688
02	11952	12	1.9008	0.002518	0.01192	0.96094	0.03125	0.039063	0.17188	0.25781	0.30469
03	10240	2	1.476	0.000286	0.01191	0.98438	0.039063	0.039063	0.13281	0.19531	0.35156
04	12213	8	1.332	0.000156	0.012	0.96875	0.046875	0.039063	0.14063	0.19531	0.35938
05	10302	6	1.8464	0.001032	0.01184	0.92345	0.039063	0.046875	0.09375	0.21094	0.30469
06	12626	4	2.0706	0.002304	0.01192	0.94223	0.046875	0.046875	0.09375	0.19531	0.29688
07	13490	10	1.475	0.000234	0.01193	0.99219	0.04234	0.05876	0.125	0.19531	0.29688
08	9291	11	1.7026	0.00096	0.01193	0.91234	0.007813	0.007813	0.14844	0.25	0.29688
09	9487	12	1.5852	0.000805	0.0117	0.95321	0.039063	0.039063	0.125	0.19531	0.32813
10	10703	12	1.9104	0.002525	0.01172	0.9810	0.039063	0.03125	0.11719	0.24219	0.36719
11	8011	8	1.739	0.001484	0.01177	0.98438	0.03125	0.03125	0.11719	0.26563	0.3125
12	10509	9	1.6174	0.000998	0.01193	0.92356	0.03125	0.03125	0.10938	0.20313	0.34375
13	9706	12	1.6627	0.000537	0.01175	0.97456	0.007813	0.03125	0.14063	0.19531	0.32031
14	13051	13	1.5005	0.000213	0.01184	0.98564	0.039063	0.039063	0.14063	0.19531	0.33594
15	10763	16	1.7429	0.000614	0.01192	0.99219	0.046875	0.046875	0.09375	0.21094	0.34375
16	14744	9	1.7683	0.000673	0.01167	0.99219	0.039063	0.039063	0.13281	0.19531	0.35156
17	9018	16	1.7176	0.002415	0.0118	0.98438	0.039063	0.039063	0.14844	0.24219	0.30469
18	9882	9	1.4643	0.000134	0.01184	0.98213	0.007813	0.015625	0.15625	0.22656	0.33594
19	13215	13	1.2675	7.57E-05	0.01181	0.92344	0.015625	0.04196	0.13281	0.19531	0.34375
20	11112	16	1.67584	0.00118	0.01185	0.9926	0.03042	0.03125	0.12788	0.21381	0.32607

Figure 3. Graph of sum of square error v/s epoch of ANN training for case-1

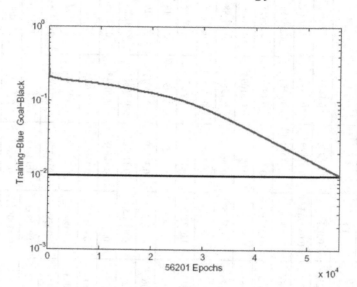

Figure 4. Fuzzy inference system for speaker identification

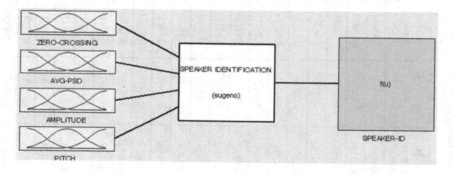

Error tolerance for the system is 0%, number of epochs are 3, number of inputs are 4, number of membership functions for each input (feature) is 3 and number of output is 1. The Number of nodes: 193; Number of linear parameters: 81; Number of nonlinear parameters: 36; Total number of parameters: 117; Number of training data pairs: 10; Number of fuzzy rules: 81. Figure 5 shows the ANFIS Model Structure for speaker identification. During training the rule sets are generated by the ANFIS editor as shown in the Figure 6. Figure 7 represents the extent of output dependency on the speech features given in the input. The model is tested for the two cases i.e.,

speaker independent and speaker dependent cases. The model is trained by speech features from 10 speakers out of 50 speakers for word number 12 from the 36 words and subsequently tested for 10 speakers from open and close sets depending upon the case 1 and 2 respectively. In open set the recognition score varies from 80% to 100% and depends upon the type of input membership function whereas in close set the recognition score is 100%. In this way an attempt has been made to develop a speaker independent system i.e. open set and to compare its performance in terms of recognition score with the speaker dependent system i.e. close set.

Figure 5. ANFIS model structure for speaker identification

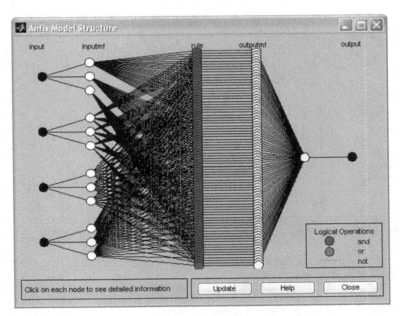

Figure 6. Fuzzy rule set for identifying speaker

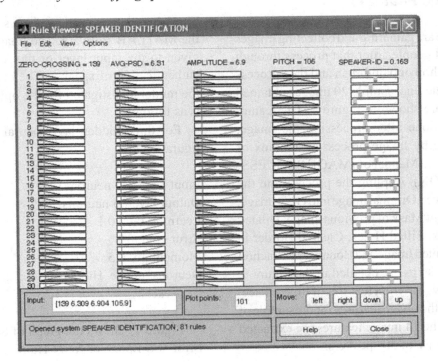

Figure 7. Surface view of zero crossing, amplitude and speaker ID (output)

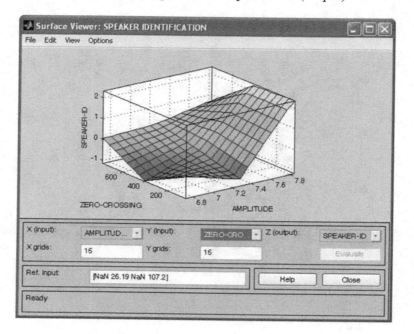

Person Identification Using Image Features

In first fold we are gathering and collecting images from different people, after that process through adobe photo shop or paintbrush and then process the images. The final sample 20 images obtained after editing are shown in Figure 8. The feature extraction is done after processing the image, which is done by Image processing toolbox of MATLAB 7.0.1 (Manual of IMAGE PROCESSING TOOLBOX). Appling the process into the sequence: convert Original image into Gray Image, Binary Gradient Mask of previous image, Dilated Gradient Mask, Filled Holes, Cleared Border in Image, Segmented Image and Boundary extraction of Image. The steps are detailed in the Figure 9. Figure 10 shows different features of Image/Face. Table 2 shows the image features for the sample of 20 speakers. The 14 image features are extracted from the database of 50 speakers.

ANN Model

The 3-layer perceptron model is simulated using the MATLAB software. The image features are given to the input layer of the ANN model for authentication of speaker. The configuration of the model investigated for the optimized results is as follows.

For three hidden layer neural network configuration are:

Input layer: 20 neurons
Output layer: 5 neurons
Learning rate: 0.1
Error goal: 0.1
Momentum: 0.5
Neurons in the Hidden layer: 20, 20, and 20 each.

Figure 11 shows the graph of Sum of Square Error V/S Epoch of ANN Training for this case.

Figure 8. Specimen for 20 images after editing from which image features are acquired

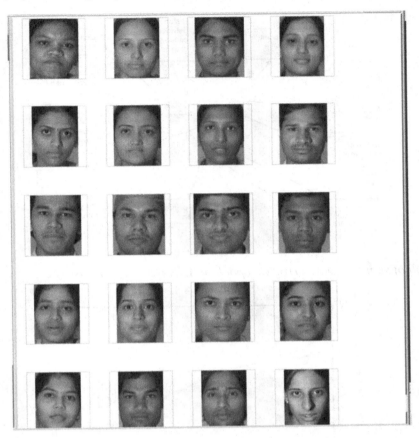

Figure 9. Different steps of image processing

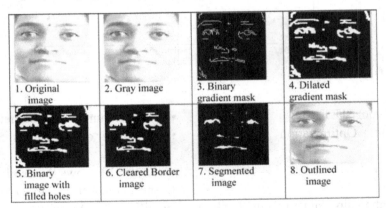

In this case the ANN model is trained for the identification of person by the image features in 19285 epochs and an extra hidden layer.

Neuro-Fuzzy Classifier Model

Neuro-fuzzy system is implemented just as in section 2.1.2, and the details of the ANFIS for person identification using face/image features are:

Figure 10. Different features of face image

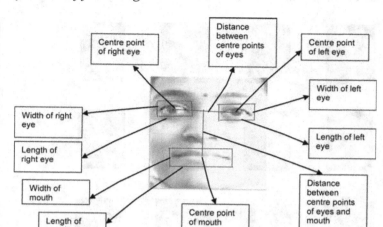

Figure 11. Graph of sum of square error v/s epoch of ANN training for case – 2

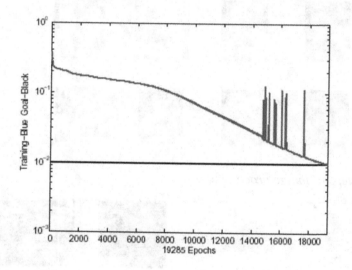

- FIS System Type: SUGENO;
- FIS Training Optimization Method: HYBRID;
- Error Tolerance: 0%;
- EPOCHS: 5;
- No. of Membership Function in Each Input(Feature): 2;
- No. of Inputs (Features): 9;
- Number of nodes: 1072;
- Number of linear parameters: 5120;
- Number of nonlinear parameters: 72;

- Total number of parameters: 5192;
- Number of fuzzy rules: 512

Figure 12 shows the detailed FIS and Figure 13 shows the ANFIS Model Structure for person identification. During training the rule sets are generated by the ANFIS editor as shown in the Figure 14. Figure 15 represents the extent of output dependency on the facial features given in the input. The recognition score varies from 96% to 100%.

Intelligent Biometric System Using Soft Computing Tools

Table 2. Sample results of 20 speakers for face/image features

No.	LE1 (pixel)	WE1 (pixel)	CE1X (pixel)	CE1Y (pixel)	LE2 (pixel)	WE2 (pixel)	CE2X (pixel)	CE2Y (pixel)	LM (pixel)	WM (pixel)	CMX (pixel)	CMY (pixel)	DE12 (pixel)	DEM (pixel)
1	38	24	69.392	23.773	26	25	69.17	85.776	61	44	126.55	54.351	62.002	71.776
2	45	29	144.93	110.47	41	30	147.01	6.4355	65	36	135.62	53.783	104.04	77.167
3	40	30	60.091	37.852	49	29	57.081	97.871	72	37	107.65	64.68	60.019	59.785
4	36	23	50.505	36.286	43	29	46.952	94.904	65	58	91.024	77.065	58.618	65.429
5	49	26	133.21	62.304	24	30	126.84	4.5536	58	44	55.857	35.866	57.75	52.428
6	39	27	65.147	25.815	32	33	67.144	80.885	70	26	137.91	56.882	55.07	84.556
7	47	33	72.989	83.947	41	26	73.651	35.794	73	38	133.63	51.485	48.154	73.758
8	35	30	76.789	85.088	32	22	73.565	35.157	56	44	123.48	59.738	49.932	63.359
9	44	38	56.229	82.482	48	28	64.048	18.066	78	43	120.98	60.022	64.416	70.704
10	47	29	66.885	86.808	48	23	69.934	38.671	69	52	116.13	57.974	48.137	53.386
11	46	30	110.79	56.362	38	23	108.47	7.0253	83	28	49.734	32.669	49.337	58.04
12	44	25	149.57	109.47	48	26	148.35	57.517	63	33	74.669	85.432	51.956	58.825
13	44	36	121.57	59.314	45	38	132.96	110.48	82	28	63.775	86.794	51.166	51.123
14	35	44	68.024	32.785	37	39	59.542	88.254	74	34	120.64	57.986	55.469	60.124
15	47	31	146.05	106.13	43	29	144.78	66.529	73	29	144.78	66.529	39.598	58.456
16	73	50	75.634	18.538	65	45	76.203	40.971	73	50	75.634	18.538	62.433	45.879
17	40	30	135.82	59.568	41	28	137.39	97.893	82	24	179.25	60.765	38.325	100.52
18	52	29	169.17	27.566	50	22	169.68	6.2264	70	42	61.507	19.127	61.34	44.611
19	50	32	64.845	38.817	44	29	77.804	35.982	79	24	18.731	37.064	62.834	48.669
20	37	28	96.717	60.177	43	23	97.39863	53.104	82	37	101.97	54.565	49.505	50.452

No. Speaker Number
WE1 Width of eye1 (left eye)
CE1Y Centre Dimension (y- coordinate) of eye1 (left eye)
WE2 Width of eye2 (right eye)
CE2Y Centre Dimension (y- coordinate) of eye2 (right eye)
WM Width of mouth
CMY Centre Dimension (y- coordinate) of mouth
DEM Distance between centre point of mouth and eyes

LE1 Length of eye1 (left eye)
CE1X Centre Dimension (x- coordinate) of eye1 (left eye)
LE2 Length of eye2 (right eye)
CE2X Centre Dimension (x- coordinate) of eye2 (right eye)
LM Length of mouth
CMX Centre Dimension (x- coordinate) of mouth
DE12 Distance between two eyes

Figure 12. Fuzzy inference system for face recognition

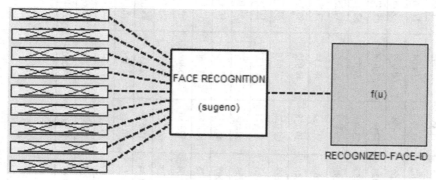

Figure 13. ANFIS model structure for face recognition

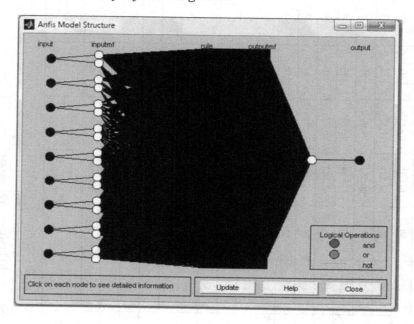

Authentication by Fusion of Speech and Image Features Using ANN

The complete scheme for speaker authentication used in the present work by fusion of speech and image data using ANN is shown in the block diagram of Figure 16. For two hidden layer neural network configuration are:

Input layer: 20 neurons
Output layer: 5 neurons

Learning rate: 0.1
Error goal: 0.01
Momentum: 0.5
Neurons in the Hidden layer: 15, 75 each.

Figure 17 shows the graph of Sum of Square Error v/s Epoch of ANN Training for this case. In this case the ANN model, simulated by fusion of speech and image features has been trained for the identification of person in 8765 epochs.

Figure 14. Fuzzy rule set for face recognition

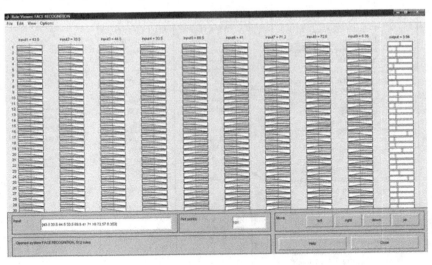

Figure 15. Surface view of Length-LE (input 1), Width-LE (input 2) and Recognized-Face-ID (output)

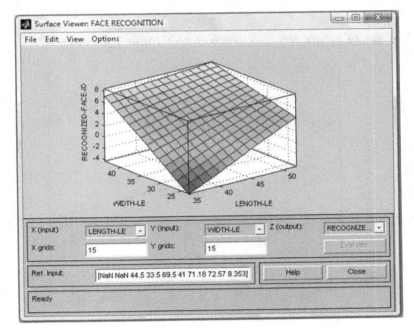

Optimized Fusion Model Using Speech and Image Features

The number of input features used in the above models has been reduced to the optimum value by selecting minimum number of speech and image features and the computer simulated ANN model has been trained with minimum number of iterations.

The features used in the present model are as follows:

Figure 16. Model for speaker authentication by fusion of image and speech features

| Speech Features
• Formant Frequency F1 To F4
• Peak & Average Power Spectral Density
• Time Duration
• Number Of Zero Crossing
• Pitch & Pitch Amplitude
• Maximum Amplitude i.e. Ceps Max
  For 20 Speakers

Image Features
• Length of both Eyes
• Width of both Eyes
• Center Dimensions (x & y coordinates) of both Eyes
• Length Of Mouth
• Width Of Mouth
• Center Dimensions (x & y coordinates) of Mouth
• Distance Between Center Points of both Eyes.
• Distance Between Center Points of Eyes & Mouth
  For 20 Persons | COMPUTER SIMULATED ANN MODEL **Training Cycle:** 3 – Layer perceptron model 20- Neurons in the input layer 15- and 75 neurons in each hidden layer and 5- Neurons in output layer Learning rate- 0.1 Momentum-0.5

To Train ANN for 20 Speakers by giving image and speech features at input layer. | COMPUTER SIMULATED ANN MODEL **Recognize Cycle:** 3 – Layer perceptron model 20- Neurons in the input layer 15 and 75 neurons in each hidden layer and 5- Neurons in output layer Learning rate- 0.1 Momentum-0.5

To Test For Any One Speaker from 20 by giving Inputs features of Desired Speaker and keeping the Weights Same as acquired From Training Cycle | Authentication Of the desired speaker |

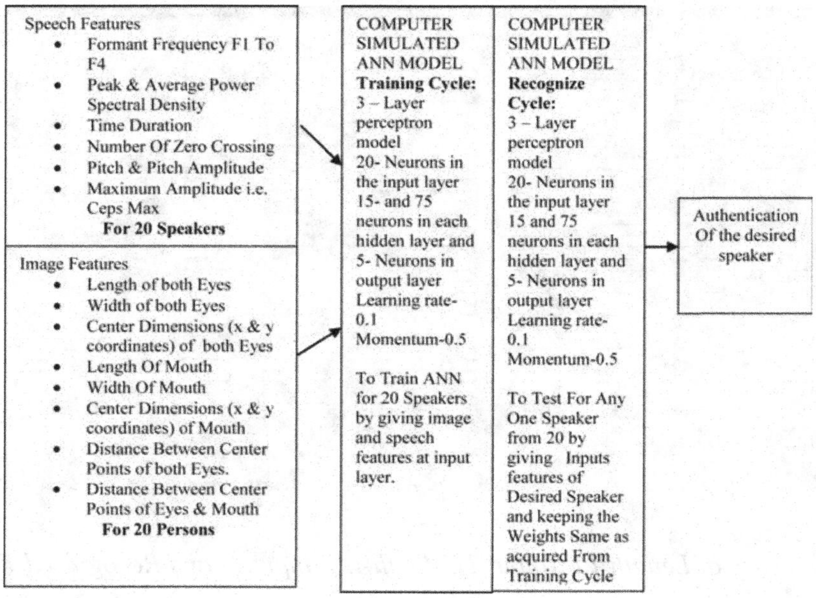

Figure 17. Graph of sum of square error v/s epoch of ANN training for case–3

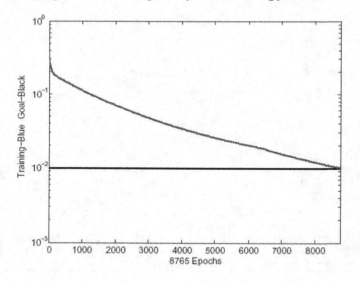

• Formant Frequency F1 to F4.
• Peak & Average Power Spectral Density.
• Length and width of the Mouth.
• Distance between Center Points of both eyes.
• Distance between Center Points of Eyes & Mouth.

The simulated ANN model is as follows. For two hidden layer neural network configuration are:

Input layer: 20 neurons
Output layer: 5 neurons
Learning rate: 0.1

Figure 18. Graph of sum of square error v/s epoch of ANN training for case-4

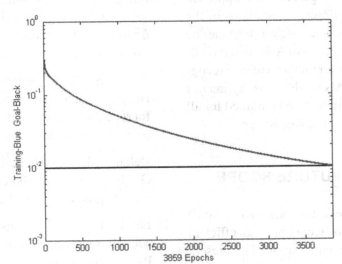

Error goal: 0.01
Momentum: 0.5
Neurons in the Hidden layer: 15, 75 each.

The Figure 18 shows the graph of Sum of Square Error v/s Epoch of ANN Training. In this case the ANN model is optimized and trained for the identification of person by the fusion of speech and image features with ANN in 3859 epochs

RESULTS & DISCUSSION

Results shows that a superior recognition is achieved using the ANN and Neuro-Fuzzy techniques. The feature extraction technique requires a long time, but recognition process is much faster than feature extraction. Reducing the size of matrices can considerably reduce the time taken in the features extraction process. The proposed method was found to perform satisfactorily in adverse conditions of exposure, illumination and contrast variations, and face pose.

This scheme is efficient because result have smoother curve as well as faster training cycle. These result furthers concludes that even a distorted image of the speaker along with few utterances of sound in noisy environment can effectively identify the person.

The variation of speech features reflects the following interpretation from the speech data:

(1) The NZC (Number of Zero Crossings) speech feature data has less variation amongst the speakers as compared to average PSD and maximum amplitude.

(2) The Pitch amplitude is not a good feature for speaker authentication.

(3) The Formant frequency data reflects that variation in F2 & F4 is small compared to F1 & F3 among the speakers.

The variation of the face image features reflects the following interpretation of the image data:

(1) The image data for the length & width of eyes and mouth indicate the large variation.

(2) The distance between two eyes is almost consistent among the persons compared to the distance between the eye and mouth feature of the image.

(3) A peculiar point regarding our approach is that among different orientations of the tested image any one single image can be utilized for the training of ANN and ANFIS as compared to other methods of face recognition in which ANN/ANFIS is, by images of different orientation, to be trained for all of the positions of the face image.

CONCLUSION & FUTURE SCOPE

From the analysis of the features and their fusion it is inferred that the fusion technique is an efficient technique for person identification. The present work contributes a new direction of research in the field of image, speech and fusion using ANN and Neuro-Fuzzy approaches.

The present work can be further extended for the multiple choice identification tasks such as for the criminal investigation. Further the work may be extended by including more biometric identity of the person like retina, finger prints etc to identify the person for the security applications and other places such as access control, telephone credit cards, and internet banking. Furthermore the system can be extended for talking faces, video sequences etc.

REFERENCES

Abraham, A. (2001). Neuro-Fuzzy Systems: State-of-the-Art Modeling Techniques. In J. Mira & A. Prieto (Eds.), *Connectionist Models of Neurons, Learning Processes and Artificial Intelligence* (LNCS 2084, pp. 269-276).

Aliev, R. A., & Aliev, R. R. (2001). *Soft Computing and its Applications*. World Scientific Publishing Co. Pvt. Ltd. Singapore.

Arbib, M. A. (2003). *Handbook of Brain Theory and Neural Networks* (2nd ed.). Cambridge, MA: MIT Press.

Bazin, A. I., & Nixon, M. S. (2004). Facial verification using probabilistic methods. In *Proc. British Machine Vision Association Workshop on Biometrics*. London.

de la Terra, A., & Perindo, M., A., et al. (2005). Histogram equalization of speech representation for robust speech recognition. *IEEE Transactions on Speech and Audio Processing*, 3.

Dellar, J. R., Jr., Hansen, H. L., & Proakis, J. G. (2000). *Discrete-Time Processing of Speech Signals* (2nd ed.). New York: IEEE Press.

Fasal, B. (2002). Robust face analysis using convolutional neural network. Proc. 7th Int.Conf. Pattern Recognition. 2. 11-15.

Fierrez-Aguilar, J. Ortega-Garcia, J. Garcia-Romero, D. & Gonzalez-Rodriguez, J. (2003). A Comparative Evaluation of Fusion Strategies for Multimodal Biometric Verification. *4th Int'l. Conf. Audio- and Video-Based Biometric Person Authentication (AVBPA 2003). Guildford* (LNCS 2688, pp. 830–837).

Fox, G. Chaza., Cohn & Reilly. (2003). Person Identification Using Automatic Integration Of Speech, Lip and Face Experts. *WBMA '03*. Berkeley, CA, USA.

Fox, N., & Reilly, R. B. (2003). Audio-Visual Speaker Identification Based on the Use of Dynamic Audio and Visual Features. In *Proc. 4th International Conference on audio and video based biometric person authentication*.

Garcia, C., & Delakis, M. (2002). A neural architecture for fast and robust face detection. In *Proc. 16th Int. Conf. Pattern Recognition (ICPR'02)* (pp. 20044-20048).

Hoffmann, F., Köppen, M., Klawonn, F., & Roy, R. (2005). *Soft Computing: Methodologies and Applications*. Birkhäuser Publications.

Jain, R. Bolle, & Pankanti, S. (1999). *Biometrics: Personal Identification in Networked Society* (2nd ed.). Kluwer Academic Publishers.

Jain & Ross. A. (2002). Learning User-Specific Parameters in Multibiometric System. In *Proc. Int'l Conf. of Image Processing (ICIP 2002), New York* (pp. 57-70).

Kittler, J. Messer, K. & Czyz, J. (2002). Fusion of Intramodal and Multimodal Experts in Personal Identity Authentication Systems. In *Proc. Cost 275 Workshop. Rome* (pp. 17–24).

Lee, C. H., & Huo, Q. (2000). On adaptive decision rules and decision parameter adaptation for automatic speech recognition. *Proceedings of the IEEE, 88,* 1241–1268. doi:10.1109/5.880082

Martin, A., & Przybocki, M. (2001). Speaker recognition in multi-speaker Environment. In *Proc. 7th Euro. Conf. Speech Communication and Technology (Eurospeech 2001) Aalborg, Denmark* (pp. 780-790).

Paplinski, A. P. (2004, July). Basic structures and properties of Artificial Neural Networks. *Neural Networks, L,* 2.

Reynolds, D. A. (2002). An overview of automatic speaker recognition technology. In *Proc. Int. Conf. On Acoustics, Speech and Signal Processing (ICASSP 2002). Orlando FL* (pp. 4072-4075).

Rutkowski, L. (2004). Flexible Neuro-Fuzzy Systems. Structures, Learning and Performance Evaluation. *The Springer International Series in Engineering and Computer Science* (771).

Sanderson, C. (2002). Information fusion and person verification using speech and face information. *IDIAP Research report 02-33.*

Sanderson, C., & Paliwal, K. K. (2000). Adaptive Multimodal Person Verification System. Proc. 1st *IEEE Pacific-Rim Conf. On Multimedia, Sydney* (pp. 210-213).

Sun, B., Liu, W., & Zhong, Q. (2003). Hierarchical speaker identification using speaker clustering. In *Proc. Int. Conf. Natural Language Processing and Knowledge Engineering 2003, Beijing, China* (pp. 299-304).

Wang, J.-S., & George Lee, C. S. (2002). Self-Adaptive Neuro-Fuzzy Inference Systems for Classification Applications. *IEEE transactions on Fuzzy Systems, 10*(6), 790. doi:10.1109/TFUZZ.2002.805880

Wu, J. & Zhou, Z.-H. (2003). Efficient face candidates selector for face detection. *The Journal of Pattern Recognition Society.*

Xiang, B., & Berger, T. (2003). Efficient text-independent speaker verification with structural gaussian mixture models and neural network. *IEEE Transactions on Speech and Audio Processing, 11*(5), 447–456. doi:10.1109/TSA.2003.815822

Chapter 16
Analysis and Modelling of Hierarchical Fuzzy Logic Systems

Masoud Mohammadian
University of Canberra, Australia

ABSTRACT

In this article the design and development of a hierarchical fuzzy logic system is investigated. A new method using an evolutionary algorithm for design of hierarchical fuzzy logic system for prediction and modelling of interest rates in Australia is developed. The hierarchical system is developed to model and predict three months (quarterly) interest rate fluctuations. This research study is unique in the way proposed method is applied to design and development of fuzzy logic systems. The new method proposed determines the number of layer for hierarchical fuzzy logic system. The advantages and disadvantages of using fuzzy logic systems for financial modelling is also considered. Conclusions on the accuracy of prediction using hierarchical fuzzy logic systems compared to a back-propagation neural network system and a hierarchical neural network are reported.

INTRODUCTION

Computational intelligence techniques such as neural networks, fuzzy logic, and evolutionary algorithms have been applied successfully in the place of the complex mathematical systems (Kosko, 1992; Cox, 1993). Neural networks and fuzzy logic are active research area (Zadeh, 1965; Kosko, 1992; Lee, 1990; Cox, 1993; Mohammadian & Stonier, 1995; Welstead, 1994). It has been found useful when the process is either difficult

to predict or difficult to model by conventional methods. Neural network modelling has numerous practical applications in control, prediction and inference.

Time series (Ruelle, 1998) are a special form of data where past values in the series may influence future values, based on presence of some underlying deterministic forces. Predictive model use trends cycles in the time series data to make prediction about the future trends in the time series. Predictive models attempt to recognise patterns and trends. Application of liner models to time series found to be inaccurate and there has been a great interest in nonlinear modelling techniques.

Recently techniques from computational intelligence fields have been successfully used in the place of the complex mathematical systems for forecasting of time series. These new techniques are capable of responding quickly and efficiently to the uncertainty and ambiguity of the system.

Fuzzy logic and neural network systems (Welstead, 1994) can be trained in an adaptive manner to map past and future values of a time series and thereby extract hidden structure and relationships governing the data. The systems have been successfully used in the place of the complex mathematical systems and have numerous practical applications in control, prediction and inference. They have been found useful when the system is either difficult to predict and or difficult to model by conventional methods. Fuzzy set theory provides a means for representing uncertainties. The underlying power of fuzzy logic is its ability to represent imprecise values in an understandable form. The majority of fuzzy logic systems to date have been static and based upon knowledge derived from imprecise heuristic knowledge of experienced operators, and where applicable also upon physical laws that governs the dynamics of the process.

Although its application to industrial problems has often produced results superior to classical control, the design procedures are limited by the heuristic rules of the system. It is simply assumed that the rules for the system are readily available or can be obtained. This implicit assumption limits the application of fuzzy logic to the cases of the system with a few parameters. The number of parameters of a system could be large.

Although the number of fuzzy rules of a system is directly dependant on these parameters. As the number of parameters increase, the number of fuzzy rules of the system grows exponentially.

In fuzzy logic systems, there is a direct relationship between the number of fuzzy sets of input parameters of the system and the size of the fuzzy knowledge base (FKB). Kosko (1992) calls this the "Curse of Dimensionality". The "curse" in this instance is that there is exponential growth in the size of the fuzzy knowledge base (FKB), where k is the number of rules in the FKB, m is the number of fuzzy sets for each input and n is the number of inputs into the fuzzy system.

As the number of fuzzy sets of input parameters increase, the number of rules increases exponentially. There are a number of ways that this exponential growth in the size of the FKB can be contained. The most obvious is to limit the number of inputs that the system is using. However, this may reduce the accuracy of the system, and in many cases, render the system being modelled unusable. Another approach is to reduce the number of fuzzy sets that each input has. Again, this may reduce the accuracy of the system. The number of rules in the FKB can also be trimmed if it is known that some rules are never used. This can be a time-consuming and tedious task, as every rule in the FKB may need to be looked at.

It has been suggested (Raju & Zhou, 1993; Mohammadian & Kingham, 1997; Mohammadian, Kingham & Bignall, 1998) using a hierarchical fuzzy logic structure for such fuzzy logic systems to overcome this problem. By using hierarchical fuzzy logic systems the number of fuzzy rules in the system are reduced, thereby reducing the computational time while maintaining the systems robustness and efficiency. In this article the design and development of a hierarchical fuzzy logic systems using genetic algorithms to model and predict interest rate in Australia is considered. Genetic algorithms are employed as an adaptive method for design and development of hierarchical fuzzy logic systems.

HIERARCHICAL FUZZY LOGIC SYSTEMS

The hierarchical fuzzy logic structure is formed by having the most influential inputs as the system variables in the first level of the hierarchy, the next important inputs in the second layer, and so on. If the hierarchical fuzzy logic structure contains n system input parameters and L number of hierarchical levels with n_i the number of variables contained in the ith level, the total number of rules k is then determined by:

$$k = \sum_{i=1}^{L} m^{n_i} \qquad (1)$$

where m is the number of fuzzy sets. The above equation means that by using a hierarchical fuzzy logic structure, the number of fuzzy rules for the system is reduced to a linear function of the number of system variables n, instead of an exponential function of n as is the conventional case. The first level of the hierarchy gives an approximate output, which is then modified by the second level rule set, and so on. This is repeated for all succeeding levels of the hierarchy. One problem occurs when it is not known which inputs to the system have more influence than the others. This is the case in many problems. In some case statistical analysis could be performed on the inputs to determine which ones have more bearing on the system.

INTEGRATED HIERARCHICAL FUZZY LOGIC AND GENETIC ALGORITHMS

Genetic algorithms (GAs) (Goonatilake, Campbell, & Ahmad, 1995; Goldberg, 1989) are powerful search algorithms based on the mechanism of natural selection and use operations of reproduction, crossover, and mutation on a population of strings. A set (population) of possible solutions, in this case, a coding of the fuzzy rules of a fuzzy logic system, represented as a string of numbers. New strings are produced every generation by the repetition of a two-step cycle. First each individual string is decoded and its ability to solve the problem is assessed. Each string is assigned a fitness value, depending on how well it performed. In the second stage the fittest strings are preferentially chosen for recombination to form the next generation. Recombination involves the selection of two strings, the choice of a crossover point in the string, and the switching of the segments to the right of this point, between the two strings (the cross-over operation). Figure 1 shows the combination of fuzzy logic and genetic algorithms for generating fuzzy rules.

For encoding and decoding of the fuzzy rule for a fuzzy logic system, first the input parameters of the fuzzy logic system is divided into fuzzy sets. Assume that the fuzzy logic system has two inputs α and β and a single output δ. Assume also that the inputs and output of the system is

Figure 1. Combination of fuzzy logic and genetic algorithms for fuzzy rule generation

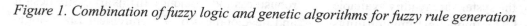
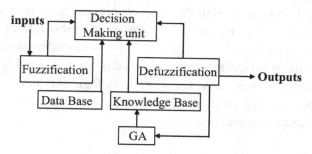

divided into 5 fuzzy sets. Therefore a maximum of twenty five fuzzy rules can be written for the fuzzy logic system.

The consequent for each fuzzy rule is determined by genetic evolution. In order to do so, the output fuzzy sets are encoded. It is not necessary to encode the input fuzzy sets because the input fuzzy sets are static and do not change.

The fuzzy rules relating the input variables (α and β) to the output variable (δ) have twenty five possible combinations. The consequent of each fuzzy rule can be any one of the five output fuzzy sets. Assume that the output fuzzy sets are: **NB** (Negative Big), **NS** (Negative Small), **ZE** (Zero), **PS** (Positive Small), and **PB** (Positive Big). Then the output fuzzy sets are encoded by assigning 1 = **NB** (Negative Big), 2 = **NS** (Negative Small), 3 = **ZE** (Zero), 4 = **PS** (Positive Small), and 5 = **PB** (Positive Big). Genetic algorithms randomly encode each output fuzzy set into a number ranging from 1 to 5 for all possible combinations of the input fuzzy variables. A string encoded this way can be represented as:

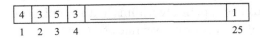

Each individual string is then decoded into the output linguistic terms. The set of fuzzy rules thus developed, is evaluated by the fuzzy logic system based upon a fitness value which is specific to the system. At the end of each generation, (two or more) copies of the best performing string from the parent generation is included in the next generation to ensure that the best performing strings are not lost. Genetic algorithms then performs the process of selection, crossover and mutation on the rest of the individual strings. Selection and crossover are the same as a simple genetic algorithms while the mutation operation is modified. Crossover and mutation take place based on the probability of crossover and mutation respectively. Mutation operator is changed to suit this problem. For mutation, an allele is selected

at random and it is replaced by a random number ranging from 1 to 5. The process of selection, crossover and mutation are repeated for a number of generations till a satisfactory fuzzy rule base is obtained. We define a satisfactory rule base as one whose fitness value differs from the desired output of the system by a very small value.

HIERARCHICAL FUZZY LOGIC SYSTEM FOR INTEREST RATE PREDICTION

There is a large interest by investors and government departments in the ability to predict future interest rate fluctuations from current economic data. Economists, and investors, have been unable to find all the factors that influence interest rate fluctuations. It is agreed however that there are some major economic indicators released by the government that are commonly used to look at the current position of the economy. These indicators used in this article are as follows:

- Interest Rate which is the indicator being predicted. The Interest Rate used here is the Australian Commonwealth government 10-year treasury bonds.
- Job Vacancies is where a position is available for immediate filling or for which recruitment action has been taken.
- The Unemployment Rate is the percentage of the labour force actively looking for work in the country.
- Gross Domestic Product is an average aggregate measure of the value of economic production in a given period.
- The Consumer Price Index is a general indicator of the rate of change in prices paid by consumers for goods and services.
- Household Saving Ratio is the ratio of household income saved to households disposable income.

- Home Loans measure the supply of finance for home loans, not the demand for housing.

  o *Average Weekly Earnings is the average amount of wages that a full time worker takes home before any taxes.*

  o *Current Account is the sum of the balances on merchandise trade, services trade, income and unrequited transfers.*

  o *Trade Weighted Index measures changes in our currency relative to the currencies of our main trading partners.*

  o *RBA Commodity Price Index provides an early indication of trends in Australia's export Prices.*

  o *All Industrial Index provides an indication of price movements on the Australian Stock Market.*

  o *Company Profits are defined as net operating profits or losses before income tax.*

  o *New Motor Vehicles is the number of new vehicles registered in Australia.*

By creating a system that contained all these indicators, we would be in a much better position to predict the fluctuations in interest rates. A fuzzy logic system that used every indicator and had five fuzzy sets for every indicator would result in a large FKB consisting of over six billion rules! As can be imagined, this would require large computing power to not only train the fuzzy logic system with a genetic algorithm, but also large storage and run-time costs when the system is operational. Even if a computer could adequately handle this large amount of data, there is still the problem in having enough data to properly train every possible rule. To overcome this problem a hierarchical fuzzy logic structure for the fuzzy logic system can be constructed. By using a hierarchical fuzzy logic system, the number of fuzzy rules of the system is reduced

hence computational times are decreased resulting in a more efficient system. A novel way to tackle this problem would be to group the relevant indicators and to build a fuzzy knowledge base for each group. The first step is to divide the indicators into smaller-related groups. This problem was investigated by Mohammadian and Kingham (1997) and Mohammadian, Kingham, and Bignall (1998) and is shown below:

1. **Employment** (Job Vacancies, Unemployment Rate)
2. **Country** (Gross Domestic Product, Consumer Price Index)
3. **Savings** (Household Saving Ratio, Home Loans, Average Weekly Earnings)
4. **Foreign** (Current Account, RBA Index, Trade Weighted Index)
5. **Company** (All Industrial Index, Company Profit, New Motor Vehicles)

The interest rate is included with each of the groups above. To learn the fuzzy knowledge base for each group, a genetic algorithm was implemented. The genetic algorithms had a population size of 500 with a crossover rate of 0.6 and a mutation rate of 0.01 and it was run for 10000 generations over 10 years (a period of 40 quarters) data. Fitness of each string of the genetic algorithm was calculated as the sum of the absolute differences from the predicted quarter and the actual quarters interest rate. The fitness was subtracted from an 'optimal' fitness amount, which was decided to be 30 as it was unlikely the error amount would be higher than this over 10 years (Mohammadian, Kingham, 1997, Mohammadian, Kingham, Bignall, 1998). The fitness of the system is calculated by the following formula:

$$fitness = 30 - \sum_{i=0}^{30} abs(PI_i - I_{i+1}) \qquad (2)$$

An elitist strategy was used in that the best population generated was saved and entered in the next generation (two copies of the string with best fitness was included to the next generation). The five fuzzy knowledge bases created form the top layer of the hierarchy are shown in Figure 2. Mohammadian and Kingham (1997) designed and connected together the fuzzy knowledge bases to form a final fuzzy knowledge base system. The final fuzzy knowledge base system shown in Figure 2 then uses the predicted interest rate from the five above groups to produce a final interest rate prediction. The number of fuzzy rules for each group is shown in Figure 2.

The final hierarchical FKB contains 3125 rules (Mohammadian & Kingham, 1997) giving the total number of rules learnt as 5250. This is a significant reduction from the 6 billion rules that would have been used previously. This allows quicker training time without the need for huge computer resources (Mohammadian & Kingham, 1997). Good prediction of Australian quarterly Interest rate can be obtained using the above system. The number of fuzzy rule are used are also reduced dramatically.

However there is still a question: Does a two layer hierarchical architecture provides the best solution?

To answer this question, one can start building three, four layer hierarchical fuzzy logic system by trial and error to possibly find the correct number of layers required. This could be cumbersome

problem. We need to know how many layers are required and which fuzzy knowledge base should be used in each layer. Genetic algorithms can be used to solve this problem by determining the number of layer in the hierarchical fuzzy logic system and the correct combination of FKBs for each layer see Figure 3.

Next the performance of genetic algorithms for design and development of hierarchical fuzzy logic systems is considered. The system is developed in such a way to provide the possible best architecture for designing hierarchical fuzzy logic systems for prediction of interest rate in Australia. Using the economic indicators five fuzzy logic systems were developed from five groups each produce a predicted interest rate for the next quarter. Genetic algorithms were then used to design and develop a hierarchical fuzzy logic system.

The hierarchical fuzzy logic system developed was then used to predicted interest rate For each of these groups, the current quarter's interest rate is included in the indicators used (Mohammadian & Kingham, 1997). The advantage of using this hierarchical fuzzy logic structure is that the number of rules used in the knowledge base of fuzzy logic systems has been reduced substantially. For encoding and decoding of the hierarchical fuzzy logic system, first a number is allocated to each fuzzy logic system developed from group of in-

Figure 2. Hierarchical fuzzy logic system (Mohammadian, Kingham, 1997, Mohammadian, Kingham, Bignall, 1998)

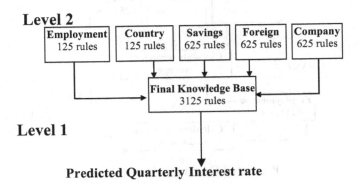

dicators. For this simulation the number allocated to each group is shown below:

1 = Employment, 2 = Country, 3 = Savings, 4 = Foreign, 5 = Company

The number of layers and the fuzzy logic system/s for each layer is determined by genetic algorithms. In order to do so a number is allocated to each fuzzy logic system. Genetic algorithms randomly encode each fuzzy logic system into a number ranging from 1 to 5 for all possible combinations of the fuzzy logic systems. The level in the hierarchy in which a fuzzy logic system is allocated to, is also encoded each string. A string is encoded this way can be represented as:

Fuzzy Logic system

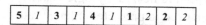

| 5 | *1* | 3 | *1* | 4 | *1* | 1 | 2 | 2 | 2 |

Level in hierarchy

Each individual string is then decoded into a hierarchical fuzzy logic system that defines the fuzzy logic system/s for each level of the hierarchical fuzzy logic system. The above string once decoded will provide a hierarchical fuzzy logic

system as shown in Figure 3 above. The set of hierarchical fuzzy logic systems thus developed, are evaluated and a fitness value is given to each string. At the end of each generation, (two or more) copies of the best performing string from the parent generation is included in the next generation to ensure that the best performing strings are not lost. Genetic algorithms then performs the process of selection, crossover and mutation on the rest of the individual strings. Crossover and mutation take place based on the probability of crossover and mutation respectively. Mutation operator is changed to suit this problem. The process of selection, crossover and mutation are repeated for a number of generations till a satisfactory hierarchical fuzzy logic system is obtained. We define a satisfactory hierarchical fuzzy logic system as one whose fitness value (predicated interest rate) differs from the desired output of the system (in this case the actual interest rate) by a very small value. We calculate the average error of the system for the training set and tests sets using the following formula (Mohammadian & Kingham, 1997):

$$E = \frac{\sum_{i=1}^{n} abs(Pi - Ai)}{n} \tag{3}$$

Figure 3. A three-layer hierarchical fuzzy logic system—3125 fuzzy rules

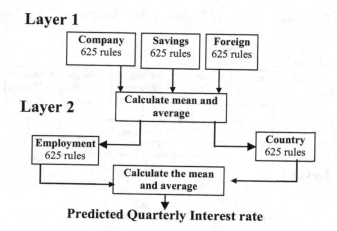

where E is the average error, *Pi* is the Predicted interest rate at time period *i*, *Ai* is the actual interest rate for the quarter and *n* is the number of quarters predicted. By using genetic algorithms to design and develop hierarchical fuzzy logic system better results were obtained. The hierarchical fuzzy logic systems developed using genetic algorithms perform predict the interest rate to different degree of accuracy. It is however interesting to see that genetic algorithms is capable of providing different hierarchical fuzzy logic system for predicting the interest rate. It is now possible to choose the best hierarchical fuzzy logic system among those suggested by genetic algorithms. The result of the top performing five hierarchical fuzzy logic systems designed by genetic algorithms is given in Table 1. Comparison of average errors of these five best hierarchical fuzzy logic systems designed and developed using genetic algorithms is also shown in Table 1.

COMPARISON OF HIERARCHICAL FUZZY LOGIC SYSTEM WITH NEURAL NETWORK SYSTEM FOR PREDICTION OF INTEREST RATE

Mohammadian and Kingham (1997) reported the use of a hierarchical neural network system using the same data inputs as described above for the hierarchical fuzzy logic system. Using these economic indicators a neural network system was created for each five groups (country group, employment group, savings group, company group and foreign group). Each neural network system was trained using back-propagation algorithms. A back-propagation neural network was used with two hidden layers, each consisting of 20 neurons, output layer consists of one node. Sigmoid learning was used to predict the following quarters interest rate. The error tolerance was set to 0.0001, the Learning Parameter (Beta) was set to 0.6, momentum (alpha) and Noise Factor were both set to 0. The neural network was trained for 10000 cycles (Mohammadian & Kingham, 1997; Mohammadian, Kingham, & Bignall, 1998). After training each neural network system for each group, all neural network systems were combined to form a hierarchical neural network system with the same structure as shown in Figure 2. The final neural network system then was trained. It used the prediction of all five neural networks for each group to predict the quarterly interest rate as its output. Table 1 shows the comparison of the average errors of hierarchical fuzzy logic systems designed and developed using GA and average errors of hierarchical neural networks by Mohammadian and Kingham, (1997).

Table 1. Average Errors of hierarchical fuzzy logic (HFL) systems designed and developed using GA and Average Errors of hierarchical neural networks by (Mohammadian, Kingham, 1997, Mohammadian, Kingham, Bignall, 1998)

	Training Error	Testing Error
Hierarchical fuzzy logic #1	0.356	0.659
Hierarchical fuzzy logic #2	0.343	0.663
Hierarchical fuzzy logic #3	0.289	0.494
Hierarchical fuzzy logic #4	0.274	0.441
Hierarchical fuzzy logic #5	0.291	0.398
Hierarchical neural network	0.354	0.607

CONCLUSION AND FURTHER INVESTIGATIONS

In this article an innovative method is used to design and develop hierarchical fuzzy logic systems. Genetic algorithms is used as an adaptive learning method to design a hierarchical fuzzy logic systems to predict the quarterly interest rate in Australia. Using a hierarchical fuzzy logic system, the number of fuzzy rules in the fuzzy knowledge base is reduced dramatically hence computational times are decreased resulting in a more efficient system. Genetic algorithms are also used to obtain the fuzzy rules for each fuzzy logic system of a hierarchical fuzzy logic system.

From simulation results it was found that the hierarchical fuzzy logic system is capable of making accurate predictions of the following quarter's interest rate. The prediction result of the top five hierarchical fuzzy logic systems were compared to a hierarchical neural network. It was found that most of the top five hierarchical fuzzy logic system designed by genetic algorithms performed better than the hierarchical neural network. It should be noted that hierarchical neural network was designed based on the intuition (Mohammadian & Kingham, 1997; Mohammadian, Kingham, & Bignall, 1998) and it may be possible to obtain better prediction results using an automated system using genetic algorithms to automatically design the hierarchical neural network system. The research work performed in this article is unique in the way the hierarchical fuzzy logic systems are developed. The application of this method to several industrial problems such as robotic control and collision avoidance of multi-robot systems is currently under consideration. Research is also currently being performed to automatically design a hierarchical neural network system for modeling and prediction.

REFERENCES

Cox, E., (1993, February). Adaptive fuzzy systems. *IEEE Spectrum*, 27-31.

Goldberg, D. (1989). *Genetic algorithms in search, optimisation and machine learning.* Reading, Massachusetts: Addison Wesley, USA.

Goonatilake, S. Campbell, J. A., & Ahmad, N. (1995). Genetic-fuzzy systems for financial decision making, advances in fuzzy logic, neural networks and genetic algorithms. *IEEE/ Nagoya-University World Wisepersons Workshop*, Springer, (LNAI), Germany.

Kosko, B. (1992). *Neural networks and fuzzy systems, a dynamic system*, Prentice-Hall: Englewood Cliff, USA.

Lee, C. C. (1990). Fuzzy logic in control systems: Fuzzy controllers - part I, part II., *IEEE Transactions on Systems, Man and Cybernetics, 2092*(404-435).

Mohammadian, M. Kingham, M., & Bignall, B. (1998). Hierarchical fuzzy logic for financial modelling and prediction, *Journal of Computational Intelligence in Finance*, UK.

Mohammadian, M., & Kingham. M. (1997). Hierarchical fuzzy logic for financial modelling and prediction, *Tenth Australian Joint Conference on Artificial Intelligence*, 147-156, Perth, Australia.

Mohammadian, M., & Stonier, R. J. (1995). Adaptive two layer control of a mobile robot systems. *Proceedings of IEEE International Conference on Evolutionary Computing*, Perth, Australia.

Raju, G. V. S., & Zhou, J. (1993). Adaptive hierarchical fuzzy controller. *IEEE Transactions on Systems, Man & Cybernetics*, 23(4), 973-980, USA.

Ruelle. D. (1998). *Chaotic evolution and strtange attractors: The statistical analysis of time series for deterministic nonlinear systems.* Cambridge Uni Press, USA.

Welstead, T. (1994). Neural networks and fuzzy logic applications in C/C++, Wiley, USA.

Zadeh, L. (1965). Fuzzy sets. *Inf. Control*, 8, 338-353.

Chapter 17
Fuzzy Logic in Medicine

Michelle LaBrunda
Cabrini Medical Center, USA

Andrew LaBrunda
University of Guam, USA

ABSTRACT

This article explores the use of fuzzy logic in the medical field. While giving a comparison of classic and fuzzy logic we present the various uses of the applications made possible by fuzzy logic, focusing on diagnosis and treatment. The ever evolving technology making the line between medicine and technology thinner every year, is helping to make the treatment of disease and the mending of injury easier for medical professionals. We also propose several questions that arise from, and may by answered by, fuzzy logic and its applications.

INTRODUCTION

In order to understand the intricacies of fuzzy logic one must build from a thorough understanding of classical logic. A basic component of classic logic is the proposition that a statement can be characterized as either true or false. An example of a proposition is "The country of France contains the Eiffel tower" or "The Eiffel tower is closed on Sundays." In classical logic, propositions are said to be either true or false. Propositions are typically connected using AND, OR, and NOT. On occasion, one might use other connections,

but they can all be derived from a combination of these three. The notation used to describe classic logic is called propositional calculus. In most computer programming languages it is common to assign numerical values to the correctness of a proposition where 1 = true and 0 = false. A proposition can either be true or it can be false. It cannot be both at the same time, nor can it simultaneously be neither. Collections of propositions can be transformed to prove truths that might not necessarily be evident on their own. The basic rules of mathematics have been transcribed into propositional calculus and as a result computers are now able to transform a series of propositions into mathematical proofs. Computers are now able to solve proofs in ways never previously conceived.

Fuzzy logic is similar to classical logic in the search for truthfulness of a proposition. Sometimes truth is subjective ill defined. As an example, it is difficult to assign a true or false value to the proposition "Andy is tall" or "Shell is old." How tall does one have to be before being categorized as "tall"? Likewise, how old does one have to be before being considered "old"? Most would agree that 100 years is old for a person but young for a planet. Like many real-world propositions, the concept of age is relative to its usage. To solve these problems there was a need to develop a more robust system of logic. Rather than assigning a proposition as either 0 or 1 the idea of variable truth was added. The variable is measured over the interval of [0, 1]. Fuzzy logic rose from this concept. One major focus of this discipline is in the development of computational models, which can accurately assign fractional values to the level of truthfulness.

Contrary to the name, the goal of fuzzy logic is to create computer programs that can accept input and provide the user a clear answer. The system is defined as "fuzzy" because it is not always evident, given the input parameters, what logic path the system will take to derive a solution. Fuzzy logic systems are frequently used as expert systems. This type of system attempts to emulate a field expert of a specific discipline. Ideally this software-based expert would be able to accept input, process the information, and output clear concise responses. Unfortunately, in emulating the thought processes of such an expert, the expert system must emulate human thought. Human thought is fuzzy in nature complete with uncertainties, ambiguities, and contradictions. Two experts might not place the same level of importance on the same piece of information. Additionally, they might not look at the same information the same way. Should a glass filled 50% be classified as half full or half empty?

Many techniques have been used to create fuzzy logic programs that function as an expert. The earliest systems used conditional statements with tolerance thresholds using if-then-else rules (Jackson, 1999). This approach, while seemingly simplistic, has been used successfully in a wide variety of medical applications including diagnostics and psychological bias (Shortliffe, 1976). Other less known approaches of fuzzy logic systems are association nets and frames, which have proven difficult to implement with only marginal results. The two most common implementations of fuzzy logic are rule-based and neural networks. Both fuzzy implementations have a diverse range of applications including medicine, avionics, security, and machine learning.

Unlike rule-based fuzzy logic, neural nets do not require thinking patterns to be explicitly specified. Typically two data sets are created to program a neural network. The first data set is the trainer. This set of input is passed into the neural network and processed. The processing phase consists of sorting the input values among an array of memory structures call nodes. Each node retains some information and sorts the remaining information between neighboring nodes. Once all the information has been processed it is evaluated and stored as the template for which all other datasets will be compared.

This technique can loosely be compared to the Japanese game Pachinko, also seen in the game show Price is Right as Plinko. The input values are represented by silver balls that are dropped into an arrangement of pins held by a board. Before the balls reach their final stop at the bottom of the board they make contact with many pins, which change the balls direction and velocity. This makes it almost impossible to predict where a ball will end up when dropped. In the real world, chaos prevents the same input from yielding a consistent output. In a computer model, the same input will always produce the same output. So as the computer receives input, these data are feed into a virtual pachinko machine. The first batch of input is called the trainer input and represents where the balls should be landing under ideal conditions. Once the machine has been trained, new input can be fed into the same virtual pachinko machine. Once processing is complete, the landing spots for the input are compared against a trainer dataset. The greater the discrepancy between the trainer set and the actual set, the greater the error in the system. To complete the analogy, computer scientists put a great deal of effort into determining the optimal location and elasticity of the pins to make sure that good input and bad input produce different results. In the case of expert systems, neural networks do not explicitly extract the rules of an expert. Rather the neural network has learned only to recognize patterns. Therefore, while the results may be good, the neural network will not know why an answer is correct other than to say it looks like other successful inputs. The strength of this approach is that it is not necessary to program each business rule. The weakness of this approach is that substantial training may be required.

Rule-based systems explicitly collect the expert's knowledge. These rules and thinking patterns are then programmed into the system. An important phase of this approach is knowledge acquisition. During this phase a team of programmers develop a rigorous and complete model of the domain rules to be implemented. Rule-based systems do not require a large training set like that of neural network solutions. This is because the domain expert has clearly specified the rules and parameters, whereas a neural network has no knowledge of domain rules, only patterns that seem to have been enforced in past successes. During testing there is usually a tuning phase, where parameters are modified based upon the results of the test data. In addition to smaller datasets, another advantage of a rule-based fuzzy logic system is that it is easier for the system to rationalize its behavior to users. Rule-based fuzzy logic system behavior is determined by rules

or parameters and changes to these parameters represent the incentives for the system to take action. This is much more easily communicated to an expert and programmer using rule-based fuzzy logic than a neural network.

FUZZY LOGIC IN THE MEDICAL FIELD

While computer scientists are refining and advancing fuzzy logic, applications within the medical field have already started to emerge. Some of these applications are rudimentary, but with time will prove invaluable. Fuzzy logic has made its way into general medicine, basic science, as well as diagnosis and treatment.

General Medicine

General medicine encompasses an enormous body of knowledge drawing from almost every field imaginable. As technology advances, the lines between medicine and technology are blurring. Fuzzy technology is a relatively new concept in computer science and few articles have been written applying fuzzy logic to medical topics. The application of fuzzy logic in general medicine has been used in addiction modeling, mapping of bruising after being shot while wearing body armor, and in the analysis and evaluation of chronic disease.

The data that are available focus heavily on the mathematics and computer science involved in applying basic fuzzy concepts to medicine. For example, an article by Nieto and Torres (2003) describes a model examining the risk of illicit drug use based on alcohol consumption and smoking habits of adolescents. Instead of labeling people as smokers or non-smokers, the degree of smoking is given a value between 0 (non-smoking) and 1 (smokes like a chimney). The same is true for alcohol consumption. Kosko's hypercube was used and a fuzzy set with a point in a unit hypercube was identified. A hypercube is an "n" dimensional figure analogous to a square. For example, if n=2 the hypercube is a square, if n=3 the hypercube is a cube. They performed a similar successful analysis looking at stroke risk factors. The article largely focuses on the engineering and mathematics behind fuzzy systems. As the utilization of fuzzy systems becomes more intuitive it is likely that articles focusing on the medical application of these systems will become available.

Lee, Kosko, and Anderson (2005) also examine a fuzzy system application to medicine. This article models gunshot bruises in soft body armor with a fuzzy system. When someone wearing soft body armor is shot, the bullet is stopped, but a bruise is produced. Analysis of the bruise and armor deformation can give information on the bullet's mass and momentum. Detailed analysis of information provided from studies such as this may allow engineers to design new types of armor better able to protect the body while minimizing armor weight. While the direct applications to medicine may be somewhat distant, the thought process involved in developing this article further combine medicine and technology bringing the real application closer to existence.

Many facets of general medicine deal with chronic disease. Chronic diseases are illnesses that last for a long time. Examples of chronic disease that will be discussed in this article are chronic kidney disease, cancer, and HIV.

The Diatelic project is a prospective randomized research project designed to test the ability of a fuzzy system to monitor chronic kidney disease patients and alert a physician of disease progression (Jeanpierre & Charpillet, 2004). In this project, patients provided daily Internet updates. These updates were analyzed by a computer using partially observable Markov decision process (POMPD) logic. POMPD is a mathematical framework from which decision-making modeling systems can be made when some of the factors are random and others are controlled. It assumes that the current state of the modeled object cannot be completely known. In the aforementioned study, a nephrologist (kidney specialist) was notified if a patient's condition appeared to be progressing. This system utilizing POMPD requires relatively low computing complexity. As the number of physicians per person continues to decline, systems of this sort will play an important roll in monitoring patient's health, disease progress, and physician alerting as problems develop.

Recent research has been done looking at fuzzy logic in diagnosing breast cancer (Polat, Şahan, Kodaz, & Güneş, 2007). The artificial immune recognition system (AIRS) has been around since 2001. It is a learning algorithm modeled after the functioning of the immune system. Polat et al. applied performance evaluation with fuzzy resource allocation mechanisms to the AIRS creating a new system, Fuzzy-AIRS. Fuzzy-AIRS was used to analyze data from a Wisconsin breast cancer dataset and predicted which samples were most likely to be cancerous. The Fuzzy-AIRS results were compared with histological diagnosis and found to be 99% accurate. Methods such as Fuzzy-AIRS can greatly reduce the time required to analyze samples and allow for more prompt diagnosis and treatment.

HIV is no longer the death sentence it once was. HIV-infected individuals in developed nations are now living nearly normal life spans thanks to advances in medication therapy and diagnosis. Many questions face infectious disease physicians when deciding how to treat HIV. These questions include when to start therapy, what medications to give, and when to change the medications. Medication is generally changed when the HIV mutates and becomes resistant to the medications that the patient is receiving. Recent research by Sloot, Boukhanovsky, Keulen, Tirado-Ramos, and Boucher (2005) utilizes multivariate analyses combined with rule-based fuzzy logic to produces a physician advice system. This system integrates a number of factors affecting the outcome of therapy and suggests a clinical course of action. As the understanding of disease, disease process, and the availability and complexity of medications increases, physicians will become more and more dependent on advice systems such as this in medical decision making. This system would also allow less skilled physicians to provide a basic level of care. This would be of enormous value in developing countries where access to physicians and therapeutic intervention is limited.

Basic Science

Taking a scientific concept and eventually developing a medical application for that concept is a long process. Basic biomedical science is the study of components of biological systems. The goals of this research do not often have direct medical applications but rather provide the building blocks for advanced biomedical diagnostic and therapeutic regimes. All medical advances have their roots in the basic sciences. Basic science includes fields such as biology, microbiology, physics, chemistry, and bioengineering. Fuzzy logic has allowed researchers to make advances that would be difficult and time consuming through other modalities, especially in the arena of modeling complex systems.

One example of the application of fuzzy logic in basic science has been done in the field of gene expression. Almost every cell in the human body contains DNA. DNA is the blueprint directing cellular functions to make each person into a human being and unique individual. On each strand of DNA are regions called genes. Genes can be thought of as the active part of DNA. Each gene contains specific directions on how to make one of the bodies many proteins. Some genes are always active. Others are only active before birth, while others are activated only under special circumstances such as pregnancy or adolescence. Genes that are activated are called expressed genes because their corresponding proteins are produced. The control of gene expression is extremely complex involving numerous chemical messengers that are not completely understood. Disregulation of gene expression has been associated with numerous diseases, most notably cancer.

A study by Du, Gong, Wurtele, and Dickerson (2005) models gene expression utilizing fuzzy logic. Because there are numerous layers of interconnecting factors regulating expression, it is amenable to fuzzy logic modeling. Cluster analysis assumes that genes with similar functions have similar mechanisms of control and produce models based on this assumption. By analyzing these repeated patterns new mechanisms of control have been elucidated.

Another related basic science topic is protein engineering. Proteins are typically built by cellular machinery that is difficult to manipulate. Engineered proteins have applications in the pharmaceutical, agricultural, and synthetic organic chemistry fields, but pure proteins must be produced. The screening of proteins to determine which synthetic proteins have desired traits is a labor intensive and expensive process involving the processing of huge amounts of data. Kato et al. (2005) developed a strategy utilizing a fuzzy neural network to screen proteins constructing a method for more quickly and efficiently screening large sets of proteins.

Diagnosis and Treatment

Once basic science has been well understood, the medical applications of this technology can be explored. Neural network and fuzzy logic have been slowly making their way into medical diagnosis and treatment as well as basic sciences. Fuzzy logic is primarily used as a modeling tool and can help to manage large sets of data while identifying individuals who follow a typical pattern of disease or disease progression. An automated system is much more efficient in processing large amounts from a number of simultaneous sources of data than the manual systems currently employed. Efforts are currently being made to determine optimal modeling systems that will allow data to be processed in an accurate and clinically meaningful manner.

A number of studies are being undertaken evaluating the role of fuzzy logic modeling in medicine. Many diseases have overlapping symptoms and the diagnosis is not always clear. John and Innocent (2005) recently published an article utilizing a fuzzy logic system to differentiate between diseases with similar symptoms. While not yet a perfect model, systems such as this may one day be of great benefit to physicians in trying to distinguish between diseases with similar symptoms. A recent review article by Grossi and Buscema (2006) looks at the application of artificial intelligence and fuzzy systems to outcomes research. As technology advances, fuzzy logic modeling systems may prove invaluable to outcomes research allowing complex data from multiple sources to be integrated into one conclusion that is accessible to patients and their healthcare providers.

Artificial intelligence and fuzzy systems have provided the opportunity to study what has traditionally fallen into the realms of philosophy and psychiatry. Sripada, Jobe, and Helgason (2005) have devised a fuzzy logic model of empathy. The ability to model complex systems may one day suggest treatments for diseases that currently have no therapies.

CONCLUSION

Computer-generated models may be highly accurate, but they will never be perfect. As many questions as answers are generated by high-powered fuzzy modeling systems. How precise must a fuzzy modeling system be before it can be implemented? If a modeling system fails and a patient is not properly diagnosed, who is at fault, the programmer, the physician, or the patient?

With these new modeling systems comes a plethora of ethical questions that will no longer be limited to science fiction films. Will we some day be able to model a person's behavior throughout their life based on their DNA? What would happen if modeling suggests that a baby is likely to become a murderer? If we can model classically human traits such as fear, love, and happiness, where will the limits between human and machine fall? Will we one day select our children based on computer modeling systems predicting their behavior, physical appearance, and aptitudes?

While these questions may seem somewhat premature, they are within the scope of reality. Fuzzy systems and neural networking provide a powerful modeling tool, the breadth of which we are only beginning to comprehend.

REFERENCES

Buchanan, B., & Shortliffe, E. (Eds.). (1984). *Rule-based expert systems*. Reading, MA: Addison-Wesley.

Du, P., Gong, J., Wurtele, E., & Dickerson, J. (2005). Modeling gene expression networks using fuzzy logic. *IEEE Transactions on Systems, Man and Cybernetics—Part B: Cybernetics, 35*(6), 1351-1359.

Grossi, E., & Buscema, M. (2006). Artificial intelligence and outcome research. *Drug Development Research, 67,* 227-244.

Jackson, P. (1999). *Introduction to expert systems*. Reading, MA: Addison-Wesley.

Jeanpierre, L., & Charpillet, F. (2004). Automated medical diagnosis with fuzzy stochastic models: Monitoring chronic diseases. *Acta Biotheoretica, 52,* 291-311.

John, R., & Innocent, P. (2005). Modeling uncertainty in clinical diagnosis using fuzzy logic. *IEEE Transactions on Systems, Man and Cybernetics—Part B: Cybernetics, 35*(6), 1340-1350.

Kato, R., Nakano, H., Konishi, H., Kato, K., Koga, Y., Yamane, T., et al. (2005). Novel strategy for protein exploration: High-throughput screening assisted with fuzzy neural network. *Journal of Molecular Biology, 351,* 683-692.

Lee, I., Kosko, B., & Anderson, F. (2005). Modeling gunshot bruises in soft body armor with an adaptive fuzzy system. *IEEE Transactions on Systems, Man and Cybernetics—Part B: Cybernetics, 35*(6), 1374-1390.

Nieto, J., & Torres, A. (2003). Midpoints for fuzzy sets and their application in medicine. *Artificial Intelligence in Medicine, 27,* 81-101.

Polat, K., , S. (2007). Breast cancer and liver disorders classification using artificial immune recogni-

tion system (AIRS) with performance evaluation by fuzzy resource allocation mechanism. *Expert Systems with Applications, 32,* 172-183.

Shortliffe, E. (1976). *Computer-based medical consultations: MYCIN.* New York: Elsevier.

Sloot, P., Boukhanovsky, A., Keulen, W., Tirado-Ramos, A., & Boucher, C. (2005). A grid-based HIV expert system. *Journal of Clinical Monitoring and Computing, 19,* 263-278.

Sripada, B., Jobe, T., & Helgason, C. (2005). From fuzzy logic toward plurimonism: The science of active and empathic observation. *IEEE Transactions on Systems, Man and Cybernetics—Part B: Cybernetics, 35*(6), 1328-1339.

This work was previously published in the Journal of Information Technology Research, Vol. 1, Issue 1, edited by M. Khosrow-Pour, pp. 27-33, copyright 2008 by IGI Publishing (an imprint of IGI Global).

Chapter 18
On Bias–Variance Analysis for Probabilistic Logic Models

Huma Lodhi
Imperial College London, UK

ABSTRACT

Deliberate exploitation of natural resources and excessive use of environmentally abhorrent materials have resulted in environmental disruptions threatening the life support systems. A human centric approach of development has already damaged nature to a large extent. This has attracted the attention of environmental specialists and policy makers. It has also led to discussions at various national and international conventions. The objective of protecting natural resources cannot be achieved without the involvement of professionals from multidisciplinary areas. This chapter recommends a model for the creation of knowledge-based systems for natural resources management. Further, it describes making use of unique capabilities of remote sensing satellites for conserving natural resources and managing natural disasters. It is exclusively for the people who are not familiar with the technology and who are given the task of framing policies.

INTRODUCTION

During the past few years, many methods have been proposed that are at the intersection of logic and probability. The distinguishing characteristic of these techniques is the provision of efficient representation for complex real world problem. For example, Stochastic Logic Programs (SLPs) (Muggleton, 1996) combine probabilistic models such as Stochastic Context Free Grammars (SCFG) and Hidden Markov Models (HMM) with first order logic. SLPs provide an efficient representation for complex biological systems such as metabolic pathways. Another competitive approach is termed Bayesian Logic Programs (BLPs) (Kersting & De Raedt) that are considered as generalization of Bayesian nets and logic programs. Newly proposed Markov logic networks (MLNs) (Richardson & Domingos, 2006) are also a useful example of combining probabilistic graphical models and logic.

More recently, there has been a growing interest in learning probabilistic logic representations. For instance, Failure Adjusted Maximization (FAM) (Cussens, 2001) is a useful tool to learn parameters in SLPs and Balios (Kersting & Dick, 2004) is a system that performs inference and learning in BLPs. While systems and techniques have been proposed for probabilistic logic learning, research has not been conducted in the important direction of analyzing the performance of probabilistic logic learners. Tools and methods to study the performance of probabilistic logical learning algorithms have not been investigated. In this article we focus on the unexplored research direction. We propose bias-variance (BV) decomposition to analyze and investigate the prediction (estimation) performance of the probabilistic logic learning algorithms for parameter estimation task.

In this article we specifically focus on a particular approach, namely Stochastic Logic Programs that provide formalism for probabilistic knowledge representation. We employ FAM to learn parameters on the SLP. In order to study and analyze the prediction performance of probabilistic logic learning algorithms such as FAM we present definitions for bias and variance.

In order to empirically analyze the BV definitions we focus on a challenging and fundamental task in computational systems biology, namely quantitative modelling of metabolic pathways. Recent research has shown critical importance of quantitative aspects of biological information stored in complex networks and pathways for the system level understanding of biology (Kitano 2002a, 2002b). We have conducted experiments using metabolic pathways in Saccharomyces cerevisiae. We have applied the proposed bias-variance definitions for estimating the rates of reactions catalyzed by enzymes in pathways using FAM.

The article is organized as follows. Section 2 briefly explains metabolic pathways. In Section 3 we describe logic programming concepts, SLPs and FAM. We present BV decomposition for pa-rameter estimation task in Section 4. Experimental results are described in Section 5 and Section 6 concludes the article.

METABOLIC PATHWAYS

Metabolic pathways, an important class of biological systems, represent chemical reactions within the confines of a cell. They comprise metabolites and enzymes and may be viewed as series of enzyme-catalyzed reactions in which product of one reaction becomes substrate for the next reaction. Dynamics of biological system and behaviour of enzymes in metabolic pathways can be studied by applying the Michaelis-Menten (MM) enzyme kinetic function, but the well-known method, namely Lineweaver-Burk or double reciprocal method (Lineweaver & Burk, 1934) is not free of problems. Dowd and Riggs (1945) analysis of the method gave discouraging and unsatisfactory results for estimating the kinetic parameters. Ritchie and Pravan (1996) have also observed that Lineweaver-Burk method can lead to unsatisfactory results. Furthermore it is computationally exhaustive to solve the MM equation using numerical methods (Duggleby 1994, 1995; Schnell & Mendoza, 2001).

In order to analyze and model metabolic pathways Petri nets have been used. Petri nets (Petri, 1962) are bipartite directed graphs. In a Petri net representation metabolites are represented by place nodes and transition nodes represent enzyme catalyzed reactions. Reddy, Mavrovouniotis, and Liebman (1993) and Hofestaedt (1994) pioneered the use of Petri nets for modelling metabolic pathways. In Angelopoulos and Muggleton (2002) SLPs have been applied to represent metabolic pathways and in order to learn metabolic pathways models FAM has been used. Lodhi and Muggleton (2004) have presented ensembles of FAM to induce quantitative models of metabolic pathways. In this article we analyze the performance of FAM for metabolic pathway modelling by decomposing the predictive error in bias and variance.

STOCHASTIC LOGIC PROGRAMS

We first give a very brief overview of logic programming concepts and then describe Stochastic Logic Programs and Failure Adjusted Maximization.

Logic Programming Preliminaries

In first order logic the alphabet comprises entities including constants, variables, function symbols, and predicate symbols. A term is a constant, variable, or a function symbol applied to terms, while an atomic formula (atom) is a predicate symbol applied to terms. A literal is an atomic formula or negated atomic formula. For example, $Q(b,f(c))$ and $\neg P(x,y)$ are examples of positive and negative literals respectively. A clause is a disjunction of literals. The clause $H \leftarrow B_1,..., B_n$ that contains at most one positive literal and zero or more negative literals is known as Horn clause. The negative literals $B_1,..., B_n$ constitute body of the clause and the positive literal H is head of the clause. The special Horn clause that contains exactly one positive literal and zero or more negative literals is called the definite clause. A Goal and a fact are the Horn clauses with an empty head and an empty body, respectively.

A Substitution θ maps variables to first order terms. For example in literal $Q(b, Z)$ mapping of variable Z to term $f(c)$ generates literal $Q(b, f(c))$. Unification is the process in which substitution is computed such that $B_1\theta = B_2\theta$, where B_1 and B_2 can be terms, literals or disjunction, or conjunction of literals. Resolution is an inference rule that is applied to clauses and each resolution step generates a new clause. The output of resolution applied to two clauses is a clause that comprises all the literals that occur in both the clauses except the pair of complementary literals. In order to obtain the complementary pair generally unification is applied. We now consider an instance of resolution for Horn clauses, Linear resolution for Definite clauses with Selection function (SLD) that is used to obtain a goal from a goal and a definite clause. An atom, selected from a goal, is unified with the head of a definite clause thus giving a new goal. An SLD-derivation of a definite goal G_0 is a sequence of goals $G_0,... G_i,... G_n$, where each goal G_i is obtained from pervious goal G_{i-1}. The sequence of goals is obtained using a set of definite clauses and a computation rule (selection function). A computation rule is a function from goals to atoms in a given goal. An SLD-derivation that ends in a non-empty goal is a failed SLD-derivation whereas a successful SLD-derivation ends in an empty goal. An SLD refutation of goal G_0 is a finite SLD-derivation $G_0,... G_n$, where G_n ends in an empty goal. An SLD-refutation is a successful SLD-derivation. Hereafter, derivation and refutation are used as synonymous to SLD-derivation and SLD-refutation respectively.

Stochastic Logic Programs

Stochastic logic programs (SLPs) (Muggleton, 1996) may be viewed as generalization of hidden markov models (HMMs) and stochastic context free grammars (SCFGs). The SLPs extend standard logic programs by combining logic and probability and efficiently represent complex probabilistic knowledge. The definite labeled logic program in which all or some of the clauses are associated with parameters (probabilities or labels) is called an SLP. The parameterization of clauses categorizes an SLP into pure SLP and impure SLP. In a pure SLP all of the clauses are labeled while an impure SLP is a set of both labeled and unlabelled clauses. An SLP is a normalized SLP if labels of the clauses with same predicate symbol in the head sum to one. In an unnormalised SLP, summands, labels of the clauses whose head have same predicate symbols, do not add to one.

Example: SLPs provide an ideal representation for metabolic pathways as they can capture dynamics of a pathway and can account for enzyme kinetics. In the SLP representation of a metabolic pathway background knowledge can comprise not only substrates and products but also co-factors and inhibitors. Figure 1 shows a simple single-enzyme-substrate reaction and Figure 2 represents an SLP representation for the reaction. It is assumed that reaction "rea" is irreversible and there is one-to-one stoichiometric relationship between reactant "O" and product "P." The transformation of reactant into product is directed via an enzyme "enz." Clauses assert the conversion and the labels assigned to the clauses represent the rate information by way of probabilities. The constant "z" represents the probability of the formations of the product P in reaction "rea" and hence enables the calculation of the enzymatic reaction rates. However the formation of product can be hindered due to factors such as reduction in enzyme, reactant concentration and defective enzyme. Such scenarios are illustrated by attaching label 1-z to the clause. The arguments "y" and "n" represent presence or non-presence (resp. formation or non-formation) of a substrate (resp. product).

Figures 3 and 4 show a simple hypothetical metabolic pathway and the SLPs for the pathway respectively. "O1," "P1," "P2," and "P3" are external metabolites, the pathway starts with "O1" whereas end products are "P1," "P2," and "P3." "rea1," "rea2," and "rea32 are reactions directed by enzymes "enz1," "enz2," and "enz3," respectively. The rate information for each reaction is represented by way of probabilities associated with each clause.

Failure Adjusted Maximization

The expectation maximization (EM) (Dempster, Laird, & Rubin, 1977) is a well-known maximum likelihood parameter estimation technique. Failure Adjusted Maximization (FAM) (Cussens, 2001) applies the EM algorithm to compute parameters on SLPs.

Given a logic program and a set of initial probabilities, FAM performs maximum likelihood parameter estimation in a two step (expectation [E] step and maximization [M] step) iterative learning process. In the E-step, FAM computes expected frequency for each parameterized clause given the current estimates of parameters and observed dataset. In the next step (M-step) the expected value for each clause is maximized and then normalized. The values associated with clauses become an input for the next iteration (round) of FAM. In this way, FAM improves current estimates of parameters at each iteration. This process is repeated till convergence.

FAM is an adaptation of EM's application to grouped truncated data. An observed dataset of atoms can be considered as a grouped truncated data derived from a complete set of derivations (successful and failed), that is truncated by discarding failed derivations and keeping only refutations (successful derivations) and then grouped to yield atoms. For the sake of simplification the atoms that have one proof are viewed as unambiguous atoms while those having more than one proof are considered as ambiguous atoms. As described in the preceding paragraph, FAM computes expected frequency for each clause in the E-step, and a clause can be invoked while yielding

Figure 2. An SLP for the reaction

```
enzyme(enz,rea,[O],[P].
z :: rea(y,y).
1-z :: rea(y,n).
```

Figure 1. Single-substrate-enzyme catalyzed reaction

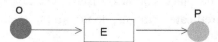

ambiguous atoms, a_0, unambiguous atoms, a_u, or failed derivations f_d. Hence the expression in the E-step is computed as a sum of three terms:

1. Expected number of times a clause C_i is used to derive unambiguous atoms,

$$\sum_{a_0} E\left(C_i | a_u\right)$$

2. Expected counts of a clause C_i in yielding ambiguous atoms,

$$\sum_{a_u} E\left(C_i | a_0\right)$$

3. Expected enumeration of a clause C_i in producing failed derivations

$$\sum_{a_0} \left(Z^{-1} - 1\right) E\left(C_i | f_d\right),$$

where Z is the normalization constant that is given by probability of successful derivation, that is, refutations.

For an underlying logic program and set of prior parameters the parameter estimation process of FAM is summarized as follows:

1. For each labeled clause compute expected counts of the clause in deriving atoms (ambiguous and unambiguous) and failed derivations (Expectation Step)

2. Perform summation of expected frequency of clauses that have same predicate symbol in the head and then divide label of each clause

by the obtained summand. (Maximization Step)

3. Repeat Step 1 and 2 till convergence

BIAS-VARIANCE ANALYSIS IN PROBABILISTIC LOGIC LEARNING

Bias-variance decomposition, a key tool to analyze predictive performance, has not been a focus of studies in probabilistic logic programming context; however, it has been extensively investigated in statistics and statistical machine learning. Simonoff (1993) studied the evaluation of the performance of an estimator by decomposing the mean squared error into bias and variance. Geman, Bienenstock, and Doursat (1992) proposed the concept of bias and variance within a regression framework for the quadratic loss function (which minimizes the mean squared error) for neural networks. The authors showed that the prediction error can be decomposed into two components: bias and variance, and there exists a trade-off between the contributors to the error. The high prediction error may be interpreted as that the predictor is highly biased or have large variance. Bias-variance decomposition has been studied by Heskes (1998) for Kullback-Leibler divergence or log likelihood. Domingos (2000) has

Figure 4. SLPs for the metabolic pathway

```
enzyme(enz1,rea1,[O1],[O2, O3].
0.75 :: rea(y,y,y).
0.25 :: rea(y,n,n).

enzyme(enz2,rea2,[O2],[P1, P2].
0.65 :: rea2(y,y,y).
0.35 :: rea2(y,n,n).

enzyme(enz3,rea3,[O3],[P3].
0.93 :: rea3(y,y).
0.07 :: rea3(y,n).
```

Figure 3. Hypothetical metabolic pathway

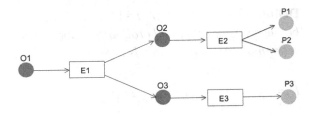

proposed definitions for arbitrary loss functions decomposing it into bias, variance and noise. The author's proposed definitions do not share the flaws that are present in some of the earlier definitions (for example, according to the definition given in (Kohavi & Wolpert, 1996) the Bayes error cannot have zero bias).

The parameter estimation problem is to compute unknown parameters given the dataset. An SLP parameter learning algorithm aims to estimate the parameters on definite clauses with high accuracy or low error probability. The error (or accuracy) measure is termed loss function, and it gives the cost of making incorrect predictions. In the SLP parameter learning Kullback-Leibler (KL) divergence or relative entropy (Cover & Thomas, 1991) seems a natural measure for the effectiveness of the estimation process.

In order to analyze and evaluate the performance of an SLP learning algorithm we give bias, variance and noise definitions by adapting the framework proposed in (Domingos, 2000). We first introduce basic terms and notations.

We first explain the terms target probability labels and estimated probability labels. Estimated probability labels are the learned SLP parameters and target probability labels are the true labels of the clauses that need to be estimated. For example, in metabolic pathway modelling task, the enzymatic reaction rates assigned according to the biological literature are target probability labels whereas the rates leaned by FAM are the estimated probability labels. The N target probability labels associated with the definite clauses are, $P = \{p_i, i = 1,...,N\}$. Given a dataset of the form $\{x_1,...,x_n\}$ an underlying logic program LP and an initial parameters P_0 the N estimated probability labels computed by a learning algorithm are given by $P' = \{p'_i, i = 1,...,N\}$. We now define entropy, relative entropy (Kullback-Leibler divergence), main probability labels, and then propose bias-variance decomposition of the prediction error in probabilistic logic learning.

Definition 1: *Let $P = \{p_i, i = 1,...,N\}$ be the target probability labels on SLPs, the entropy of P is*

$$-\sum_{i=1}^{N} p_i \log(p_i).$$

Shannon entropy is a measure of uncertainty. Given that the noise component of error is independent of the learning process; hence can be calculated by computing entropy of the target probability labels on SLPs. KL-divergence measures the difference between the target probability labels and the estimated probability labels and is defined as follows

Definition 2: *Let $P = \{p_i, i = 1,...,N\}$ be the target probability labels on SLPs and $P' = \{p'_i, i = 1,...,N\}$ be the estimated probability labels. KL divergence between the target and the estimated probability labels is given by*

$$KL(P\|P') = \sum_i p_i \log\left(\frac{p_i}{p'_i}\right).$$

KL divergence between P and P' is zero if P and P' are equal otherwise it is non-negative. Formally

$KL(P\|P') = 0$ *iff* $P = P'$
$KL(P\|P') > 0$ *iff* $P \neq P'$
$KL(P\|P') \neq KL(P'\|P)$, *when* $P \neq P'$

The parameters on the SLP for which KL divergence is minimum between the target and the estimated labels are termed main probability labels. The main probability labels are obtained by combining the estimated probabilities produced by individual predictors. The main probability labels are defined as follows

Definition 3: *Let $P'_r = \{\{p'_i, i = 1,...,N\}, r = 1,...,R\}$ be the r sets of estimated probability labels. The set of main probability labels is given by*

$$\hat{P} = \left\{\hat{p}_i = \sum_{r=1}^{R} \frac{1}{r} p'_{r_i}, i = 1,...,N\right\}.$$

The main probability label $\hat{p}_i$ of a clause C_i is a weighted linear combination of the individual labels of the clause that are produced by r different predictors. The weights are assigned according to a uniform distribution. In order to combine the estimated labels we use simple arithmetic average. In the literature on aggregation of expert opinions arithmetic mean has been successfully used to combine the probabilities and is termed linear opinion pool (Clemen & Winkler, 1999; Genest, 1984; Stone, 1961). We now give definitions for bias and variance.

Definition 4: *Let P be the target probability labels and $\hat{P}$ be the main probability labels. The bias of an SLPs predictor is the KL divergence between the target probability labels and the main probability labels.*

$$bias = LK(P\|\hat{P})$$

Definition 5: *Let $\hat{P}$ be the main probability labels and P' be the estimated probability labels. The variance of an SLPs predictor is the expected KL divergence between the main probability labels and the estimated probability labels.*

$$variance = E[LK(\hat{P}\|P')]$$

The bias term measures the amount by which main probability labels on an SLP differ from the target probability labels and the amount by which the main probability labels differ from the estimated probability labels is given by variance.

RESULTS AND ANALYSIS

We conducted a set of experiments to study the proposed bias-variance decomposition.

We performed experiments to perform modelling of amino acid pathway of Saccharomyces cerevisiae (baker's yeast, brewer's yeast). Yeast is a well understood eukaryotic organism. It was the first organism whose chromosome III was completely sequenced (Oliver, van der Aart, Agostoni-Carbone, Aigle, Alberghina, Alexandraki, Antoine, Anwar, Balleta, & Benit, 1992,) and its entire genetic code was determined (Goffeau, Barrell, Bussey, Davis, Dujon, Feldmann, Galibert, Hoheisel, Jacq, Johnston, Louis, Mewes, Murakami, Philippsen, Tettelin, & Oliver, 1996). Yeast is viewed as model system for the development of the emerging field of computational systems biology.

In order to conduct experiments we used the pathways and the corresponding SLPs described in (Angelopoulos & Muggleton, 2002). For inducing quantitative models we generated data using SLPs where SLPs represent the pathways. In the SLP metabolic pathway representation the underlying set of definite clauses incorporates information about enzymes, metabolites (reactants and products), and enzyme catalyzed reactions. The clause probability labels represent reaction rates. Twenty-one enzymatic reactions in the pathway are represented by stochastic clauses. Experiments have also been conducted on branching metabolic pathway that has been obtained by adding a branch in the same pathway. The phenomenon of adding a branch gives a new set of 27 stochastic clauses (for details see Angelopoulos & Muggleton, 2002).

Datasets

We generated datasets using SLPs representing chain and branching metabolic pathways. The datasets hereafter are referred to as Chain dataset (non-branching metabolic network) and Branch dataset (branching metabolic network). The size of the dataset has been set to 300 so that the evaluation of bias and variance is reliable. In order to understand the bias-variance phenomenon of an SLP learner we sampled 100 datasets comprising 300 examples from SLPs representing branching and non-branching (chain) amino acid pathways in yeast.

Experimental Methodology

The coordinates described below can control the performance of FAM.

Convergence criterion for FAM: In FAM convergence criterion can be specified. It can be set using log likelihood or by specifying the number of rounds. We seek to study bias and variance of FAM as a function of number of iterations k, we therefore varied the number of iterations from 1 to 10.

Initial Parameters: The initial parameters can be set randomly or can be set to a uniform distribution (nonrandomly). We performed bias-variance decomposition setting initial parameters both randomly and nonrandomly.

Results

We now present results for bias-variance analysis in the SLP parameter learning using FAM. Figures 5 through 8 illustrate the results. The figures depict bias, variance, and KL divergence as a function of number of rounds that are varied from 1 to 10. The tradeoff between bias and variance is illustrated in the figures which show decrease in bias and increase in variance with the increasing number of iterations. The behaviour produces maximal reduction in divergence to target probability labels at about halfway. The results show that the performance of FAM can be improved by reducing the error variance and demonstrate the need to study the methods that generally reduce the variance and do not change the bias.

We first focus on non-branching metabolic pathways and consider the scenario in which initial parameters are set to a uniform distribution (Figure 5). A significant decrease in bias can be observed in the first six rounds, after that the decrease is too small and bias is almost stabilized. Regarding variance a slow and gradual increase can be observed with number of iterations. Figure 6 represents bias-variance results for the Chain dataset where the initial parameters of FAM are set randomly. Bias shows the same pattern that has been observed in Figure 5 but there is an irregular increase in variance.

Figures 7 and 8 illustrate the bias, variance and KL divergence for branching metabolic

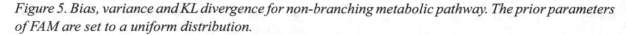

Figure 5. Bias, variance and KL divergence for non-branching metabolic pathway. The prior parameters of FAM are set to a uniform distribution.

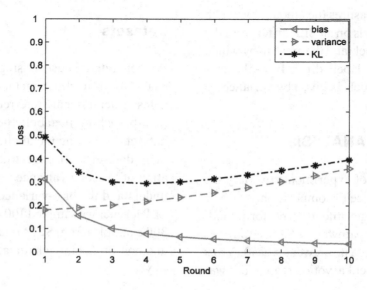

pathways. The results presented in Figure 7 have been obtained by setting FAM's initial parameters nonrandomly while Figure 8 depicts the experimental findings for random initial probabilities. The figures show that substantial bias reduction occurs within 6 iterations. However during these iterations there is an increase in variance. The results show that the higher number of parameters has increased bias and variance for branching metabolic pathways as compared to the bias and variance numbers for non-branching metabolic pathway.

Figure 6. Bias, variance and KL divergence for non-branching metabolic pathway. The prior parameters of FAM are set randomly.

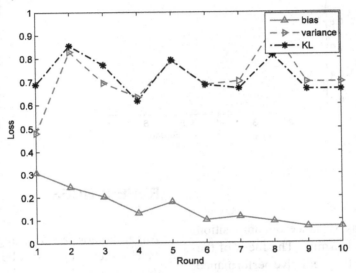

Figure 7. Bias, variance and KL divergence for branching metabolic pathway. The initial parameters of FAM are set to a uniform distribution.

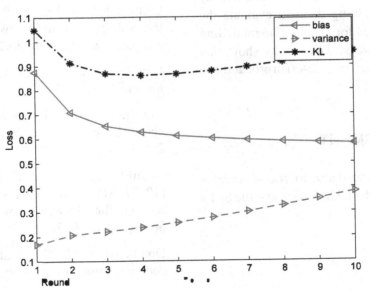

Figure 8. Bias, variance and KL divergence for branching metabolic pathway. The initial parameters of FAM are set randomly.

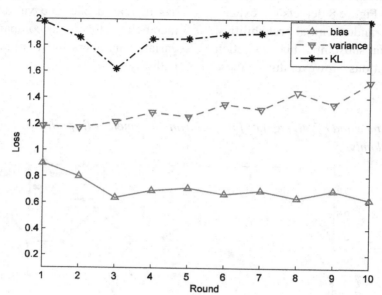

CONCLUSION

We have studied bias variance decomposition in probabilistic logic learning. The focus of the article is on analyzing the predictive performance of a learning algorithm for the task of parameter computation in Stochastic Logic Programs. The bias-variance definition has been empirically investigated by applying them to evaluate the performance of FAM for quantitative modelling of metabolic pathways. The results show that there exists bias-variance trade-off in probabilistic logic learning.

ACKNOWLEDGMENT

The author wishes to thank to Nicos Angelopoulos for making the FAM's code and the SLPs available.

REFERENCES

Angelopoulos, N. & Muggleton, S. H. (2002). Machine learning metabolic pathway descriptions using a probabilistic relational representation. *Electronic Transactions in Artificial Intelligence, 6.*

Clemen, R. T. & Winkler, R. L. (1999). Combining probability distributions from experts in risk analysis. *Risk Analysis, 19*(2), 187 – 203.

Cover, T. M. & Thomas, J. A. (1991). *Information theory.* Wiley.

Cussens, J. (2001). Parameter estimation in stochastic logic programs. *Machine Learning, 44*(3), 245 – 271.

Dempster, A. P., Laird, N. M., & Rubin, D. B. (1977). Maximum likelihood from incomplete data via the EM algorithm. *J. Royal statistical Society Series B, 39,* 1 – 38.

Domingos, P. (2000). A unified bias-variance decomposition for zero-one and squared loss.

Proceedings of Seventeenth National Conference on Artificial Intelligence, 564 – 569.

Dowd, J. E. & Riggs, D. S. (1945). A comparison of estimates of Michaelis-Menten Kinetic constants from various linear transformation. *The Journal of Biological Chemistry, 240*(2) 863 – 869.

Duggleby, R. G. (1994). Analysis of progress curves for enzyme-catalyzed reactions: Application to unstable enzyme, coupled reactions and transient-state kinetics. *Biochimica et Biophysica Acta, 1205*(2), 268 – 274.

Duggleby, R. G. (1995). Analysis of enzyme progress curves by nonlinear regression. *Methods in Enzymology, 249*, 61 – 90.

Geman, S., Bienestock, E., & Doursat, R. (1992). Neural networks and the bias/variance dilemma. *Neural Computation, 4*, 1 – 58.

Genest, C. (1984). Pooling operators with the marginalization property. *Candian Journal of Statistics, 12*, 153 – 163.

Goffeau, A., Barrell, B. G., Bussey, H., Davis, R.W., Dujon, B., Feldmann, H., Galibert, F., Hoheisel, J. D., Jacq, C., Johnston, M., Louis, E. J., Mewes, H. W., Murakami, Y., Philippsen, P., Tettelin, H., & Oliver, S. G. (1996). Life with 6000 genes. *Science, 274*(5287), 563 – 567.

Heskes, T. (1998). Bias/variance decomposition for likelihood-based estimators. *Neural Computation*, 1425 – 1433.

Hofestaedt, R. (1994). A Petri net application of metabolic processes. *Journal of System Analysis, Modelling and Simulation, 16*, 113 – 122.

Inductive Logic Programming (ILP-2001), LNCS, 2157. Springer.

Kersting, K. & De Raedt, L. (2001). Towards combining inductive logic programming and Bayesian networks. Proceedings of the Eleventh Conference on

Kersting, K. & Dick, U. (2004). Balios - The engine for Bayesian logic programs. *Proceedings of the 8th European Conference on Principles and Practice of Knowledge Discovery in Databases (PKDD-2004)*, 549 – 551.

Kitano, H. (2002a). Systems biology: a brief overview. *Science, 295*, 1662 – 1664.

Kitano, H. (2002b). Computational systems biology. *Nature, 420*, 206 – 210.

Kohavi, R. & Wolpert, D. (1996). Bias plus Variance decomposition for zero-one loss function. *Proceedings of the 13th International Conference on Machine Learning*, 275 – 283.

Lineweaver, H. & Burk, D. (1934). The determination of enzyme dissocistion constants. *Journal of the American Chemical Society, 56*, 658 – 666.

Lodhi, H. & Muggleton, S. H. (2004). Modelling metabolic pathways using Stochastic Logic Programs-based ensemble methods. *Proceedings of the International Conference on Computational Methods in Systems Biology (CMSB04), LNBI 3082*, Springer, 119 – 133.

Muggleton, S. H. (1996). Stochastic logic programs. *Advances in Inductive Logic Programming*, 254 – 264.

Oliver, S. G., van der Aart, Q. J., Agostoni-Carbone, M. L., Aigle, M., Alberghina, L., Alexandraki, D., Antoine, G., Anwar, R., Balleta, J. P., Benit, P., et al. (1992). The completer DNA sequence of yeast chromosome III. *Nature, 357*, 38 – 46.

Petri, C. A. (1962). *Kommunikation mit automaten*. University of Bonn.

Reddy, V. N., Mavrovouniotis, M. L., & Liebman, M. N. (1993). Petri net representations in metabolic pathways. *Proceedings of the 1st International Conference on Intelligen Systems for Molecular Biology (ISMB)*, 328 – 336.

Richardson, M. & Domingos, P. (2006). Markov logic networks. *Machine Learning, 62*, 107 – 136.

Ritchie, R. J. & Prvan, T. A. (1996). Simulation study on designing experiments to measure the

Km of Michaelis-Menten kinetics curves. *J. Theor. Biol., 178*, 239 – 254.

Schnell, S. & Mendoza, C. (2001). A fast method to estimate kinetic constants for enzyme inhibitors. *Acta Biotheoretica, 49*, 109 – 113.

Simonoff, J. S. (1993). The relative importance of bias and variability in the estimation of the variance of a statistic. *The Statistician, 42*, 3 – 7.

Stone, M. (1961). The opinion pool. *Annals of Mathematical Statistics, 32*, 1339 – 1342.

Compilation of References

A. T. Kearney. (2004, September). *Outsourcing among pharamaceutical and biotech firms: The growing imperative for a more aggressive approach*. Boston: Author.

Aaron, R., Clemons, E. K., & Reddi, S. (2005). Just Right Outsourcing: Understanding and Managing Risk. *Journal of Management Information Systems, 22*(2), 37–55.

Abraham, A. (2001). Neuro-Fuzzy Systems: State-of-the-Art Modeling Techniques. In J. Mira & A. Prieto (Eds.), *Connectionist Models of Neurons, Learning Processes and Artificial Intelligence* (LNCS 2084, pp. 269-276).

Accenture. (2004). *Driving high-performance outsourcing: Best practices from the masters*. Executive survey results. Retrieved March 26, 2006, from http://www.accenture.com/xdoc/en/services/outsourcing/ps/global/landing_ps.pdf

Aggarwal, A., & Pandey, A. (2004). Offshoring of IT services—Present and future. *Evalueserve*. Retrieved from http://www.evalueserve.com

Aguiar, A., & David, G. (2005). WikiWiki weaving heterogeneous software artifacts. In *Proceedings of the 2005 International Symposium on Wikis (WikiSym '05)*. Retrieved November 16, 2007, from http://doi.acm.org/10.1145/1104973.1104980

Alavi, M., & Leidner, D. E. (2001). Review: Knowledge Management and Knowledge Management Systems: Conceptual Foundations and Research Issues. *MIS Quarterly, 25*(1), 107–136. doi:10.2307/3250961

Alchian, A. A., & Demsetz, H. (1972). Production, Information Costs, and Economic Organization. *The American Economic Review, 62*(5), 777–795.

Aliev, R. A., & Aliev, R. R. (2001). *Soft Computing and its Applications*. World Scientific Publishing Co. Pvt. Ltd. Singapore.

Allen, L., Fernandez, G., Kane, K., Leblang, D., Minard, D., & Posner, J. (1995). Clearcase multisite: Supporting geographically-distributed software development. In *International Workshop on Software Configuration Management: ICSE SCM-4 and SCM-5 Workshops Selected Papers* (pp. 194-214).

Allison, G. (1971). Essence of Decision. Boston: Little, Brown.

Altman, D. G. (1991). *Practical statistics for medical research*. London: Chapman & Hall.

Amdahl, G. M., Blaauw, G. A., & Brooks, F. P., Jr. (2000). *Architecture of the IBM System/360*. Retrieved November 12, 2007, from http://www.research.ibm.com/journal/rd/441/amdahl.pdf

Ang, S., & Straub, D. (1998). Production and Transaction Economies and Information Systems Oursourcing: A Study of the US Banking Industry. *MIS Quarterly, 22*(4), 535–552. doi:10.2307/249554

Angelopoulos, N. & Muggleton, S. H. (2002). Machine learning metabolic pathway descriptions using a probabilistic relational representation. *Electronic Transactions in Artificial Intelligence, 6*.

Anonymous. (2006). Create Successful International Mergers and Alliances. *Strategic Direction, 22*(1), 25–28. doi:10.1108/02580540610635915

Anonymous. (2004). Managing long-term relationships with Laura. *Communication of the ACM, 47*(4), 42.

Anonymous. (2005). Briefly noted. *Computerworld, 39*(20), 14.

Anonymous. (2007). Call and response. *Economist, 382*(8519), 8-9.

Aranha, H., & Wheelwright, S. (2007). Transition from Business Process Outsourcing to Knowledge Process Outsourcing. *Biopharm International, 20*(5), 58.

Arbib, M. A. (2003). *Handbook of Brain Theory and Neural Networks* (2nd ed.). Cambridge, MA: MIT Press.

Arbore, A., & Ordanini, A. (2006). Broadband divide among SMEs: The role of size, location and outsourcing strategies. *International Small Business Journal, 24*(1), 83-90.

Argote, L., Beckman, S., & Epple, D. (1990). The persistence and transfer of learning in industrial settings. *Management Science, 36*, 140–154. doi:10.1287/mnsc.36.2.140

Austin, J. L. (1963). *Gothenburg studies in philosophy I*.

Bachmann, D., & Elfrink, J. (1996). Tracking the progress of e-mail versus snail-mail. *Marketing Research, 8*(2), 31–35.

Baggot, J. (1992). *The meaning of quantum theory*. Oxford University Press.

Bahill, A. T., & Dean, F. (1999). Discovering system requirements. In A. P. Sage & W. B. Rouse (Eds.), *Handbook of systems engineering and management* (pp. 175-220). New York: Wiley.

Bakhle, D. (2003). Global clinical trials: Challenges and opportunities. *Business Briefing: Pharmatech*.

Baldwin, C. Y., & Clark, K. B. (2000). *Design rules, Vol. 1: The power of modularity*. Cambridge, MA: The MIT Press.

Bardhan, I., Whitaker, J., & Mithas, S. (2006). Information technology, production process outsourcing, and manufacturing plant performance. *Journal of Management Information Systems, 23*(2), 13-25.

Barney, J. (1991). Firm Resources and Sustained Competitive Advantage. *Journal of Management, 17*(1), 99–120. doi:10.1177/014920639101700108

Barney, J. (1995). Looking inside for competitive advantage. *The Academy of Management Executive, 9*, 49–61.

Barrett, D. R. (2006). Offshore outsourcing: Key commercial and legal issues. In C. Evans (Ed.), *The Euromoney outsourcing handbook* (pp. 39-48).

Barthélemy, J., & Quélin, B. V. (2006). Complexity of Outsourcing Contracts and *Ex Post* Transaction Costs: An Empirical Investigation. *Journal of Management Studies, 43*(8), 1775–1797. doi:10.1111/j.1467-6486.2006.00658.x

Bartneck, C. (2005). Subtle emotional expressions of synthetic characters. *International Journal of Human-Computer Studies, 62*(2), 179-192.

Bartneck, C., Suzuki, T., Kanda, T., & Nomura, T. (2007). The influence of people's culture and prior experiences with Aibo on their attitude towards robots. *AI & Society, 21*(2), 217-230.

Bauer, J., Tanner, S. J., & Neely, A. (2004). Developing a Performance Measurement Audit Template – A Benchmark Study. *Measuring Business Excellence, 8*(4), 17–25. doi:10.1108/13683040410569370

Bazin, A. I., & Nixon, M. S. (2004). Facial verification using probabilistic methods. In *Proc. British Machine Vision Association Workshop on Biometrics*. London.

Beamon, M. (1999). Measuring Supply Chain Performance. *International Journal of Operations & Production Management, 19*(3), 275–292. doi:10.1108/01443579910249714

Beck, K. (1999). Embracing change with extreme programming. *IEEE Computer, 32*(10), 70-77.

Beck, K. (1999). *Extreme programming explained: Embrace change*. Reading, MA: Addison-Wesley.

Beiling, Y. (2006). Demand for skills in Canada: The role of foreign outsourcing and information-communication technology. *The Canadian Journal of Economics, 39*(1), 53-60.

Berger, P. L., & Luckmann, T. (1966). The Social Construction of Reality. Harmondsworth: Penguin.

Berk, L. E. (1997). Ethics in Research on Children *Child development* (4ᵗʰ ed., pp. 64-69). Allyn and Bacon.

Berliner, B. (1990). CVS II: Parallelizing software development. In *USENIX Winter 1990 Technical Conference* (pp. 341-352).

Berry, A. J., Coad, A. F., Harris, E. P., Otley, D. T., & Stringer, C. (2009). Emerging Themes in Management Control: A review of Recent Literature. *The British Accounting Review, 41*, 2–20. doi:10.1016/j.bar.2008.09.001

Billings, C., Clifton, J., Kolkhorst, B., Lee, E., & Wingert, W. B. (1994). Journey to a mature software process. *IBM Systems Journal, 34*(1), 46.

Bisdikian, C. (2005). A framework for building Bluetooth scatternets: A system design approach. *Pervasive and Mobile Computing, 1*, 190-212.

Bititci, U. S., Mendibil, K., Martinez, V., & Albores, P. (2005). Measuring and Managing Performance in Extended Enterprises. *International Journal of Operations & Production Management, 25*(4), 333–353. doi:10.1108/01443570510585534

Blanchard, E. (2001). Introduction to networking and data communications. *Commandprompt, Inc.* Retrieved from http://www.w3.org/2004/12/rules-ws/paper/105/

Boehm, B. (1988). A spiral model of software development and enhancement. *Computer, 21*(5), 61-72.

Botterell, A., & Addams-Moring, R. (2007). Public warning in the networked age. *Communications of the ACM.*

Bourne, J. K., Jr. (2004). Gone with the water. *National Geographic*, 888-105.

Bremser, W. G., & Chung, Q. B. (2005). A Framework for Performance Measurement in the e-business Environment. *Electronic Commerce Research and Applications.*

Brinkley, D. (2006). *The great deluge: Hurricane Katrina, New Orleans, and the Mississippi Gulf Coast.* New York: HarperCollins.

Brown, C. V. (2003). Performance Metrics for IT and Human Resource Alignment. *Information Systems Management, 20*(4), 36–42. doi:10.1201/1078/43647.20.4.20030901/77291.6

Brown, T. (2001). Modernization or failure? IT development projects in the UK public sector. *Financial Accountability & Management, 17*(4), 363-381.

Buchanan, B., & Shortliffe, E. (Eds.). (1984). *Rule-based expert systems.* Reading, MA: Addison-Wesley.

Burmeister, O. K. (2000). HCI Professionalism: ethical concerns in usability engineering *Usability testing: revisiting informed consent procedures for testing internet sites* (Vol. 1).

Burmeister, O. K. (2001). *Usability Testing: Revisiting Informed Consent Procedures for Testing Internet Sites.* Paper presented at the Proceedings of Australian Institute of Computer Ethics Conference, Canberra, Australia.

Cadiz, J. J., Gupta, A., & Grudin, J. (2000). Using Web annotations for asynchronous collaboration around documents. In *Proceedings of the 2000 ACM conference on Computer supported cooperative work* (p. 309).

Capability Maturity Model Integration (CMMI) Overview. (2005). Retrieved May 7, 2006, from http://www.sei.cmu.edu/cmmi/general/general.html accessed 5/8/06

Carmel, E. (1999). *Global software teams: Collaborating across borders and time zones.* Upper Saddle River, NJ: Prentice Hall.

Carnegie Mellon University. (2001, October 4). *Determining capabilities of IT-enabled outsourcing service providers: A capability model and methods.* Retrieved May 25, 2007, from http://www.globaletp.com/images/clientExecSum_1.0_100401

Carver, L., & Turoff, M. (2007). Human-computer interaction: The human and the computer as a team in emergency management systems. *Communications of the ACM*, 33-38.

Cassell, J. (2000). Embodied conversational interface agents. *Communications of the ACM, 43*(4), 70-78.

Cassell, J., & Bickmore, T. (2000). External manifestations of trustworthiness in the interface. *Communications of the ACM, 43*(12), 50-57.

Cassell, J., & Bickmore, T. (2003). Negotiated collusion: Modeling social language and its relationship effects in intelligent agents. *User Modeling and User - Adapted Interaction, 13*(1), 89-132.

Cassell, J., & Thórisson, K. R. (1999). The power of a nod and a glance: Envelope vs. emotional feedback in animated conversational agents. *Applied Artificial Intelligence, 13*, 519-538.

Cavalla, D. (1997). *Modern strategy for pre-clinical pharmaceutical R&D: Towards the virtual research company.* Chichester, England: Wiley.

Chakrabarty, S. (2007). Strategies for Business Process Outsourcing: An Analysis of Alternatives, Opportunities and Risks. In J. Sounderpandian, & T. Sinha (Eds.), E-Business Process Management: Technologies and Solutions (pp. 204-229). Hershey, PA: IGI Publishing.

Chakrabarty, S. K., Gandhi, P., & Kaka, N. (2006). The untapped market for offshore services. *The McKinsey Quarterly,* 16-22.

Chamberlin, J. R., Cohen, J. L., & Coombs, C. H. (1984). Social Choice Observed: Five Presidential Elections of the American Psychological Association. *The Journal of Politics, 46*(2), 479–502. doi:10.2307/2130971

Chan, S. S. (2005). *IT outsourcing in China: How China's five emerging drivers are changing the technology landscape and its industry.* Retrieved April 9, 2006, from http://www.outsourcing, com/china_trends/index.html

Chang, E., Dillon T. S., Sommerville, I., & Wongthongtham, P. (2006). Ontology-based multi-site software development methodology and tools. *Journal of Systems Architecture, 52*(11).

Charai, S. (June, 2002). Pharmaceutical outsourcing. *American Pharmaceutical Outsourcing.*

Childe, S. J. (1998). The Extended Enterprise: A Concept for Co-operation . *Production Planning and Control, 9*(4), 320–327. doi:10.1080/095372898234046

Chopra, S. & Meindl, P. (2001). *Supply Chain Management, Strategy Planning and Operations.* Pearson Education

Clark, R. A. (2004). *Against all enemies.* New York: Free Press.

Clemen, R. T. & Winkler, R. L. (1999). Combining probability distributions from experts in risk analysis. *Risk Analysis, 19*(2), 187 – 203.

Clinically speaking, India is becoming a hub for clinical trials and insight. (2005, March 31). *India Business Insight.*

Cockburn, A. (2004). *Crystal clear: A human-powered methodology for small teams.* Addison-Wesley.

Cohen, L., Manion, L., & Morrison, K. (2000). *Research methods in education* (5ᵗʰ ed.). New York: Routledge Falmer.

Cohen, W. M., & Levinthal, D. A. (1990). Absorptive Capacity: A New Perspective on Learning and Innovation. *Administrative Science Quarterly, 35*(1), 128–152. doi:10.2307/2393553

Coleman, G., & Verbrugge, R. (1998). A quality software process for rapid application development. *Software Quality Journal, 7,* 107-122.

Collins-Sussman, B. (2002) The subversion project: Building a better CVS. *Linux Journal,* 3.

Commonwealth Government of Australia. (2005). *National Statement on Ethical Conduct in Research Involving Humans*: National Health and Medical Research Council.

Connecting for Health. (2004). *Business plan.* Retrieved May 2005, from http://www.connectingforhealth.nhs.uk

Convention of the Rights of the Child. (1989). *General Assembly Resolution, 44*(25), 1–15.

Cook, C., Heath, F., & Thompson, R. (2000). A Meta-Analysis of Response Rates in Web- or Internet-Based Surveys. *Educational and Psychological Measurement, 60*(6), 821–836. doi:10.1177/00131640021970934

Cooper, M. (2000). Web Surveys: A Review of Issues and Approaches. *Public Opinion Quarterly, 64*(4), 464–494. doi:10.1086/318641

Covaleski, M. A., Dirsmith, M. W., & Michelman, J. (1993). An institutional theory perspective on the DRG framework, case mix accounting systems and healthcare organizations. *Accounting, Organizations and Society, 18*(1), 65-80.

Cover, T. M. & Thomas, J. A. (1991). *Information theory.* Wiley.

Cox, E., (1993, February). Adaptive fuzzy systems. *IEEE Spectrum*, 27-31.

Coyle, D. A. (2009). *Computers Are Your Future.* Upper Saddle River, NJ: Pearson Hall.

Craig, R. T. (1981). Generalization of Scott's index of intercoder agreement. *Public Opinion Quarterly, 45*(2), 260-264.

Currie, W. L., & Guah, M. W. (2006). IT-enabled healthcare delivery: The UK National Health Service. *Information Systems Management, 23*(2), 7-22.

Currion, P., De Silva, C., & Van der Walle, B. (2007). Open source software for disaster management. *Communications of the ACM.*

Cussens, J. (2001). Parameter estimation in stochastic logic programs. *Machine Learning, 44*(3), 245 – 271.

D'Aveni, R. A. (1994). *Hypercompetition: Managing the dynamics of strategic maneuvering.* New York: Free Press.

Danait, A. (2005). Agile offshore techniques—A case study. In *Proceedings of the IEEE Agile Conference* (pp. 214-217).

De Angeli, A., & Carpenter, R. (2005). Stupid computer! Abuse and social identities. *Proceeding of Abuse: The dark side of Human-Computer Interaction: An INTER-ACT 2005 workshop.* Rome, September 12, 2005, pp 19-25.

De Angeli, A., Johnson, G.I., & Coventry, L. (2001). The unfriendly user: Exploring social reactions to chatterbots. Proceedings of International Conference on Affective Human Factor Design, Singapore, June 27-29, 2001, pp 467-474. London: Asean Academic Press.

de la Terra, A., & Perindo, M., A., et al. (2005). Histogram equalization of speech representation for robust speech recognition. *IEEE Transactions on Speech and Audio Processing*, 3.

DeGrace, P., & Stahl, H. (1998). *Wicked problems, righteous solution: A catalog of modern engineering paradigms.* Prentice Hall.

Dekleva, S. (1992). Delphi study of software maintenance problems. 10-17.

Dellar, J. R., Jr., Hansen, H. L., & Proakis, J. G. (2000). *Discrete-Time Processing of Speech Signals* (2nd ed.). New York: IEEE Press.

Dempster, A. P., Laird, N. M., & Rubin, D. B. (1977). Maximum likelihood from incomplete data via the EM algorithm. *J. Royal statistical Society Series B, 39*, 1 – 38.

Denny, N., Crk, I., Sheshu, R., & Gupta, A. (in press). Agile software processes for the 24-hour knowledge factory environment. *Journal of Information Technology Research.*

Denny, N., Mani, S., Sheshu, R., Swaminathan, M., Samdal, J., & Gupta, A. (in press). Hybrid offshoring: Composite personae and evolving collaboration technologies. *Information Resources Management Journal.*

Denscombe, M. (2006). Web-Based Questionnaires and the Mode Effect. *Social Science Computer Review, 24*(2), 246–254. doi:10.1177/0894439305284522

Department of Health (DoH) (UK). (2000). *NHS plan: An information strategy for the modern NHS*. London: Author.

Dhar, S. (2008). Global IS outsourcing: Current trends, risks, and cultural issues. In M. S. Raisinghani (Ed.), *Global information technology management in the digital economy*. Hershey, PA: IGI Global.

DiMaggio, P. J., & Powell, W. W. (1983). The iron cage revisited: Institutional isomorphism and collective rationality in organizational fields. *American Sociological Review, 48,* 147-160.

DiMaggio, P. J., & Powell, W. W. (Eds.). (1994). *The new institutionalism in organizational analysis*. Chicago: University of Chicago Press.

DiMasi, J. (1995). Trends in drug development costs, times, and risks. *Drug Information Journal.*

Dolan, K. A. (2006). Offshoring the offshorers. *Forbes, 177*(8), 1-12.

Domingos, P. (2000). A unified bias-variance decomposition for zero-one and squared loss. *Proceedings of Seventeenth National Conference on Artificial Intelligence,* 564 – 569.

Doolin, B. (2004). Power and resistance in the implementation of a medical management information systems. *Information Systems Journal, 14,* 343-362.

Dowd, J. E. & Riggs, D. S. (1945). A comparison of estimates of Michaelis-Menten Kinetic constants from various linear transformation. *The Journal of Biological Chemistry, 240*(2) 863 – 869.

Druin, A., & Hourcade, J. P. (2005). Interaction design and children: Introduction. *Communications of the ACM, 48*(1), 33–34. doi:10.1145/1039539.1039565

Du, P., Gong, J., Wurtele, E., & Dickerson, J. (2005). Modeling gene expression networks using fuzzy logic. *IEEE Transactions on Systems, Man and Cybernetics— Part B: Cybernetics, 35*(6), 1351-1359.

Duggirrala, R., Ashok, R. L., & Agrawal, D. P. (2003). BEAM: A framework for bridge negotiation in Bluetooth scatternets. In *12th ICCCN Conference* (pp. 339-344).

Duggleby, R. G. (1994). Analysis of progress curves for enzyme-catalyzed reactions: Application to unstable enzyme, coupled reactions and transient-state kinetics. *Biochimica et Biophysica Acta, 1205*(2), 268 – 274.

Duggleby, R. G. (1995). Analysis of enzyme progress curves by nonlinear regression. *Methods in Enzymology, 249,* 61 – 90.

Dunlop, A., & Smith, C. (2005). *Outsourcing: Know your legal position*. Retrieved April 2, 2006, from http://www.computing.co.uk//computing/features/2072392/outsourcing-know-legal-position

Dursch, A., Yen, D. C., & Shih, D. (2004). Bluetooth technology: An exploratory study of the analysis and implementation frameworks. *Computer Standards & Interfaces, 26,* 263-277.

Eaton, C. E., & Wierenga, D. E. (1999). *The drug development and approval process*. Pharmaceutical Research Association, Office of Research and Development.

Eisenhardt, K. M. (1989). Agency Theory: An Assessment and Review. *Academy of Management Review, 14*(1), 57–74. doi:10.2307/258191

Elliott, G., & Phillips, N. (2003). *Mobile commerce and wireless computing systems*. Addison-Wesley.

Ellis, K. (2002). *Modelling interface metaphors: developing multimedia for young children*. Monash University, Melbourne.

Ellis, K. (2008). *Tools for inclusive play: multimedia for children learning Australian Sign Language*. Monash University, Melbourne.

Ellis, K. A., & Blashki, K. M. (2004). Toddler Techies: A Study of Young Children's Interaction with Computers. *Information Technology in Childhood Education Annual,* 77–96.

Ellis, K., & Blashki, K. (2007). The Digital Playground: Kindergarten Children Learning Sign Language via multimedia. *AACE Journal, 15*(3), 225–253.

Erasala, N., & Yen, D. C. (2002). Bluetooth technology: A strategic analysis of its role in 3G wireless communication era. *Computer Standards & Interfaces, 24,* 193-206.

Ernst & Young. (2004). *Progressions 2004: Global pharmaceutical report, industry defining events.* New York: Author.

Evans A. G., & Varaiya, N. (2003, Fall). Assessment of a biotechnology market opportunity. *Entrepreneurship Theory and Practice.*

Evans, A., Martin, K., & Poatsy, M. A. (2009). *Complete Technology in Action.* Upper Saddle River, NJ: Pearson Hall.

Expanding global access to HIV/AIDS treatments: An overview of the issues. (2005). *American Newsletter.*

Farrell, D. (2005). Offshoring: Value creation through economic change. *Journal of Management Studies, 42*(3), 675-683.

Farrell, D., (Ed.). (2005, June). *The emerging global labor market.* Washington, DC: McKinsey Global Institute Press.

Farrell, D., Dibbern, J., Goles, T., Hirschheim, Rudy & Jayatilaka, B. (2004). Information systems outsourcing: A survey and analysis of the literature. *The DATABASE for Advances in Information Systems, 35*(4), 6-102.

Fasal, B. (2002). Robust face analysis using convolutional neural network. *Proc. 7th Int.Conf. Pattern Recognition. 2.* 11-15.

Feeny, D. F., Lacity, M. C., & Willcocks, L. P. (1995). IT outsourcing: Maximize flexibility and control. *Harvard Business Review, 73*(3).

Fergusson, N. (2004, April 12). Survival of the biggest. *Forbes 2000,* p. 140.

Field, M. J., & Behrman, R. E. (2004). *Ethical Conduct of Clinical Research Involving Children.* Washington, D.C.: The National Academies Press.

Fierrez-Aguilar, J. Ortega-Garcia, J. Garcia-Romero, D. & Gonzalez-Rodriguez, J. (2003). A Comparative Evaluation of Fusion Strategies for Multimodal BiometricVerification. *4th Int'l. Conf. Audio- and Video-Based Biometric Person Authentication (AVBPA 2003). Guildford* (LNCS 2688, pp. 830–837).

Finin, T., Weber, J., Wiederhold, G., Genesereth, M., Fritzson, R., McKay, D., et al. (1993). *Specification of the KQML agent-communication.* Darpa Knowledge Sharing Effort.

Finkbeiner, D. (1966). *Matrices and linear transformations.* Freeman.

Fish, R. S., Chaljonte, B. L., & Kraut, R. E. (1991). Expressive richness: A comparison of speech and text as media for revision. In *Conference on Human Factors in Computing Systems Proceedings of the SIGCHI Conference on Human factors in computing systems: Reaching Through Technology* (pp. 1-6).

Fjermestad, J., & Saitta, J. N. (2005). A Strategic Framework for IT Outsourcing: A Review of Literature and the Development of a Successful Factors Model. *Journal of Information Technology Cases and Applications, 7*(3), 42–60.

Flewitt, R. (2005). Conduction research with young children: some ethical considerations. *Early Child Development and Care, 175*(6), 553–565. doi:10.1080/03004430500131338

Flores, F. (1982). *Management and communication in the office of the future.* Unpublished dissertation, University of California, Berkeley.

Fowler, M., & Highsmith, J. (2001). The agile manifesto. *Software Development,* 28-32.

Fox, G. Chaza., Cohn & Reilly. (2003). Person Identification Using Automatic Integration Of Speech, Lip and Face Experts. *WBMA '03.* Berkeley, CA, USA.

Fox, N., & Reilly, R. B. (2003). Audio-Visual Speaker Identification Based on the Use of Dynamic Audio and Visual Features. In *Proc. 4th International Conference on audio and video based biometric person authentication.*

Freeman, E., & Gelertner, D. (1996). Lifestreams: A storage model for personal data. *ACM SIGMOD Record, 25*(1), 80-86.

Fulk, J., & DeSantis, G. (1995). Electronic Communication and Changing Organizational Forms. *Organization Science, 6*(4). doi:10.1287/orsc.6.4.337

Garcia, C., & Delakis, M. (2002). A neural architecture for fast and robust face detection. In *Proc. 16th Int. Conf. Pattern Recognition (ICPR'02)* (pp. 20044-20048).

Gattorna, J. (1998). *Strategic Supply Chain Alignment – Best Practice in Supply Chain Management.* Gower

Geman, S., Bienestock, E., & Doursat, R. (1992). Neural networks and the bias/variance dilemma. *Neural Computation, 4*, 1 – 58.

Genest, C. (1984). Pooling operators with the marginalization property. *Candian Journal of Statistics, 12*, 153 – 163.

Gerhard, M., Moore, D., & Hobbs, D. (2005). Close encounters of the virtual kind: Agents simulating copresence. *Applied Artificial Intelligence, 19*(4), 393-412.

Gilley, M., & Rasheed, A. (2000). Making More by Doing Less: An Analysis of Outsourcing and its Effects on Firm Performance. *Journal of Management, 26*(4), 763–790. doi:10.1016/S0149-2063(00)00055-6

Gillis, A. (2005). *The future of outsourcing.* Retrieved August 9, 2005 from http://www.ababj.com/futureoutsourcing.html.

Go, R. (2005). *Deloitte white article: India meets Doha: Changing patent protection.* New York: Deloitte Touche Tohmatsu.

Goffeau, A., Barrell, B. G., Bussey, H., Davis, R.W., Dujon, B., Feldmann, H., Galibert, F., Hoheisel, J. D., Jacq, C., Johnston, M., Louis, E. J., Mewes, H. W., Murakami, Y., Philippsen, P., Tettelin, H., & Oliver, S. G. (1996). Life with 6000 genes. *Science, 274*(5287), 563 – 567.

Goldberg, D. (1989). *Genetic algorithms in search, optimisation and machine learning.* Reading, Massachusetts: Addison Wesley, USA.

Gonzalez, R., Gasco, J., & Llopis, J. (2006). Information systems outsourcing: A literature analysis. *Information & Management, 43*(7), 821-834.

Goodwin, F., & Goldberg, R. (2001, July 7). New drugs: The right remedy. *The Washington Post,* p. A21.

Goonatilake, S. Campbell, J. A., & Ahmad, N. (1995). Genetic-fuzzy systems for financial decision making, advances in fuzzy logic, neural networks and genetic algorithms. *IEEE/Nagoya-University World Wisepersons Workshop,* Springer, (LNAI), Germany.

Gopal, A., Krishnan, M. S., Mukhopadhyay, T., & Goldenson, D. R. (2002). Measurement Programs in Software Development: Determinants of Success. *IEEE Transactions on Software Engineering, 28*(9), 863–875. doi:10.1109/TSE.2002.1033226

Gottfredson, M., Puryear, R., & Phillips, S. (2005). Strategic sourcing: From periphery to the core. *Harvard Business Review,* 132-139.

Gottschalk, P. (2006). Research propositions for knowledge management systems supporting IT outsourcing relationships. *The Journal of Computer Information Systems, 46*(3), 110-116.

Gould, J. D. (1978). An experimental study of writing, dictating, and speaking. In J. Requin (Ed.), *Attention and performance: Vol. 7* (pp. 299-319).

Grabowski, M., & Lee, S. (1993). Linking information systems application portfolios and organizational strategy. In R. D. Banker, R. J. Kauffman, & M. A. Mahmood (Eds.), *Strategic information technology management: Perspectives on organizational growth and competitive advantage* (pp. 33-54). Hershey, PA: IGI Global.

Grabowski, M., & Roberts, K. (1997). Risk mitigation in large scale systems: Lessons from high reliability organizations. *California Management Review,* 152-162.

Graesser, A. C., McNamara, D. S., & VanLehn, K. (2005). Scaffolding deep comprehension strategies through Point&Query, AutoTutor, and iSTART. *Educational Psychologist, 40*(4), 225–234.

Graham-Rowe, D. (2004). Software agent targets chatroom pedophiles. *New Scientist, 181*(2439), 225–234.

Grant, R. M. (1996b). Toward a knowledge-based theory of the firm. *Strategic Management Journal, 17*, 109–122.

doi:10.1002/(SICI)1097-0266(199602)17:2<109::AID-SMJ796>3.0.CO;2-P

Greaver, M., & Kipers, K. (2005). *Outsourcing*. Retrieved on March 26, 2006, from http://www.valuecreationgroup.com/outsourcing_advantages.html

Green, I., Raz, T., & Zviran, M. (2007). Analysis of active intrusion prevention data for predicting hostile activity in computer networks. *Communications of the ACM*, 63-68.

Green, N., & Lehman, J. F. (2002). An integrated discourse recipe-based model for task-oriented dialogue. *Discourse Processes, 33*(2), 133–158.

Greenfield, P. M. (1984). *Mind and media: the effects of television, video games, and computers*. Cambridge, MA.: Harvard University Press.

Grossi, E., & Buscema, M. (2006). Artificial intelligence and outcome research. *Drug Development Research, 67*, 227-244.

Grover, V., Cheon, M., & Teng, J. (1996). The effect of service quality and partnership on the outsourcing of information systems functions. *Journal of Management Information Systems, 12*(4), 89–116.

Guah, M. W., & Currie, W. L. (2004). Application service provision: A technology and working tool for healthcare organization in the knowledge age. *International Journal of Healthcare Technology and Management, 6*(1), 84-98.

Guah, M. W., & Currie, W. L. (2005). *Internet strategy: The road to Web services*. Hershey, PA: IGI Global.

Gunasekaran, A., Patel, C., & Tirtiroglu, E. (2001). Performance Measures and Metrics in a Supply Chain Environment. *International Journal of Operations & Production Management, 21*(1/2), 71–87. doi:10.1108/01443570110358468

Gupta, A. K., & Govindarajan, V. (2000). Knowledge flows within multinational corporations. *Strategic Management Journal, 21*, 473–496. doi:10.1002/(SICI)1097-0266(200004)21:4<473::AID-SMJ84>3.0.CO;2-I

Gupta, A., & Seshasai, S. (2007). 24-hour knowledge factory: Using Internet technology to leverage spatial and temporal separations. *ACM Transactions on Internet Technology, 7*(3).

Gupta, A., Seshasai, A., Mukherji, S., & Ganguly, A. (2007, April-June). Offshoring: The transition from economic drivers toward strategic global patnership and 24-hour knowledge factory. *Journal of Electronic Commerce in Organizations, 5*(2), 1-23.

Gupta, A., Seshasai, S., Mukherji, S., & Ganguly, A. (2007). Offshoring: The transition from economic drivers toward strategic global partnership and 24-hour knowledge factory. *Journal of Electronic Commerce in Organizations, 5*(2), 1-23.

Gupta, U. G., & Gupta, A. (1992). Outsourcing the IS function: is it necessary for your organization? *Information Systems Management, 9*(3), 44–50. doi:10.1080/10580539208906881

Hall, J. A., & Liedtka, S. L. (2007). The Sarbanes-Oxley Act: Implications for large-scale IT outsourcing. *Communications of the ACM, 50*(3), 12-20.

Hanakawa, N. Matsumoto, K., & Torii, K. (2002). A knowledge-based software process simulation model. *Annals of Software Engineering, 14*(1-4), 383-406.

Hand, A., Cardiff, J., Magee, P., & Doody, J. (2006). An architecture and development methodology for location-based services. *Elsevier Electronic Commerce Research and Applications, 5*, 201-208.

Hanna, L., Risden, K., & Alexander, K. (1997). Guidelines for usability testing with children. *Interactions (New York, N.Y.), 4*(5), 9–12. doi:10.1145/264044.264045

Haslam, S. A., & McGarty, C. (1998). Experimental Design *Doing psychology: an introduction to research methodology and statistics* (pp. 60-91): Sage.

Hatch, P. J. (2005). *Offshore 2005 research preliminary findings and conclusions*. Retrieved on March 26, 2006, from http://www.ventoro.com/Offshore2005Research-Findings.pdf

Heathfield, H., Pitty, D., & Hanka, R. (1998). Evaluating information technology in healthcare barriers and challenges. *British Medical Journal, 316,* 1959-1961.

Hedde, R., Manoj, B. S., Rao, B. D., & Rao, R. R. (2006). Emotion detection from speech signals and its application to supporting enhanced QoS in emergency response. In *Proccedings of the 3rd International ISCRAM Conference,* Newark, NJ.

Hedges, H. (2001). A Right to Respect and Reciprocity: Ethics and Educational Research with Children. *NZ Research in ECE, 4*(1), 1–18.

Heib, B. R. (2006, May). *Characteristics of successful care delivery: Organization IT cultures* (pp. 2-3). Gartner Industry Research.

Hendy, J., Reeves, B. C., Fulop, N., Huchings, A., & Masseria, C. (2005). Challenges to implementing the national program for information technology: A qualitative study. *British Medical Journal, 420,* 1-6.

Herper, M., & Kang, P. (2006, March). The world's ten best-selling drugs. *Forbes.*

Herzlinger, R. E. (1989). The failed revolution in healthcare—The role of management. *Harvard Business Review,* 95-103.

Heskes, T. (1998). Bias/variance decomposition for likelihood-based estimators. *Neural Computation,* 1425 – 1433.

Higgins, M. J., & Rodriguez, D. (2004, December). *The outsourcing of R&D through acquisitions in the pharmaceutical industry* (SSRN Working Article).

Highsmith, J. (2000). *Adaptive software development: A collaborative approach to managing complex systems.* New York: Dorset House.

Highsmith, J. (2002). *Agile software development ecosystems.* In A. Cockburn & J. Highsmith (Eds.), *The agile software development series.* Boston: Addison-Wesley.

Hofestaedt, R. (1994). A Petri net application of metabolic processes. *Journal of System Analysis, Modelling and Simulation, 16,* 113 – 122.

Hoffmann, F., Köppen, M., Klawonn, F., & Roy, R. (2005). *Soft Computing: Methodologies and Applications.* Birkhäuser Publications.

Horan, T. A., & Schooley, B. (2007). Time-critical information services. *Communications of the ACM,* 73-79.

Hsu, L. M., & Field, R. (2003). Interrater agreement measures: Comments on Kappan, Cohen's Kappa, Scott's it, and Aickin's α. *Understanding Statistics, 2*(3), 205-219.

Hughes, M. A., & Garrett, D. E. (1990). Intercoder reliability estimation approaches in marketing: A generalizability theory framework for quantitative data. *Journal of Marketing Research, 27*(2), 185-195.

Humphrey, W. S. (1995). Introducing the personal software process. *Annals of Software Engineering, 1.*

Hunt, T. (2006, March 7). *Concern over data security on the rise in outsourcing industry.* Retrieved April 30, 2006, from http://www.marketwire.com/mw/release-html

Hyder, E. B., Kumar, B., Mahendra, V., Siegel, J., Heston, K. M., Gupta, R., et al. (2002, October 21). *eSourcing capability model for IT-enabled service providers v. 1.1.* Retrieved May 25, 2007, from http://reports-archive.adm.cs.cmu.edu/anon/2002/CMU-CS-02-155.pdf

India can become significant global player by 2010. (2006, November, 14). *Biospectrum India.*

Inductive Logic Programming (ILP-2001), LNCS, 2157. Springer.

Institute of Medicine. (2002). *Crossing the quality chasm: A new health system for the 21ˢᵗ century.* Washington, DC: National Academy Press.

Ireland, R., Hitt, M., & Vaidyanath, D. (2002). Alliance Management as a Source of Competitive Advantage. *Journal of Management, 28,* 413–446. doi:10.1177/014920630202800308

IT outsourcing destination: Russia. (2005). Retrieved April 16, 2006, from http://www.sourcingmag.com/outsource_by_region/russia_central_eastern_europe.html

Iyengar, P., & Rolf, J. (2007). *Factors to weigh before going offshore*. Retrieved April 30, 2007, from http://outsourcing.weblog.gartner.com/weblog/index.php?blogid=9

Jackson, P. (1999). *Introduction to expert systems*. Reading, MA: Addison-Wesley.

Jain & Ross. A. (2002). Learning User-Specific Parameters in Multibiometric System. In *Proc. Int'l Conf. of Image Processing (ICIP 2002), New York* (pp. 57-70).

Jain, R. Bolle, & Pankanti, S. (1999). *Biometrics: Personal Identification in Networked Society* (2nd ed.). Kluwer Academic Publishers.

Jamieson, S. (2004). Likert scales: how to (ab)use them. *Medical Education*, *38*, 1217–1218. doi:10.1111/j.1365-2929.2004.02012.x

Jeanpierre, L., & Charpillet, F. (2004). Automated medical diagnosis with fuzzy stochastic models: Monitoring chronic diseases. *Acta Biotheoretica, 52,* 291-311.

Jogernsen, H. (2005). Methods & Elements of a Solid Risk Management Strategy. *Risk Management, 52*(7), 53.

John, R., & Innocent, P. (2005). Modeling uncertainty in clinical diagnosis using fuzzy logic. *IEEE Transactions on Systems, Man and Cybernetics—Part B: Cybernetics, 35*(6), 1340-1350.

Johnson & Scholes. (1999). *Exploring Corporate Strategy*. Prentice Hall

Johnson, K. (2000). Research Ethics and Children. *Curriculum Perspectives*, (November): 6–7.

Johnson, W. H. A., & Medcof, J. W. (2007). Motivating Proactive Subsidiary Innovation: Agent-Based Theory and Socialization Models in Global R&D. *Journal of International Management*, *13*, 472–487. doi:10.1016/j.intman.2007.03.006

Kakabadse, A., & Kakabadse, N. (2003). Outsourcing Best Practice: Transformational and Transactional Considerations. *Knowledge and Process Management*, *10*(1), 60–71. doi:10.1002/kpm.161

Kanka, M. (2001). *A paper on semantics*. Berlin, Germany: Institut für deutsche Sprache und Linguistik.

Kaplan, R. S., & Norton, D. P. (1992). The Balanced Scorecard – Measures that Drive Performance. *Harvard Business Review, 70*(1), 71–79.

Kaplan, R. S., & Norton, D. P. (1996). The Balanced Scorecard: Translating Strategy into Action. *Harvard Business Review*. Boston, MA

Kaplowitz, M., Hadlock, T., & Levine, R. (2004). A Comparison of Web and Mail Survey Response Rates. *Public Opinion Quarterly, 68*(1), 94–101. doi:10.1093/poq/nfh006

Kaptelinin, V. (2003). UMEA: Translating interaction histories into project contexts. In *Proceedings of CHI 2003*.

Kato, R., Nakano, H., Konishi, H., Kato, K., Koga, Y., Yamane, T., et al. (2005). Novel strategy for protein exploration: High-throughput screening assisted with fuzzy neural network. *Journal of Molecular Biology, 351,* 683-692.

Kavan, C., Saunders, C., & Nelson, R. (1993). The information systems outsourcing bandwagon. *Sloan Management Review*, 73–86.

Keeler, J., & Newman, J. (2001). Paperless success: The value of e-medical records. *HIMSS Proceedings, 2*(45).

Kellehear, A. (1993). Simple Observations *Unobtrusive Researcher: a guide to methods* (pp. 115-138): Allen and Unwin.

Kelly Scientific Resources. (2004). Management of clinical trials in an era of outsourcing. *Issues and Trends*.

Kermani, F., and Bonacossa, P. (2003). Outsourcing Clinical trials in the pharmaceutical industry. *Chiltern International Business Briefing: Pharmatech*.

Kern, T., Kreijger, J., & Willcocks, L. (2002b). Exploring ASP as sourcing strategy: theoretical perspective, propositions for practice. *The Journal of Strategic Information Systems*, *11*, 153–177. doi:10.1016/S0963-8687(02)00004-5

Kern, T., Willcocks, L. P., & Heck, E. v. (2002). The Winner's Curse in IT Outsourcing: Strategies for Avoiding Relational Trauma. *California Management Review, 44*(2), 47–69.

Kersting, K. & Dick, U. (2004). Balios - The engine for Bayesian logic programs. *Proceedings of the 8th European Conference on Principles and Practice of Knowledge Discovery in Databases (PKDD-2004),* 549 – 551.

Kingston, J. (2002). Merging top level ontologies for scientific knowledge management. *Proceedings of the AAAI Workshop on Ontologies and the Semantic Web.* Retrieved from http://www.inf.ed.ac.uk/publications/report /0171.html

Kishore, R., Rao, H. R., Nam, K., Rajagopalan, S., & Chaudhary, A. (2003). A Relationship Perspective on IT Outsourcing. *Communications of the ACM, 46*(12), 87–92. doi:10.1145/953460.953464

Kitano, H. (2002a). Systems biology: a brief overview. *Science, 295,* 1662 – 1664.

Kitano, H. (2002b). Computational systems biology. *Nature, 420,* 206 – 210.

Kittler, J. Messer, K. & Czyz, J. (2002). Fusion of Intramodal and Multimodal Experts in Personal Identity Authentication Systems. In *Proc. Cost 275 Workshop. Rome* (pp. 17–24).

Klein, R. L., Bigley, G. A., & Roberts, K. H. (1995). Organizational culture in high reliability organizations. *Human Relations, 48*(7), 771-792.

Knuth, D. E. (1984). Literate programming. *Computer journal, 27*(2), 97-111.

Koch, C. (2007, February 1). IT builds a better. *CIO,* 34-40.

Kogut, B., & Zander, U. (1992). Knowledge of the Firm, Combinitive Capabilities, and the Replication of Technology. *Organization Science, 3*(3), 383–397. doi:10.1287/orsc.3.3.383

Kohavi, R. & Wolpert, D. (1996). Bias plus Variance decomposition for zero-one loss function. *Proceedings of the 13th International Conference on Machine Learning,* 275 – 283.

Korgaonkar, P., & Wolin, L. (1999). A Multivariate Analysis of Web Usage. *Journal of Advertising Research, 39*(2), 53–68.

Kosko, B. (1992). *Neural networks and fuzzy systems, a dynamic system*, Prentice-Hall: Englewood Cliff, USA.

Kraemer, K., & Dedrick, D. (2004). *Offshoring in Orange County: Leader, follower, or mirror of international trends?* University of California Irvine, Personal Computing Industry Center, Graduate School of Management.

Kraemer, R., & Schwander, P. (2003). Bluetooth based wireless Internet applications for indoor hot spots: Experience of a successful experiment during CeBIT 2001. *Computer Networks, 41,* 303-312.

Kramer, D. (1999) API documentation from source code comments: A case study of javadoc. In *Proceedings of the 17th Annual International Conference on Computer Documentation (SIGDOC '99)* (pp. 147-153).

Krebsbach, K. (2004). Outsourcing Dominates As Banks Seek Savings. *Bank Technology News, 17*(9), 16.

Kripalani, M., Foust, D., Holmes, S., & Enga, P. (2006). Five offshore practices that pay off. *Business Week, 30*(3969), 60.

Krippendorff, K. (2004). Reliability in content analysis: Some common misconceptions and recommendations. *Human Communication Research, 30*(3), 411-433.

Kussmaul, C., Jack, R., & Sponsler, B. (2004). Outsourcing and offshoring with agility: A case study. In C. Zannier et al. (Eds.), *XP/Agile Universe 2004* (LNCS 3132, pp. 147-154). Springer.

Lacity, M. C., & Willcocks, L. P. (1998). An empirical investigation of information technology sourcing practices: lessons from experience. *MIS Quarterly, 22*(3), 363–408. doi:10.2307/249670

Lacity, M. C., & Hirschheim, R. (1993). The information systems outsourcing bandwagon. *Sloan Management Review, 35*(1), 73–86.

Lacity, M. C., Hirschheim, R., & Willcocks, L. (1994). Realizing outsourcing expectations: incredible expectations, credible outcomes. *Information Systems Management, 11*(4), 7–18. doi:10.1080/07399019408964664

Lacity, M. C., Willcocks, L. P., & Feeny, D. F. (1996). The value of selective IT outsourcing. *Sloan Management Review, 37,* 13–25.

Lacity, M., Willcocks, L., & Feeny, D. (2004). Commercializing the Back Office at Lloyds of London: Outsourcing and Strategic Partnerships Revisited. *European Management Journal, 22*(2), 127–140. doi:10.1016/j.emj.2004.01.016

Lally, L. (1996). Enumerating the risks of reengineered processes. In *Proceedings of 1996 ACM Computer Science Conference* (pp. 18-23).

Lally, L. (1997). Are reengineered organizations disaster prone? In *Proceedings of the National Decision Sciences Conference* (pp. 178-182).

Lally, L. (2002). Complexity, coupling, control and change: An IT based extension to normal accident theory. In *Proceedings of the International Information Resources Management Conference* (pp. 1089-1095).

Lally, L. (2005). Information technology as a target and shield in the post 9/11 environment. *Information Resources Management Journal, 18*(1), 14-28.

Lally, L. (2005a). Applying the target and shield model to wireless technology. In *Proceedings of the International Information Resources Conference.*

Langfield-Smith, K. (2008). The Relations Between Transactional Characteristics, Trust and Risk in the Start-Up Phase of a Collaborative Alliance. *Management Accounting Research, 19,* 344–364. doi:10.1016/j.mar.2008.09.001

LaPorte, T. R., & Consolini, P. (1991). Working in practice but not in theory: Theoretical challenges of high reliability organizations. *Journal of Public Administration, 1,* 19-47.

Lash, J., & Wellington, F. (2007). Competitive advantage on a warming planet. *Harvard Business Review,* 95-107.

Lassar, W. M., & Kerr, J. L. (1996). Strategy and Control in Supplier-Distributor Relationships: An Agency Perspective. *Strategic Management Journal, 17,* 613–632. doi:10.1002/(SICI)1097-0266(199610)17:8<613::AID-SMJ836>3.0.CO;2-B

Layman, S. (2005). Strategic Goal Alignment at CMP Technologies. *Strategic HR Review, 4*(4), 24–27.

Leavy, B. (1996). Outsourcing strategy and learning a dilemma. *Production and Inventory Management Journal, 37* (4).

Lee, C. C. (1990). Fuzzy logic in control systems: Fuzzy controllers - part I, part II., *IEEE Transactions on Systems, Man and Cybernetics, 2092*(404-435).

Lee, C. H., & Huo, Q. (2000). On adaptive decision rules and decision parameter adaptation for automatic speech recognition. *Proceedings of the IEEE, 88,* 1241–1268. doi:10.1109/5.880082

Lee, I., Kosko, B., & Anderson, F. (2005). Modeling gunshot bruises in soft body armor with an adaptive fuzzy system. *IEEE Transactions on Systems, Man and Cybernetics—Part B: Cybernetics, 35*(6), 1374-1390.

Lee, J. N., Miranda, S. M., & Kim, Y. M. (2004). IT Outsourcing Strategies: Universalistic, Contingency, and Configurational Explanations of Success. *Information Systems Research, 15*(2), 110–131. doi:10.1287/isre.1040.0013

Lee, M. H., & Lacey, N. J. (2003). The influence of epistemology on the design of artificial agents. *Minds and Machines, 13,* 367-395.

Linder, J. (2004). Transformational Outsourcing. *MIT Sloan Management Review,* Winter, 52-58

Lineweaver, H. & Burk, D. (1934). The determination of enzyme dissociation constants. *Journal of the American Chemical Society, 56,* 658 – 666.

Littlejohn, S. W. (1983). *Theories of human communication (*2nd ed.). Belmont, CA : Wadsworth Pub. Co.

Lodhi, H. & Muggleton, S. H. (2004). Modelling metabolic pathways using Stochastic Logic Programs-based ensemble methods. *Proceedings of the International Conference on Computational Methods in Systems Biology (CMSB04), LNBI 3082*, Springer, 119 – 133.

Loh, L. & Venkatraman, N. (1992b). Determinants of IT outsourcing: a cross-sectional analysis, 9, 7-24.

López-Bassols, V. (1998). Y2K. *The OECD Observer*, **214.**

Louwerse, M. M., Graesser, A. C., Lu, S., & Mitchell, H. H. (2005). Social cues in animated conversational agents. *Applied Cognitive Psychology, 19,* 693-704.

Lowndes, V. (1996). Varieties of new institutionalism—A critical appraisal. *Public Administration, 74,* 181-197.

Lucas, H. C. (1993). The business value of information technology: A historical perspective and thoughts for future research. In R. D. Banker, R. J. Kauffman, & M. A. Mahmood (Eds.), *Strategic information technology management: Perspectives on organizational growth and competitive advantage* (pp. 359-3744). Hershey, PA: IGI Global.

Luftman, J. (2000). Assessment business IT alignment maturity, *Communications of the AIS, 4*(14), 1-51.

Majeed, A. (2003). Ten ways to improve information technology in the NHS. *British Medical Journal, 326,* 202-206.

Mangiameli, P. M., & Roethlein, C. J. (2001). An Examination of Quality Performance at Different Levels in a connected Supply Chain: A Preliminary Study. *The International Journal of Manufacturing Technology Management, 12*(2), 126–133.

Manoj, B. S., & Baker, A. H. (2007). Communication challenges in emergency response. *Communications of the ACM,* 51-53.

March, J. G., & Olsen, J. P. (1989). *Rediscovering institutions: The organizational basis of politics.* New York: Free Press.

Markus, L. M. (2001). Toward a theory of knowledge reuse: Types of knowledge reuse situations and factors in reuse success. *Journal of Management Information Systems, 18*(1), 57-93.

Markus, M. L. (1983). Power, politics and MIS implementation. *Communications of the ACM, 26*(6), 430-445.

Marr, B., & Stephen, P. (2004). Performance Management in Call Centers: Lessons, Pitfalls and Achievements in Fujitsu Services. *Measuring Business Excellence, 8*(4), 55–62. doi:10.1108/13683040410569415

Martin, A., & Przybocki, M. (2001). Speaker recognition in multi-speaker Environment. In *Proc. 7th Euro. Conf. Speech Communication and Technology (Eurospeech 2001) Aalborg, Denmark* (pp. 780-790).

Martin, J. B. (2003). Effectiveness, efficiency, and the value of IT. *Journal of Healthcare Information Management, 17*(2).

Massaro, D. W., Cohen, M. M., Beskow, J., Daniel, S., & Cole, R. A. (2001). Developing and evaluating conversational agents. In J. Cassell, J. Sullivan, S. Prevost, & E. Churchill (Eds.), *Embodied conversational agents* (pp. 287-318). Boston: MIT Press.

McAdam, R., & McCormack, D. (2001). Integrating Business Processed for Global Alignment and Supply Chain Management. *Business Process Management Journal, 7*(2), 19–23. doi:10.1108/14637150110389696

McFarlan, F. W., & Nolan, R. L. (1995). How to manage an IT outsourcing alliance. *Sloan Management Review, 36,* 9–22.

McLaughlin, T. (2004). The Shape of Banks to Come. Retrieved August 9, 2005 from http://www.gtnews.com.

McLean, J. (2006). Slaves to technology? *The British Journal of Administrative Management,* 16.

McMurray, A., Pace, R. W., & Scott, D. (2004). *Research: a commonsense approach.* Southbank, Vic.: Thomson Learning.

Melnyk, S. A., Stewart, D. M., & Swink, M. (2004). Metrics and Performance Measurement in Operations Management: Dealing with the Metrics Maze. *Journal of Operations Management, 22,* 201–217. doi:10.1016/j.jom.2004.01.004

Mendonca, D., Jefferson, T., & Harrald, J. (2007). Collaboration adhocracies and mix and match technologies in emergency management. *Communications of the ACM*, 53-54.

Meyer, J. W., & Rowan, B. (1991). Institutionalized organizations: Formal structure as myth and ceremony. In W. W. Powell & P. J. DiMaggio (Eds.), *The new institutionalism in organizational analysis*. Chicago: University of Chicago Press.

Miranda, S. M., & Saunders, C. S. (2002). The social construction of meaning: An alternative perspective on information sharing. *Information Systems Research*.

Misic, J., Misil, V. B., & Chan, K. L. (2005). Talk and let talk: Performance of Bluetooth piconets with synchronous traffic. *Ad Hoc Networks, 3,* 451-477.

Misra, R. B. (2004). Global IT Outsourcing: Metrics for Success of all Parties. *Journal of Information Technology Cases and Applications*, 6(3), 21–34.

MIT's *Magazine of Technology Innovation*. (2005).

Mitra, A., & Gupta, A. (2005). *Agile systems with reusable patterns of business knowledge*. Artech House.

Mitra, A., & Gupta, A. (2006). *Creating agile business systems with reusable knowledge*. Cambridge University Press.

Mitroff, I. (2005). *Why companies emerge stronger and better from a crisis: 7 essential lessons for surviving disaster*. New York: American Management Association.

Mohammadian, M. Kingham, M., & Bignall, B. (1998). Hierarchical fuzzy logic for financial modelling and prediction, *Journal of Computational Intelligence in Finance*, UK.

Mohammadian, M., & Stonier, R. J. (1995). Adaptive two layer control of a mobile robot systems. *Proceedings of IEEE International Conference on Evolutionary Computing*, Perth, Australia.

Mohan, J. (2002). *Planning, markets and hospitals* London: Routledge.

Mohrman, S. A., & Mohrman, A. M. (1997). *Designing and Leading Team-Based Organizations: A Workbook for Organizational Self-Design*. San Francisco: Jossey-Bass.

Moitra, D., & Ganesh, J.Web Services and Flexible Business Processes: Towards the Adaptive Influence Of A Learning Culture On It Investments. *Information & Management*, 42, 921–933.

Mourik, O. V. (2006). Can't quit? Go online. *Psychology Today, 39*(5), 27-28.

Muggleton, S. H. (1996). Stochastic logic programs. *Advances in Inductive Logic Programming*, 254 – 264.

Munshi, J. (1990). A Method for Constructing Likert Scales. Retrieved June 2004 from http://www.munshi.4t.com

Murphy, T. B., & Martin, D. (2003). Mixtures of distance-based models for ranking data. *Computational Statistics & Data Analysis*, 41, 645–655. doi:10.1016/S0167-9473(02)00165-2

Myopolous, J. (1998). Information modeling in the time of revolution. *Information Systems, 23*(3-4).

Nair, N. T. (2002). *eServices capability model (eSCM)— A new quality standard for outsourcing activities*. Retrieved May 23, 2007, from http://ewh.ieee.org/r10/kerala/April_June_2002.htm

Nallanathan, A., Feng, W., & Garg, H. K. (2006). Co-existence of wireless LANs and Bluetooth networks in mutual interference environment: An integrated analysis. *Computer Communications, 30,* 192-201.

Narasimhan, R., & Jayaram, J. (1998). Causal Linkages in Supply Chain Management: An Exploratory Study of North American Manufacturing Firms. *Decision Sciences, 29*(3), 579–605. doi:10.1111/j.1540-5915.1998.tb01355.x

Nardi, B. (Ed.). (1995). *Context and consciousness: Activity Theory and human-computer interaction*. Cambridge, MA: MIT Press.

National Audit Office (NAO). (2004). *Improving IT procurement*. Report by the Comptroller and Auditor General, HC 877 Session, 2003. London: The Stationary Office.

Neely, A. (2005). The Evolution of Performance Measurement Research, Developments in the Last Decade and a Research Agenda for the Next. *International Journal of Operations & Production Management, 25*(12), 1264–1277. doi:10.1108/01443570510633648

Neely, A. D., Gregory, M., & Platts, K. (1995). Performance Measurement System Design: A Literature Review and Research Agenda. *International Journal of Operations & Production Management, 15*(4), 80–116. doi:10.1108/01443579510083622

Neely, A. D., Mills, J. F., Platts, K. W., Gregory, M. J., & Richards, A. H. (1994). Realizing Strategy through Measurement. *International Journal of Operations & Production Management, 14*(3), 140–152. doi:10.1108/01443579410058603

Neely, A., & Adams, C. (2001). The Performance Prism Perspective. *Journal of Cost Management, 15*(1), 7–15.

Neuwirth, C. M., Chandhok, R., Charney, D., Wojahn, P., & Kim, L. (1994). Distributed collaborative writing: A comparison of spoken and written modalities for reviewing and revising documents. *Proceedings of the SIGCHI Conference on Human Factors in Computing Systems: Celebrating Interdependence* (p. 51).

Newman, L., & Pollnitz, L. (2002). *Ethics in action: Introducing the Ethical Response Cycle.* ACT: Australian Early Childhood Association Inc.

Nieto, J., & Torres, A. (2003). Midpoints for fuzzy sets and their application in medicine. *Artificial Intelligence in Medicine, 27,* 81-101.

Nonaka, I. (1994). *A Dynamic Theory of Organizational Knowledge Creation, 5*(1), 14-37.

North, D. (1990). *Institutions, institutional change and economic performance.* Cambridge, UK: Cambridge University Press.

Norwood, J., Carson, C., Deese, Ms., Johnson, N. J., Reeder F. S., Rolph J. E., et al. (2006, January). *Offshoring: An elusive phenomenon.* A Report of the Panel of the National Academy of Public Administration for the U.S. Congress and the Bureau of Economic Analysis.

Nunan, D. (1992). *Research methods in language learning.* Cambridge, MA: Cambridge University Press.

Nyrhinen, M., & Dahlberg, T. (2007, January). Is transaction cost economics theory able to explain contracts used for and success of firm-wide IT-infrastructure outsourcing? In *40th Annual Hawaii International Conference on System Sciences (HICSS).*

O'Brien, P. D., & Nicol, R. C. (1998). FIPA—Towards a standard for software agents. *BT Technology Journal, 16*(3).

"Offshoring R&D activity." (2007 , January 1). *Genetic Engineering and Biotechnology News.*

O'Leary, D. E. (2001). How knowledge reuse informs effective system design and implementation. *IEEE Intelligent Systems, 16*(1), 44-49.

Oliver, S. G., van der Aart, Q. J., Agostoni-Carbone, M. L., Aigle, M., Alberghina, L., Alexandraki, D., Antoine, G., Anwar, R., Balleta, J. P., Benit, P., et al. (1992). The completer DNA sequence of yeast chromosome III. *Nature, 357,* 38 – 46.

Orlikowski, W., Yates, J., Okamura, K., & Fujimoto, M. (1995). Shaping Electronic Communication: The Metastructuring of Technology in the Context of Use. *Organization Science, 6*(4), 423–444. doi:10.1287/orsc.6.4.423

Pabuwal, N., Jain, N., & Jain, B. N. (2003). An architectural framework to deploy scatternet-based applications over Bluetooth. *IEEE International Conference on Communications, 2,* 1019-1023.

Palen, L., Hiltz, S. R., & Lui, S. B. (2007). Online forums supporting grassroots participation in emergency preparedness. *Communications of the ACM,* 54-58.

Palvia, S. (2006). A model for choosing a destination country for outsourcing of IT and IT enabled services. In C. Evans (Ed.), *The Euromoney outsourcing handbook* (pp. 39-48).

Paplinski, A. P. (2004, July). Basic structures and properties of Artificial Neural Networks. *Neural Networks, L,* 2.

Park, R. (2002). The international drug industry: What the future holds for South Africa's HIV/AIDS patients. *Minnesota Journal of Global Trade*.

Parker, T., & Idundun, M. (1988). Managing Information Systems in 1987: The Top Issues for IS Managers in the UK. *JIT, 3*(1), 34–42. doi:10.1057/jit.1988.6

Pascal, R., & Rosenfeld, J. (2005). *The demand for offshore talent in services*. Washington, DC: McKinsey Global Institute Press.

Pastons, C. (2007). Web-Based Surveys. Best Practices Based on the Research Literature. *Visitor Studies, 10*(1), 1064-5578. Retrieved July 15, 2007, from http://www.informaworld.com/10.1080/10645570701263404

Pati, N., & Desai, M. S. (2005). Conceptualizing Strategic Issues in Information Technology Outsourcing. *Information Management & Computer Security, 13*(4), 281–296. doi:10.1108/09685220510614416

Patterson, D. A. (2006). Offshoring; Finally facts vs. folklore. *Communications of the ACM, 49*(2), 41-49.

Peddemors, A. J. H., Lankhorst, M. M., & De Heer, J. (2003). Presence, location and instant messaging in a context-aware application framework. In *4th International Conference on Mobile Data Management* (LNCS 2574, pp. 325-330). Springer.

Pell, F. (2005). Use and misuse of Likert scales. *Medical Education, 39*, 970. doi:10.1111/j.1365-2929.2005.02237.x

Penrose, E. (1959). *The Theory of the Growth of the Firm*. London: Basil Blackwell.

Pentland, B. T. (1995). Read me what it says on your screen: The interpretative problem in technical service work. *Technology Studies, 2*(1), 50–79.

Perrow, C. (1984). *Normal accidents: Living with high risk technologies*. New York: Basic Books.

Petershack, R. (2005, July 18). *Consider the legal issues before outsourcing offshore*. Retrieved April 9, 2006, from http://www.wistechnology.com/article.php?Id=2007

Petri, C. A. (1962). *Kommunikation mit automaten*. University of Bonn.

"Pfizer to set up academy for clinical excellence." (2002, February, 16). *Business Line*.

Pharmaceutical Research and Manufacturers of America (PhRMA). (2003). *Incentives to discover new medicines: Pharmaceutical patents*. Washington, DC: Author.

Pharmaceutical Research and Manufacturers of America (PhRMA). (2003). *The 2003 pharmaceutical industry profile*. Washington, DC: Author.

Pisano Gary, P. (1990). The R&D boundaries of the firm: an empirical analysis. *Administrative Science Quarterly, 35*, 153–176. doi:10.2307/2393554

Plant, R., Willcocks, L., & Olson, N. (2003). Measuring e-business Performance: Towards a Revised Balanced Scorecard Approach. *Information Systems and e-Business Management* (pp. 265-281). Springer Verlag.

Plass, J., L. (1998). Design and Evaluation of the User Interface of Foreign Language Multimedia Software: A Cognitive Approach. *Language Learning & Technology, 2*(1), 35–45.

Polat, K. S. (2007). Breast cancer and liver disorders classification using artificial immune recognition system (AIRS) with performance evaluation by fuzzy resource allocation mechanism. *Expert Systems with Applications, 32*, 172-183.

Poppendieck, M., & Poppendieck, T. (2003). *Lean software development: An agile toolkit for software development managers*. Addison-Wesley.

Porter, S., & Whitcomb, M. (2005). E-mail Subject Lines and Their Effect on Web Survey Viewing and Response. *Social Science Computer Review, 23*(3), 380–387. doi:10.1177/0894439305275912

Powell, T. C., & Dent-Micallef, A. (1997). Information technology as competitive advantage: the role of human, business, and technology resources. *Strategic Management Journal, 18*(5), 375–405. doi:10.1002/(SICI)1097-0266(199705)18:5<375::AID-SMJ876>3.0.CO;2-7

Prasad, R., & Munoz, L. (2003). WLANs and WPANs towards 4G wireless. *Artech House*.

Prechelt, L., Unger-Lamprecht, B., Philippsen, M., & Tichy, W. F. (2002, June). Two controlled experiments assessing the usefulness of design pattern documentation in program maintenance. *IEEE Transactions on Software Engineering, 28*(6), 595-606.

Preston, G., & Singh, A. (2003, November). Rebuilding big pharma's business model. *Vivo, the Business and Medicine Report, 21*(10).

Puccinelli, R. (2003, October). BPO meets BPM. *Supplement to KM World*.

Quelin, B., & Duhamel, F. (2003). Bringing together Strategic Outsourcing and Corporate Strategy: Outsourcing Motives and Risks. *European Management Journal, 21*(5), 647–661. doi:10.1016/S0263-2373(03)00113-0

Quigley, M. (2004). *Cyberporn Panics: Policing Pre/Pubescent Peeping*. Paper presented at the Information Resources Management Association International Conference. Innovations through information technology.

Quinn, J. B. (1999). Strategic Outsourcing: Leveraging knowledge capabilities. *Sloan Management Review*, 9–21.

Quinn, J. B., & Hilmer, F. G. (2004). Make versus buy: Strategic outsourcing. *McKinsey Quarterly*.

"Quintiles moves data management work to india." (2005, April 11). *Associated Press*.

Raju, G. V. S., & Zhou, J. (1993). Adaptive hierarchical fuzzy controller. *IEEE Transactions on Systems, Man & Cybernetics, 23*(4), 973-980, USA.

Ramanujan, S., & Jane, S. (2006). A legal perspective on outsourcing and offshoring. *Journal of American Academy of Business, 8*(2), 51-58.

Ravichandran, T. (2005). Organizational assimilation of complex technologies: An empirical study of component-based software development. *IEEE Transactions on Engineering Management, 52*(2)

Raysman, R., & Brown, P. (2005). Computer Law; Sarbanes-Oxley's 404 and Business Process Outsourcing. *New York Law Journal, 233*(34), 23–35.

Razavi, R., Fleury, M., Jammeh, E. A., & Ghanbari, M. (2006). An efficient packetization for Bluetooth video transmission. *Electronic Letters, 42*(20), 1143-1145.

Read, J. C., & MacFarlane, S. (2006, June 7-9). *Using the Fun Toolkit and Other Survey Methods to Gather Opinions in Child Computer Interaction*. Paper presented at the Proceedings of Interaction design for children, Tampere, Finland.

Reddy, V. N., Mavrovouniotis, M. L., & Liebman, M. N. (1993). Petri net representations in metabolic pathways. *Proceedings of the 1st International Conference on Intelligen Systems for Molecular Biology (ISMB)*, 328 – 336.

Reynolds, D. A. (2002). An overview of automatic speaker recognition technology. In *Proc. Int. Conf. On Acoustics, Speech and Signal Processing (ICASSP 2002). Orlando FL* (pp. 4072-4075).

Richardson, M. & Domingos, P. (2006). Markov logic networks. *Machine Learning, 62*, 107 – 136.

Rifkin, S. (2001). What makes measuring software so hard? *IEEE Software, 18*(3), 41-45.

Rising, L., & Janoff, N. S. (2000). The scrum software development process for small teams. *IEEE Software, 17*(4), 26-32.

Ritchie, R. J. & Prvan, T. A. (1996). Simulation study on designing experiments to measure the Km of Michaelis-Menten kinetics curves. *J. Theor. Biol., 178*, 239 – 254.

Roethlien, C., & Ackerson, S. (2004). Quality Communication within a Connected Supply Chain. *Supply Chain Management, 9*(3/4), 323–330.

Ross, R. G. (1997). *The business rule article: Classifying, defining and modeling rules*. Database Research Group.

Ruelle. D. (1998). *Chaotic evolution and strtange attractors: The statistical analysis of time series for deterministic nonlinear systems.* Cambridge Uni Press, USA.

Rutkowski, L. (2004). Flexible Neuro-Fuzzy Systems. Structures, Learning and Performance Evaluation. *The Springer International Series in Engineering and Computer Science* (771).

Ruuska, I., Artto, K., Asltonen, K., & Lehtonen, P. (2009). Dimensions of Distance in a Project Network: Exploring Olkiluoto 3 Nuclear Power Plant Project. *International Journal of Project Management, 27,* 142–153. doi:10.1016/j.ijproman.2008.09.003

Ryokai, K., Vaucelle, C., & Cassell, J. (2003). Virtual peers as partners in storytelling and literacy learning. *Journal of Computer Assisted Learning, 19,* 195-208.

Sackman, H., Erickson, W., & Grant, E. (1968). Exploratory experimental studies comparing online and offline programming performance. *Communications of the ACM, 11*(1).

Sagan, S. (1993). *The limits of safety.* Princeton, NJ: Princeton University Press.

Sakthivel, S. (2007). Managing risk in offshore systems development. *Communications of the ACM, 50*(4), 69-75.

Salmoni, A. J., Coxall, S., Gonzalez, M., Tastle, W., and Finley, A. (under review). Defining a postgraduate curriculum in dermatology for general practitioners: a needs analysis using a modified Delphi method.

Sambamurthy, V., & Zmud, R. W. (1994). *IT management competency assessment: A tool for creating business value through IT.* Working paper. Financial Executives Research Foundation.

Sanderson, C. (2002). Information fusion and person verification using speech and face information. *IDIAP Research report 02-33.*

Sanderson, C., & Paliwal, K. K. (2000). Adaptive Multimodal Person Verification System. Proc. 1st *IEEE Pacific-Rim Conf. On Multimedia, Sydney* (pp. 210-213).

Saunders, C., Gebelt, M., & Hu, Q. (1997). Achieving success in information systems outsourcing. *California Management Review, 39*(2), 63–79.

Schmidt, J., Calantone, R., Griffin, A., & Montoya-Weiss, M. (2005). Do Certified Mail Third-Wave Follow-ups Really Boost Response Rates and Quality? *Marketing Letters, 16*(2), 129–141. doi:10.1007/s11002-005-2291-7

Schnell, S. & Mendoza, C. (2001). A fast method to estimate kinetic constants for enzyme inhibitors. *Acta Biotheoretica, 49,* 109 – 113.

Schwaber, K., & Beedle, M. (2002). *Agile software development with scrum.* Series in agile software development. Upper Saddle River, NJ: Prentice Hall.

Schwartz, E. (2005). Flash apps for phones. *InfoWorld, 27*(20), 21.

Scott, D., Sharp, R., Madhavapeddy, A., & Upton, E. (2005). Using visual tags to bypass Bluetooth device discovery. *ACM Mobile Computing and Communications Review, 9*(1), 41-53.

Scott, W. R., Ruef, M., Mendel, P. J., & Caronna, C. A. (2000). *Institutional change and healthcare organizations: From professional dominance to managed care.* Chicago: University of Chicago Press.

Seabrook, J. (2004, October 30). *Offshore outsourcing.* Retrieved March 30, 2006, from http://www.countercurrents.org/glo-seabrook301003.html

Searle, J. R. (1975). A taxonomy of illocutionary acts. *Language, Mind and Knowledge, Minnesota Studies in the Philosophy of Science,* 344-369.

Seewald. (2005, February 2004). Best countries for U.S. outsourcing, 2004. *Wired,* 101.

Segil, L. (2005). Metrics to Successfully Manage Alliances. *Strategy and Leadership, 33*(5), 46–52. doi:10.1108/10878570510616889

Sepulveda, C. (2003, June). Agile development and remote teams: Learning to love the phone. In *Proceedings of the Agile Development Conference* (pp. 140-145).

Shaked, Y., & Wool, A. (2005). Cracking the Bluetooth PIN. In *3rd International Conference on Mobile Systems, Applications and Services* (pp. 39-50).

Sherman, P., & Oakley, E. (2004). Pandemics and panaceas: The WTO's efforts to balance pharmaceutical patents and access to AIDS drugs. *American Business Law Journal, 41*(2/3).

Sheshu, R., & Denny, N. (2007). *The nexus of entrepreneurship & technology (NEXT) initiative* (Tech. Rep. 20070220). Unpublished manuscript.

Shortliffe, E. (1976). *Computer-based medical consultations: MYCIN*. New York: Elsevier.

Simonoff, J. S. (1993). The relative importance of bias and variability in the estimation of the variance of a statistic. *The Statistician, 42*, 3 – 7.

Skinner, W. (1971). The Anachronistic Factory. *Harvard Business Review*, (January-February): 61–70.

Sloot, P., Boukhanovsky, A., Keulen, W., Tirado-Ramos, A., & Boucher, C. (2005). A grid-based HIV expert system. *Journal of Clinical Monitoring and Computing, 19*, 263-278.

Smarter offshoring. (2006). *Harvard Business Review,* 85-92.

Smith, H., & Fingar, P. (2002). *The next fifty years*. Retrieved from http://www.darwinmag.com/read/120102/bizproc.html

Solomon, D. (2001). Conducitng Web-Based Surveys. *Practical Assessment Research and Evaluation, 7*(19).

Sparling, M. (2000). Lessons learned through six years of component-based development. *Communications of the ACM, 43*(10), 47-53.

Spender, J. C. (1996). Competitive advantage from tacit knowledge? Unpacking the concept and its strategic implications. In B. Moingeon & A. Edmondson (Eds.), *Organizational learning and competitive advantage*. London: Sage Publications.

Sripada, B., Jobe, T., & Helgason, C. (2005). From fuzzy logic toward plurimonism: The science of active and empathic observation. *IEEE Transactions on Systems, Man and Cybernetics—Part B: Cybernetics, 35*(6), 1328-1339.

Sriram, R. (2002). *Distributed and integrated collaborative engineering design*. Glenwood, MD: Sarven.

Stanek, M. B. (2004). Measuring Alliance Risk and Value – A Model Approach to Prioritizing Alliance Projects. *Management Decision, 42*(2), 180–204. doi:10.1108/00251740410511252

Stanton, J. (1998). An Empirical Assessment of Data Collection Using the Internet. *Personnel Psychology, 51*(3), 709–725. doi:10.1111/j.1744-6570.1998.tb00259.x

Steeples, C. (2000). Reflecting on group discussions for professional learning: Annotating videoclips with voice annotations. 251-252.

Steeples, C. (2002). Voice annotation of multimedia artifacts: Reflective learning in distributed professional communities, 10.

Stein, E., & Zwass, V. (1995). Actualizing organizational memory with information systems. *ISR, 6*(2), 85–117. doi:10.1287/isre.6.2.85

Stephen, A., & Coote, L. V. (2007). Interfirm Behavior and Goal Alignment in Relational Exchanges. *Journal of Business Research, 60*, 285–295. doi:10.1016/j.jbusres.2006.10.022

Stevens, P., Schade, A., Chalk, B., & Slevin, O. (1993). *Understanding research: A scientific approach for health care professionals*. Edinburgh, UK: Campion Press.

Stone, M. (1961). The opinion pool. *Annals of Mathematical Statistics, 32*, 1339 – 1342.

Streiner, D. L., & Norman, G. R. (1995). *Health measurement scales: A practical guide to their development and use* (2nd ed.). Oxford: Oxford University Press.

Suchan, J., & Hayzak, G. (2001). The communication characteristics of virtual teams: A case study. *IEEE Transactions on Professional Communication, 44*(3), 174-186.

Sun, B., Liu, W., & Zhong, Q. (2003). Hierarchical speaker identification using speaker clustering. *In Proc. Int. Conf. Natural Language Processing and Knowledge Engineering 2003, Beijing, China* (pp. 299-304).

Szyperski, C. (1997). *Component software: Beyond object-oriented programming.* ACM Press.

Takeuchi, H., & Nonaka, I. (1986). The new product development game. *Harvard Business Review,* 137-146.

Tanner, K. (2000). Survey Research. In K. Williamson (Ed.), *Research methods for students and professionals: information management and systems* (pp. 71-91). Wagga Wagga, N.S.W.: Centre for Information Studies, Charles Sturt University.

Tastle, W. J., & Wierman, M. J. (2006). An information theoretic measure for the evaluation of ordinal scale data. *Behavior Research Methods,* (3): 487–494.

Tastle, W. J., & Wierman, M. J. (2006). Consensus and dissension: A new measure of agreement. In *NAFIPS 2006,* Montreal, Canada.

Tastle, W. J., & Wierman, M. J. (2007). Consensus: A new measure of ordinal dispersion measure. *International Journal of Approximate Reasoning.*

Tastle, W. J., & Wierman, M.J. (2007). The development of agreement measures: From general to targeted. *Int. J. of Approximate Reasoning,* Invited Submission.

Tastle, W. J., & Wierman, M.J. (2007). Determining Risk Assessment Using the Weighted Ordinal Agreement Measure. *Journal of Homeland Security,* July 2007.

Teece, D., & Pisano, G. (1994). The Dynamic Capabilities of Firms: an Introduction. *Industrial and Corporate Change, 3*(3), 537–556. doi:10.1093/icc/3.3.537-a

Telecoms & Technology Forecast Americas. (2005, June). *Forecast on the telecommunications and technology sector* (pp. 10-16).

The British Psychological Association: Code of ethics and conduct (2006). Liecester: The British Psychological Association.

Thompson, K. R., & Mathys, N. J. (2008). The aligned Balanced Scorecard: An Improved Tool for Building High Performance Organizations. *Organizational Dynamics, 37*(4), 378–393. doi:10.1016/j.orgdyn.2008.07.006

Tolbert, P. S., & Zucker, L. G. (1994). Institutional analysis of organizations: Legitimate but not institutionalized. Institute for Social Science Research working paper. University of California, Los Angeles.

Tomlinson, H. (2004, November 1). Drug giant moves trials abroad: Glaxo lured by security and low cost of trials overseas. *The Guardian.*

Trambert, M. (2006). PACS voice clips enhance productivity, efficiency; radiologists, referrers, front offices, and patients benefit from reporting in reader's own voice. *Diagnostic Imaging,* S3.

Treinen J. J., & Miller-Frost, S. L. (2006). Following the sun: Case studies in global software development. *IBM Systems Journal, 45*(4).

Tucci, L. (2005, April 5). *Outsourcing needs strong RX.* Retrieved April 9, 2006, from http://searchcio.techtarget.com/originalContent/0,289142,sid19_gci1075783,00.html

Turner, B. M. (1976). The organizational and interorganizational development of disasters. *Administrative Science Quarterly, 21,* 378-397.

U.S. Department of Commerce. (2006). *U.S. industrial outlook: 2006.* Washington, DC: U.S. Government Printing Office.

Understanding the WTO—Intellectual property: Protection and enforcement. (n.d.). Retrieved April 9, 2006, from http://www.wto.org/english/theWTO_e/whatis_e/tif_e/agrm7_e.htm

Urrutia, I., & Eriksen, S. D. (2005). Insights from Research: Application of the Balanced Scorecard in Spanish Private Healthcare Management. *Measuring Business Excellence, 9*(4), 16–26. doi:10.1108/13683040510634808

Van Heerden, I. (2006). *The storm—What went wrong and why during Hurricane Katrina—The inside story from one Louisiana scientist.* New York: Viking Press.

Van Hoek, R. I. (1998). Measuring the Unmeasurable – Measuring and Improving Performance in the Supply Chain. *Supply Chain Management, 4*(4), 187–192.

Van Zyl, J., & Corbett, D. (2000). Framework for comparing methods for using or reusing multiple ontologies in an application. In *Proceedings of the Eighth International Conference on Conceptual Structures.*

Vanguri, S., & Rajput, V. (2002). Patents and biotechnology. *Indian Journal of Medicine*, (3).

Vanwelkenhuysen, J., & Mizoguchi, R. (1995). Workplace-adapted behaviors: Lessons learned for knowledge reuse. In *Proceedings of KB&KS* (pp 270-280).

Venkataraman, N., & Camillus, J. (1984). Exploring the Concept of Fit in Strategic Management. *Academy of Management Review, 9*, 513–525. doi:10.2307/258291

Verdu, S. (1998). *IEEE Transactions on Information Theory, 44*(6).

Vestdam, T. (2003). Elucidative programming in open integrated development environments for java. In *Proceedings of the Second International Conference on Principles and Practice of Programming in Java (PPPJ '03)* (pp. 49-54).

Vin, H. M., Chen, M.-S., & Barzilai, T. (1993). Collaboration management in DiCE. *The Computer Journal, 36*(1), 87-96.

Vining, A., & Globerman, S. (1999). A Conceptual Framework for Understanding the Outsourcing Decision. *European Management Journal, 17*(6), 645–654. doi:10.1016/S0263-2373(99)00055-9

Violino, B. (2006). *Power play. Baseline.* Retrieved from www.documentum.com

Vogel, L. (2003). Finding value from IT investments: Exploring the elusive ROI in healthcare. *Journal of Healthcare Information Management, 17*(4).

Wade, M., & Hulland, J. (2004). Review: The Resource-Based View and Information Systems Research: Review, Extension and Suggestions for Future Research. *MIS Quarterly, 28*(1).

Walker, G. (1988). Strategic Sourcing, Vertical Integration, and Transaction Costs. *Interfaces, 18*(3), 62–73. doi:10.1287/inte.18.3.62

Walsh, J., & Ungson, G. (1991). Organizational Memory. *Academy of Management Review, 16*(1), 57–91. doi:10.2307/258607

Wang, J.-S., & George Lee, C. S. (2002). Self-Adaptive Neuro-Fuzzy Inference Systems for Classification Applications. *IEEE transactions on Fuzzy Systems, 10*(6), 790. doi:10.1109/TFUZZ.2002.805880

Wanless, D. (2002). *Securing our future health: Taking a long-term view.* London.

Wanless, D. (2004, February). *Securing good health for the whole population.* London.

Weber, R. P. (1990). *Basic content analysis* (2nd ed.). Newbury Park, CA: Sage.

Weick, K. E., & Roberts, K. (1993). Collective mind in organizations: Heedful interrelating on flight decks. *Administrative Science Quarterly, 38*, 357-381.

Welstead, T. (1994). Neural networks and fuzzy logic applications in C/C++, Wiley, USA.

Wernerfelt, B. (1984). A Resource-Based View of the Firm. *Strategic Management Journal, 5*(2), 171–180. doi:10.1002/smj.4250050207

Whittaker, S., Hyland, P., & Wiley, M. (1994). FILOCHAT: Handwritten notes provide access to recorded conversations. In *Proceedings of the SIGCHI Conference on Human Factors in Computing Systems: Celebrating Interdependence* (p. 271).

Wierman, M. J., & Tastle, W. J. (2005). Consensus and Dissention: Theory and Properties. *North American Fuzzy Information Processing Society (NAFIPS) Conference, Ann Arbor, MI.*

Wilks, Y. (2005). Artificial companions. *Interdisciplinary Science Reviews, 30*(2), 145-152.

Willcocks, L. P., & Feeny, D. (2006). IT outsourcing and core IS Capabilities: Challenges and lessons at Dupont. *Information Systems Management, 23*(1), 49-57.

Willcocks, L. P., Lacity, M., & Kern, T. (1999). Risk mitigation in IT outsourcing strategy revisited: longitudinal case research at LISA. *The Journal of Strategic Information Systems, 8*(3), 285–341. doi:10.1016/S0963-8687(00)00022-6

Willcocks, L., & Lacity, M. (1998). *Strategic Sourcing of Information Systems: Perspectives and Practices.* New York: John Wiley & Sons.

Willcocks, L., Feeny, D., & Olson, N. (2006). Implementing core IS capabilities: Feeny-Willcocks IT governance and management framework revisited. *European Management Journal, 24*(1), 28-37.

Willcocks, L., Hindle, J., Feeny, D., & Lacity, M. (2004). IT and Business Process Outsourcing: The Knowledge Potential. *Information Systems Management, 21*(3), 7–15. doi:10.1201/1078/44432.21.3.20040601/82471.2

Williams, L., Maximilien, E., & Vouk, M. (2003, November 17-20). Test-driven development as a defect-reduction practice. In *International Symposium on Software Reliability Engineering (ISSRE 2003)* (pp. 34-45).

Williamson, O. E. (1975). *Markets and Hierarchies.* New York: Free Press.

WIPO-administered treaties, WIPO treaties, treaties and contracting parties: General information. (n.d.). Retrieved April 9, 2006, from http://www.wipo.int/treaties/en/

Wu, J. & Zhou, Z.-H. (2003). Efficient face candidates selector for face detection. *The Journal of Pattern Recognition Society.*

Xiang, B., & Berger, T. (2003). Efficient text-independent speaker verification with structural gaussian mixture models and neural network. *IEEE Transactions on Speech and Audio Processing, 11*(5), 447–456. doi:10.1109/TSA.2003.815822

Xiaohu, Y., Bin, X., Zhijun, H., & Maddineni, S. (2004). Extreme programming in global software development. In *Canadian Conference on Electrical and Computer Engineering* (Vol. 4).

Yang, Z., & Peterson, R. (2004). Customer perceived value, satisfaction, and loyalty: The role of switching costs. *Psychology and Marketing, 21*(10), 799–822. doi:10.1002/mar.20030

Yap, M. (2005). Follow the sun: Distributed extreme programming environment. In *Proceedings of the IEEE Agile Conference* (pp. 218-224).

Zadeh, L. (1965). Fuzzy sets. *Inf. Control, 8*, 338-353.

Zaheer, A., & Venkatraman, N. (1994). Determinants of Electronic Integration in the Insurance Industry: An Empirical Test. *Management Science, 40*(5), 549–566. doi:10.1287/mnsc.40.5.549

Zeadally, S., & Kumar, A. (2005). Design, implementation, and evaluation of the audio/video distribution transport protocol (AVDTP) for high quality audio support over Bluetooth. *Computer Communications, 28*, 215-223.

About the Contributors

Mehdi Khosrow-Pour (DBA) received his Doctorate in Business Administration from the Nova Southeastern University (FL, USA). Dr. Khosrow-Pour taught undergraduate and graduate information system courses at the Pennsylvania State University – Harrisburg for 20 years where he was the chair of the Information Systems Department for 14 years. He is currently president and publisher of IGI Global, an international academic publishing house with headquarters in Hershey, PA and an editorial office in New York City (www.igi-global.com). He also serves as executive director of the Information Resources Management Association (IRMA) (www.irma-international.org), and executive director of the World Forgotten Children's Foundation (www.world-forgotten-children.org). He is the author/editor of over twenty books in information technology management. He is also the editor-in-chief of the Information Resources Management Journal, the Journal of Cases on Information Technology, the Journal of Electronic Commerce in Organizations, and the Journal of Information Technology Research, and has authored more than 50 articles published in various conference proceedings and journals.

* * *

Yun-Ke Chang is an assistant professor in the School of Communication and Information at Nanyang Technological University. She taught information technology related topics and several research method courses. Her research areas include search engines, digital image retrieval, Web site evaluation, instructional design, human visual perception, learning organization and knowledge management. Dr. Chang also has served in several academic program committees of international conferences as well as a paper reviewer for journals.

Mark Chavez received a Bachelor's of Fine Arts from Arizona State University and Master's of Fine Arts from the University of California at Los Angeles. He specializes in creating stylized cartoon animation and photorealistic visual effects. Before joining the School of Art, Design, and Media at Nanyang Technological University, Mr. Chavez worked on many Academy-Award nominated projects. His professional experiences include serving as technical and art director for television broadcast projects in Tokyo Broadcasting System, lead animator/modeler in Dreamworks Feature Animation, and visual effects specialist at Rhythm and Hues.

Igor Crk is currently pursuing a doctoral degree in computer science at the University of Arizona. He holds a master's degree in computer science from the University of Arizona. Current research interests include context-driven energy management in operating systems and the 24-Hour Knowledge Factory model for distributed agile software development.

Nathan Denny is currently pursuing a doctoral degree in computer engineering at the University of Arizona. He holds a master's degree in computer science from Southern Illinois University and has previous publications in design automation for reliable computing, knowledge management, and computer and Internet security. His current interests include the 24-Hour Knowledge Factory and distributed agile software development.

Kirsten Ellis is a lecturer in the Faculty of Information Technology, Monash University. Her research specialisation is in the design and development of multimedia software for children with particular interest in interactions and behaviour. Her research has involved the investigation of children as young as two using computers. Her recent work includes research focused on the possibilities for teaching hearing children sign language using computers to create a more inclusive society.

Panayotis Fouliras is a lecturer at the Department of Applied Informatics, University of Macedonia, Greece. He received his BSc in physics from Aristotle University of Thessaloniki, Greece and MSc and PhD in computer science from the University of London, UK. His primary research interests are in computer networks, multimedia streaming, network services and applications.

Preeti Goyal is currently a research candidate at the Management Development Institute, Gurgaon, India. She has about 10 years of industry experience. Prior to starting her PhD, Preeti worked for leading firms in the area of Financial Services and Technology in India and the US. Her domain has been the implementation of technology solutions for financial services' operations. She has been on consulting assignments to leading Wall Street firms. She has a Bachelor's degree in Commerce from the University of Delhi, India and an MBA in Finance from The George Washington University, US.

Matthew Waritay Guah is assistant professor at Erasmus School of Economics, Erasmus University Rotterdam. Research focuses on organizational issues surrounding emerging technologies (i.e., Web services and SOA) in the healthcare and financial industries. His research interests include neo-institutional theory, socio-economic impacts of e-business on government services delivery, resistance to IS, organizational structure, IS infrastructure, strategic planning for IS—with a more general interest in the cognitive, material and social relationships between science, technology and business as well as their implications for present-day understandings of creativity and innovation. Dr. Guah has his PhD in information systems from Warwick Business School, MSc in technology management from University of Manchester, and BSc (Honours) from Salford University, in United Kingdom. He came into academia with a wealth of industrial experience spanning over ten years (including Merrill Lynch, CITI Bank, HSBC, British Airways, and United Nations). Authored books include Managing Very Large IT Projects and Internet Strategy: The Road to Web Services (with W.Currie). Recent journal publications include JIT, ISM, IJST&M, IT&I, IJKM, IJHT&M, IJT&HI. Editorial membership of JCIT, SJI, JIQ, JMIS and IJEC. Reviewer for major IS journals and conferences. Also a member of ERIM, AIS, UKAIS, BMiS, and BCS.

Jaime Jimenez-Guzman is the head of the Department of Mathematic Modeling of Social Systems in the Institute of Applied Mathematics and Systems in the National University of Mexico. His research addresses the issues of large social systems with multiple stakeholders and their interests in which ambiguity and confusion prevail. He also studies human information needs in the context of socio-technical problems.

Mahesh Kulkarni is Programme Co-ordinator, CDAC-GIST Group, at Centre for Development of Advanced Computing, Pune, India. After obtaining his Masters degree in Science (M.Sc) –Special Electronics, he has worked in both Public and Private sectors. He represented C-DAC at World Hindi conference at Paramaribo and New York. He has worked on Supermini systems, telecommunications systems and executed research projects on Natural language processing, OCR, Online handwriting recognition, Text to speech and mobile computing. As a part of the EU funded projects, he spearheaded international conference and EU workshops. He has several publications and patent on implementation of Indian Language Inputting on Mobile Handset with limited keys.

Andy LaBrunda is currently the vice president of IT at GTA, the largest telephone company on Guam. He holds an MS in computer science from the Southeastern University of Florida, with a specialization in computational geometry, 2003. Areas of research include optimization techniques for computing Voronoi diagrams and shader tree synthesis using genetic algorithms. He is been an adjunct professor at the University of Guam teaching mathematics and computers. He has also worked as a telecommunication analyst for the Computer Science Corporation and as a software developer for Bank of America.

Michelle LaBrunda is currently chief medical resident at Mount Sinai: Cabrini Medical Center in New York City. She holds an MS in biology from Portland State University and an MD from Universidad de Monterrey in Monterrey, Mexico. She has diverse research interests, but primarily focuses on infectious disease in developing countries as well as technology in medicine. She has extensive international experience and will be entering a geographic medicine/infectious disease fellowship at Tufts New England Medical Center in 2008.

Laura Lally received her PhD in information systems from New York University's Stern School of Business. For the past twelve years, the primary focus of her research has been the on information technology as a target, shield, and weapon against disasters. Her work has appeared in numerous conference proceedings including AMCIS, IRMA, and the DSI. A seminal article on her work has appeared in the Journal of the Information Resources Management Association, and as an updated version in the IGI Global advances series, Advanced Issues in Information Technology Management. She has also published an article on this topic in the International Journal of Technology, Knowledge and Society. Her other research interests focus on the use of consumer involvement theory to enhance e-commerce applications.

Huma Lodhi obtained her PhD in computer science from University of London in 2002. She is working as researcher in Department of Computing, Imperial College London. She has a strong background in machine learning and data mining. Her research interests lie in designing, analyzing and applying learning and data mining techniques for solving complex and challenging biological and chemical problems.

Jason McCoy is a vice president of Global Seawater, Inc., a private economic development firm with projects in Mexico and sub-Saharan Africa. He works primarily on business development, investor relations, strategy, and project operations with partners and governments in host countries. He holds a BA from the University of Arizona in economics and international relations and graduated summa cum laude. Additionally, he was selected as a USA Today Academic All-Star, which is an annual honor bestowed to the top 20 graduating seniors nationwide.

B. Dawn Medlin is the Chair and an Associate Professor in the Department of Computer Information Systems, John A. Walker College of Business, and Appalachian State University in Boone, NC. Her teaching and research activities have mainly been in the area of security, health care informatics, and e-commerce. She has published in journals such as The Journal of Information Systems Security, Information Systems Security, International Journal of Electronic Marketing and Retailing, and the International Journal of Healthcare Information Systems and Informatics.

Bhimaraya A. Metri received his Ph.D. from IIT, Bombay, India. He has over 18 years of teaching/ research experience. Currently he is working as an Associate Professor (Operations) and the Chairman, Post Graduate Program in Management at Management Development Institute, Gurgaon, India. He has provided Executive Education and Consulting Services to several leading organizations. He has published over 65 papers in scholarly journals and conference proceedings. Dr. Metri is on the editorial board of the journal on 'Consultancy Ahead'. His consulting/research interests are quality management, service management and supply chain management. Dr Metri is a Life Member of ISTE and IETE.

Amit Mitra is a senior manager at TCS Global Consulting Practice. Prior to TCS he was the senior vice president for process improvement and enterprise architecture at GalaxE solutions. He also holds a black belt certification in the six-sigma, and is the author of several ground breaking books and papers on knowledge management and process improvement to support business agility and innovation. Amit is also a visiting faculty member at the University of Arizona, which introduced a new course based on his work, and teaches executive classes at the University of California at San Diego on process modeling and service oriented architecture. He led the executive round table on business agility at BPMI's process improvement think tank 2006 in Washington DC, and has been an invited speaker at several national and international conferences on business modeling and business-IT alignment. Previously Mitra was a manager of architecture and e-commerce at Bearing Point, the former chief methodologist at AIG and a former director of architecture at Verizon. He currently provides thought leadership and consulting services on process improvement, methodology, IT governance, enterprise architecture and IT strategy to some of America's leading firms.

Masoud Mohammadian's research interests lie in adaptive self-learning systems, fuzzy logic, genetic algorithms, neural networks and their applications in industrial, financial and business problems which involve real time data processing, planning and decision making. His current research also concentrates on the application of computational intelligence techniques for learning and adaptation of intelligent agents and web-based information filtering and data mining. He has received a number of awards from USA, Austria and Australia for his research activities. He has been the chair and program committee of a large number of conference in the area of computational intelligence and intelligent agent systems. He has edited and co-authored over 12 books in computational intelligence and intelligent agent systems.

Miguel Angel Morales-Arroyo received his bachelor's degree in EEE and his master's degree in engineering (planning) from the National University of Mexico, and his PhD in information science from the University of North Texas. His research area is in decision making and problem-solving methods, including identifying stages and factors related to the nature of collaborative projects. He has worked as a freelance consultant in several projects in Mexico, including transportation problems, project feasibility of a recreational club, and identification of information system failures. Currently, Dr. Morales is lecturing in the School of Communication and Information at Nanyang Technological University.

Katharina O'Toole is currently working with two start up companies. GreenSun is focused on renewable energy and Kastle Data Systems is focused on network attached storage. She holds an MBA from the Eller College of Management at the University of Arizona and masters degree in electrical and computer engineering from the University of Arizona.

A.B. Patki obtained his M Tech from Indian Institute of Technology (IIT), Kharagpur in 1975. Presently, he is working as Scientist —G & HoD with the Department of Information Technology (DIT), Government of India. He has been a referee for IEEE Transactions on Reliability for over twenty years. His research areas include soft computing, software engineering, outsourcing, productivity enhancement and cyber forensics & security. He has been trained in VLSI Design at Lund University, Sweden and Mentor Graphics, USA. He holds a copyright for FUZOS©- Fuzzy Logic Based Operating Software. His hobbies include Hindustani music, homoeopathy and vedic studies.

Tapasya Patki is a Graduate student at the Department of Computer Science at University of Arizona, Tucson. She obtained her Bachelor of Technology in Computer Science & Engineering. She is Gold medallist from GGS Indraprastha University, New Delhi, India. She has an internship experience of over six months at the Department of Information Technology, Government of India, where she specialized in applications of Fuzzy Logic and Rough Set Techniques. She has formally studied graduate level professional outsourcing course at Eller College of Management, University of Arizona. Her areas of interest include software engineering, artificial intelligence, outsourcing technologies, surreptitious computing, and bio-informatics. Presently, she is exploring potentials of soft computing to knowledge management practices and software code obfuscation. She is also a violin soloist and an amateur poet.

Mark Power is a lecture at the Faculty of Information Technology. Current teaching and research interest are video and sound production, special effects (post production) and animation. Mark's research area examines the impact of emerging technologies on the production process. Recent works include contributions to the chapter 3D avatars and collaborative virtual environments (Idea Group Inc, Hershey, PA USA, 2007) and Evaluation ICT in Education: A comparison of the Affordance of the iPod, Ds and Wii (Ascilite conference, Nanyang Technological University, Singapore, 2007).

Marian Quigley is an honorary research fellow in the faculty for Information Technology, Monash University. Her major research interests are the social effects of ICTs; animation and writing. Her recent publications include Encyclopaedia of Information Ethics and Security (IGI Global, Hershey, PA, USA, 2007) and Women Do Animate: Interviews with 10 Australian Women Animators (insight Publications, Mentone, Australia, 2005).

Mahesh S. Raisinghani is an associate professor at Texas Woman's University's College of Management. He is also the president and CEO of Raisinghani and Associates International, Inc., a diversified global firm with interests in software consulting and technology options trading. Dr. Raisinghani earned his PhD from the University of Texas at Arlington and is a certified e-commerce consultant (CEC). Dr. Raisinghani was the recipient of the 1999 UD Presidential Award, the 2001 King Hagar Award for excellence in teaching, research and service; and the 2002 research award. As a global thought leader on e-business and global information systems, he has served as the local chair of the World Conference on Global Information Technology Management in 2001 and the track chair for e-commerce technologies management at the Information Resources Management Association since 1999. Dr. Raisinghani has published in numerous leading scholarly and practitioner journals, presented at leading world-level scholarly conferences and has served as an editor of two books, E-Commerce: Opportunities and Challenges and Cases on Worldwide E-Commerce: Theory in Action. He serves as the associate editor for JGITM and IRMJ and is a member of the editorial review board of leading information systems/e-commerce academic journals. He has also served as the editor of three special issues of the Journal of Electronic Commerce Research on Intelligent Agents in E-Commerce and eBusiness Security. Dr. Raisinghani was also selected by the National Science Foundation after a nationwide search to serve as a panelist on the Information Technology/E-Commerce Research Panel and Small Business Innovation Research panel. He has also been involved in consulting activities and frequently participates in news media interviews on IS issues. Dr. Raisinghani serves on the board of directors of Sequoia, Inc. and is included in the millennium edition of Who's Who in the World, Who's Who Among America's Teachers and Who's Who in Information Technology.

Chandra Prakash Rathore is working at Tata Consultancy Services, Noida. He has done M. Tech. in Software Engineering from ABV-Indian Institute of Information Technology and Management, Gwalior. His areas of research are Artificial Intelligence, Speech Processing, Soft Computing, and Software Quality Economics. He has received RSR scholarship on securing 1st position in B.E and Top Performer's award in Initial Learning Program of Tata Consultancy Services, Greater NOIDA.

Adriana Romaniello is currently serving as an Associate Professor in the Department of Management in Universidad Rey Juan Carlos in Madrid, Spain. She earned her PhD at Universidad Complutense de Madrid. Her teaching and research activities have been in the area of knowledge management, strategic management and information and communication technology. She has participated in many international conferences and in various projects supported with governmental funds.

Nikolaos Samaras is a lecturer at the Department of Applied Informatics, University of Macedonia, Greece. He received his BSc and PhD in applied informatics from the University of Macedonia, Greece. His primary research interests are in mathematical programming, experimental evaluation of algorithm performance, computer and network applications and computational operations research.

Johannes Sarx is a strategic consultant with Alcimed, a Paris-based European consultancy with focus on life sciences and chemistry. He works primarily on corporate, marketing, pricing, and R&D strategy projects for multinational biotechnology and pharmaceutical companies. He holds a MBA from the University of Arizona and received his undergraduate degree in molecular biotechnology from the Dresden University of Technology in Germany.

Anupam Shukla is an Associate Professor in the Information and Communication Technology Department of ABV-Indian Institute of Information Technology and Management, Gwalior, India. He has 20 years of teaching experience. His research interest includes Artificial Intelligence, Soft Computing, Biometrics, Bio-Medical Engineering, Bioinformatics Robotics, Animation and Signal processing. He has published around 80 papers in various national and international journals. He is the editor and reviewer for international journals; and also member of program and technical committees in international conferences. He received Young Scientist Award from Madhya Pradesh Government and Gold Medal from Jadavpur University.

Dane Sorensen is employed by Raytheon Missile Systems, and works with the operations business team providing financial analysis, performance and summary data to operations, supply chain and mission assurance directorates. He is a graduate of the Eller College of Management of the University of Arizona, and was awarded a certificate for being the outstanding graduating student the Management and Policy department. While attending this university, he was the president of the Society for Human Resource Management (SHRM). Sorensen has also authored papers related to offshore activities in the Philippines and the outsourcing of human resources functions.

Srividhya Subramanian is pursuing her master's in computer science at the University of Arizona. She is currently working with Intel under the Mobility group with the Graphics Software Validation team, as part of her Summer Internship. Her interests and associated academic projects lie in Firmware Validation and Software Development, more precisely, the 24-Hour Knowledge Factory and the use of Agile Processes in this scenario.

William J. Tastle received his PhD in advanced technology with specialization in systems science from the Thomas J. Watson School of Engineering and Applied Science of the State University of New York, University Center at Binghamton in 1994 and an MBA in MIS from the School of Management at Binghamton. He is Associate Professor of Information Systems in the business school at Ithaca College, Visiting Research Professor at the University of Iceland, and is active in the IS community having served as the president of the Association for Information Technology Professionals, Education Special Interest Group (EDSIG), and on many other committees. He is the managing editor of the International Journal of General Systems. Currently he serves on the board of directors of the North American Fuzzy Information Processing Society and is its treasurer. Dr. Tastle's current areas of interest involve measures of consensus, dissention, agreement and disagreement, requirements analysis elicitation, and outsourcing.

Ritu Tiwari is an Assistant Professor in the Information and Communication Technology Department of ABV-Indian Institute of Information Technology and Management, Gwalior, India. She has 09 years of teaching experience. Her field of research includes Artificial Intelligence, Soft Computing, Biometrics, Bio-Medical Engineering, Robotics and Speech Signal processing. She has published around 30 papers in various national and international journals/conferences. She is the editor and reviewer for international journals and also member of program and technical committees in international conferences. She received Young Scientist Award from Chhattisgarh Council of Science & Technology and also received Gold Medal in her post graduation.

Mark J. Wierman is an Assistant Professor of Computer Science at Creighton University in Omaha, Nebraska. He received his Ph.D. in Systems Science from Binghamton University. His current research interests are the application of the Mathematics of Uncertainty to Political Science and Generalized Information Theory. He has published over 30 papers and his second book, Applying Fuzzy Mathematics to Formal Models in Comparative Politics (with TD Clark, JM Larson, JN Mordeson, and JD Potter) will be published in spring 2008.

Index